"The story of Willie McGee was one of the murkiest and most haunting cases to come out of the violence-ridden South in the years following World War II. Alex Heard uses McGee's story to shed light on an America we'd like to forget—a time when mob rule and lynching prevailed. This is a magisterial book."

—Susan Brownmiller, author of *Against Our Will*

"*The Eyes of Willie McGee* recreates a drama of race, class, crime, and politics that helped set the stage for both the McCarthy era and the civil rights revolution. Heard's story reads like *Radical Chic* set in 1940s Mississippi. It's a gripping, disturbing treat."

—Jacob Weisberg, author of *The Bush Tragedy*

"Engrossing, thoroughly researched, moving, intense, instructive, and masterfully written, *The Eyes of Willie McGee* grabs hold of the past and makes it vivid and remarkably relevant. A brilliant powerhouse of a book." —Martin Clark, author of *The Many Aspects of Mobile Home Living*

"In this gripping story of a world at once remote yet painfully familiar, Alex Heard has crafted a memorable narrative of a civil rights case that deserves a larger place in American memory."

—Jon Meacham, author of *American Lion*

"Alex Heard has peeled back the tarp on the American South ten long years before Rosa Parks boarded the bus. Willie McGee was and remains a powerful symbol of corruption and racism, but he is far more than that. He's the epicenter of an addictive mystery that draws you in even as it repels you. The story, as Heard masterfully tells it, belies our easy assumptions—about race, human nature, and the notion of justice. This is an extraordinary book."

—Mary Roach, author of *Stiff*

"The story of Willie McGee—a tale as rich and important as any in the history of the American civil rights movement—deserves a writer as brilliant as Alex Heard. With humanity, subtlety, and persistence, Heard cracks open this Jim Crow mystery and shows how it foreshadowed, and shaped, the massive shakeup in the American South that would occur in the decades after McGee's death."

—David Plotz, author of *Good Book*

"As a son of Mississippi and a knowledgeable student of its conflicted past, Alex Heard presents a gripping account of one of the most controversial legal dramas of the civil rights era, in a volume that provides intriguing insight into the broader complexities of race relations in the South at that time. It reads like a novel, but with real-life characters who are unforgettable."

—William Winter, former governor of Mississippi
and founder of the William Winter Institute
for Racial Reconciliation

"An iconic criminal case—a black man sentenced to death for raping a white woman in Mississippi in 1945—exposes the roiling tensions of the early civil rights era in this provocative study. . . . Heard finds no easy answers, but his nuanced, evocative portrait of the passions enveloping McGee's case is plenty revealing."

—*Publishers Weekly*

"A thorough revisiting of the 1945 Mississippi black-white rape case that ended in the electric chair. . . . Heard does a fine job presenting horrific documentation of the practice of lynching in the South. . . . He undertakes painstaking detective work to engagingly explore an era of deep-seated racial hatred." —*Kirkus Reviews*

THE EYES OF
WILLIE McGEE

A Tragedy of Race, Sex, and Secrets in
the Jim Crow South

ALEX HEARD

HARPER PERENNIAL

NEW YORK • LONDON • TORONTO • SYDNEY • NEW DELHI • AUCKLAND

HARPER ● PERENNIAL

Grateful acknowledgment for permission to reproduce illustrations is made to the following: The Hawkins Family: insert page 1, bottom; page 2, top; page 2, middle; page 16, top; page 16, bottom. The Jensen Family: insert page 2, bottom. The University of Southern Mississippi: insert page 3, top; page 4, top; page 4, bottom. The Mississippi Department of Archives and History: insert page 3, bottom. The Associated Press: insert page 4, middle; page 6, top; page 6, bottom; page 7, bottom. The Pyles Family: insert page 5, top. Getty Images: insert page 5, middle; page 12, top; page 14, top; page 14, bottom; page 15, top; page 15, bottom. The Burnham Family: insert page 5, bottom. The Communist Party of the United States Photograph Collection, Tamiment Library, New York University: insert page 7, top; page 9, top; page 9, bottom right; page 10, top; page 11, top left; page 13, top. The Abzug Family: insert page 8, top. The London Family: insert page 8, bottom right. The Poole Family: insert page 8, bottom left. The Popham Family: insert page 9, bottom left. The Schomburg Center for Research in Black Culture, New York Public Library: insert page 10, bottom. The Stoll Family: insert page 11, middle right. The Ordower Family: insert page 11, middle left. The Feise Family: insert page 11, bottom. The Mitford Collection, Ohio State University: insert page 12, bottom. The Cohen Family: insert page 13, bottom.

A hardcover edition of this book was published in 2010 by HarperCollins Publishers.

HarperCollins books may be purchased for educational, business, or sales promotional use. For information, please e-mail the Special Markets Department at SPsales@harpercollins.com.

FIRST HARPER PERENNIAL EDITION PUBLISHED 2011.

Designed by Leah Carlson-Stanisic

The Library of Congress has catalogued the hardcover edition as follows:

Heard, Alex.
 The eyes of Willie McGee : a tragedy of race, sex, and secrets in the Jim Crow South / by Alex Heard.
  p. cm.
 Summary: "A saga of race and retribution in the deep South that says as much about Mississippi today as it does about the mysteries of the past"—Provided by publisher.
 ISBN 978-0-06-128415-1 (hardback)
 1. McGee, Willie, 1915-1951—Trials, litigation, etc. 2. Capital punishment—Mississippi—History—20th century. 3. Capital punishment—Social aspects—Mississippi—History—20th century. 4. Discrimination in capital punishment—Mississippi—History—20th century. 5. Discrimination in criminal justice administration—Mississippi—History—20th century. 6. Executions and executioners—Mississippi—History—20th century. 7. Race discrimination—Mississippi—History—20th century. 8. Mississippi—Race relations—History—20th century. I. Title.
 HV8699.U6M744 2010
 364.66092—dc22   2009051769

ISBN 978-0-06-128416-8 (pbk.)

HB 10.06.2020

For Jim Leeson

I can hear Rosalee
See the eyes of Willie McGee
My mother told me about
Lynchings
My mother told me about
The dark nights
And dirt roads
And torch lights
And lynch robes . . .
The
Faces of men
Laughing white
Faces of men
Dead in the night.
sorrow night
and a
sorrow night

—Lorraine Hansberry, "Lynchsong," 1951

Contents

THE EYES OF
WILLIE McGEE

one

THE HOT SEAT

On May 8, 1951, a thirty-five-year-old African American named Willie McGee was electrocuted in Laurel, Mississippi, on a much-disputed charge that he raped a white housewife named Willette Hawkins. A few days later Eleanor Roosevelt, who was traveling in Europe, received a protest letter about the execution, sent by a Swiss citizen who identified himself as Mr. F. Aegerter.

Aegerter didn't know Roosevelt and she didn't know him. But he knew she was in Geneva for a meeting of the United Nations Commission on Human Rights, so he took a moment to sound off about the human rights of Willie McGee, a man whose death he deeply mourned. During a legal battle that lasted more than five years, McGee's story had risen from obscurity to fame, and Aegerter, who probably read about McGee in French-language newspapers, felt certain he was innocent. As he knew, the former First Lady had avoided taking part in a widely publicized campaign to stop the execution. He wanted to know why.

Roosevelt didn't apologize. Just the opposite, she pushed back. In a reply written on the 18th, she told Aegerter she was very familiar with the facts of the McGee saga—unlike him. "[Y]ou do not seem to have much understanding of the case about which you write," she informed him coolly. "It is quite true that all of us oppose a law which is applied differently to white and colored and that happens to still be in effect in some southern states. . . .

"In the case of Willie McGee, while I regret there should be this discrimination in the law, I have to add that he was a bad character and so was the white woman, so there was very little that one could feel personally about."

That sounded definite, as if she had inside information. But the truth was that Roosevelt knew very little about McGee or "the white woman." A lot of what she thought she knew—and this was true for Aegerter as well—was rumor mixed with fact, unproven allegations, or simply wrong, since the story produced more than its share of inaccurate reporting, lies, and colorful but useless folklore.

The "bad character" phrase makes it clear she'd heard about and believed the most explosive allegation of all: McGee's claim that his sexual encounter with Willette wasn't a rape but an act of consensual sex, part of a long-standing love affair that she had instigated. As for Roosevelt's observation that the story lacked elements that could stir the soul, she couldn't have been more off base, because Aegerter wasn't the only person who cared. By 1951, hundreds of thousands of people knew McGee's name and what it represented, and many had passionate opinions about what had happened to him inside Mississippi courtrooms.

———

The story began in November 1945, when McGee, a longtime Laurel resident who worked as the driver of a wholesale grocery-delivery truck, was charged with breaking into a home in a middle-class white neighborhood and raping Mrs. Troy Hawkins, a thirty-two-year-old housewife and mother of three.

The rape allegedly happened in the predawn hours of November 2, a warm autumn Friday. As the still-traumatized Mrs. Hawkins told police after daybreak that morning, she was asleep in a front bedroom with a sick twenty-month-old girl at her side. Her thirty-seven-year-old husband was in a room near the back of the house, having gone there after spending several hours helping Willette take care of the child. She said she woke up and heard a man crawling toward her on the floor. In an instant, he was on top of her, smelling like whiskey and threatening to kill her and the child if she didn't shut up and submit. Once he was done, he told her never to say a word about what happened or he would come back and kill her. Then he ran out the front door. Mrs. Hawkins said it was too dark to see the rapist's face, but she knew he was black by the texture of his hair.

McGee became a suspect in part because he didn't show up for work on Friday, but also because Laurel police found witnesses—including two male friends of his—whose statements seemed to place him in the vicinity at the time of the assault. He was arrested the next day in a nearby city, Hattiesburg, briefly taken back to Laurel, and then driven to jail ninety miles away in Jackson, the state capital. Jackson was home to a massive county courthouse with a two-floor, upper-story lockup that was considered safe from attacks by lynch mobs. Often in cases like this, black defendants were whisked away from wherever they'd been arrested and taken straight to the Hinds County jail.

The trial was held in early December, amid so much local hostility that the governor of Mississippi sent McGee back to Laurel under heavily armed guard. It lasted only a day, with an all-white jury sentencing him to death after deliberating for less than three minutes. There would be two more circuit-court trials—the first two verdicts were reversed on procedural grounds by the Mississippi Supreme Court—followed by a three-year period of state and federal appeals, including multiple appeals to the U.S. Supreme Court.

For a long time—through all three trials, in fact—the McGee case was barely noticed outside Mississippi, but by the end that had changed dramatically. People all over the United States, Canada, South America, Europe, and Asia had read or heard about his death sentence and were convinced he was either the victim of a racist frame-up or, if guilty, had been condemned unfairly, since Mississippi's death penalty for rape was only applied to blacks, never to whites. In 1950 and 1951, thousands of individuals sent letters, postcards, and telegrams to public officials who had the authority to halt the execution—including Mississippi's governor and chief justice, the justices on the U.S. Supreme Court, and President Harry S. Truman—demanding either a new trial, a prison term instead of death, or outright clemency. A week before the execution, Truman even heard from McGee's children, who pleaded with him in a letter to save their father.

Dear Mr. President,

We are writing to you about our daddy Willie McGee who have been in jail five years and on May eight they are going to put our daddy on the hot seat. Will you please not let him die, Mr. Truman. You is our president.

My name is Gracie Lee McGee. I have two sisters and one brother. My poor mother is somewhere trying to get my daddy home. She may come by your house. Please help her.

Like F. Aegerter, most people who spoke out weren't public figures, but several were—or soon would be. McGee's lead defense attorney during the appeals was Bella Abzug, a young labor lawyer from New York who was destined for fame in the 1960s and 1970s as a feminist and politician. Long before that, the McGee case put her in the national spotlight for the first time. In March 1951, William Faulkner, the recent recipient of the Nobel Prize for Literature, signed off on a press release that said that McGee was probably innocent and should be spared. In April, Albert Einstein issued a statement in which he asserted, with utmost confidence, that "any unprejudiced human being must find it difficult to believe that this man really committed the rape of which he has been accused. Moreover, the punishment must appear unnaturally harsh to anyone with any sense of justice."

There was a lot more besides—support from people like Paul Robeson, Josephine Baker, Jessica Mitford, Norman Mailer, Richard Wright, and Frida Kahlo, along with protests from labor unions, political groups, and foreign governments. As McGee's last day approached, the U.S. State Department sent a staffer to monitor the case in Jackson because many foreign embassies, prompted by inquiries from citizens back home, were demanding to know why Mississippi seemed determined to kill an innocent man. By the end, news organizations all over the world—including the *New York Times*, the *Washington Post*, *Time*, *Life*, *Newsweek*, the *Nation*, and newspapers overseas—were covering McGee intensively. The day after his electrocution, the French paper *Combat* spoke for many when it declared that "the Mississippi executioner has won out over the world conscience . . . Yesterday morning a little of the liberty of all men and a little of the solidarity between the peoples died with Willie McGee."

What prompted much of this was McGee's claim about interracial sex, a real-life version of a fictional theme that, nearly a decade later, would be at the heart of Harper Lee's Pulitzer Prize–winning novel; *To Kill a Mockingbird*. In the novel, Mayella Ewell, a lower-class white woman, sets up a deadly chain of events when she and her father tell the sheriff of a Depression-era Alabama town that she was raped by a black man, Tom Robinson, who narrowly escapes lynching just before his trial starts. In court, Atticus Finch, a local white attorney of flawless integrity, presents a convincing case that Mayella lied—that she'd made a pass at Tom, was rejected, and went along with the false accusation to save herself from her father's violent rage. An all-white jury finds Robinson guilty anyway and sentences him to death. He's shot and killed while attempting to escape from jail.

McGee's story was just as grim but much more carnal. In *Mockingbird* there was no sex, just fabricated accusations about it. In the McGee case, the sex—if it happened—was rampant and insanely risky, given the time and place. According to McGee, it all started when he was waxing floors in Mrs. Hawkins's home one afternoon and, he said, "she showed a willingness to be familiar." With small children in the house and her husband at work, she took him to a bedroom, stripped, and flopped down on a mattress. This wouldn't be their only encounter: in a story that evolved considerably over time, McGee said they had sex frequently during an affair that lasted for several years.

Though McGee said he tried to break off the relationship, knowing he'd be lynched if they were found out, Mrs. Hawkins supposedly wouldn't let go. She publicly harassed him and his wife, Rosalee, accosting them both on the streets of Laurel and calling Rosalee a "Negro whore." She turned up at his house to knock on his door, drove him to a graveyard for midnight encounters, and left a note in a gas-pump nozzle at a service station where he worked.

Her final misdeed was to condemn McGee to death by crying rape once the affair came to light, and for this she would be pilloried in the years ahead. A few months after McGee died, an African-American poet and actress named Beaulah Richardson—who, under the stage name Beah Richards, was nominated for an Oscar in 1968 for her supporting role in *Guess Who's Coming to Dinner*—set the tone in a poem called "A Black Woman Speaks." One of its chief villains was Mrs. Hawkins, "the depraved, enslaved, adulterous woman, whose lustful demands denied, lied and killed what she could not possess."

Tennessee Williams weighed in too, years later, in his 1957 play *Orpheus Descending*. In act one, Carol Cutrere, an eccentric white Mississippian, talks about her early involvement in civil rights causes, saying, "I delivered stump speeches, wrote letters of protest about the gradual massacre of the colored majority in the county. . . . And when that Willie McGee thing came along—he was sent to the chair for having improper relations with a white whore—I made a fuss about it. I put on a potato sack and set out for the capitol on foot. This was in winter. I walked barefoot in this burlap sack to deliver a personal protest to the Governor of the State. . . . You know how far I got? Six miles out of town—hooted, jeered at, even spit on!—every step of the way—and then arrested!"

———

Eleanor Roosevelt may not have known all the lurid details, but she knew the basics. In the end, though, the reason she ignored McGee was more about politics than personal distaste, and from her perspective this was the only wise choice she had.

Roosevelt was no coward about civil rights. Among much else, she'd faced down her husband and his advisers in 1934, when she supported federal anti-lynching legislation that FDR refused to get behind, fearing the loss of white Democratic support in the South. But she could only push it so far, and the McGee case was beyond the pale because it involved a third color along with black and white: red. Many of McGee's supporters were Communists, and during his long legal ordeal, his defense was paid for by the New York–based Civil Rights Congress (CRC), a group whose staff and supporters included radioactive far-left figures like Robeson, CRC head William L. Patterson, Communist

Party chief William Z. Foster, and the writers and editors of the *Daily Worker*, the contentious organ of the Communist Party USA.

Throughout 1950 and 1951, a lot of the pro-McGee protest noise came from Communist governments overseas. The ruling officials of Red China denounced Truman for allowing McGee's death, while the Soviet Union sent out crackling radio broadcasts that railed against the United States for its racial hypocrisy. On the home front, domestic Communists and radical union members marched through the streets of major cities like New York, Chicago, Los Angeles, San Francisco, and Washington, D.C., where a group of men wearing FREE WILLIE MCGEE T-shirts chained themselves to the columns of the Lincoln Memorial. News of the execution was a blow to one of the most famous American Communists of the era, Julius Rosenberg. Just after it happened, in a letter to his wife, Ethel, written from his prison cell, the accused atomic spy lamented the evils of a system that would allow such an injustice to occur.

"Ethel I was terribly shocked to read that Willie McGee was executed," he wrote. "You know how I am affected by these things. . . . My heart is sad [and] my eyes are filled with tears. Shame, America!! Shame on those who perpretrated [sic] this heinous act!! Greater Shame on those who did not lift their voices and hands to stop the . . . Mississippi executioner."

Roosevelt knew all about the Communist connection. As letters between her and her contacts at the National Association for the Advancement of Colored People show, her opinions about McGee were essentially dictated to her by the NAACP, which stiff-armed him because the CRC had gained control of the case.

The NAACP's hostility had its roots in the spring of 1946, when the group, along with many other liberal, progressive, and left-wing outfits, was invited to Detroit to participate in a two-day "Initiating Committee for a Congress on Civil Rights." The NAACP sent observers who reported that the gathering ended with the merger of previously existing organizations into an ambitious new entity called the Civil Rights Congress. CRC leaders vowed to become a major new force in turning post–World War II agitation for civil rights and Cold War–era civil liberties into a movement that would sweep the nation.

That meeting took place in April; within days, NAACP personnel were already brooding about the new competition. "Gloster Current telephoned my house from Detroit last night, saying he felt we should watch very carefully the newly set up National Congress of Civil Rights Organizations," NAACP executive secretary Walter White wrote in a May 1, 1946, memo to a colleague. ". . . He opened up the conversation by saying that the so-called civil rights conference had been called by the Comrades. I regard Gloster as an expert on the activity of the Comrades and on their various 'fronts.' "

The upshot was a blanket policy of noncooperation. Throughout the ten-year history of the CRC, the NAACP almost always balked at joint effort on cases, like McGee's, that involved allegations of racially motivated judicial railroading.

The NAACP conveyed its feelings directly to Roosevelt in July 1950, when the McGee case began making national news in advance of a July 27 execution date that was later postponed by the U.S. Supreme Court. "This is, unfortunately, another one of those cases where the Communists persuaded an apparently innocent family to turn over the case to them," White wrote her on the 24th. With the case approaching its climax in the spring of 1951, Roosevelt received an appeal from a CRC lawyer named Aubrey Grossman. She promptly wrote to tell him that he didn't have his facts straight. It could be reasonably argued, she said, that McGee's punishment fit the crime, but in any event such matters were best left to the wiser heads at the NAACP. Do that, she advised, and unfortunates like McGee "would not have added suspicions aroused against them."

I didn't know any of this when I first started researching McGee's story a few years ago, but it didn't take long to see that the case, after all these decades, was still full of mysteries that warranted a fresh look. I got interested one summer day in 2004, when I was browsing in a used bookstore and came across Philip Dray's *At the Hands of*

Persons Unknown, a history of lynching published in 2002. The book contains a brief account of the McGee case, and as I skimmed it, I realized I'd heard of McGee long before, in 1979.

Back then, I was a junior at Vanderbilt University in Nashville, Tennessee, studying English and history and working on student publications. The school provided us with the guidance of a part-time adviser named Jim Leeson, a former civil rights reporter who was originally from Hattiesburg, the town near Laurel where McGee was arrested in 1945. One night, as he often did, Leeson invited a few students over for dinner. Late in the evening, he played a tape he'd recorded himself in 1951, from a broadcast by Hattiesburg radio station WFOR. It was a live, half-hour news report that went out from the execution scene on the night McGee died.

The electrocution happened a few minutes after midnight on Tuesday, May 8, on the second floor of the Jones County Courthouse. As required by Mississippi law—for a condemned man of any race—McGee was put to death in a portable electric chair that was set up in the same courtroom where he'd been convicted. Inside, official onlookers—including local and state law enforcement people, prosecutors, newsmen, and a few male relatives of Mrs. Hawkins, who wasn't there—waited for McGee to be brought over from the city jail next door and strapped in to the clumsy-looking wood-and-metal contraption. Outside, a crowd of roughly a thousand white adults and children milled around, talking, laughing, and looking up at the courthouse's second-floor windows for a sign that the execution was about to happen.

A truck housing a generator was parked near the jail on a courthouse driveway. The electrical current would travel from the truck through long lines that snaked up to a second-story window and over the courtroom floor. The radiomen were outside too, using a portable transmitter they'd set up near the truck. There wasn't much to see, so they made do by talking about the scene in the courtyard.

"Time is rapidly running out for Willie McGee," said one of the broadcasters, a Mississippi radio veteran named Granville Walters. ". . . [T]hey are opening the truck, getting it all set, ready to turn it on, so that the juice will be funneled up through these cables . . . to the chair."

Leeson didn't play this tape to be morbid. He was twenty when he recorded it—about my age when I heard it—and he shared it as an example of how much things had changed since his years in college. He grew up in Mississippi before the civil rights era began, when segregation and Jim Crow were the ironclad law of the land. I was born in Mississippi too—in Jackson in 1957—but my experiences were completely different. He lived in a small town in the 1940s, a decade when lynchings were still common in the South, public interracial romances were forbidden by law and custom, and famous political demagogues like Mississippi senator Theodore G. Bilbo still rolled into towns and delivered live, courthouse-square speeches promising that white supremacy would endure forever.

I grew up in the 1960s, on a suburban street that could have been almost anywhere. And although I was able to understand, dimly, that major changes were happening, it would be a pose to say that I really grasped what was going on. I was only four when James Meredith enrolled at the University of Mississippi, sparking fatal riots; five when Medgar Evers was assassinated in Jackson; and seven when Chaney, Goodman, and Schwerner were murdered in the central Mississippi town of Philadelphia.

I reamined oblivious, even when the changes started affecting me directly. I was in seventh grade in 1970, when Jackson's public schools were finally desegregated after sixteen years of resistance. By the time I started paying attention to current events—in ninth grade, which was also the year I first read *To Kill a Mockingbird*—my Mississippi years had come to an end. My father took a new job in Kansas and we moved in 1972. I've been back to the state many times since—I have family there—but only as a visitor, never a resident.

Seeing Dray's book made me want to know more, not only about McGee, but about the history of Mississippi and the South as a whole between the end of World War II and the mid-1950s. It was an important and violent period—notable for the front-line activities of

Communists and other radicals—and it's usually skipped in standard histories of the civil rights movement.

I looked around for a full-length account of the McGee case, but I couldn't find one, just a few pages here and there in books, old magazine and journal articles, and on Web sites. McGee was the subject of a chapter in Carl Rowan's *South of Freedom*, a 1952 collection of reporting about race issues below the Mason-Dixon Line, and in Jessica Mitford's 1977 memoir, *A Fine Old Conflict*. The case also came up in *Against Our Will*, Susan Brownmiller's 1975 study of the history and politics of rape.

From these and other accounts, I could see that the question of "what really happened" between McGee and Mrs. Hawkins was still a moving target. Dray seemed convinced that the affair story was true, as did Mitford, a former Communist Party member who was involved in McGee protests in Jackson in 1951. Brownmiller took the opposite view, pointing out that the affair was an allegation, not proven fact. She thought Mrs. Hawkins might have been telling the truth, and that she could have been defamed by people who found it easier to blame her than the Mississippi justice system, or who could not accept that, sometimes, black men accused of rape in the bad old days had actually done something wrong. Brownmiller didn't mean this excused mob action or one-sided trials. She did mean that it was possible for a woman like Mrs. Hawkins to be turned into a caricature—that of a soulless, evil sex fiend who didn't care who had to die to cover up her lust and lies.

Rowan, a prominent black journalist originally from Tennessee, didn't seem sure either way. At times posing as a drifter, he traveled to Laurel in early 1951, where he heard juke-joint talk to the effect that everybody in town knew McGee and Mrs. Hawkins were carrying on. However, he had no way of knowing whether this was truth or fiction. Politically, Rowan was a middle-of-the-roader who didn't care for McGee's Communist defenders, and he believed their interference did more harm than good. In a chapter called "Run! The Red Vampire!" he wrote, "The Reds, shedding crocodile tears, put a fatal 'curse' on McGee, for non-Communist liberals began to shy away. A Negro leader explained that the 'case would warrant the support of the general public, but because the Communists are connected with it, the people are afraid to say anything.' "

From where I was based—Santa Fe, New Mexico—it was hard to do much research, but I did notice that the case's basic facts didn't match up from one telling to the next. For whatever reason, nobody spelled Willette Hawkins's first name right, using variations like Wiletta, Willett, and Willametta. There was also confusion about McGee's children. One book said he had four, named Willie Earl, Della, Gracie Lee, and Mary. Another said there were two, named Adolphus and Marjorie. Those were small mistakes, but they hinted at something significant. It seemed possible that, like Eleanor Roosevelt, the people who had written about the McGee case really didn't know much about him or Mrs. Hawkins.

The other glaring problem was missing information. The three circuit-court trials were never summarized in much detail, which was probably a sign that the transcripts hadn't survived. It was unclear whether Bella Abzug had argued the case in trial court or had come in later, during appeals. It was evident that some of the defense work was handled by in-state lawyers—I saw the names Dixon Pyles and John Poole, Mississippians both—but there were few facts about who they were or what they did.

At some point that summer, I realized that if I wanted to know more, I had to start over, diving in to see if I could find comprehensive newspaper coverage and primary documents—transcripts, appeals, letters, organizational papers, FBI files, and so forth. If the information wasn't available, I'd probably hang it up, because there was no reason to keep reading secondhand accounts.

At the same time, I would try to find any surviving children of McGee and Mrs. Hawkins, and if I couldn't locate them—or if they refused to talk—I'd probably quit for that reason as well. They were sure to know indispensable things. If they wouldn't open up, I'd never feel confident that I knew the whole story.

Of the two main tasks, I suspected that finding family members would be harder. McGee's wife, Rosalee, became a public figure during the case, because the CRC sent her on speaking tours that took her all over the North, Midwest, and West. But then she dropped out of sight, appearing in only a couple of newspaper stories after 1952. I had no idea where she ended up, what happened to her children, or whether they numbered two, four, or six.

I had less to go on with the Hawkins children: All I knew was that, circa 1945, there were three young girls. What were their names? And were they or their parents still alive?

It took months to find out, and as I did so—through trial, error, and luck—I became convinced that the old, long-dormant story of Willie McGee deserved a complete reexamination. Partly because it was an important civil rights episode that had never been explored in full. Partly because, as I soon found out, some of the mistakes about the case were game changers.

———

I found the Hawkins daughters first—sort of. For months, I didn't know what their names were, and it would be a while before I communicated with any of them directly. A Web search led me to a woman named Mary Mostert, a Utah-based freelance journalist in her seventies who had written about McGee for the *Nation* back in 1951, when she was a young progressive based in Memphis, Tennessee. Mostert, who had moved to the right politically since then, was still working, and she'd recently written a Web article that used her old *Nation* story as an example of how the political bias of editors can distort what a journalist intends to say.

Her sense in 1951 was that the case was too confusing for her to know whether McGee was guilty or not. But the *Nation*, she said, had changed her words to emphasize his innocence. Just the opposite happened to a colleague who filed a report for *Time*. He was unsure too, but since *Time* was known for its strong anti-Communist line, his editors manipulated his copy to underscore McGee's guilt.

I called Mostert, who told me her piece had prompted two of the Hawkins's grown grandchildren to e-mail her, asking for tips on researching the case. Later, she heard from one of the daughters, who explained that it was she who had inadvertently aroused the curiosity of the grandkids. This woman—Mostert wouldn't give me her name at first—had gotten upset when she happened to see an HBO documentary profiling Beah Richards, in which Richards read from "A Black Woman Speaks." She had heard about the affair story, but she didn't know until seeing this program that it was so widely accepted as fact. She mentioned this to her sisters, who told their children about it. Some of the grandkids decided to do Web research on their own, which led them to Mostert.

I asked Mostert what the family's goal was. She wasn't sure, and she wouldn't give me contact information. Instead, she passed my name along to the daughter. For months, I communicated with her indirectly, using Mostert as a go-between and occasionally seeing snippets of what she'd written in her e-mails. It was no surprise that she believed McGee was guilty.

"When I was eight years old, Willie McGee broke into our home and raped my mother," she wrote in one. "My twenty-month-old sister was in bed with her. My [other] sister and I were in the next room. My father was in the back bedroom, trying to rest after a late shift at work and helping my mother comfort a sick child. Our lives changed forever."

Sometimes, through Mostert, I would pass along a piece of information I had come across, and during one of these exchanges I made a mistake that almost shut down the conversation for good. Since I didn't have any sources in Mississippi—just friends and relatives—I was cold-calling all over the place at first, talking to anybody from old civil rights activists like Ed King (a white Jacksonian who'd worked with Medgar Evers and who shared a home with one of Dixon Pyles's sons, Todd) to Richard Barrett, a New Jersey transplant who had made a name as Mississippi's most outspoken modern segregationist. Barrett had some useful thoughts about sources, but I should have been more careful. In an e-mail to Mostert, I mentioned him in connection with something he'd said about libel law. She sent the Hawkins daughters

only a fragment of what I'd written, and for a long time they thought
he and I might be colleagues on the extreme right. Given the nature of
the McGee case, they wanted nothing to do with that.

I found the McGees in an equally roundabout way. After spending weeks trying to track them down without success, I wrote a letter to the editor of the *People's World*—a Chicago-based newspaper
descended from the *Daily Worker*—hoping that some old-timer who
remembered Rosalee McGee would call. Several months later, I got an
e-mail from Bridgette McGee Robinson, a woman from Las Vegas who
said she was Willie McGee's granddaughter. The *People's World* ran
my letter online, so my name turned up in a Web search she'd done
while looking into the case. She also told me about another relative
who was interested: Tracey McGee, the granddaughter of McGee's
late brother, Jasper McGee Jr.

I reached Tracey first. A longtime Bay Area resident, she said that
she and Bridgette had only recently learned of each other's existence.
Now they were doing research with an eye toward co-writing a family
history about the case. She added that two of McGee's children, Willie
Earl and Della, were still around, both of them living in Las Vegas.
And then she left me hanging with a cryptic statement. "I have to tell
you that some of the things people say about this case are wrong,"
she said.

Like what?

"I shouldn't talk about that on the phone. Can you get out to Las
Vegas and talk to Bridgette and Della?"

My wife, Susan, and I made that trip in February 2005, traveling by
car and arriving on a Friday night. The next morning, we rolled onto
the endless pavement of North Las Vegas, following one of the city's
racetrack boulevards, Camino Al Norte, and taking a series of quick
turns that put us on a side street called Jose Leon. The street was in
a quiet development of middle-class homes that baked blandly under
the winter sun.

Bridgette, who was in her thirties, greeted us at a side-door entrance and took us into a small beige living room that merged with a dining room where she'd laid out finger food and drinks. She was plump, funny, and friendly, as was her husband, Harold, a cheerful man who came bounding off a couch to shake our hands. Willie Earl wasn't there. He either couldn't show up (because of health reasons) or didn't want to; I was never sure which. Della was on a couch, sitting silent and stone-faced. She was in her late sixties, but she hadn't retired. At the time, she was working at the Stardust Hotel.

We settled in around the table, Della at the far end, Harold on the couch, and Bridgette next to me and Susan, her pile of old newspaper stories and family photos within easy reach. She started showing us things, beginning with an old colorized photographic portrait of a light-skinned black woman. I'd never seen a picture of Rosalee McGee before and assumed this was she. But as Bridgette told me, this woman's name was Eliza Jane Payton McGee, and she, not Rosalee, was the mother of all of Willie McGee's children. There were four: Willie Earl, Della, Gracie Lee, and Mary. Bridgette and Della had never heard of an Adolphus or Marjorie. Whoever Adolphus and Marjorie were, they weren't part of this family.

The Eliza Jane Payton news was a stunner. Rosalee McGee—loyal wife, selfless mother, brave CRC spokesperson—had been central to how Willie's story was presented to the public during his appeals. She and Willie always acted as if the four children were theirs, and as if Rosalee had custody of them throughout the duration of the case. But Della said that she, her siblings, and her mother left Mississippi after McGee's arrest. Among other things, this meant the "Gracie Lee" letter to President Truman was faked.

Why did Rosalee and Willie lie about their relationship?

Bridgette and Della didn't know, but solving this mystery was very important to them. To Della, Rosalee was an identity thief, and she said there had been an episode long ago—she couldn't remember when—in which Rosalee had tried to collect Social Security payments that belonged to McGee's biological children.

While we all puzzled over this, Bridgette asked Della if she thought

Rosalee might have been a girlfriend of Willie's rather than a wife. Apparently, he got around. "Couldn't it have been possible," Bridgette said, "that he was going with . . . whatever, Willameeta, whatever her name was—"

"The woman that he was supposed to rape?" Della said.

". . . That he was going with her, and then he could have been going with a black woman too? And he could have been with grandma. He was that type of man."

There was no particular response to that. Maybe Della didn't want to talk about what type of man he was in front of me. I tried an easier question, asking if she had clear memories of him. She was in grade school when he was arrested in 1945.

"Um . . . hmm, I remember him," she said.

"Can you tell me what was he like?" I mentioned that, in one account I'd read, McGee was depicted as being simpleminded, but that this didn't seem right. I'd seen a picture of him published in *Life*. He didn't look mentally impaired.

"He wasn't that," she said. Then she abruptly started talking about Mrs. Hawkins. "What I was told, as a young woman in my twenties, was that he and this lady were going together and they got caught. And that's when they had her say rape." She tried to think of who told her this but couldn't. "Because you see, in them days, you couldn't go with no white woman," she said. "Not down in Mississippi."

Bridgette cut in with a theory I hadn't heard before: that McGee and Mrs. Hawkins had had a child together—the twenty-month-old girl, who supposedly was conceived during their affair. The reason McGee crawled into Willette's room that night, she said, was to visit his own offspring. Bridgette said the baby was starting to show "the black heritage" and that this triggered the frame-up.

"So it shows up in this child?" I said.

"Yeah. But they wouldn't allow that to be submitted into the trial."

That sounded far-fetched, and it was the first example of something I would encounter often as I learned more about the McGee case: Somewhere along the line, it stopped being only about verifiable facts. It had become a ghost story, a malleable myth whose realities, lessons, and undercurrents varied tremendously, depending on the perspective of the teller.

At the same time, it was a true story with a terrible ending: McGee lost his life in a humiliating public execution. Della wasn't ready to open up to me about how it felt to have that in her past—I wondered if she ever would be—but Bridgette was less reticent. I asked her why she was doing this research and what she hoped to accomplish with it.

"I want it to be exposed," she said. "I think it's time. I want it to be exposed. I want the truth to be known. I know he wasn't a perfect man. But if he was killed that way, I want it to be known."

She said her mother, on her deathbed, had made Bridgette promise to keep looking into the case until she found out what really happened. She wasn't sure yet what to do about the things she learned; that was something she was praying over.

At this point, Harold cut in and asked, "Would there be something they would do as far as, um, the state of Mississippi maybe acknowledging that the trial was, like, pretty much set up?"

"That's what we're thinking," Bridgette said. "I mean, we know half the people are dead that were involved in the trial. So we're saying . . . it does not bring him back, but just the recognition that they committed a crime. . . . Because they never proved any rape. It was her word against his word."

I went to Mississippi on my first research trip in the spring of 2005, driving from Santa Fe to Laurel, detouring south for a weekend-long stopover in pre-Katrina New Orleans. It wasn't the smartest way to get there—total road time, twenty-two hours—but it was worth it. I love the terrain of southern Louisiana and Mississippi, where you can see everything from cypress swamps to blinding sun-and-sand panoramas to highway stretches where the trees are so thick and close that it feels like you're spinning down a giant green hallway.

I took I-59 out of New Orleans on a Sunday afternoon, heading north and east through the west side of Mississippi's boot heel, past small towns like Picayune, Poplarville, and Lumberton. The first real city you come to is Hattiesburg, followed by Laurel, which is only about 140 miles from New Orleans. I stopped long enough to drop my stuff at a hotel, then I drove to a place thirty miles farther north: a tiny town, a few miles off the interstate, called Pachuta. I had a fragment of an old newspaper story, published in an African-American newspaper in 1951, that said McGee was buried there somewhere.

In 1951, cemeteries were segregated, and I'd called ahead looking for a funeral home director who might know where the old black graveyards were. I found somebody in a nearby town, Quitman, who said the place I wanted was called Campbell's. But he couldn't give me directions. He just knew the name.

Where was Campbell's? There was nothing in the phone book, so I started knocking on doors, driving back and forth over country roads on a warm, soft-breezed spring afternoon. I banged on the door of a beat-up trailer home with a deputy sheriff's car parked out front. No answer. I startled a white man in the back office of an empty church. I went inside a convenience store and approached the first person I saw, a tall, heavy black woman in her fifties who was dressed in shorts, bedroom slippers, and a tentlike T-shirt.

"Campbell's?" she said, frowning and thinking. "Naw. Hold on." She rounded up every person in the place, as if I were on an important mission. "This man needs to find *Campbell's* cemetery. Anybody know?" Nobody knew. She looked perplexed that she couldn't help.

A few minutes later, I was driving around lost when I pulled up beside a middle-aged black man riding down a woodsy side road on a bike. He said he knew people who knew where Campbell's was, but could I give him two dollars first? Sure, I said. He pointed down the road and said to go that way and "look for the Jordans."

A half mile farther in, I found Cleaven Jordan, a short, wiry black man in his late sixties who was working on a car in front of a ranch house. Two younger men looked on and a small dog wiggled and whined as I rolled down the window to explain myself.

"Yeah, I know Campbell's," he said, tilting his head and smiling. "But why do you want to find it?" I told him I was researching the Willie McGee case. Maybe he'd heard of it?

"Oh, yes," he said softly.

I talked on, telling him I'd recently met one of McGee's two surviving children and one of his granddaughters. They were gathering information, and we were sharing what we found out.

"OK," he said, as if that was all anybody needed to hear. "Well, the thing is, I know all about Willie McGee. So you might want to just pull over."

After I parked, Jordan walked us a few paces down the road, heading south, and then stopped. Standing there, which was nowhere in particular, he took a deep breath and started in on a capsule history of the case.

"Willie McGee was a man who liked women and they liked him," he began. "Along in there after the war, he got messed up with a white woman and her husband found out. So she called rape on Willie to save her own neck." I waited for more but that was it. He paused to try and retrieve additional details about where McGee was executed and buried.

"Hold on a second," he said, pulling out a cell phone. "I'm going to call my uncle. He might know something more."

The uncle said Campbell's wasn't the right place. He told Jordan to send me to a pair of rural church cemeteries a few miles west of the interstate. "He thinks he's in one of those," Jordan said cheerfully. "You have to remember that when people say Pachuta, they mean them little country places too."

Twenty minutes later, I pulled up to a redbrick Baptist church called Mt. Pleasant. Nobody was there and the chapel door was locked. In a big downward-sloping lawn behind the building, backed by a thicket of swishing hardwoods, pines, and scrub trees, sat an austere old graveyard. There were dozens of headstones scattered around, many inscribed with the name McGee: Cecil C. McGee, Father Burkie Mc-Gee Sr., Elzie Mae McGee. But no Willie McGee or Jasper McGee Sr.—Willie's father, who's supposed to be buried there near him. About a third of the graves were unmarked, nothing more than dents in the earth or sunken concrete slabs without headstone or label.

Was McGee in there? I inspected every grave I could find, crawling around to read hidden markers and finger worn lettering. Nothing. I felt sure he was, but he was still out of reach.

———

Over time, I was able to locate the materials I needed to understand the McGee case better—including a complete transcript of the first trial, which had been missing for years—but there were moments during that initial trip when it seemed like there were nothing left to find but rumors.

Early in the morning on Monday, I started out at the Jones County Courthouse, a two-story building made of brick and stone with tall entryway doors, wide hallways, and big wavy-paned old windows. The courthouse is positioned between Laurel's now depressed downtown and its nicest residential neighborhoods, streets built up during the city's bygone glory days as an agricultural-industrial center fueled by the harvesting and processing of pine trees. For block after block running north, the streets were lined with beautiful homes and a few outright mansions.

The courtroom where McGee died was locked, so I spent most of my time in a side room off the circuit clerk's office, a small, crowded space where the large bound ledgers of marriage licenses are kept. In McGee's time, the records were maintained separately by race, and I started with a ledger from the 1930s labeled MARRIAGE RECORD COLORED. It didn't take long to find the paperwork. McGee and Eliza Jane Payton got their license on April 15, 1935, when he was twenty-one and she was eighteen. She was from Collins, a small town twenty-seven miles to the west. Her parents were named Joe and Eliza Payton. McGee's parents were named Jasper and Bessie.

There was also a wedding license for Troy and Willette Hawkins, whose maiden name was Dorothy Willette Darnell. They were married on March 16, 1934, when he was twenty-five and she was twenty. Later that day, at the public library, I found a front-page story in the local newspaper, the *Laurel Leader-Call*, which explained what became of them: On March 25, 1967, Mrs. Hawkins was killed in a car accident inside the Laurel city limits, with Troy at the wheel. He survived the impact but died later at the hospital. There wasn't a word about the McGee case, and no picture of either of the deceased.

After looking at the licenses, I asked a clerk to bring me whatever she had on McGee. She came back with a folder containing a few scattered pages, including the original indictment, the witness list, verdict slips, and a motion for a continuance from the second trial, which was held in Hattiesburg after a judge ordered it moved out of Laurel. The lead defense lawyer for that one was Jackson-based attorney Dixon Pyles.

Pyles died in 2000, but later that day in Hattiesburg, I met one of his sons, Todd, a retired lawyer who was nice enough to drive down from Jackson and escort me to an archives building at the University of Southern Mississippi, where papers from Pyles's legal career are kept. The collection was still being processed and was off-limits to researchers, so Todd—a friendly man with a bushy moustache and a courtly Southern accent—spent an hour looking at the finding aid to see if the McGee case was referenced in there. He saw no sign of it.

"To tell you the truth, I don't think you're going to find it in here," he said. "I think he would have given all that stuff to the next lawyer who worked the case."

Later, the circuit clerk in Hattiesburg, a woman named Lou Ellen Adams, took me to an off-site storage facility where older court records were kept, material that was originally moved as a result of a courthouse fire years earlier. As she'd confided when I phoned her, I wasn't the first person to ask about McGee. One of Mrs. Hawkins's daughters had come through months before, looking for the second-trial transcript.

She didn't find it, and once we got to the facility I could see why.

The site was a defunct commercial space in an old shopping center miles from the courthouse. The interior was dark and dusty; mildew in the air stung my throat. On makeshift shelves, in disintegrating boxes, and heaped on the floor in crazy piles, were thousands of old indictments and trial transcripts. It would have taken weeks to look at it all, so I gave up and left.

———

The next day, back in Laurel, I spent the morning with a sixty-four-year-old African-American woman named Evelyn Smith McDowell, whom I'd been introduced to by a local author named Cleveland Payne. Payne has written several books about the history of blacks in Laurel, and he said he thought McDowell was related to McGee—a distant cousin or something like that.

She lived in a poor part of town, in a long, run-down brick apartment building on the south side of the railroad tracks that split Laurel in two. After greeting me at her front door, she marched me straight through her apartment to a tiny outdoor patio, took a seat in the blazing morning sun, and started shouting answers to my questions. McDowell was short, heavy, and hard of hearing, and had lost most of her front teeth. She was wearing a shiny dirty-blonde wig and a stretched-out gold T-shirt. She did most of the talking.

She started by telling me about a long-dead aunt who had owned a neighborhood grocery store when she was a child. "She lived at 239 South Eighth Avenue," she said, "and she was the first black lady that had a grocery market on that end of town." This aunt used to hold evening dances at the store, and Willie McGee, as a young man, would come to them. McDowell claimed to remember seeing him in the early 1940s, when she would have been, at most, a preschooler.

"What was he like?" I asked at one point.

"He was a soft-spoken person," she said. "To me, he was kinda shy. You would have to kinda force him into talking. He was handsome! But he was very neat. He had deep creases in his pants, he wore white, pretty shirts, and he smelled good all the time. Women liked that he was very clean and kept his hair cut. He was a very handsome man.

He wasn't pretty, but he was handsome enough for you to notice. . . . The ladies were after him. He wasn't after them."

The story she'd heard about the affair represented yet another variation: McGee, she said, was having sex with both the white woman and the woman's maid. He went away for a while at some point—to Las Vegas or Los Angeles with a friend named T-Bone. When he returned, his plan was to marry the maid and move west, but the white woman wouldn't allow it. She didn't mind him messing around with the maid, but she would never let him leave the state.

"When the lady found out about Willie was having a personal affair with this black lady, it was all well and good as long as it was going to be here in Mississippi," Evelyn said. "But when they decided to leave and go to California together, she got all upset about this rape thing."

I told her I'd heard that everybody in the black sections of Laurel knew the affair was going on.

"Yeah, we *did* know. Everybody knew, but wasn't nothing we could do about it."

"How did they know?"

"Hey, they would be out in the car, and she'd be kissing him! They would come down through here and there wasn't anything anybody could do about it, because this is what she wanted to do."

"But wasn't that dangerous?"

"Not really. At that particular time, whatever white people said was all right. . . . The only way you'd get lynched was if she hollers about that you raped her. . . . If you were black and I was white, as long as I didn't bother saying you were trying to rape me, it was all right."

McDowell also talked about the execution, which happened when she was nine. On the afternoon of May 7, 1951, she darted around in downtown Laurel, staying out of the way but peeking here and there to see what was going on. "It was just like something was waiting to happen," she said, with awe in her voice. "It wasn't noisy, it wasn't nobody demonstrating anything. But you could *feel* it, the tension in the air."

McDowell didn't go near the courthouse that night, but she said she clearly remembered that the lights in her part of town went out every time the current was applied to the electric chair, a signal to the downtrodden blacks of Laurel about what would happen if they crossed the line. That didn't sound possible—the chair was powered by a generator—but I shut up and listened. McDowell went on to say that, the next day, black schoolchildren, including her, were taken in groups to "the Pete Christian funeral home" to view McGee's body. This was done to teach them a lesson.

"My third-grade teacher, Miss Della Hodge, had us children all in line, and we was just like a couple of ducks, walking across the street," she said. "They had us to go and look. They said, 'This is an example to black boys, if they mess with white women.'

"I was terrified," she said. "You could see that he was a human being, but he was just like a piece of charcoal. He was just black, black, black—burnt black."

─────

The following Sunday, at a bookstore in a suburban shopping center in Jackson, I finally met two of the Hawkins sisters: Sandra, the middle daughter and the person who had kept in contact with Mary Mostert, and Dorothy, who was the baby in the bed on the night of the rape. They agreed to meet me after I sent a long e-mail explaining my interest in the case and how I proposed to handle researching it.

Dorothy lived in Mississippi; Sandra was passing through with her husband. Both sisters were in their sixties, and both were the kind of tastefully dressed Southern women I'd seen a thousand times before. I had aunts, now mostly gone, who looked like both of them.

Even before we sat down, I knew which one was Sandra thanks to a high-school yearbook photo I'd found in Laurel. A former majorette, she had big eyes and a friendly face and a manner that made her easy to talk to. Dorothy was more closed-off, though she opend up some as we talked. When I could, I sneaked glances at her, looking for outward signs of "the black heritage." There weren't any.

Dorothy worked in a public school system and was nearing retire-

ment, one of several reasons why she was leery about discussing the
McGee case in any kind of media context. In tune with that, I didn't
take notes. They were interviewing me, not vice versa, and during
a two-hour grilling about my motives, I felt as if I were making, at
best, modest progress toward getting them to believe that I could tell
their story without bias. Richard Barrett came up early on, and they
accepted my explanation about him. The harder part was convincing
them that I wasn't a professional liar. Journalists weren't high on their
list of trustworthy people.

Dorothy, especially, seemed scarred by having lived with the case.
At one point, she asked if I had any idea where the McGee children
were. When I said yes, she looked shocked and went silent. She didn't
ask for additional details.

Though meeting the sisters was difficult, it was a valuable reminder
of how explosive the case still was for both families. Like Bridgette,
the Hawkins sisters believed that they owed it to their parents' memory to correct lies about who they really were, yet they were smart
enough to see how risky it was for them to go anywhere near this
subject. After all, their side won: McGee was put to death. Half a
century later, who would want to listen to a couple of Deep South
white women complain that their mother got a raw deal?

By the time we parted company, I had no idea what they were
thinking. Eventually, they did decide to talk to me, but that didn't
happen for more than a year. As those months went by and we sporadically kept in touch, I started to believe that they would eventually
choose to talk. To do nothing would mean, by default, condemning
their mother to an eternal reputation as an adulteress, liar, and murderer. Sandra, for one, couldn't tolerate that. As she put it to me later
in an e-mail: "My mother was a victim. She's become the accused."

two

A MAN WASN'T BORN
TO LIVE FOREVER

There's an undated picture of Willie McGee that looks like it was probably taken at the time of his arrest in November 1945. It was shot by a now deceased Laurel man who sometimes photographed accused criminals in hopes of selling images to a newspaper or magazine. His brother, who held on to it, says there's no record of when it was made. But, notably, McGee is dressed in street clothes: a checked jacket with dark sleeves and pointed collars, and, under the jacket, a light-colored shirt, unbuttoned at the neck. The picture shows a handsome young man with smooth skin, piercing eyes, a strong jaw, and a broad nose. He's standing in front of a cell door, staring into the camera with a serious but calm expression on his face. If the photo is from 1945, he looks remarkably composed for a man in his position.

McGee would have known what was in store if he fell into the hands of a lynch mob. As a black man accused of raping a white woman in Mississippi in 1945, he would, at the very least, have been killed. At worst, he would have been tortured by an enraged gang of white men who might have taken their time before finishing him off with a knife, gun, or rope. There weren't nearly as many lynchings in the South in the 1940s as there had been in the period between 1890 and 1930, but they still happened, and they could still be medieval in their intensity.

As McGee may have known, there had been a gruesome double lynching in 1942 near Shubuta, a small town about thirty-five miles northeast of Laurel. There, two fourteen-year-olds named Charles Lang and Ernest Green were taken from jail and killed by a mob for allegedly trying to assault a thirteen-year-old white girl. They were found hanging from a rusty old bridge over the Chickasawhay River, but they'd been mutilated first. Madison S. Jones, an NAACP field operative who filed a report on the incident, wrote that the boys' "reproductive organs were cut off. Pieces of flesh had been jerked away from their bodies with pliers and one boy had a screwdriver rammed down his throat so that it protruded from his neck."

In an earlier era, McGee's chances of living long after a rape charge would have been slim to none. But by the mid-1940s, he had a reasonable shot of surviving to face trial, because local and state law enforcement officials often made serious efforts to keep potential lynching victims out of mob hands. A lot depended on who was governor at the time, and McGee was arrested during the term of a chief executive who cared about law and order: Thomas Bailey.

Still, the prospect of a trial couldn't have been much comfort. In many cases from that era, the court proceedings were only formalities, with all-white, all-male juries virtually guaranteed to deliver guilty verdicts and death penalties when a black person was accused of raping or killing a white, whether the evidence was strong or weak. Civil rights people in the North had a rueful term for it: "legal lynching."

A typical legal-lynching episode occurred in early 1934, in the northwest Mississippi town of Hernando, when three black men from Memphis—Isaac Howard, Johnny Jones, and Ernest McGehee— were tried on charges of robbery and the alleged sexual assault of a seventeen-year-old white schoolgirl. Like McGee, they were hurried off to Jackson after their arrest and kept there until it was time for them to appear in court. When they were delivered to Hernando on February 12, 400 National Guard troops were assembled to provide safe escort. "Rifles, sidearms, grenades, gas guns and gas masks were issued to them," the Associated Press reported, "and they were accompanied by engineers who will be available to build barricades."

Even with all that firepower—and barbed-wire tangles circling the courthouse—several locals tried to force their way in. One old man sliced his hand on the wire and was asked by a reporter if he'd cut himself accidentally. "Hell, no," he said. "We want those Negroes."

Inside, the prisoners were kept in a vault until they emerged just long enough to plead guilty. They were taken back to Jackson in a steel-barred train; one month later, they were returned to Hernando for hanging. (Mississippi's portable electric chair wasn't put into use until 1940.) Even then, it was necessary to have a 200-man guard on duty and circulate false stories about their arrival time.

Were these men guilty of anything? They might have been, but it's hard to know since the judicial process was so corrupted. As they died on the gallows, they issued a stream of statements, prayers, and confessions that sounded like scripted warnings to members of their race. Their last words were widely quoted in Mississippi newspapers, including the *Laurel Leader-Call*, which, coincidentally, ran a front-page story about the execution on the same day Troy and Willette Hawkins got married. The message was clear: Don't touch white women, or this, most definitely, will happen to you.

"Tell others of my kind never to attack none who don't belong to them," Howard said. "Tell 'em never to do that. I believe in my God— goodbye."

"I want to warn others of my race," said Jones. "I wish some of them were here to see how we go. It's awful."

Though, technically, these men weren't lynched, they took a very fast ride to oblivion: only eighty days passed between their arrests and deaths. This brand of speedy retribution is what McGee was looking at, and in early December, when state troopers brought him back to Laurel for his arraignment, he didn't look calm anymore.

———

The crime that put McGee in the crosshairs happened sometime after 4 a.m. on November 2. At first, any details about what took place were slow in coming, skimpy, and controlled by the police chief, sheriff, and local prosecutors.

The *Leader-Call* wrote about the alleged rape the same day it occurred, in a short item headlined "Forcible Entry, Criminal Assault, Reported." The victim wasn't named, just described. She was a white woman living with her family on South Magnolia Street, and she'd been taken away to recover at a hospital in "a nearby city." (The story didn't say, but it was Hattiesburg.) She was raped by an attacker who threatened her life if she made a sound.

This story and a follow-up said there was a suspect, but it wasn't Willie McGee. The first man arrested was a thirty-four-year-old laborer named Floyd Nix, who was described as "a former employe [sic] of the woman." Sheriff Luther Hill and Chief of Police Wayne Valentine had rounded up several black men for questioning and released them that day. With Nix, they felt confident enough that he was their man that they sent him to Jackson for safekeeping. The reports never said what evidence this decision was based on.

On Saturday, November 3, everything changed with the arrest of a man identified in the *Leader-Call* as "Willie Magee, 30-year-old Laurel negro." The paper spelled his name wrong but got his age right: McGee was born on November 4, 1915, so he turned thirty the day after he was picked up. He was arrested in Hattiesburg on a larceny charge, stemming from unauthorized use of a truck owned by his employer, the Laurel Wholesale Grocery Company. The report correctly said—though police initially denied—that McGee had confessed to the rape after being taken back to Laurel from Hattiesburg. He didn't stay in Laurel long. Like Nix, he was taken to Jackson for protection and questioning. During all this time—and for the next thirty days—he was held without benefit of counsel.

One week later came another major development: "Magee" had confessed in writing, to Jones County Attorney Albert Easterling, who took down his statement at the Hinds County jail. In addition, the *Leader-Call* reported, physical evidence and fingerprints had been gathered and "sent to Washington to the Federal Bureau of Investigation laboratory for analysis."

There were no further details, but they wouldn't be long in coming, since the trial, predictably, got fast-tracked. The next circuit-court session in Laurel wasn't scheduled until February 1946, but the presiding judge, F. Burkitt Collins, didn't want to wait. He ordered a special session starting on the first Monday in December, with the trial to be held at the circuit-court building in downtown Laurel.

In some ways, Laurel wasn't a typical Mississippi town—it had a different backstory than many Magnolia State communities, and, in 1945, a very different feel, because it was a highly industrialized place in an agricultural state. The population was 31,000—with whites outnumbering blacks roughly 65 to 35—and there was a booster spirit in the air before and after World War II, with a sense that growth and expanding wealth were the city's inevitable destiny.

The resources that mattered most were pine trees and oil, not cotton. Laurel was in the heart of south Mississippi's Piney Woods region, a vast sea of trees that covered all or part of twenty-five counties. The woods were originally inhabited by Choctaws and Chickasaws; by the early 1800s, white settlers originally from South Carolina were coming in to what was then the Mississippi Territory, settling on lands that the Choctaws ceded in treaties with the United States. Jones County was founded in 1826, nine years after Mississippi entered the Union. It was a place of small settlements and subsistence farming, not of the big plantations associated with the Mississippi Delta, the flat, rich-soiled agricultural crescent in the northwest part of the state.

Consequently, Jones was never a major slaveholding county—there were only about 400 slaves there just before the start of the Civil War—and this distinction was, and still is, significant to the area's lore and self-image. Jones was home to a sizable amount of pro-Union feeling; during the war this gave rise to a guerrilla movement that was later mythologized into something nobler than it really was. The renegades were led by a Confederate deserter named Newton Knight, whose men were elusive because they knew the woods and rivers like no one else. Their motives were a mix of Union loyalty, a desire not to get shot fighting on behalf of plantation owners, and the freebooting spirit of frontier adventurers.

The legend, which isn't quite true, is that Jones County formally seceded from the Confederacy, reestablishing itself as a Union stronghold called the Free State of Jones. James Street, a novelist from Lumberton, Mississippi, fictionalized the Knight story in a 1942 novel called *Tap Roots*, which Universal made into a motion picture in 1948.

Tap Roots is an interesting old book, but it's also a little duller than it could have been, because Street softpedaled the most compelling theme connected to Newton Knight: interracial sex. Knight had children with both his white wife, Serena, and (probably) with an ex-slave named Rachel. Children of Newton and Rachel intermarried, starting a line of "white negroes" who were a fixture of the Piney Woods. One of Rachel's great-grandsons, Davis Knight, was fated for a starring role in a Jones County courtroom the same year the *Tap Roots* movie was released. In 1948, after marrying a local white girl named Junie Lee Spradley, Knight was charged with breaking Mississippi's law against mixed-race marriage.

Laurel wasn't founded until 1882, when the building of the New Orleans and Northeastern railroad—later acquired by the Southern Railway—created a demand for timber to complete the line. The first mill was opened that year by a man named John Kamper, who later sold out to Midwesterners whose investments changed Laurel from outpost to town: George and Silas Gardiner, and Charles Eastman. In April 1891, they, along with Lauren Eastman, began Jones County operations of the Eastman Gardiner lumber company, a major Jones County employer. The mills were why Willie McGee lived in Laurel to begin with. He was born in the country near Pachuta, but his father relocated to Laurel after World War I. Jasper Sr. turned up in the Laurel city directory in 1922, as a laborer at Eastman Gardiner. In the 1936 directory, he was still with the company. Willie's brother, Jasper, was listed as a student, and Willie was listed as an unspecified laborer. Their address was "64 3d Red Line." The red line was an area of red-colored company housing.

By 1939 the first-growth pines had been gone for years, but Laurel was getting more product out of less wood with a boost from science. A special edition of the *Leader-Call* called Laurel "the Chemurgic City," explaining that this coined word conveyed the magic that took place when technology, applied to agriculture, yielded products that had never existed before.

Since "chemurgy" is not in the dictionary as yet, Laurel feels she must act the part of Noah Webster:

Pronounce it thus:

Chem-urg'-y: accent on the second syllable. (Kem-urg'-y.)

Meaning: A movement to find industrial uses for products of the soil.

The prime example was the Masonite Corporation, an important Laurel employer—founded in 1926—whose economic might earned an eight-column headline in the *Leader-Call* supplement: "Chemurgic Development of Masonite Rivals Aladdin's Story." The Masonite process was invented by a transplanted West Virginian named William H. Mason. It involved taking scrap wood pieces and using high-pressure steam to reduce them to wood fiber that could be reconstituted into sturdy boards and panels.

Perfecting this involved some hard-knock experimentation. In one early attempt, Mason crammed wood chips into a homemade cannon, plugged it, steam-heated the contents to 800 degrees, and knocked off the plug with a pole, releasing a tremendous explosion of wet, wood-fiber shrapnel. A separate pressing process formed the fibers into a solid mass that was surprisingly strong. As a result, Masonite was good for more than just paneling and insulation. During World War II, many of the army tanks made at the American Car & Foundry plant in Berwick, Pennsylvania, were lined with two thicknesses of Masonite boards.

The various things that made Laurel unusual—the romanticized history, the modern industry, and an early influx of Yankee cash—were a source of local pride, and for many they fed a belief that Jim Crow–era Laurel was an easier place for a black person to exist than was the Delta. "Bi-racial investment and philanthropy displayed by the city's benefactors stood in stark contrast to the views of most white Mississippians," David Stanton Key, a Laurel native, wrote in a 2001 master's thesis on the city. "The . . . progressive outlook transcended traditional racial divisions and helped create a town of the 'New South' in the heart of the Piney Woods."

This was true only up to a point, because Laurel in 1945 was still rigidly segregated, still ruled by the same sexual taboos and voting-rights suppression as any other Mississippi town. Even so, there were tangible differences, like the existence of the Oak Park Vocational High School, which stood out as one of the best schools in Mississippi in the 1930s through the 1950s, producing prominent graduates like opera singer Leontyne Price and Olympic long jumper Ralph Boston. To Cleveland Payne, who attended the school and wrote a history about it called *The Oak Park Story*, everything good about Laurel was embodied there.

"An affluent class of northern whites had become part of the fabric of community life and influenced greatly the character of the town by setting the tone for cultural values and aesthetic appreciation," he wrote. "Too, a black middle class had emerged." In 1928, with donations of land, money, and buildings from wealthy local philanthropists, Oak Park was opened as a school that gave eager, motivated black students a chance to aim high in both vocational and academic course work.

Boston, a 1957 graduate of Oak Park, shares Payne's strong feelings about the school. "Oak Park was the lifeblood of everything," he told me in a phone interview. "Everything that was African-American in Laurel revolved around it." But he wasn't so sure about Laurel's exceptionalism. The main Oak Park building burned down in '57, and, in his opinion, "It was not spontaneous combustion. We were pretty sure that somebody set it afire.

"For quite a while," he added, "I understand that Laurel was known as 'liberal Laurel.' . . . But if you understand Laurel, you understand that Sam Bowers was from there. How liberal could you be if you have a man like that living there and who had a following there?"

Bowers, who wasn't born in Laurel, was around during the tail end of the McGee case, but he made his mark at a later time: He was Mississippi's most powerful Klan leader in the 1960s and the architect of the Philadelphia murders. Even so, Boston's point applies just as well to the McGee era. It was true: Laurel was a different sort of town, the existence of Oak Park proved that. But when the McGee trial got going, New South Laurel suddenly became a very Old South place.

———

On December 3, when McGee was brought back to Jones County for his arraignment and plea, he was under protective armed guard, requested by the sheriff, Luther Hill, and provided by Governor Bailey. During his monthlong stint in Hinds County, nothing was published about what he said and did—or what was said and done to him. It must have been a stark experience, because McGee came home a transformed man, scared out of his wits and unable, or unwilling, to speak, even to his lawyers. From the time of his first trial until the end of his third—more than two years later—he would not utter a single intelligible word in public, and he gave every indication of having lost his mind.

"The negro arrived shortly after 3 o'clock under guard of approximately fifty state troopers," the *Leader-Call* reported. "He was dressed in clothing similar to that worn by the guardsmen, including a helmet, and was chained. The officers had to drag him from the car and the prisoner was evidently either crazy or putting on a good act, say witnesses. He was shaking all over and jibbering, unable to answer intelligently the questions of the court."

The guard detail arrived in three army trucks, "a reconnaissance car," and a heavily armed jeep. The troopers were equipped with bayoneted rifles, machine guns, and tear gas. Outside the courthouse, men were arrayed at the entrances and on the lawn. Inside the big courtroom, which was kept breezy with help from windows and balconies on the south and north sides, deputies searched spectators for firearms before letting them in. The first three rows of benches were cleared to create a buffer between the people and the prisoner.

McGee's lawyers were court-appointed locals, M. W. Boyd and Harry Koch, who didn't want anything to do with the case and who weren't experienced criminal defenders. The presiding judge was F. Burkitt Collins, a member of a pioneering Jones County family who had served as a combat infantryman in France during World War I. Collins started practicing law in 1915 in Ellisville—along with Laurel, the second of Jones County's two county seats—and he was elected to the circuit-court bench for the first time in 1940. He was middle-aged when the McGee case started, a gray-haired, thin-lipped man with sharp features and a reputation for being, as the *Leader-Call* once put it, "quiet, studious, and unassuming, possessed of that rare quality known as judicial temperament."

Everybody knew the McGee case was combustible—the *Leader-Call* labeled it "the strongest charge" of Collins's career—and that first morning, speaking to prospective jurymen, the judge gave a speech that was intended not just for the townspeople in the room, but for anybody outside who might be harboring creatively violent ideas.

"The great war is over and our country is saved," he said. "It is a country of law, governed by law, a law under which all are considered equal. We need bow to none. The only majesty we recognize is 'His Majesty, the Law.'"

Soon enough, he got to the point: The trial and punishment were the exclusive business of him, the lawyers, and the jury. Spectators and other interested parties were not to interfere. "We are called today to see that the law is properly administered, to see that those who have transgressed are brought to justice," he said. "We cannot do this by taking the law into our own hands, and running over the law. We must follow the law in every particular. We must do this, whether it suits us or not. . . ."

———

Calling any case "the strongest charge" of Collins's career was saying something, since he had been involved in two of the most famous courtroom spectacles in Laurel history. He served as a defense attorney in the first of them, the sensational 1935 trial of a local woman named Ouida Keeton, a thirty-three-year-old who was accused of murdering her mother, Daisy Keeton—killing her inside the home they shared and then chopping her up and dumping the parts in the woods.

Some of the parts, that is. People called it "the legs murder" because the only remains ever found were a pair of hefty female hips and two thighs. The legs turned up on January 21, 1935, wrapped in old sugar sacks. They were spotted by a black tenant farmer named Don Evans Jr., who was out hunting rabbits in the woods of Jasper County, about fourteen miles north of Laurel. Evans was terrified that he'd be blamed—and lynched—but later that day he told a white man what happened, and together they flagged down a motorist who notified the police.

Policeman Wayne Valentine, a central figure in the McGee case, helped solve the mystery and later co-wrote a true-crime article about it called "Unraveling the Ouida Keeton 'Legs' Murder." Step one was identifying the remains; all the medical examiner could say was that the victim was probably over thirty-five, probably weighed around 155 pounds, had given birth, and appeared to be "a woman of refinement."

The first break came on the 24th, when a farmer north of town reported having seen a "highly excited woman" in a red car coming up his farmhouse lane before turning around. He recalled seeing a "large bundle" in the car. Newspaper coverage brought forth another witness, a wreckerman who'd been called to pull a red Willys-Knight sedan out of the mud on the morning of the 21st. He told police it belonged to Ouida Keeton.

Questioned at home, Ouida said her mother was in New Orleans. Police Chief J. E. Brown arrested her after spotting blood on a fender of the car. Valentine found bloodstains on the floor in front of the hearth, which had been vigorously scrubbed, along with a stained iron poker and cleaving instruments in the kitchen.

Pressed, Ouida offered a preposterous story, saying her mother had been kidnapped while they were driving together in the country. Eventually she confessed, shocking the town by naming an accomplice: W. M. Carter, a prominent sixty-seven-year-old Laurel businessman with whom Ouida was having an out-of-wedlock romance. Ouida said Carter killed Daisy because Daisy objected to their relationship. He ordered her to dispose of the legs while he took care of the upper half.

Carter was brought in and questioned (he denied everything), arrested, and taken to Jackson, because there was concern that even he, a white man, might get lynched thanks to the barbarity of the crime. They were tried separately. Ouida, represented by Collins, pleaded insanity, and she came to court every day in a wheelchair, presenting the image of a swooning invalid who had lost her mind. But the evidence was overwhelming and included an extremely graphic exhibit: the legs themselves, which were displayed to the jury inside a small, gray-painted box with a glass cover.

Before the jury went out, Collins delivered an eloquent speech that pinned the blame on Carter and asked for mercy for the second person whose life he had destroyed: Ouida. Carter, he said, had killed Daisy with a poker and then forced Ouida to be his accomplice. Ouida was like a "mighty oak that stands in the forest, unshakened and unmoved," while Carter was a malevolent wind that roared in to knock her down. "She saw this dominating mind take this poker and destroy the life of the best friend she ever had," he said. "Why wouldn't it destroy her mind?"

The jury didn't go for it. Ouida was found guilty and sentenced to life at the state prison at Parchman. She was later transferred to the state mental hospital, where she lived out her days. Carter was tried twice but he got off, one reason being that the portion of the body he was responsible for never turned up. Forever after, many people believed he dumped Daisy's torso in the Gulf of Mexico.

———

Over time, Ouida Keeton became Laurel's version of Lizzie Borden: ghastly but quaint. Eudora Welty, a connoisseur of Mississippi murder stories, loved to titillate friends with the bloody details. Even now, the case is still a guilty pleasure in Jones County. If you're ever in the courthouse, and you ask politely, the women there might show you a tucked-away folder that contains photographs of Daisy's legs, along with an original copy of Ouida's mail-order course in butchering.

However, there never was, and never will be, any nostalgia attached to another famous case Collins played a part in, this time as the judge: the October 1942 lynching of a convicted African-American killer named Howard Wash. Collins presided over Wash's trial and over a subsequent grand jury that refused to indict the men accused of lynching him. The jury's inaction opened the door to an early attempt by the federal government to step in on a Mississippi lynching case, prosecuting it as a criminal violation of Wash's right to equal protection under the Fourteenth Amendment. At McGee's first trial, when Collins talked about the perils of "taking the law into our own hands," it was probably the Wash case, with all its associated headaches, that he had in mind.

Wash was a middle-aged tenant laborer who worked for a white dairy farmer named Clint Welborn. Early in the morning on May 18, 1942, the two had an argument that apparently started because Wash overslept. Welborn yelled at him not to bother getting up—he was fired.

Nobody saw what happened next, but several people heard it from their beds. Wash's fourteen-year-old son, Howard Jr., testified that he heard the sound of a metal milk bucket slamming into something solid— "four licks," he recalled. Welborn's daughter, Patricia, said she heard three blows and a "peculiar gurgling." Wash went back to his house, changed his shoes, and calmly told his son and fifteen-year-old daughter, Frozine, that they would have to fend for themselves. Their mother was gone—at the trial, it wasn't made clear why, or where she was. Wash walked off and eluded capture for six weeks. He was arrested seventy miles away in the south Mississippi town of Poplarville.

At the trial, Wash claimed self-defense during brief testimony that was halting, mumbling, and hard to believe. Yes, he said, he'd been late for work, but Welborn went into a rage, cursed him, and raised a shovel to strike him. He used the bucket to block the shovel and he

hit Welborn once, by accident. Though Wash claimed he didn't realize he'd struck Welborn fatally—he lived for two more days—he ran
away because he was scared of what the Welborn family would do in
revenge.

The prosecution insisted he was lying. A doctor who treated Welborn said his skull was "broken . . . in many various and sundry
directions," indicating a purposeful beating. Wash was convicted on
October 16. In a surprise development, the jurors didn't give him the
death penalty. Instead he was sentenced to life in prison.

For friends and relatives of Clint Welborn, this manslaughter-style
sentence wasn't enough. At around 1 a.m. on the 17th, a group of
roughly fifty men showed up at the Laurel jail and demanded to be
let in. Luther Holder, a deputy sheriff and jailer, was asleep inside,
along with his three children and two other deputies. He phoned the
sheriff, J. Press Reddoch, who rushed over and tried to talk the mob
into dispersing. They pushed him aside and forced Holder to unlock
a heavy door that sealed off the cell areas. Wash was taken away just
after 2 a.m.; he was found the next morning hanging from the "Welborn bridge," which spanned a creek near the dairy farm.

Wash's lynching was one of three in south Mississippi that month.
Around 1:30 a.m. on October 12, the teenagers Lang and Green had
been killed near Shubuta, under mysterious circumstances that are
still impossible to sort out. There's no reliable account of the events
that got the boys lynched. There was little public investigation at the
time, and the newspaper stories that appeared offered conflicting details.

But a story in the *Chicago Defender*, a prominent African-American
newspaper, may have come closest to being accurate. Six months after
the incident, the paper published a report by a black journalist named
Enoc P. Waters, who traveled to Shubuta to piece together what he
could. Lang and Green, he was told by local blacks, were poor, barely
literate boys who worked hard doing odd jobs and collecting scrap
metal and rubber. On October 6, a Tuesday, they were scavenging
under a concrete highway bridge south of town when a girl named
"Martin" walked by on her way home from school. The three appar-

ently knew one another and started talking. A passing white driver, apparently a male, saw them and proceeded to tell the girl's father that she was being pursued by Lang in an inappropriate way.

What happened next is unknowable: Some accounts said Lang and Green freely confessed to attempted rape at their arraignment; some said they were chasing the girl around harmlessly, as any play-mates would. The boys were arrested and taken to jail at Quitman, the county seat. The next few days passed uneventfully. But on Monday, after midnight, a mob went in, threw a blanket over the jailer's head, and took Lang and Green off to their horrifying deaths.

———

The Wash, Lang, and Green killings were all covered nationally, al-though more so in African-American papers and the *Daily Worker* than in mainstream publications like the *New York Times*. In the black press and on the left, there was intense interest and a call for a coor-dinated federal response. The *Daily Worker* reported on the creation of a new National Emergency Committee to Stop Lynching, chaired by left-wing New York congressman Vito Marcantonio, who vowed to keep pressure on until the lynchers were identified and arrested.

There was a reasonable chance of that happening, since Missis-sippi's governor at the time, Paul Johnson Sr., promised to do some-thing and seemed to mean it. He publicly criticized the local sheriff for not notifying him about Lang and Green's arrest—Johnson would have moved them to Hinds County immediately—called the lynchers murderers, and promised to hunt them down. After Wash was killed, Johnson sent a state guard contingent to Laurel to help maintain order while suspects were brought in and questioned. During that period, the scene around the Jones County Courthouse looked remarkably similar to the opening days of the McGee trial.

"The courtyard is bristling with soldiers, who, at the instigation of Judge Burkitt Collins, were sent here by Governor Johnson," the *Leader-Call* reported. "Tear gas bombs, hand grenades and riot guns, bristling bayonets, are in readiness to cope with any trouble that may come up."

The state's effort produced five firm suspects in the Wash lynching but nothing on Lang and Green. Then, on October 20, it was reported that the Federal Bureau of Investigation would help investigate the case, and that Johnson publicly welcomed its input. That was significant in 1942. To invite federal intrusion into a Mississippi criminal case with racial overtones was risky politics, but Johnson followed through. He told his own investigator, John Byrd, to share anything he knew with the FBI.

Bureau field agents from Jackson spent several days asking questions in Jones County, filing a thick report on November 4 that described the Wash lynching in great detail. Mack Lee Lewis, an African-American prisoner who was also in the Laurel jail on October 16, told the FBI that Wash seemed to know what was coming. Earlier in the evening, he said, Wash's wife had visited him with a three-year-old child in her arms. "[Lewis] said he heard WASH say to her: 'Well, a man wasn't born to live forever,' " the report said. "Then he kissed his baby and told it goodbye. WASH lay down on the cot and never got up until they came after him."

Somehow, every lawman in town failed to anticipate what Wash had easily intuited. "Officials had no indication of mob violence prior to the mob first endeavoring to enter the jail about 1 a.m.," the report said. Jones County sheriff J. Press Reddoch was at home asleep when he got a call from the jail saying a mob had formed. Reddoch told FBI agents he loaded a rifle with sixteen hollow-point bullets, drove to the jail, stood in front of the crowd, and spent nearly half an hour urging them to disperse. "He appealed from a patriotic viewpoint," the report said, "from a family viewpoint, and even requested the crowd to get on its knees and pray with him."

Reportedly, a mob member told Reddoch the discussion could continue if he would put down his rifle. He handed it over to a colleague and was quickly grabbed and dragged out of the way. Later, Reddoch vowed that he would find and arrest all the members of the mob, but as Byrd reported, he soon got bodychecked by powerful men in Laurel. The morning after the lynching, Reddoch had already arrested three men when he was summoned to lunch with a trio of unnamed businessmen at Laurel's Pinehurst Hotel.

"BYRD later returned to the sheriff's office and found the sheriff there," the report said. ". . . [T]he sheriff seemed to have completely reversed his prior decision to arrest all members of the mob." As he told Byrd, "The local business men advised me to go slow on this."

There were no state criminal indictments in the Wash lynching, but federal charges were filed in Jackson in early 1943 against five men, including Luther Holder, the jailer, and two relatives of Welborn's, Allen Welborn Pryor and Nathaniel T. Shotts. The charges against Shotts and another man were later dropped for lack of evidence.

In April, the three remaining defendants were tried before a twelve-man federal jury in Hattiesburg. The defense, led by a prominent Hattiesburg lawyer named Earle Wingo, stressed the issue of government intrusion, arguing that the FBI's role represented unwarranted interference with a state-level judicial proceeding. Prior to the verdict, Judge Sidney Mize reminded jurors that the case wasn't about states' rights, but about whether the prosecution had presented enough evidence to warrant a conviction. Whatever factors the jurors weighed, the result was a rebuke to the federal government: All three men were acquitted.

———

McGee's first trial was held on December 6, a Thursday. The prosecution, led by Albert Easterling and District Attorney Homer Pittman, had had plenty of time to prepare and, in fact, presented a case that offered more substance than later critics cared to admit. But the trial wasn't remotely fair, since the defense was nullified by handicaps that no judge should have allowed.

It took place in a town full of angry people who wanted to kill the defendant, a man who was so frightened that he apparently couldn't communicate or function. His lawyers, Boyd and Koch, weren't given any time to put a case together, so they had no witnesses to speak of, and their cross-examinations were almost nonexistent. Even so, they managed to do a few things right, filing motions related to issues like sanity and venue that would give them (or somebody else) grounds for appeal later on.

Once again, McGee was brought to town under armed guard, dressed in fatigues and wearing a helmet until he was offloaded from a military truck into the courthouse. A newspaper photographer snapped a picture of him inside the courtroom, capturing an expression of pure terror that gripped McGee during the entire trial. "He was trembling, wild-eyed, unsteady on his feet and jibbered continually and inaudibly throughout the day," the *Leader-Call* said. "He showed no recognition of his mother when she took the stand, and none of her when she prayed over him. . . ."

The first order of business was a sanity hearing, to determine whether McGee was mentally fit to be tried. Boyd told Judge Collins that, while he was no expert on mental health, something was wrong with McGee, because he and Koch had been unable to get him to speak at all.

"It becomes our painful duty to announce that we cannot get one word in the world out of this man," Boyd said. "I do not state what is the matter with him. I never saw him to know him until Monday morning. If I ever saw him I didn't know it, I probably have, he has been here all these years, was raised here, but we take him in the room and try to get something out of him and can't. We get his mother in there and she can't get a word out of him, and she prays over him. . . . Of course, he looks more to me like a wild hyena than anything else. I don't know why, and I'm not saying why. He may be sane and may not be. I'm not a mental specialist."

During Keeton's trial, Collins was given time to solicit expert opinion on her mental state. But McGee's sanity hearing had to happen immediately, using only the witnesses at hand. None were psychiatrists or psychologists, and most had already prejudged McGee as being both sane and guilty. Horace McRae, Laurel's postmaster, said McGee had worked for him and his brothers for several years, and that he saw McGee in the Hinds County jail during his monthlong incarceration. He agreed with Homer Pittman's suggestion that his behavior in court was some of kind of "horse play."

Robert B. Taylor, a captain in the guard unit that transported McGee, had watched him at the jail too. He said McGee responded to orders "just like a mule heading for his stall when you turn him aloose."

"Do you think he is feigning over there now, or what we call horse play?" Pittman asked.

"He is putting on a pretty good act, sir."

The Reverend M. L. Davis, a preacher from Jackson who had conducted a worship service with Hinds County prisoners, said McGee seemed to comprehend the words of the hymns they sang. "On . . . the song of 'Swing Low Sweet Chariot'—I am a vocalist myself . . . I noticed the movement of the cords of his throat and the movement of his lips as he hummed and sang part of the song. . . ."

"From your observation there," Pittman said, "tell the court and jury whether or not he knew what was going on then."

"Sure, he knew what was going on."

The only witness to take McGee's side was his mother, Bessie, who said she'd seen him upset in the past, but not like this. "I never have seen him in that shape before and I been knowing him ever since he been in the world," she said. ". . . I know he is easy to get upset, especially if white folks are around him. If you scold him the least bit he goes all over himself, but I never seen him in the shape he's in now— not like he is now.

"To my notion," she said, "he been over there in jail and just sat there and stayed worried until he just about done lost his mind. That's my notion."

Pittman wasn't interested in her notions. "Aunty, you say you don't know yourself?"

"No, sir, I don't know myself."

"That's the truth about it, isn't it?"

"Yes, sir, when a fellow don't know, he just don't know."

McGee was pronounced sane and fit for trial.

———

Willette Hawkins was put on the stand first, after Judge Collins, honoring her request, cleared the courtroom of spectators and reporters.

There was no description in the local newspaper stories about her demeanor, clothing, or physical appearance, but the jury must have been struck by how thin she was. Mrs. Hawkins was five feet eight inches tall, but she weighed only around ninety-two pounds at the time of the rape, a result of chronically poor health that, she said, had nagged her since she'd been married.

She was thirty-two when she testified the first time. She had dark hair and beautiful eyes—big, dark irises under narrow, arching eyebrows. In a photo taken around the time of her high school graduation, she looked happy, pretty, and perfectly relaxed. Three children, a dozen years, and the strain of recent weeks had probably added a few stress lines to her appearance.

Pittman started with basic questions, and Mrs. Hawkins mentioned that she'd resided in Laurel most of her life, not counting "the two years we were in Indiana." Pittman didn't ask when those two years were—as far as he knew, there was no need, but, much later, that information would turn out to be important. Instead, he moved straight to her account of the rape. She described the circumstances of that night—the sick baby, Troy's retreat to a back room—along with the layout of her bedroom at the front of the house, her various actions before falling asleep, and the moment when she woke up and sensed that somebody was in the room with her.

"I heard something crawling along by the bed whispering, and I thought, 'My goodness, what could this be? Has Troy lost his mind?' Because no other man had ever been in the house and the doors were locked, I felt sure, and I just never dreamed of such a thing, just imagine. And I smelled whiskey, or I smelled beer or something, and I said, 'That's not Troy,' and I reached out and I said, 'Oh, Troy, what do you want?' and I put my hand on a bushy Negro head. . . ."

She went on, saying that she saw the man on his hands and knees but couldn't see his face. She reached for a bedside lamp but he told her not to bother—he'd broken the electrical line at the back of the house. She asked what he wanted and he told her in the crudest terms.

"Miss, Miss, I come for you," he said. "I want your pussy and I am going to have it." When she said "no, no," he told her to shut up or he would cut her throat.

"I was just scared to death, that's all, not so much for myself," she said. "If he had killed me, I never would have felt it, because I was just petrified. But I had that baby, my two-year-old baby girl in the bed with me, and in the next room my two little girls, one eight and one ten . . . and I didn't know what he would do to them or what he would do to the baby, and he said 'shut your mouth' every time I called Troy. I called him, not loud, because I didn't want to wake the children up in the next room, and I didn't know but what he had already killed Troy. And when I called Troy, he said, 'He's back there asleep, Miss.' I said, 'Why did you come here?" And he said, 'I came to fuck you.' Well, then, I thought, 'Well, if that's all I can take it.'"

Pittman said, "Mrs. Hawkins, he told you what he came for, and then did he rape you?"

"Yes, and all the time he was there, he was talking, talking, whispering to me, telling me what he wanted to do and what he was going to do, and he did it, he did it all."

A few questions later, Pittman asked if it were true that she was menstruating that night. "I was," she said. "It was right about the end of my period. I was not menstruating a great deal, but I had to take that off, and he mentioned that."

"He mentioned that?"

"He said, 'You lied to me, why did you lie to me? Why did you tell me that lie?' And he was laying up there, just as if he was—"

"He finally, though, penetrated your female organs with his male organ? He did that?"

"Yes. . . ."

Toward the end, she described a vow the rapist extracted from her once he was through. "He said, 'Will you promise me—all I want now is one thing. I want you to promise me you will never tell it.'" She agreed, but he emphasized how serious he was, threatening her again.

"If you never tell it, things will be all right," he said. "[O]therwise, I will cut your head off. I won't just cut your throat, I will cut your head off."

She promised and he finally left. Moving silently, she found her way back to Troy's room, woke him, and said, "Troy, get up, wake up. The worst thing in the world that ever happened has happened to me."

———

There were only two other witnesses whose testimony touched on the rape itself: Troy Hawkins and Dr. Grady Cook, a Hattiesburg physician. It would be said in coming years that, suspiciously, Mrs. Hawkins was never examined by a doctor. But unless Dr. Cook was lying on the stand, that was untrue. He owned a small private hospital in Hattiesburg called the South Mississippi Infirmary, which is where Mrs. Hawkins was kept under sedation for a week. On the stand, he sounded credible, reporting what he observed and nothing more. A pelvic exam, he said, had revealed "some minor, slight abrasions of the lining of the vagina."

"To the layman that would be what we call bruises?" Easterling asked.

"Scratches, you might say. Little pieces of tissue were scratched off of the surface." Dr. Cook said he made a slide and saw live spermatozoa, but he had no way of knowing where they originated. For all he knew, they could have come from Troy. He stopped short of declaring that Mrs. Hawkins had been raped. "I know that some trauma had occurred in the vagina," he said. "I don't know how the trauma occurred nor how the cells got there."

Troy testified too, describing the moment when Willette woke him up. In this trial, neither of them said much about what they did immediately after Troy came to—that happened in later trials—but he did touch on the mysterious matter of the lights, which weren't working when he got up. As he explained, a single wire came in from a back-alley utility pole, was fastened to the eave of the house, dropped down, and went through the edge of the siding boards into a switch box.

"Where was the wire broken?" Pittman asked.

"Where it fastened to the wire going to the alley," Troy said. "It was the little short wire that went down to the house."

The point was that this wire was something an intruder could break rather than cut, and that a man on an impromptu mission to commit a rape could have simply jimmied it. He wouldn't have had to think ahead to bring a wire-cutting tool.

———

That was it in terms of proving that a rape had happened, and the weaknesses in the case were obvious. Mrs. Hawkins hadn't seen the rapist's face—all she knew was that he was black and that he smelled like alcohol. Despite the *Leader-Call* story that said evidence had been shipped to an FBI lab, no forensic evidence was introduced that tied any individual to the crime. There was a confession, but anybody familiar with Mississippi justice had to figure that beatings and coercion came into play.

The remainder of the prosecution's case consisted of testimony from eleven witnesses, including two African-American friends of McGee. The prosecution used them to lay out a circumstantial case that Mc-Gee was drunk that night, had lost money gambling, and appeared to be in the vicinity at the time of the rape.

After Troy Hawkins, the next witness was Harold Elliot, a white manager with the Laurel Wholesale Grocery Company. Elliot said that, as of Thursday, November 1, McGee had been working there for only four days as a delivery driver. He was driving a "1941 ton-and-a-half Ford truck with a stake body" with a sign on the side that said LAUREL WHOLESALE GROCERY. After his rounds on Thursday, McGee didn't come back in the evening. Elliot said he next saw him at 6:10 a.m. on Friday, in the company parking lot, asleep in the truck cab.

Tal Porter, a black employee of the company, testified that he saw McGee that morning just after 7 a.m., near a bus station.

"I asked him where he was going," Porter said, "and he said he had to run to the house a minute, and I turned around and said, 'You haven't messed up none of the boss's money have you?' And he said, "No, I'll be back in a few minutes.'" He didn't come back, so Elliot called Wayne Valentine to report the theft of company cash.

Where had McGee been? Two acquaintances, Bill Barnes and George Walker, testified that they'd been with him during a long night of driving, drinking, and gambling. Barnes said that on Thursday afternoon he'd helped McGee do some unloading before they knocked off and bought a half-pint of bootleg whiskey in Laurel. Soon they hit the highway, heading west and driving around in the vicinity of small towns like Hot Coffee, Mt. Olive, Mize, and Collins. They were looking for McGee's "daddy-in-law," Joe Payton, and his brother-in-law, Johnny Payton. Barnes said they made two more stops to buy whiskey and a fourth when they returned to Laurel after 11 p.m.

At 11:20 p.m., at a cafe on Pine Street, they ran into George Walker, a Masonite employee who was "eating lunch" after his 3–11 shift. They drove to a house in a black part of Laurel called Queensburg and found a game.

"Did you gamble with Willie that night?" Easterling asked.

"Yes, sir."

"Did he have any money?"

"Yes, sir, he had money. After he got broke he said, 'George, lend me some money until tonight. I had $15.35 of the company's money.'" Walker gave him a few bucks and they went to a house in "the K.C."— the K.C. Bottom, a tough neighborhood near the railroad tracks— where he won some of his cash back. Walker walked home by himself at 3:00. Barnes said McGee dropped him near his house at 3:45. McGee then drove up Masonite Drive and back toward town.

Boyd cross-examined Barnes, asking several inconclusive questions about a woman named Hettie or Hattie Johnson. According to Barnes, her house at 424 East Oak Street was the last place they'd gambled that night.

Nobody saw McGee after that. But two people, both white, said they saw a truck that fit the description of the Laurel Wholesale Grocery vehicle. Rose Marie Imbragulio, a young woman who lived with her parents a block away from the Hawkins home, was up, as usual, by 4:30, getting ready to go to work at her father's business. On her way out, she said, she "heard a lot of noise before I opened the door, and when I opened the door, I saw the truck. . . ." She didn't see the person driving it or the company name on the side, only that it had "a built-up body."

Paul Britton, who worked the night shift at a filling station on Ellisville Boulevard, a main drag parallel to Magnolia Street, said he saw a "Laurel Wholesale Grocery truck, stake body" go by at a few minutes past 5:00. But it was too dark to see the driver.

Much of the case hinged on these two sightings, but the bottom line was that nobody inside or near the Hawkins home was able to positively identify McGee as the man at the scene.

———

McGee was arrested on Saturday, November 3, at around 2:40 p.m. in downtown Hattiesburg. Based on Elliot's phone call, Valentine had put out a bulletin that went all over Mississippi and into Louisiana. Hattiesburg policeman Hugh Herring testified that he and a patrolman named E. C. Harris were parked on South Main Street when they saw a man who matched McGee's description.

They followed him on foot for a few paces and then Harris sneaked up and quietly said, "Willie." McGee jumped, so they grabbed him and took him in. Both Herring and Hattiesburg police chief M. M. Little testified that McGee looked scared, like a man who had something to hide.

"I told Willie what he was charged with and told him Mr. Valentine would be down after him in a very few minutes," Little said, "and he swallowed two or three times and said, 'Boss, they got me wrong,' and perspiration popped out on him, on his face. And I asked him what he was so hot about and he says, 'Boss, it's hot back here,' so I went back to the office and in a few minutes a trusty, a negro boy, came back and reported that this boy was trying to break out of jail. . . ." McGee, he said, was caught clawing at heavy mesh wire on the window of his cell.

Valentine testified next. He began by describing the scene at the Hawkins home on the morning of the crime. After getting a call at 5:30 a.m., he went to the house and saw signs that someone had gone in through a side window. He said the lights were working by the time he arrived. He didn't say why he came to suspect McGee, only that he'd pursued "every lead I could get hold of" and "finally, I run into this lead on Willie McGee." After talking to McGee's employer and getting a report that he had stolen "a zoot suit" from "a negro house," he put out his bulletin. He said he'd known McGee for more than fifteen years and had never had trouble with him before.

When the call came from Hattiesburg, Valentine drove down with two other officers, Jack Anderson and Jeff Montgomery. Inside the jail, Valentine ordered McGee to drop his pants so he could look at his underwear. "I examined the shorts he had on, and the shorts had what I call blood," he said. His belief was that McGee's genitals were stained with Mrs. Hawkins's menstrual blood, but he never had the blood matched in a lab.

In Valentine's account—which would be challenged by the defense in the years ahead—McGee confessed voluntarily when they got back to Laurel. At first, he said, McGee reversed the chronology of his whereabouts, saying he'd gambled in Laurel until 2:30 and then cruised around in the country until 6:00.

"I told Willie that I wanted him to tell me the truth," Valentine said. "If he was the one that done it, just tell me the truth and we would know then—no one was going to harm him, nobody was going to lay a hand on him, it was our duty to protect him and we were going to protect him. And he said he went into the house."

The officers drove McGee to Magnolia Street, and he showed them where he'd parked. They drove to the next block, parked in front of the Hawkins home, and McGee pointed to two houses, saying, "It was one of those two."

In McGee's written confession, he corroborated the prosecution's version of his movements. After dropping Barnes, he said, he drove back toward town, drove down Magnolia, and parked "near a stucco house."

"I got out of the truck, walked back north on South Magnolia Street until I came to a house where I saw a light, and saw a white woman lying on the bed," his confession said. "I then entered the front door and before I got into the room where the woman was, someone had turned out the lights. I then removed my outer clothes, or coveralls, and then removed my shoes, and got in bed with the woman. I then forcibly assaulted her, or had relations with her, and put on my clothes, [and] got in the truck. . . .

"I don't remember what I said to the woman, or what she said to me," he said, "as I was drinking very heavy."

———

When you look at the prosecution's case and McGee's confession, the dots don't all connect. It's a bit unclear from the confession whether McGee stopped and parked because he saw a light or if he parked first and then happened to see a light (and a woman) while walking up the street.

McGee doesn't mention tampering with the lights, but Troy Hawkins said someone did. However, Valentine said the lights were on when he got there, and at the first trial there was no mention of anybody fixing them. (That would be rectified later, with testimony from a power company repairmen who said he'd performed the job.) Also, Valentine thought the intruder went in through an unlocked window. McGee said he walked through the front door.

And then there was the matter of the "bloody shorts," which were introduced as evidence during the trial. Just one month after the crime, there was already a problem with this piece of material evidence: The bloodstains were disappearing. Pittman produced the shorts while questioning Valentine.

"I will ask you whether or not you found any blood on them?" he said. Valentine said he had. "Could you point out to the jury now where that blood is, or if there is any there now?"

"It is faded away," Valentine said, pointing, "but it is right in this part right in here. There was quite a bit more on them than what is on there now, but you can tell by looking at it right there what it is."

Boyd barely questioned Valentine. He didn't bother to ask why the underwear hadn't been sent to a lab.

When their turn came, the defense lawyers called no witnesses and said very little. Before resting his case, Boyd said to McGee, "Willie, do you want to go confer with us a while?" No answer. "Boy, if you have got any sense, you better be using it."

The jury went out at 5:55 p.m. and came back two and a half minutes later. The verdict: guilty as charged. McGee was sentenced to die by electrocution on January 7, 1946. If that held up, he would be dead only sixty days after his arrest—faster even than the Hernando Three.

three

TAKE YOUR CHOICE

The irregularities of McGee's first trial made it ripe for appeal, and the job fell to a white Mississippi lawyer named Forrest B. Jackson. At first glance, Jackson might seem like a strange pick, since he also did frequent legal work for Mississippi's most powerful and flamboyant racist, Senator Theodore G. Bilbo. But he had a reputation for fairness in dealing with black criminal defendants, and it extended outside the state.

Jackson, forty-five, was a friendly looking, slightly jug-eared former farm boy from southwest Mississippi whose father had died before he was ten. In a biography he distributed when he ran unsuccessfully for the U.S. Senate in 1947, he prided himself on a hardworking childhood ("newspaper carrier, laundry worker, railroad laborer and clerk . . . salesman, Page in Mississippi Legislature . . .") that was capped by his graduation from the University of Mississippi in 1923.

By the early 1940s, Jackson had built up a general law practice in the capital city, occasionally doing work for the NAACP. In a 1943 letter from Carsie A. Hall, president of the group's Jackson branch, to the national office in New York, Hall mentioned him in connection with two trials, one involving three blacks who were charged with murdering an elderly white man in the town of Madison. "In this case Mr. Jackson has had no financial help," Hall wrote, "yet he has spent his [own] money in getting the case appealed and he promises to go through with the case because he feels that the youths were not given a chance."

Starting in 1944, Jackson represented Willie Carter, an accused murderer whose appeal was paid for by the NAACP. Though the effort failed——Carter was retried, found guilty a second time, and electrocuted in 1946—Thurgood Marshall, who worked with Jackson during this process, said he did "a splendid job."

On the heels of McGee's guilty verdict, Jackson was approached by Louis E. Burnham, a thirty-year-old African American from New York who had moved to Birmingham, Alabama, in 1941, where he served as organizational secretary for a civil rights group called the Southern Negro Youth Congress. Roughly ten days after McGee's conviction, Burnham went to Mississippi on a fact-finding mission, interviewing the principal players in Laurel. He summarized what he learned in a December 26 report to George Marshall, head of the National Federation for Constitutional Liberties, a New York–based group that would be folded into the mix when the Civil Rights Congress launched in the summer of 1946. His memo was detailed and accurate—in fact, it was one of the most reliable things ever written about the case—and it opened with special praise for Jackson, who struck Burnham as "an unusually fair-minded and dependable man."

In addition to taking on the appeal, Jackson agreed to help Bessie McGee recover money she'd paid to Earle Wingo, the man who had successfully defended the accused lynchers of Howard Wash. Willie was aware of Wingo's reputation for winning cases; according to Bessie's first-trial testimony, he'd asked her to hire him for the defense— which, if true, indicates that his mind was working all right before the trial started.

Wingo said no, but he told Bessie he would write the appeal if she paid him $1,000, half of it up front. (In 2008 dollars, $1,000 would be more than $11,000. Jackson charged $100 for the same service.) She somehow scraped together $205 and gave it to Wingo, who then made himself difficult to find. "Obviously, he was taking advantage of Mrs. McGee's extremity and seeking to milk her for all she could beg or borrow," Burnham concluded.

In his memo, Burnham discussed both of McGee's lawyers, Boyd and Koch, sizing them up as precisely the wrong men for the job. "Koch played no role whatsoever in the trial," he wrote. "Boyd went through the motions of defending his client. However, Boyd has no competence as a criminal lawyer, by his own admission to me. In addition, he does little practice of any kind, most of his time being spent in managing the Southern Hotel which he owns."

Bessie sketched out McGee's basic biography, telling Burnham that he was separated from his wife and four children, none of whom was named. He said McGee lived with Bessie at 105 Elm Street, in a "dilapidated two-room shack with outdoor toilet situated in a slum neighborhood. McGee's earnings were the main support of his mother; some part of them were contributed for the upkeep of his children. Mrs. McGee (Bessie) helped by taking in washing." Bessie's house (which no longer exists) stood in a poor part of town known as the Neck, just east of the railroad tracks that bisected Laurel, and near another rough area named in the first trial, the K.C. Bottom.

Burnham also mentioned that, a few days after McGee's indictment, Forrest Jackson—at the request of the NAACP office in Mobile, Alabama—tried to see McGee in the Hinds County jail but was turned away. Burnham tried to get in two days before Christmas but was also refused.

"These facts are important in light of Mrs. McGee's description of her son's behavior during her visits," Burnham wrote. "The first time she saw him in jail was a few days after the indictment. At that visit she asked him if he was guilty. He said no. She then asked why he had signed a confession. McGee replied, 'I signed to be living when you got here. You just don't know what it was like.'" McGee said the confession had been written for him by his captors and that "they told me to sign or else," thus contradicting the prosecution's claim that he confessed voluntarily.

Willie didn't say a word during Bessie's subsequent visits. Burnham assumed this was explained by the "terrific beating and intimidation to which he has been subjected or . . . his state of sanity, or both." Bessie, he said, spoke of "a strong possibility" that McGee had lost his mind. She talked about an aunt and two great-aunts who were "insane at death" and an uncle on Willie's father's side, Governor Mc-

Gee, who "was recently confined in a mental ward at Tuskegee Veterans Facility."

Burnham closed by ticking off some of the case's oddities—"Why didn't the woman cry out . . . ?"—and noting possible grounds for review, including the issues of venue and race-based jury exclusion. Jackson got right to work: On December 28, 1945, he served notice of his intent to appeal. That action, filed in early January, automatically stayed the January 7 execution.

———

Maybe it's not a surprise that Jackson provided honest service to his client; that's what lawyers are supposed to do, after all. Still, the contrast between McGee and Jackson's other client couldn't have been greater. By the mid-1940s, Senator Bilbo was more than just another segregationist politician. He was the gold standard of the breed, and his last name, slightly tweaked, had become a nationally recognized label for racism and demagoguery: "Bilboism." In a 1946 story published in *Life*, Senator Robert Taft, a powerful Republican conservative, called Bilbo "a disgrace to the Senate." Bilbo countered that *Life* was a "pink colored mongrel magazine."

Though Bilbo played no direct role in the McGee case—he died before it took off as a national news story—Jackson's involvement wasn't the only connection. The opening months of the case overlapped with Bilbo's final months as America's least-loved senator. The CRC was well positioned to work on McGee's appeal that summer and fall because, thanks to Bilbo, the group was already focused on Mississippi: Its first national project was a campaign to deny Bilbo his Senate seat after the election of 1946.

By that point, Bilbo—who brayed as loudly as radio's Senator Claghorn and immodestly called himself "the Man"—was a fat target, a walking caricature who was routinely trashed by everyone from newspaper editors to folk singers to filmmakers. He was denounced for his racism in the 1946 song "Listen, Mr. Bilbo" and cited by name as an anti-Semite in the 1947 movie *Gentleman's Agreement*. He was the partial inspiration for a mixed-race college football game played in the mid-1940s at the Polo Grounds in New York, pitting black teams like the Tuskegee Warhawks against the U.S. Navy's all-white New London Undersea Raiders. In a preview of the 1946 contest, the *Daily Worker* promised "a nice afternoon watching the Bilbo white-supremacy myth get booted all over the lot."

That year, Bilbo was called "America's most notorious merchant of hatred" by the *Saturday Evening Post*, which published a summertime profile about his primary campaign. "The 68-year-old senator . . . who has become so widely known as a fountainhead of intolerance, is a little man who attempts to offset his undistinguished appearance with a red necktie and diamond stickpin," the *Post*'s Milton Lehman wrote. ". . . His big head, set with squinty blue eyes and thin lips, is scarred by a blow from a pistol butt. . . .

"Like his personal appearance, Bilbo's political record is also undistinguished. During the New Deal he tied himself to the Administration, originating nothing, but taking credit at home for every piece of favorable legislation."

The *Post* neglected to mention that Bilbo's long career had seen a few finer moments. Was he a racist? Down to the marrow. But as his most thorough biographer, Chester M. Morgan, points out, Mississippi voters originally responded to Bilbo not because of race-baiting, but because he promised, and sometimes delivered, progressive reforms that were a bright spot in state politics during the first quarter of the twentieth century.

On a gut level, Bilbo's supporters also loved him because he was colorful and bombastic, in an era when politicians had to show their stuff in front of live crowds in small-town settings. "With incantation from the Bible and the plays of Shakespeare, he held his audience spellbound," wrote his first biographer, A. Wigfall Green. "Perched high on the porch or on the balcony of a courthouse . . . he seemed not five feet two in height but a giant: 'On the stump,' said one of his disciples, 'he's 7 feet 10 inches tall.'"

Sometimes he was legitimately funny, in ways that did no harm and showed an inventive mind at work. As a young state senator in 1910, Bilbo decided to attract attention to himself with a mock legislative attack against a certain popular, stimulating soft drink and its many imitators. So he introduced a bill banning "the manufacture, sale, barter, or giving away of . . . coca cola, afri cola, ala cola, caffi cola, carre cola, celery cola," and thirty other imaginary variations, including "mellow nip," "revive ola," and "french wine of coca wise ola." He was so proud of his joke that he introduced the bill three times.

At his worst, Bilbo used the same verbal talents to attack and defame, and his mouth almost got him killed the next year. Some of the scars on his head came from a 1911 pistol-whipping he suffered after calling one political opponent, a former Mississippi prison warden named John J. Henry, "a cross between a hyena and a mongrel, begotten in a nigger graveyard at midnight, suckled by a sow and educated by a fool."

This was the Bilbo that so many people came to hate, the snapping-turtle loudmouth who would say anything for a laugh, a gasp, or a vote. By 1946, unfortunately, this was the only Bilbo left. And in the context of the McGee case, it's important to keep one thing in mind: Though Bilbo had plenty of opposition inside Mississippi, he was still one of the most popular elected officials in the state.

———

Born in 1877, the Man came from southern Mississippi's Pearl River County, a backwoods area far from the state's traditional power centers. His rise was made possible by changes in Mississippi election law in the early 1900s that opened the Democratic Party nominating process—previously controlled by a convention of wealthy planters and their allies—to white primary voters of all economic levels. Poor white farmers, called rednecks and peckerwoods by their political betters in the Delta, were soon able to hoist a few champions, including Bilbo's leather-lunged predecessor, James K. Vardaman. After serving in the state senate and as lieutenant governor starting in 1912, Bilbo ran a gubernatorial primary campaign in 1915 that promised a host of progressive changes in how Mississippi was managed, and he followed through when he won.

"The governor early established good relationships with most law-makers and then implored, prodded, cajoled, and pressured them into passing a legislative program that remains unsurpassed by any four-year period in modern Mississippi history," Morgan wrote. "Under Bilbo's whip hand the legislature gave Mississippi a board of bank examiners, a highway commission, a pardoning board, a tuberculosis hospital . . . a tougher antilobby law . . . and the largest appropriation ever for education." Bilbo's second gubernatorial term—from 1928 to 1932—was a bust, weighed down by his futile campaign to move the University of Mississippi from Oxford to Jackson. But when he won his first of three Senate terms in 1934, he found fresh life as a New Deal loyalist, supporting FDR almost in lockstep throughout his first four years.

Because of this record, Morgan labeled Bilbo a "redneck liberal," using "liberal" in the sense that he supported an active, progressive federal government. No other meaning could reasonably apply. Bilbo didn't always play the race card on the stump—for much of his political career, Mississippi blacks were so marginalized that there wasn't much need to bring them up—but when you look at his actions and speeches in the 1920s, 1930s, and 1940s, there's no doubt where he was coming from.

In 1928, in support of Al Smith's presidential bid, Bilbo reportedly spread a rumor that Republican candidate Herbert Hoover, during a flood-relief trip to the Delta the year before, had flouted Mississippi conventions by dancing in public with Mary Booze, a Mississippi African American and GOP committeewoman. During a flurry of arguments over what Bilbo had actually said, he tried to trap Hoover by asking him to state clearly whether it would be "indecent, infamous or disgraceful for you to come in contact with or dance with a woman of the negro race."

That year, one of the most notorious lynchings in Mississippi history occurred under Bilbo's watch, the mob murder of an escaped black convict named Charley Shepherd, who ran away from Parchman prison after allegedly killing his supervisor, J. D. Duvall. Bilbo didn't do anything to stop it, and he had plenty of time to get organized. In the aftermath, his only response to this hellish event was a wisecrack.

The Shepherd case started at 3:30 a.m. on Friday, December 28, when Duvall's wife found his body on the floor of their dining room, his throat cut and his skull crushed by a hammer. Shouting for help, she realized that their eighteen-year-old daughter, Ruth, was missing. The early assumption was that Ruth had been murdered by the forty-one-year-old Shepherd, who lived among the family as a trusty, cooking and cleaning. A multi-county Delta manhunt ensued that lasted three days and involved airplane surveillance, bloodhounds, and hundreds of armed men driving country roads and marching through forests.

Ruth came out of woods alone on Saturday, dazed and bruised and telling rescuers that Shepherd had kidnapped her and forced her to stagger along with him while he tried to escape. Shepherd gave himself up on Monday morning to a plantation owner, Laura Mae Keeler, after securing her promise that she would turn him over to a jailer instead of vigilantes. Keeler tried to make good on that; she and a few local men attempted to drive Shepherd to jail in the Delta town of Cleveland. But they were stopped on the road by unidentified men who took Shepherd away.

Shepherd may well have been guilty—the evidence certainly pointed that way, and he was in prison for the murder of his wife and mother-in-law—but he deserved his right to due process instead of the prolonged horror show that followed. He was driven through country towns for seven hours to draw a crowd for the ritualistic lynching that everybody knew was coming. Early in the evening of December 31, near the town of Rome—about thirty miles away from Cleveland—some 4,000 to 6,000 people assembled in a forest clearing. Shepherd was tied to a five-foot-high pile of wood, doused with gasoline, and set ablaze. Mob members had crammed mud in his mouth and nostrils so the smoke wouldn't kill him before the flames did, and he reportedly stayed alive for close to an hour. One newspaper report said his screams could be heard from half a mile away.

Throughout the days of search, capture, and lawlessness, Bilbo made only token attempts to exert executive authority. On Sunday afternoon, he sent three dozen state troops to Parchman, with orders to help with the search but not to take charge. That day, Bilbo left Jackson by car with his son, Theo Jr., en route to Theo's boarding school in Tennessee. He checked in at Parchman, made an empty comment or two, and left Mississippi. When Shepherd was seized by the mob, the state guard, obeying Bilbo's orders, made no attempt to find the lynchers or intervene. A spokesman said their job was not "to kill a lot of people trying to take away the murderer. . . ."

Bilbo swung through Parchman on his return trip, looked at Shepherd's remains—little more than a charred torso with stumps—and announced that his role in the matter was over. "I have neither the time nor the money," he said, "to investigate 2,000 people."

———

The McGee case also featured a dramatic escape attempt, though this was little noticed at the time, was never addressed by McGee's defenders, and was quickly forgotten once the story ended. On February 20, 1946, inside the Hinds County jail, McGee masterminded a violent jailbreak that involved two other condemned black prisoners, Sherman Street and Charlie Holloway.

Or so it was reported in both Jackson newspapers. It's possible that the whole thing was a put-on by the jailers, designed to erase McGee's ability to pursue an insanity defense.

This isn't as implausible as it sounds. During and after the first trial, McGee was depicted as a terrified imbecile who couldn't put two words together. But the person behind this escape plot was anything but helpless. He was crafty bordering on brilliant, and ruthless enough to kill his way to freedom.

A faked escape would have served an obvious need for people who wanted to see McGee die. Anyone familiar with the first trial knew that an insanity-based appeal was coming, and there was dread that it might actually work. Jones County prosecutor Albert Easterling was worried that "Jackson doctors and witnesses" would be more gullible or lenient about diagnosing McGee than their Laurel counterparts, so

he tried to pressure Sheriff Luther Hill into bringing him back to the
Laurel jail. Hill refused. He said it was too dangerous to keep McGee
down there for any reason.

News of the escape attempt was splashed across the front pages of
both Jackson newspapers, which shouted the underlying message in
case anybody missed it. "Willie McGee Faked Dumbness Until Time
of Attempted Break from Hinds Jail Cell," said the *Clarion-Ledger*'s
headline. The story's lead offered more of the same.

"Willie McGee, convicted rapist waiting an appeal of his death
sentence on the grounds of insanity, is crazy—like a fox," it said.
"This was agreed yesterday by Hinds county officials investigating
the Wednesday night attempted jail break which revealed McGee had
been putting on an act of helplessness."

Of course, it could have happened exactly as the jailers described
it, because McGee wasn't mentally deficient. Whether he was faking insanity or was temporarily incapacitated by fear, he found his
voice before long: By the time of his second trial in late 1946, he was
communicating, haltingly, with his new defense lawyers, and he testified at length during the third trial. McGee, Street, and Holloway all
faced imminent execution, so they had good reason to want to escape.
And despite the jail's reputation for being "escape proof," it wasn't.
McGee's alleged attempt sounds similar to a pair of successful escapes
that happened before and after his incarceration. Prisoners probably
knew about the first of these.

The old Hinds County jail no longer exists, but the reason it was
considered secure is that it sat on the fourth and fifth floors of the
Hinds County Courthouse, a fortresslike art deco structure opened in
1930. You had to take an elevator to get to it, a design that by definition choked off the possibility of easy escapes or rapid mob action. For
anyone hoping to get out, the key was overpowering the jailer and
getting to the lift.

In February 1944, three "youthful desperadoes" who'd been arrested for trying to rob downtown Jackson's Robert E. Lee Hotel—
white men in their early twenties named Lawrence Motari, Ralph

Ward, and Roy Drake—ran past a jailer and trusty, rode down the
elevator, stole a car, and kidnapped a high-school girl before being
captured. In 1954, Gerald Gallego, a Californian who'd killed a Mississippi policeman on the Gulf Coast, and Minor Sorber, a Parchman
inmate who'd killed a fellow prisoner, threw floor-cleaning fluid in
the eyes of jailer J. C. Landrum and then beat him with a heavy strip
of metal. They too rode the elevator down and fled. Landrum died a
few days later; the escapees, both white, were captured and subsequently executed.

According to the *Jackson Daily News* story about McGee's attempt,
he had playacted his way through an elaborate con, pretending for
thirty days straight to be a bedridden invalid, so shell-shocked by
his arrest, abuse, and trial that he wouldn't eat unless he was fed by
hand. The jailers had allowed Street, a labor organizer who'd gotten
the death penalty for allegedly raping a thirteen-year-old white girl
from Jackson—a disputed case that Louis Burnham was also investigating—and Holloway, who'd been condemned to death in the town
of Holly Springs, to enter McGee's cell to feed and wash him.

On the night of the 20th, Street and Holloway went back to their
cells after attending to McGee, who then "slipped out of his cell before
the master switch could be thrown, locking all the doors of the cell
block." Next, he sneaked over to collect fifteen keys that Holloway
had made, supposedly using a file (never found) to grind away at
pieces of weather-stripping he'd torn loose from around his cell window. McGee worked his hands through the bars that sealed off the
cell block, picked a lock protecting the switch box, and used a coat
hanger to throw a lever that opened the main door. Once he accessed
the switch box, he opened the doors to Street's and Holloway's cells.

After that, the three men hid and called out to the jailer, C. M.
Herring, saying McGee needed medical attention. Herring unwittingly
walked in, "only to be met by a heavy blow from an iron strip weighing about eight pounds, in the hands of McGee."

Herring was a large man, 215 pounds, and he put up a "terrific
struggle, knocking two of the negroes down several times." But he

was soon beaten to the floor, hit so hard that he suffered five "deep gashes" on the back of his head. He pretended to be unconscious while Holloway begged McGee and Street to stop hitting him with the iron, yelling, "He's dead!"

Two lawmen, Chief Deputy J. T. Naugher and highway patrolman Sam Moorhead, were downstairs in the sheriff's office when they heard about the disturbance by way of a phone call from a trusty on another floor. They hopped in the elevator and headed up to stop whatever was going on. Seeing the top of the elevator as it ascended, the three escapees despaired and ran back into their cells, locking themselves in and throwing the keys into the jail's main corridor.

Neither newspaper ran a picture of the prisoners, but both ran photos of Herring, sitting up in a hospital bed the next day, less than twenty-four hours after the attack. He was smoking a cigarette, and though his head was wrapped in bandages, he looked chipper for a man who'd had his skull bashed in the night before. The stories said he suffered badly bruised arms and a dislocated right shoulder. In the photographs, he was shirtless, and no bruises or scratches were visible. His left arm, not his right, was in a sling, and his face was unmarked. The *Jackson Daily News* may have understated things when it said he was responding "nicely" to treatment.

As for McGee, with the plot foiled, he reportedly reverted to his old ways. "All during the morning," the *Daily News* said, he "howled like an animal in his solitary cell. He was quiet whenever no one was around, but if someone passed his cell door and made any noise, he would put up a heart-rending cry and moan."

If McGee did howl, he had good reason. In those days, Mississippi kept its executions moving: Street and Holloway were both dead within six months. McGee knew he might not be far behind.

———

Lynching statistics are an inexact science, but there had been a time when something like the Charley Shepherd killing happened every week in a Southern state, and Mississippi, running neck and neck with Georgia, probably had the highest rate of them all. According to *Lynchings in Mississippi*, a 2006 study by Julius E. Thompson, roughly 500 of the 5,000 or more U.S. lynching victims between 1865 and 1965 died in Mississippi. Between 1890 and 1920, the state saw at least 450 lynchings, an average of more than one a month. A few victims were white men or black women, but the overwhelming majority were black men, who were killed without trial for alleged crimes ranging from murder and rape—murder, or a charge of murder, being the most common by far—to arson, assault, burglary, counterfeiting, and non-crimes like "insulting a white woman" and "informing."

The South, of course, wasn't the only place where lynchings occurred, and they didn't happen only to blacks. According to Thompson's figures, the number of blacks lynched nationally in the 1880s was actually less than the total number of whites, because lynching was still a common form of frontier justice in the West. But in Mississippi the practice was primarily a tactic of racial control and revenge, and that pattern solidified as the years went by. Thompson counted 280 Mississippi lynchings in the 1880s, 20 of which where of whites. In the 1890s, there were 195 lynchings, only 5 involving whites. By the 1930s, a decade that saw 52 lynchings, only 2 had white victims, and in the 1940s there were 15, none involving whites.

As lynching totals went down overall, Southern politicians and newspaper editors often proclaimed that the region was solving the problem on its own, so there was no need for interference in the form of federal anti-lynching legislation. In one sense this was true: 1895 was a lot worse than 1945, when the Tuskegee Institute—the Alabama-based academic research center that kept an official tally of American lynchings—counted just one Southern lynching, of a Florida man named Jesse James Payne. But groups like the CRC often argued that Tuskegee's counting methods were too conservative, and that they missed cases that should have been tabulated.

No doubt they were right. Tuskegee's own clip files on lynching— a massive collection of several decades' worth of newspaper stories and reports on lynchings, legal lynchings, and similar incidents—sometimes contain newspaper stories about racial atrocities that didn't show up in its own year-end statistics.

For example, a few months after McGee's alleged jailbreak in 1946, in the Mississippi Delta town of Indianola, a twenty-eight-year-old black man named Alonzo Rush was reportedly lynched with the full cooperation of officials in the surrounding county, Sunflower. According to a story published in the *Afro-American* newspaper, Rush had been accused of having an affair with a white woman, who admitted to the affair but refused to press charges. Rush was kidnapped, taken off into some woods, executed in what the paper described as a "home-made electric chair," and delivered to a black undertaker, who gave a reporter a grisly description of his remains.

"Electricity of high voltage had passed through the body for about five minutes," the story said. "The scalp where the cap fitted was cooked thoroughly in barbecue fashion. Flesh around the knee, where the knee band was placed, was cooked to the bone."

Did this really happen? That's hard to say, but the detailed account makes it seem likely. Even so, Tuskegee didn't include Rush in its lynching totals for 1946.

In 1950, a year when Tuskegee reported only two lynchings, its annual roundup didn't count the notorious Attala County massacre, which happened southwest of the central Mississippi town of Kosciusko on January 8, 1950. The trouble began on December 22, 1949, when three white men who'd been drinking moonshine—Malcum Whitt, Windol Whitt, and Leon Turner—went on a spree that involved harassing three black families in their rural cabins. At the home of sharecropper Thomas Harris, they tried to rape Harris's wife, Mary Ella, and were arrested at the scene by the county sheriff, who'd been alerted by one of the other families. They escaped from jail about a week later, hid in the woods several days, and descended on the Harris cabin on the night of the 8th, apparently believing Harris had turned them in. Turner went inside with a pistol, wounding two people and killing three: Frankie Thurman, 12, Mary Burnside, 8, and Ruby Nell Harris,

4. Though the prosecution pressed hard for a death penalty in the cases of Turner and Windol Whitt, all three men got prison terms.

By the mid- to late 1940s, with lynching on the wane, groups like the CRC were paying just as much attention to legal lynching, which they said Tuskegee also undercounted. "In its 1947 report on lynchings in America the Tuskegee Institute notes that there has been a decrease in deaths by mob action during the past 10 years," said a *Daily Worker* story from 1947. "In that period the Alabama Negro college states that 273 lynchings have been prevented by officials or citizens. . . .

"The report does not show, though, what happened to those who were 'saved' from the intended extralegal executioners." The story went on to argue that many of these people wound up just as dead, following one-sided trials before all-white juries.

"Legal lynching" cases are even harder to quantify than lynchings, but the best measure is probably state-by-state executions for rape—an offense for which black men were disproportionately condemned—and there, the available statistics support the view of the CRC. According to one tally, between 1800 and 1964, Mississippi executed 29 men for rape or attempted rape, all of them black.

In this category, though, Mississippi wasn't the leader: The numbers were much higher in other Southern states, including Texas, Georgia, and Virginia. In Texas, the estimated execution total over the same time period was 137; in Georgia it was 108; and in Virginia it was 136. Not long before McGee's execution, Virginia executed 7 black men accused of taking part in a rape of the same woman. They were known as the Martinsville Seven, and their case would join his as a rallying cause for the left.

Because the CRC didn't trust Tuskegee's statistics, the group, from the start of its existence, began compiling clips and records of its own. Years later, the CRC would make explosive use of this material, generating headlines around the world about the unjust practices of Southern courts.

News of McGee's jailbreak rattled Forrest Jackson. In late February, he sent the local newspaper stories to Abraham J. Isserman, a labor lawyer affiliated with the National Federation for Constitutional Liberties. "I regret that this disturbance occurred and may prove most unfortunate on appeal results," he wrote. "This apparently demonstrates that Willie McGee has been faking as to his mental condition and as to his inability to talk."

Nonetheless, Jackson filed the appeal on March 28, arguing that the lower court should have granted McGee's lawyers more time, a change of venue, and a proper examination by a qualified physician or psychiatrist.

"The futility of their hurried effort at defense without his help, without investigation or the searching out of witnesses, is apparent from the record," Jackson wrote. ". . . The proceeding pressed on relentlessly to conviction and sentencing, with no opportunity for unprepared counsel to catch their breath, or to remedy their enforced lack of prior preparation. An ignorant negro pauper on trial for his life was, through lack of time, denied effective counsel and left defenseless in the face of death."

The Mississippi Supreme Court ruled on June 10, granting McGee a new trial on venue grounds but ignoring all the other claims. Citing cases in Mississippi and other states, the court said it was well established that when "the public is so aroused against [the] accused that it [is] necessary to call out the militia or otherwise protect him from violence or to remove him from the county," a change of venue should be automatic.

As a precedent, the judges mentioned a Texas case that involved an African-American man who had killed a white man during a fight, which reportedly started with a show of "impertinence and insolence" by the killer. The case aroused fury among local whites—necessitating a militia escort at the trial similar to the one that safeguarded McGee and the Hernando defendants—and the Texas court noted that verbal disrespect, by itself, had compounded the danger to the defendant.

The Mississippi judges agreed, adding that McGee's crime involved an even greater insult: interracial sexual assault. "It will be noticed that . . . the [Texas] court referred to impertinence and insolence on the part of negroes towards white people as fruitful sources of aggravation," the opinion said. "How much more so is a charge, and reasonable grounds to believe it, of rape by a negro against a white woman."

Now that McGee was getting a new trial, he needed a new lawyer, because Forrest Jackson was bowing out. Why? Most likely, he got cold feet after the alleged jailbreak. Or he may have been too busy. By November 1946, when the second McGee trial took place, Senator Bilbo was embroiled in the last big battle of his life.

———

Bilbo's final exit was a theatrical event that made for an irresistible spectacle in newspapers all over the nation. It combined new forms of organized protest involving Mississippi blacks and their Southern and Northern allies; political fireworks; the Man's legendary mouth; and the wrathful hand of fate, which hit Bilbo hard during his remaining months.

Fueling everything was the fight over African American voting rights in Southern states, which had been at issue in an important U.S. Supreme Court decision from 1944, *Smith v. Allwright*. In that case, argued before the Court by Thurgood Marshall, the justices ruled eight to one that an all-white Democratic primary held in Texas was unconstitutional. This set the stage for attempts by African-Americans to vote in Mississippi's Democratic primary on July 2, 1946. That prospect, as much as anything, sent Bilbo over the edge.

He'd been heading that way for a while. In 1938, railing against one of several anti-lynching bills that stalled in the Senate—thanks to Southern filibusters—Bilbo said, "If you succeed in the passage of this bill, you will open the floodgates of hell in the South. Raping, mobbing, lynching, race riots, and crime will be increased a thousandfold; and upon your garments and the garments of those who are responsible for the passage of the measure will be the blood of the raped and outraged daughters of Dixie. . . ."

In 1944, he promised to make Eleanor Roosevelt "queen of Greater Liberia" once he succeeded in his quest to send American blacks "back" to West Africa. In the summer of 1945, he shadowboxed with his longtime enemy, New York congressman Vito Marcantonio. A woman from Brooklyn named Josephine Piccolo wrote Bilbo to criticize him for opposing the extension of the Fair Employment Practices Committee, part of Roosevelt's wartime push to ban discriminatory hiring in national defense industries. "I find it very hard to believe that you are an American citizen," she wrote. Bilbo returned serve with a letter that began, "My Dear Dago," followed by, "If I am mistaken in this, please correct me."

Marcantonio wrote Bilbo to demand an apology. In his reply, Bilbo denied that "dago" was a slur against Italians—it was no more offensive than "Hoosier," he insisted—even as he piled on the Italian slurs. "It is through you and your gang," he wrote, "and I dare say many of them are gangsters, from the sin-soaked, communistic sections of the great metropolis of New York, that practically all the rotten, crackpot, communistic legislative schemes are being thrown into the congressional 'mill.' . . ."

In March 1947, with Mississippi politicians busily trying to figure out new legal impediments to black voting rights, Bilbo published a book called *Take Your Choice: Separation or Mongrelization?* in which he argued that the only solution to the looming race crisis was permanent segregation and eventual repatriation. Quoting from an earlier tract by another writer, he pushed the old, discredited idea that African Americans, whom he called "anthropoid apes," were members not just of a different race, but a different species.

"[T]he hair is short, black, and frizzly—in fact, distinctly wooly," *Take Your Choice* said. "Soft and velvety to the touch, the negro epidermis is, for the most part, quite free from hair, and would be interesting were it not for the outrageous odor it emits, especially under heat and excitement. This is sometimes so strong that I have known persons of our own race brought almost to the stage of emesis when compelled to inhale it for any length of time."

At the heart of *Take Your Choice*, which flew off the shelves in Jackson, was the same taboo subject that made the McGee case so dangerous: interracial sex. Bilbo didn't deny that it had happened in the South, but he believed, or pretended to believe, that the contact had always been one-way: white men having relations with black women.

In South America, he argued, the situation was different and disastrous—unchecked, two-way race-mixing there had debased the entire continent with a population of "mestizos, mulattoes, zambos, terceroones, quadroons, cholos, musties, fusties, and dusties." But in America, "[a]s disgraceful as the sins of some white men" had been, "[S]outhern white women have preserved the integrity of their race, and there is no one who can today point the finger of suspicion in any manner whatsoever at the blood which flows in the veins of the white sons and daughters of the South."

In the summer of 1946, Bilbo cranked it up as the Democratic primary approached. Reporters followed him around Mississippi, taking down his most outrageous statements. Much of it was the same old stuff, but with black voting rights now on the table, he broke new ground.

"Mississippi is white," he said. "We got the right to keep it that way. . . . [I'm] calling on every red-blooded American who believes in the superiority and integrity of the white race to get out and see that no nigger votes. . . . And the best time to do it is the night before!"

Bilbo kept it up as the primary approached. On June 22, speaking in Jackson, he argued that every "red-blooded Anglo-Saxon man in Mississippi" should use any means necessary to keep blacks away from polling places. "And if you don't know what that means," he said, "you are just not up on your persuasive measures."

Even before election day, people started acting on such words. On June 6, Etoy Fletcher, an army veteran attending Jackson College on the G.I. Bill, was seized by four white men after attempting to register in the town of Brandon. In an affidavit, he said they drove him to a stand of woods, stripped him, and flogged his legs with a wire cable, threatening to kill him if he tried to register again.

Bilbo won the election on July 2, narrowly avoiding a runoff in a crowded field but beating his nearest opponent by nearly 40,000 votes. The "night before" line wasn't forgotten, however. The Senate initially declined to act, but on September 6, the Campaign Investigating Committee announced that it would look into complaints about Bilbo's statements. His enemies were confident that they were incendiary enough to get him booted out of Congress.

———

Bilbo had gone too far plenty of times. Why was 1946 any different? One factor was purely political. The GOP had won House and Senate majorities in the 1946 election. Going after Bilbo was a no-lose proposition.

But there were other reasons too. The country was changing, slowly but perceptibly, and people were paying more attention to his excesses. More than a million African Americans had served in World War II, 85,000 of them from Mississippi, and they came back with a pent-up demand for basic rights in areas like voting and jury selection. The July primary was the first since Reconstruction in which significant numbers of black Mississippians voted; despite Bilbo's threats, roughly 1,000 cast a ballot.

Meanwhile, Bilbo had picked a bad year to get caught inciting midnight attacks on black people, because too much of that was going on already. The wartime dip in Southern lynchings ended in 1946, a year that saw a new outbreak of violence, much of it directed at returning black soldiers.

Some of these cases became famous, including the February 1946 beating and blinding of Sergeant Isaac Woodard Jr., a twenty-seven-year-old veteran of the Pacific theater, on his way home from military service, who was arrested in Batesburg, South Carolina, after a disturbance on a Greyhound bus. During a stop about an hour north of Atlanta, Woodard asked the bus's white driver if he had time to run inside and use a restroom. The driver said no and cursed him; Woodard cursed him back, and the driver told him to go ahead but make it fast. At the next stop, Batesburg, the driver contacted the police and told them Woodard was drunk and disorderly. He was taken off the bus by Police Chief Lynwood Shull, clubbed, and hauled into jail, where he was punched in the eyes with the end of a billy club. By the next morning, he'd permanently lost his eyesight.

The Woodard blinding became a national symbol of the injustices being committed against black veterans. Orson Welles talked about it repeatedly on his ABC-Radio show *Orson Welles Commentaries*, and Woody Guthrie wrote a protest song called "The Blinding of Isaac Woodard." In August, 20,000 people turned out at a Harlem rally to raise money for his medical care and living expenses. In an interview, Woodard, a Bronx resident, echoed a theme heard again and again that year.

"Negro veterans that fought in this war don't realize that the real battle has just begun in America," he said. "They went overseas and did their duty, and now they're home and have to fight another struggle, that I think outweighs the war." Woodard's personal struggle was an exercise in frustration. In November, Shull was acquitted of federal civil rights charges at a trial in Columbia, South Carolina. In 1947, Woodard sued Greyhound—and lost.

Other notorious 1946 incidents occurred in Columbia, Tennessee; Walton County, Georgia; and Webster Parish, Louisiana. In Columbia, on February 25, an argument and fight involving a navy veteran named James Stephenson, his mother Gladys, and William Fleming, a white radio repairman, led to the Stephensons' arrest and release on bail. In short order, a mob formed near the black part of town, known as Mink Slide. That night, residents of the neighborhood doused lights and loaded weapons, anticipating a vigilante attack. Many of these men were returning soldiers, and it was rumored later that several white mob members did in fact charge into Mink Slide, only to be wounded or killed, their deaths attributed locally to "heart failure."

"It is felt that white Columbia can't admit, even to this day, that it took a beating when colored decided to protect themselves and prevent one of the most dastardly crimes known to humanity," the *Afro-American* reported. "Mink Slide stood . . . as a solid wall. . . ."

What is known is that four white policemen, patrolling the streets that night, were wounded by shotgun pellets. The next morning, hundreds of police and state patrolmen went in to arrest the shooters and get some payback. They ransacked businesses, searched homes, seized weapons, and arrested upwards of one hundred people. Two days later, two prisoners, William Gordon and James Johnson, were shot to death by guards at the Columbia jail, allegedly while trying to escape. Only the black rioters were charged, most of them with attempted murder. The case went to trial later that year, with Thurgood Marshall leading the defense. In October, to the surprise of nearly everyone, an all-white jury acquitted twenty-three of the twenty-five defendants.

In Georgia, one of the most notorious lynchings of the postwar era happened on July 25, when two young tenant-farmer couples—Roger and Dorothy Malcom and George and Mae Dorsey—were shot to death in broad daylight by two dozen white men who waited for them in an ambush. Roger Malcom had been jailed in the north-central Georgia town of Monroe after he had a fight with Barney Hester Jr., the son of the landowner he worked for. What started the fight was unclear—one rumor had it that Hester took a romantic interest in Dorothy Malcom—but it ended when Malcom wounded Hester with a pocketknife. He was arrested and jailed. After a week behind bars, he was bailed out by a local landowner named J. Loy Harrison, who was supposed to drive him, Dorothy, and the Dorseys back to their homes. Instead he took a different road and handed them over to a mob, claiming that he was taken by surprise. All four were taken into a stand of woods, lined up four abreast, and gunned down with dozens of rounds from pistols, rifles, and shotguns. The case became a national scandal and prompted a major probe by the Georgia Bureau of Investigation and the FBI, but no one was ever charged with murder or federal civil rights violations.

Finally, there was the August 1946 lynching of army veteran John C. Jones near Minden, Louisiana. Jones and a cousin, Albert Harris

Jr., were arrested for allegedly prowling around the home of a white woman named Maddry. This appeared to be a frame-up, and it came out later that Jones had been asking questions about oil-producing land that his grandfather owned, which the old man had leased out for a pathetically low amount. After being held for several days, Jones and Harris were freed when Mrs. Maddry declined to press charges. Upon their release, a group of armed men abducted them, threw them into separate cars, and drove into the country. Harris was beaten severely but survived and managed to escape. Jones died, reportedly after being tortured with a meat cleaver and a blowtorch. Subsequent investigation pointed to a conspiracy involving local law enforcement officials, but there were no criminal indictments. The federal government later brought civil rights charges against five men, including two deputy sheriffs and three oil-field workers. All were found not guilty in 1947.

Senator Bilbo had no role in any of these killings, but many people believed his rhetoric and style had everything to do with them. Speaking at a protest rally in Washington after the Malcom-Dorsey lynchings, Max Yergan, president of the National Negro Congress, said that Bilbo and others like him "stand with bloody hands in the murders of these men and women of Georgia. . . ." In Yergan's view, they should be "brought to the bar of justice as the stooges of Hitler were brought to the bar of justice at Nuremberg."

That fall, two investigations of Bilbo took shape. One centered on voter intimidation; the other was a probe by a Senate subcommittee into alleged kickbacks paid to Bilbo by defense contractors.

The Man also faced very serious health problems. He was a cigar smoker, and that summer he developed a gum irritation that led to a diagnostic procedure in New Orleans. It revealed a malignancy and infection that required the removal of part of his jaw. He bragged that the operation gave him "more mouth" and said that all traces of the cancer were gone, but in fact the disease made rapid progress as the new year approached.

The voting-rights challenge marked the first major crusade by the

Civil Rights Congress, which spent thousands on its national "Un-seat Bilbo" Campaign. Novelist Dashiell Hammett, who served as the CRC's New York president during the organization's early years, wrote Bilbo to invite him to a Manhattan dinner—set up to raise funds for his removal—telling him to "feel free to come" but to leave "your klansman's outfit home."

It also marked the first time the CRC crossed paths with the NAACP during a cause, and the NAACP kept its distance. Both groups had a hand in organizing testimony by Mississippi blacks regarding voter intimidation, but NAACP head Walter White ruled out the idea of cooperating with the CRC, arguing that "it is imperative that this . . . be done under non-Communist auspices lest there be support for Bilbo as a victim of the 'Reds.'"

Ultimately, both groups got help from in-state organizers who rounded up witnesses. The CRC's point man was Percy Greene, editor of the *Jackson Advocate*, the state's leading black newspaper. Greene would be heard from again as the Willie McGee case gained traction.

In early December, a five-member Senate committee traveled to Jackson to take testimony from Mississippi citizens, among them several blacks and black veterans who described the threats and violence they'd experienced while trying to vote. In a hearing held at the federal building downtown, Etoy Fletcher repeated his story about the beating he took at Brandon. Varnado R. Collier, who tried to vote in Gulfport, said he was swarmed by ten or fifteen men who knocked him senseless. Joseph Parham of McComb testified that, after he registered, an unidentified white man came up to him and said, "What kind of flowers do you want?" In all, roughly one hundred witnesses were called between December 2 and 4. Forrest Jackson was there throughout, counseling Bilbo and challenging testimony.

Bilbo was there for it all, looking cadaverous but feisty, dressed as usual with his diamond stickpin. He rallied enough to read a prepared statement, take questions, and cackle at his enemies. He admitted that, yes, he favored any lawful means of prohibiting blacks from voting, denying that he had advocated any unlawful acts. He also denied saying, as the *Clarion-Ledger* summarized his words, "that negroes try-

ing to vote should have gasoline poured on them, or that the leaders
of the Mississippi Progressive Voter's League . . . should be atomically
bombed and exterminated from the surface of the earth."

Questioners like Iowa senator Bourke Hickenlooper confronted
him with other things he'd said, including this statement: "The white
people of Mississippi are sitting on a volcano. . . . We are faced with
a nationwide campaign to integrate the nigger with the social life of
this country."

"I subscribe to that," Bilbo replied. "If I didn't say it, I wish I
had."

Did he also say, "The nigger is only 150 years from the jungles of
Africa, where it was his great delight to cut him up some fried nigger
steak for breakfast"?

"Yes."

Had he also said that Clare Booth Luce, the author and wife of *Time*
founder Henry Luce, was "the greatest nigger-lover in the north except Old Lady Eleanor Roosevelt"?

"I said that," he agreed with a smile, ". . . that is true too."

The committee's Democratic chairman, Allen J. Ellender of Louisiana, shrugged off any link between Bilbo's rhetoric and violent acts,
saying that he hoped Bilbo would be unanimously exonerated. The
senators' vote broke three to two in Bilbo's favor, along party lines,
and the committee dutifully forwarded its report to Congress.

When the new Senate convened in January 1947, leaders of the
Republican majority organized to try to deny Bilbo his seat, pending
further investigation into the charges. Southerners began a filibuster,
and pro- and anti-Bilbo forces were still fighting it out when a "com-
promise" was reached on January 4.

In truth, it was a stalemate. Bilbo had to go back to New Orleans
for a new round of jaw surgery, so final resolution of the fight was
tabled until he returned. He left, by car, before dawn the next day,
with Forrest Jackson loyally on hand to drive him home. "If I live I
will be back with my fighting clothes on," he vowed before leaving
Washington. "And if I die I'll come back and haunt you."

Bilbo spent the next few months in Jackson and New Orleans,

8 0] THE EYES OF WILLIE McGEE

dealing with medical procedures and rallying for one last show of public defiance. In March 1947, he held a barbecue for 10,000 people in his hometown of Poplarville, the site of a beloved estate he called the "Dream House." One of his guests was Gerald L. K. Smith, a nationally prominent white supremacist who called Bilbo "the most persecuted man in the world."

The Man died in New Orleans on August 21, 1947. During his final hospital stay, he either had a last-minute conversion or forgot his most cherished beliefs. In an interview done a few weeks before his death, he told African-American journalist Leon P. Lewis, of the *Negro South*, "I hold nothing personal against the Negroes as a race." He probably thought he meant it.

four

HER JITTERBUG

McGee's second circuit-court trial started on October 7, 1946, in the Jones County Courthouse. After the Mississippi Supreme Court's reversal, a change of venue seemed like a given. But on the 9th, Judge Collins said no to the defense's motion for a shift in locale, accepting the state's claim that a "fair and impartial" jury could be assembled in Laurel.

Collins was just being stubborn. He knew nothing had changed, and it was obvious the trial had to be moved. For three days in a row, McGee was transported from Hinds County to Jones by armed state troops who were there for one reason: to keep him from getting lynched. "Twenty troopers were stationed inside the courthouse and thirty were ranged about the yard with machine guns in trucks, while the negro was placed in jail," the *Leader-Call* reported after the first of the transfers.

This time, McGee's defense was in the hands of a more formidable lawyer: Dixon Pyles, a short, burly, balding thirty-three-year-old who took over at Forrest Jackson's recommendation and whose fees and expenses were paid by the CRC. Jackson and Pyles knew each other from political and legal circles. Both had been Bilbo supporters—during the Depression, Bilbo had gotten Pyles a much-needed federal patronage job—and both kept offices in the Century Building, a structure in the heart of downtown Jackson, no longer standing, that was popular with attorneys.

Pyles became a prominent figure in Mississippi and was known for representing labor unions, including locals affiliated with the Congress of Industrial Organizations (CIO). That was another small irony, since Bilbo, Pyles's onetime mentor, hated the CIO. Bilbo could be pro-labor in his way—he supported the 1935 passage of the Wagner Act, which protected the rights of workers to join unions and engage in collective bargaining—but his loyalties were to railroad unions and the craft-oriented American Federation of Labor (AFL). To him, the industrial workers' union was too friendly to both blacks and Reds, and the CIO alienated him further when its political action committee targeted him for defeat in 1946.

"Bilbo was convinced that the Communists were in back of [the CIO]," Pyles told historian Chester M. Morgan in an interview, "and that if they . . . became as well-organized as he thought they would, then Communism would take over through them. So he fought the industrial unions tooth and nail."

In 1946, Pyles was less worried about labor-union preferences than about finding paid labor for himself. He'd served in the army during World War II, landing in Normandy shortly after D-day and seeing action in five major European campaigns. He was still rebuilding his practice when Jackson approached him. "I had no business, and so in order to give me some business, Forrest Jackson persuaded me to become the defense counsel for Willie McGee," Pyles recalled. "And I persuaded, against his will, a young lawyer named Dan Breland to assist me in it."

Over the years, Pyles sat for several interviews in which he talked about what it was like to defend McGee. Describing packed courtrooms and a "wrought up" public mood, he said he had no doubt that he and Breland could have gotten McGee or themselves killed if they'd said or done the wrong thing in court.

He meant this seriously, but he also joked about it as time went by. For the rest of his life, Pyles entertained colleagues with a well-practiced anecdote about a death threat he got in Jones County, after he presented arguments for a change of venue. The way he told it, a group of surly local white men was waiting for him and Breland at the bottom of the courthouse stairs, angry that he was trying to get the trial moved. One of them called Pyles a son of a bitch and told him he had exactly thirty minutes to get out of Jones County.

Tossing his keys to Breland, Pyles said, "You take care of the car." Not wanting to waste a second, he started running toward the county line, moving so fast that he skimmed over the surface of a mill pond. As for that thirty-minute time limit? "I've still got twenty-nine of them left," he laughed in his loud, raspy voice.

In the end, Pyles got his way about venue. Cooler heads in Laurel persuaded Collins that he had to step aside and let someone else make the decision. "[M]embers of the bar down there told him he was making a fool of himself, that he would be reversed again," Pyles said. ". . . [H]e excused himself on the grounds that his wife was sick."

By the time the trial opened, a circuit judge from a different part of the state—John Stennis, who replaced Bilbo in the Senate in 1947—had taken over temporarily, and he quickly decided Laurel was too dangerous. At the start of the day's proceedings on October 16, heavily armed state guardsmen were ordered to assemble inside the courtroom to form a protective barrier between McGee, 150 potential jurymen sitting inside, and a sizable number of muttering men who were outside but wanted in. Spectators were barred, but the *Leader-Call* said another 150 people were gathered on the other side of the courtroom doors, along with "scores" more on the courthouse lawn.

"I don't like the idea of trying a case behind guns," Stennis grumbled. He said he'd received reports about citizens making angry remarks in the presence of guardsmen. So he shut the whole thing down and sent it to Hattiesburg, a similarly sized pine-belt town thirty miles southwest of Laurel, in Forrest County.

———

Challenging the venue was one thing, but there was another line of attack that Pyles wouldn't touch: McGee's claim that he'd had consensual sex with Mrs. Hawkins, and that she started it. Contrary to some published accounts of the case, this allegation was not introduced at any of the circuit-court trials—in fact, it wasn't made public until very late in the appeals process—but McGee definitely told his lawyers that the real story involved seduction, not rape. He conveyed this to Forrest Jackson in late 1945 or early 1946 in a statement that he either wrote himself or dictated to a fellow inmate in the Hinds County jail.

Pyles first talked about the statement in 1952, sharing its contents with a private investigator from New York who had been sent to Mississippi after the case ended by a law firm representing the *Daily Worker*. The investigator, whose name was only given as "Mr. Spivak," was assigned to dig up new evidence that McGee's affair story was true, because by then the paper had a potentially expensive problem on its hands: a libel suit for $1 million filed by Willette Hawkins in 1951 at the federal district court in Manhattan.

After the McGee case ended, Mrs. Hawkins hired the Jackson law firm of future governor Ross Barnett—one of the best in Mississippi—to pursue a libel action against the *Daily Worker*, claiming that it had defamed her by writing about the affair as if it were proven. *Daily Worker* editors and Communist Party officials realized with a gulp that the affair story was never argued before a jury, just alleged and denied during appeals, so they opened their own investigation. Spivak went to Jackson and Laurel for several days in June and July of 1952, where he spoke with at least four of McGee's defense lawyers—Pyles, Breland, and third-trial counsel John Poole and Alvin London—and to Mrs. Hawkins's preacher, the Reverend Grayson L. Tucker. The interviews survive as blurry carbon copies in the CRC's files.

Spivak talked to Pyles on June 30 at his law office in Jackson. "I'll tell you what the problem is," he said as they settled in. "We've got a million-dollar suit on our hands as a result of the McGee case. . . . I'm looking for some leads about some information—about the lady in question whose honor has been impugned."

Pyles knew about the lawsuit, so it's surprising he opened up to a stranger who for all practical purposes was taping a deposition. But, to varying degrees, most of the lawyers spoke frankly about their experiences defending McGee. It was as if they relished the chance to show off their battle scars.

By that point, Pyles couldn't remember whether McGee first gave the statement to him or to Forrest Jackson. But he thought he must have inherited it from Jackson, because throughout the pretrial and trial periods, Pyles was unable to get McGee to say more than a handful of words to him.

Why this resistance to his own lawyer? Pyles speculated that McGee had experienced so much stress and terror, and had bonded so strongly with Jackson, that he was unable to transfer his trust to another white attorney. "Forrest Jackson . . . had developed a good rapport with Willie McGee," he said. "McGee somehow got the impression that I was part of the establishment that was attempting to take his life, and he refused to talk with me, to give me any facts, at all."

Jackson told McGee he ought to have faith in Pyles, but it didn't help: "[H]e did not tell me anything and I think it was out of fear, complete, paralyzing fear and distrust."

Pyles decided to say nothing about the affair claim at the trial. As he told Spivak, to make such an accusation in a Mississippi court was extremely dangerous, but there was another problem: He couldn't find independent evidence to support it. Pyles used two investigators of his own to poke around Laurel in search of fresh intelligence about this or anything else that might help McGee's defense. One was Laurent Frantz, a white CRC attorney from Knoxville, Tennessee, who had been part of the anti-Bilbo push. Another was an African-American attorney from Mississippi named Dan Williams. Pyles and Breland also got research help from two Jackson colleagues, E. T. Calhoun and Tom Watkins. Nobody turned up witnesses about the affair.

It's an open question whether they tried very hard. Pyles said he doubted that any Laurel citizens, of either race, would have talked or testified about a love affair between a black man and a white woman, and it seems unlikely he would have called them to the stand, even if he had the goods. Many years later, he told an interviewer that, in retrospect, he found the affair story "hard to believe."

"I'll tell you why I never raised the story," he told Spivak. ". . . [I]f you introduced this thing down there—that court room was packed—[it] would have started a riot, would have had no appreciable difference in the outcome of the jury. They wouldn't have believed it. . . . Those people couldn't have done otherwise and lived in that community. Of course, you don't know how high that feeling gets. You're from New York. . . . You don't know how high a feeling can get in a community like that down there."

"It was pretty . . . pretty explosive," Spivak said.

"Oh, it was. Completely so . . . [T]here would have been a near riot in the courtroom, no doubt about that. Whenever you charge a white woman in the south with having sexual relations with a nigger in this part of the country, why, you better be God-damn sure."

"I see."

"We wouldn't have lived to have gotten out of town."

Spivak paused on that, to make sure Pyles meant it. "You wouldn't have lived to have gotten out of town?"

"Well, if we had used that. Unless we would have had the facts absolutely. Then she probably wouldn't have lived. They would have killed her."

". . . So, in other words, the situation was such that even if everybody believed that this was so, it just wasn't wise to introduce it."

"[You] couldn't have—and lived."

"So [you] followed the procedure that it's best to forget it?"

"Well, there was no evidence to back it up. There was just his words and him in a state where he couldn't testify. The only way we could have brought it up was in cross-examination of her. In an atmosphere like that, why, they would have chewed us up like cotton."

Dan Breland—who, unlike Pyles, didn't relish talking about the case—made similar points with Spivak, calling the trial's atmosphere "very frightening." If McGee had talked about interracial sex in court, he said, "[H]e probably wouldn't have got off the stand. He would have been killed there."

"And the lawyers with him?"

"Yeah, that's sure," Breland said. He returned to this theme later, saying that if he and Pyles had known what they were getting into, "money couldn't have hired us" to take the case.

"Was it that much of a danger?"

"Yeah. We're lucky we got out of it."

═══

There was another angle to McGee's story that never became public knowledge, even after 1951. As Pyles explained to Spivak, McGee claimed the affair was tied into an elaborate murder plot. He said Mrs. Hawkins had told him she was pregnant with his child and had pressured him to kill her husband, so she could collect what Pyles described as "a fifteen thousand dollar double indemnity" life-insurance policy that Troy had taken out.

"Her husband had what?" Spivak said.

Pyles told him again. Spivak asked if he knew which company wrote the policy.

"I don't know what company it was."

"Indemnity policy . . . and she wanted McGee to—"

"She wanted McGee to kill her husband so that she could get the thirty thousand dollars; and that, in place of paying him any money, that he could have sexual intercourse with her."

While Pyles kept talking, it occurred to him that he might have the original letter—he'd handed some of his McGee files over to the lead third-trial lawyer, John Poole, but not all—so he looked around until he found it. The statement, written in childish handwriting, filled three sheets of yellow tablet paper.

"Now, here, I don't know whether Willie wrote this or not, but here is a statement that came down into our hands and we were told it was written by Willie," Pyles said. "It shows—tell[s] you the whole story—gives you everything. I think it's his own writing." He started reading it into the tape recorder.

Willie McGee, born November 4, 1915, at Pachuta, Miss. Came to Laurel, Miss. at four years old. Went to school at Laurel until I got to 7 grade and got married 1935 to Eliza Jane Payton in Laurel, Miss. Have four children. Lived with my mother in Laurel until worked for McRae Service Station, 1936 to 1937. Worked at Eastman Garden [Gardiner] Company until cut out and went to work for Masonite in 1938 and quit then. Went to work in 1939 with Bethea Grocery. . . .

That was the style throughout: conversational, rambling, moving through time in sudden leaps. McGee mentioned other jobs and

moves—he went off to New Orleans for a while, worked on the river-
front, then returned to Laurel in 1941 to work at Bethea again—after
which there was a gap of several years and a confusing section in
which he seemed to say he'd enlisted in the army but was discharged
because of "something on the brain." By that point, suddenly, it was
1944.

McGee said the affair started in August of that year, but that he had
encountered Mrs. Hawkins before then. Once or twice in the past, he
said, as he walked through her neighborhood, she had acted friendly
and tried to get him to come inside her house to do chores.

> *Every time she would see me she would smile and pick on me. She
> would call me her jitterbug. So one morning . . . as I passed her
> house on South Magnolia she called me and I went up to her porch
> and she asked me to come on in and I went on in. She told me she
> had wanted a little work that she wanted did so [she] asked me
> what would I charge to wash windows and wax the floors. Then
> she said that seem like I was afraid of white folks. I told her I was
> not. She said to me you must be, you must be. You act like you are
> ready to run. So she caught hold of my arm and pulled me up to
> her. So I caught around her and kissed her. And she said to me, Do
> you want to love me? And I said: My, oh—yes. And she walked
> on back in the bedroom and laid across the bed and I pulled my
> pants down and got on her. . . . This was on Saturday morning,
> one morning in August. Cannot give the exact date but it was in
> August 1944.*

Abruptly, without providing dates, McGee said, "I left Laurel and
went to Nevada for a while." When he came back—he didn't say
when—Mrs. Hawkins presented him with shocking news. "I went to
see her one night and she told me that she was in the family way and
that I had done it," he said.

According to McGee, the murder plot was hatched at this moment.
He claimed that Mrs. Hawkins was in love with him and wanted them
to run away together. "She said that she would get the insurance

money and we'd go to California together and get married," he wrote. The plot fell apart, McGee said, only because he didn't want to do the killing. He left Laurel again and went to California, and then came back sometime in 1945, at which point the insatiable Mrs. Hawkins started badgering him again.

In this part of the statement, McGee sidetracked into logistical details about how the affair worked. Sometimes he would sneak into the back of the Hawkins home, with Troy either out of the house or in the front room, asleep. Twice, Mrs. Hawkins picked him up on the street and drove him to a "Negro cemetery" where they had sex in her car. Twice she showed up at a service station where he worked—"Mr. Joe Newson Service Station in Laurel," he said. He quit that job because he was scared her carelessness would get him in serious trouble.

Everything came to a head in October and November of 1945. McGee said he went to Mrs. Hawkins's home on a Wednesday night—October 31—to borrow $20. "She got at me again about killing her husband and I told her I would be back Thursday night and would do it," he said.

McGee admitted that on Thursday he drank, gambled, lost his company's money, and then parked his truck near the Hawkins home—just as the prosecution had sketched it at the first trial. But all similarities ended there. The prosecutors said he crawled through a window and took Mrs. Hawkins by surprise in the dark. McGee said she was eagerly awaiting his arrival. He scratched on a window screen and she let him in the front door, thinking he was there to murder Troy. But he told her he wasn't prepared to do it.

"So she began to fuss," he said. "She told me that I was not doing a thing but lying. I told her I did not have to lie. She asked me was I going to love her and I kissed her and hugged her. . . . She even unbuttoned my overalls for me and we got into bed. And when I started to get up I told her I wanted some money. She got angry again and began to raise sam. She said that I was taking her money, me and my Negro whores having a big time. But she went on in the back room and got me $5.50. It was $4 in bills, $1.50 in halves."

The rest of the statement was repetitive, so it may be that McGee wrote it down twice. But there were a few new tidbits: He claimed there were three "Negro witnesses" who saw him and Mrs. Hawkins at a roadhouse one night, and that his wife found and tore up a picture of her that he secretly kept at home. In all, he estimated, they had sex "over a dozen times."

McGee never spelled out the cause-and-effect of why his failure to murder Troy led to his arrest. He didn't seem to be sure, but said Mrs. Hawkins had told him once that "you are going to do what I say or something is going to happen to you bad."

"I didn't know just what happened after I left," he wrote. "I don't know whether [Troy] heard me or she told him or not. . . .

"She tried to force me to kill Mr. H.," he reiterated. "She seem that she was plum insane. She told me she did not care anything about him any more. . . . In the beginning she told me to never tell no one about our plans. I tried everything to get rid of her but she being white lady I had to do what she said. . . . She told me that I was the one who got her in pregnancy. She kept me worried at all times."

———

Dixon Pyles doesn't get much stage time in existing accounts of the McGee case. Writers like Carl Rowan and Jessica Mitford tended to skip details of the circuit-court trials in favor of higher-profile years like 1950 and 1951, when the verdict was under appeal and Bella Abzug was overseeing the defense.

More recently, Philip Dray's *At the Hands of Persons Unknown* covers the three trials in a single paragraph and doesn't mention Pyles at all. Dray, by necessity, had to compress the story—his book is a complicated narrative that touches on dozens of lynching and legal lynching cases—but it's a shame Pyles didn't make the cut. Dray writes that "the CRC" raised the issue of race-based jury exclusion in the second trial, which is true but incomplete. It was Pyles who did that, and it required grilling a cavalcade of county officials about fraudulent voting-rights practices that were integral to the Jim Crow system. In the process, he helped force a historic, unpopular change in Mississippi jury selection that came about in 1948, at the start of McGee's third trial.

When Pyles does come up, the reviews aren't always kind. Abzug seemed to like him—in an interview done nearly fifty years later, she remembered him as "a decent guy, a labor lawyer"—but others have assumed he was a lightweight, a shyster, or a one-dimensional bigot who, like Boyd and Koch, didn't care enough about McGee to give the case his best. In a letter sent to the CRC's Milton Kemnitz two weeks before the second-trial preliminaries in Laurel, Laurent Frantz—a CRC staffer from Tennessee who was involved in the case—said Pyles wasn't up to the job, calling him "inexperienced in this sort of work" and saying he lacked "an adequate theoretical foundation to find his own way in it. . . ."

In *Communist Front?*, Gerald Horne's 1988 history of the Civil Rights Congress, Horne concluded that Pyles's use of "nigger" proved he was a racist whose heart wasn't in it. Later, he thumped him again while discussing another Mississippi case Pyles handled for the CRC in 1947—a tricky one that involved members of an African-American family named Craft, who fired on four law enforcement officers as they approached the family's home in rural Smith County, apparently thinking they were part of a lynch mob.

"As had happened in many of their other cases in the South, CRC had incredible difficulties with local counsel, this time the familiar Dixon Pyles," Horne wrote. "By early in 1947 they had already paid him $2,130 and had agreed to pay him $3,000 more."

That's phrased to sound like price-gouging, but Pyles never pretended he took these cases to be charitable. As for his word choice, it's offensive now and it was offensive then, but that's the way white people often talked in the 1940s. A better-known transgressor was President Truman, who in 1945 referred to Harlem congressman Adam Clayton Powell as "that damn nigger preacher" during a White House staff meeting.

Pyles was an establishment figure in a segregated society, so his views on race and society wouldn't resemble today's norms. But he was also a lawyer who'd taken an oath, and every indication is that he did the best he could with the tools he had. The CRC's leaders must have agreed, because after the second trial they hired him to help write the second appeal to the Mississippi Supreme Court. They also pleaded with him to stay on the job when the third trial approached.

Finally, Frantz's point about Pyles's "theoretical foundation" raises a question of its own: Which theory would equip you to walk into a courtroom where the men inside would rather kill your client than look at him? Though it wasn't reported at the time, it was stated convincingly in later interviews and appeal documents that Troy Hawkins was caught sneaking a pistol into court, and that he said he was prepared to shoot McGee or his lawyers if he didn't like what he heard.

What the job required, as much as anything, was courage, and Pyles had plenty of that. Originally from Little Rock, Arkansas, he graduated from Central High School in Jackson and attended Millsaps College, also in Jackson, from 1930 to 1933. Standing five feet three inches tall and weighing 150 pounds, he was compact, physically strong, and mulishly determined. His mother and stepfather moved away from Jackson when he was sixteen, but he stayed behind, living in a boardinghouse and working to support himself. The summer after graduating from Millsaps, in a typical adventure, he headed off to the 1933 Chicago World's Fair, where he earned money by pulling fairgoers around in a rickshaw.

"He had broad shoulders and was built like a fireplug," says his son, Todd. "He had what you call 'short-man attitude.' He had a friend named Weaver Ellis Gore III, who used to say that if he could just get Dixon's vote, it would be unanimous that Dixon was a son of a bitch."

After the World's Fair, Pyles went back to Jackson, where he started out in journalism. He got a job writing for the *Clarion-Ledger*, which led to a job on radio station WJDX, where he became what he proudly called "the first radio news commentator in Mississippi." He'd met Bilbo as a high-school student, came to know him better during his newsman days, and traveled to Washington in the mid-1930s to ask for a Mississippi-based job with the Federal Housing Authority, which he got. Later, he bounced around in short-term posts in Louisiana and Mississippi and contributed unsigned writing for *Mississippi: The WPA Guide to the Magnolia State*, reporting on subjects like the Gulf Coast shrimp-fishing industry.

Pyles entered law school in Jackson in 1937 and opened his practice in early 1940. One of his first clients was a famous central Mississippi gambler and bootlegger named Dewey Swor, who was still a public scourge as late as 1948, when he was arrested for numerous bookmaking violations. Pyles said Swor put him on retainer mainly because he didn't drink. "He told me, 'Jackson has some good lawyers, criminal lawyers particularly, but when it gets dark they all get drunk,'" he said. "'If they get arrested and put in jail, I cannot depend on those that I have on my payroll.'"

Pyles went into the army in 1942 and became a gunner in an antiaircraft artillery battalion, part of the Sixth Armored Division of the Third Army under General George Patton, which punched its way through some of the worst campaigns in Europe. He took part in major battles in Normandy, the Rhineland, and the Ardennes, commanding a half-track with two 37 mm antiaircraft guns mounted on a turret in the center of the bed.

"When I was growing up," Todd told me, "we had a .45-caliber service weapon that had Plexiglas in place of the usual brown handles, with a family photograph mounted behind the glass. My dad personally shot down an ME-109"—a Messerschmitt Bf-109, the workhorse fighter plane of the Luftwaffe—"and went over and took a souvenir, which was the glass out of the cockpit."

Todd makes it clear, in his funny, rueful way, that Dixon could be a rough parent, but that didn't negate his admiration. "He is *still* my hero," he said. "You must understand that. He was not sweet and kind. He had a tendency to piss people off. Hell, he used to win cases by pissing people off. He'd get his witnesses up there and ask smartass questions until they lost their temper."

Todd is well aware of Dixon's role in the McGee case, which he calls "an extraordinary act of courage in enemy territory." He thinks he took it on for a combination of reasons. One being that, yes, he needed the work. But another was genuine conviction. "He was a progressive who really did care about the little guy," Todd said. But there was something more elemental at work too: "He just didn't like anybody telling him what to do."

———

Like Laurel, Hattiesburg was a small city that owed its existence to the nineteenth-century timber boom. It wasn't incorporated until 1884, but it had become a busy place by the 1940s, a crossroads of highways, railroads, and manufacturing nicknamed Hub City. Hattiesburg's numbers had swollen a bit during World War II, thanks to Camp Shelby, a huge army base southeast of town, but Shelby was downsized after the war ended. Another notable institution was Mississippi Southern College, a former teacher training school that was still a few years away from a period of growth and construction that would later turn it into a sizable campus.

The Forrest County Courthouse was similar to Laurel's—a big, brick-clad building at the edge of the downtown business district, with a Confederate soldier out front, standing guard on top of a pillar. From Pyles's perspective, the two locations weren't any different. He'd hoped to get as far away from Laurel as he could, to a north Mississippi town like Tupelo. Instead, he would have to present his case before the same judge, Burkitt Collins, and McGee's fate would be decided by an all-white, all-male jury that was certain to have unforgiving opinions about black men putting their hands on white women. Mrs. Hawkins wasn't a local, but there were local connections to the case. McGee had been arrested in Hattiesburg, and Mrs. Hawkins spent ten days there in a hospital. She also had a sister, LaVera Hooks, who lived in town.

Not surprisingly, McGee—who was jailed in Hattiesburg for the trial's duration—was still in a state of great personal distress. He looked terrified whenever he had to enter the courtroom, and he continued to say nothing. "[H]e was crazy at the time we tried [the case]," Dan Breland told Spivak, the *Daily Worker*'s investigator. "He didn't open his mouth. . . . Never did get a word out of him. Not one word."

Pyles pursued three lines of defense, in all instances looking past the trial and toward what he assumed would be a second appeal. First, unlike Boyd and Koch, he tried to put meat on the insanity plea. Step one was to get McGee examined by a qualified psychiatrist. During proceedings held in Laurel before the venue shift, he told Judge Collins that every psychiatrist in Mississippi—all of whom were employed by the state mental hospital in Jackson—had refused to examine his client. So he called on a psychologist from the capital named N. B. Bond, who performed hurry-up jailhouse examinations and concluded that McGee had the mind of "a normal eight-year-old child." Pyles wanted to get a second opinion from a psychiatrist in New Orleans, a Dr. Charles E. Holbrook, but Holbrook told him he wouldn't be available for three or four days. Could he have that much time?

Collins ruled that this was too long; the court couldn't recess "while the defense was out fishing for witnesses." Later, both sides agreed that insanity arguments would be presented during direct testimony, not at a separate hearing.

In another move, Pyles said he had been told that Willie had tried to enlist in the army but was taken out of training because his mind was shot. He'd called around and had been "advised upon reliable information" that McGee had served in the army briefly—he didn't say when or where—and had been put in "a ward set aside for the observation of mentally deficient patients" before being discharged. Specifically, Pyles said, "records will show that the defendant is suffering from syphilis of the brain." He asked for additional time and the court's assistance to obtain the army records. This too was denied.

Most of Pyles's effort went into a challenge of the jury-selection systems in Jones and Forrest counties, which, like those in every other Mississippi county, were designed to exclude African Americans from serving. The issues he raised had come up, with strikingly similar details, in Alabama in 1933, during the second set of circuit-court trials involving the Scottsboro Boys, a group of nine black males— most of them teenagers—who'd been accused of raping two white women on a freight train. Their lawyers asked the court to quash the indictment based on the systematic exclusion of blacks from juries. The judge refused and the state supreme court upheld him, but the U.S. Supreme Court reversed the verdicts, saying the county's reasons for exclusion—basically, that it happened because there weren't any blacks with sufficient judgment or qualifications to serve—wouldn't wash.

That was Alabama in the 1930s. By 1946, jury exclusion was still the rule in Mississippi, though it was under assault there as well. Pyles may have known that the same questions were already before the state supreme court in a case called *Patton v. Mississippi*, an appeal of a murder conviction of a black defendant in Meridian, a railroad town sixty miles northeast of Laurel. Either way, he knew that, to lodge a successful appeal, he and Breland had to get it on the record that blacks were kept off juries in Laurel and Hattiesburg— and why.

To do this, they put one official after another on the stand, including circuit clerks, members of the county boards of supervisors (whose job it was to place names of potential jurors in the jury box), and other city officials involved in compiling jury lists. All agreed that they'd never seen a black serve on a grand or petit jury during their combined decades of public service. Luther Hill, the Jones County sheriff, was asked whether, at any time during a career that stretched back forty-six years, he had served a jury summons on an African American. "I don't remember that I did," he said.

Generally, the reasons given had to do with raw statistics. To serve on a jury, you had to be a registered voter, and there weren't many registered blacks. With a straight face, the officials said this was just the way things had worked out, and that no pressure was applied to keep blacks from registering. And if they did happen to be registered and were called? They voluntarily elected not to serve.

During questioning by District Attorney Homer Pittman, Bill Hosey, a former Laurel mayor and Jones County prosecutor, insisted that the names of black voters were sometimes drawn from the jury box, but these men declined to take part of their own free will.

"We have always had in this county about 35 to 50 negroes that were qualified electors," he said. "They were the better class of Negroes and when they were drawn for jury service . . . they would ask to be excused." Why was that? Because they were "of that class of intelligent Negroes that didn't want to appear as a juror in court."

That was double-talk, and Hosey seemed to be enjoying his time on the stand. Under cross-examination by Pyles, he boasted that, in his experience, white jurors often went easier on black criminals than on white criminals—one of those surprising facts of Southern life that they didn't tell you about up north. "I have had more Negro defendants turned aloose, that is, acquitted, in my eight years as prosecutor, by white jurors than I have white defendants acquitted," he said.

"Did you ever have any white defendants turned aloose by negro jurors in your eight years of office?" Pyles asked.

"No, sir," Hosey said, "and I would rather not answer that question, because I thought my forefathers settled that question in Jasper County in 1876 with a negro sheriff when they stole—"

This caused a commotion, and it was never explained what happened to the negro sheriff. Collins banged his gavel and excused Hosey. Though he let Pyles keep going—asking the same questions of Forrest County officials—he'd already made up his mind.

"[T]here isn't a scintilla of testimony offered by the defendant in this case to show that there was any legal fraud in drawing jurors for Forrest County, either actual or legal," he said at the end. "[T]he testimony shows that they were drawn by the Board of Supervisors as contemplated by law. . . ." He overruled both motions to quash the jury panels.

"Note our exception," Pyles said. He would have more to say on the subject later.

The last chore was jury selection, a process of questioning and win-
nowing that was limited by a simple fact: No matter how deep you
went into the pool, the candidates weren't going to change much. No
women. No blacks. Just white males who were primarily blue-collar.
Among the potential jurors at the start, there was a postal clerk, a
woodworker, a student at Southern, an auto mechanic, a piano repairman, a farmer, a pulp-mill machinist, and a truck driver. Almost to a
man, they said they could listen to the case and make up their minds
without prejudice against McGee.

Pyles didn't believe it, but he'd had his say about the jury's makeup.
He rejected a few candidates—as did Judge Collins—but he didn't
seem interested in a long selection battle. Three men were excused
because they said they'd already decided McGee was guilty; two because they were over sixty; and one because he opposed the death
penalty.

"I have been thinking, sitting here studying about that," this man
said, "and I would hate—I'm not trying to shirk my duty, but . . .
I would hate to bring in any verdict that takes a man's life." That
was enough to get him bounced. The jurors had to set the sentence,
and they had to be open to one of three possible outcomes: innocent,
guilty with a penalty of life in prison, and guilty with a penalty of
death.

Direct testimony began on November 11, a Monday. The prosecution, led by Homer Pittman, presented the same case as before, with
a few variations and in more detail. They put Willette on the stand
first, and she repeated the story she'd told in December 1945. Lying in
bed with her infant daughter, she'd heard something crawling on the
floor, reached out in the dark, and felt "a human being. . . . I felt along
and finally got up on his head and there was that old, the kinkiest hair
I have ever felt. . . . I asked him, 'What do you want? Go away. Why
did you come here?'"

Mrs. Hawkins said she called out to her husband but knew he
wouldn't hear her because he was in the back and was a heavy sleeper.
("He has changed now," she said.) She told the attacker she was men-

struating, but said he didn't care, and that he ordered her to "get them goddamned rags off, and them goddamned britches off." She said she could smell him ("like old beer") but couldn't see him. The rapist said that if she didn't shut up and give him what he wanted, he would start killing people. "All the time I was trying to protect the baby with one hand and trying to shove him away with the other hand," she testified.

Pyles was aggressive when he cross-examined Mrs. Hawkins, starting on Monday afternoon. This session was long and emotional—she was already drained from revisiting the crime, and Pyles kept her on the stand for three hours. "The witness faltered several times in telling her story," the *Hattiesburg American* reported, "and then, during the cross-examination by defense attorney Dixon Pyles, became so visibly upset that Judge Burkitt Collins ordered court recessed shortly after 5 p.m."

Pyles had decided to make Mrs. Hawkins the centerpiece of his third courtroom strategy. In a move that would cause confusion in the years ahead, he pursued the idea that she had legally "consented" to having sex with McGee. But this had nothing to do with the love-affair story. It was about her failure to scream loud enough or fight hard enough during the rape. According to a motion introduced by the defense, this failure tended to "raise a presumption that no rape was committed upon her. . . ." Why? Because Mississippi law said that if a rape victim didn't fight as hard as she could during an assault, what happened technically wasn't a rape.

Breland, during his interview with Spivak, talked about why Pyles went down this road. "She testified that she said . . . 'Oh. All right. If that's all I can do it.' You'll find in that first [trial] record . . . that she testified that she didn't holler because she didn't want to arouse her children—didn't want to wake her children up. That . . . shows that he didn't rape her, by her own testimony."

It was a weak argument—Mrs. Hawkins thought the rapist was going to kill her and her family, a state of mind that would seem to constitute "fear"—but Pyles hammered away, obviously planning to bring the matter up on appeal.

"What did you say when you screamed?" he asked her.

"I said, 'What do you want?'"

"I believe that you testified under oath at the former trial that after he told you what he wanted, you said, 'Well, if that is all, I can take it.'"

"That is a lie. No, I didn't, not in my right mind."

". . . I will ask you if, at a former trial, you did not testify, 'I called him, not loud, because I did not want to wake the children up in the next room, as I didn't know but what he had already killed Troy. And when I called Troy, he said, 'He is back there asleep, Miss,' and then you said he told you what he came for. And you said, 'Well, if that's all I can take it.'"

"I don't remember that I did," she said.

———————

As the trial went on, Pyles did what he could to attack the prosecution's case. He argued that the testimony placing a Laurel Wholesale Grocery truck near the scene of the crime at the right hour—and McGee along with it—was purely circumstantial. Did Paul Britton see a truck roll by his service station at 5 a.m.? So what? He didn't see the driver. Did Rose Imbragulio see a truck on the street that "looked like Wholesale Grocery" to her? Fine, but she didn't clearly see anybody inside it. The prosecution didn't bother denying that none of the witnesses or the victim could identify McGee by sight, and that there was no physical evidence proving that he was the rapist.

Dr. Grady Cook testified again, saying he'd examined Mrs. Hawkins at his clinic in Hattiesburg, had found "living spermatozoa," but had no way of knowing whose cells they were. Mrs. Lonnie Meador, the Jones County circuit clerk, produced the bloodstained boxer shorts again, which had been stored in a file cabinet inside a vault. But by now the bloodstains were gone. During cross-examination, Pyles held up the shorts and asked Police Chief Wayne Valentine to show him where the stain had been.

Valentine pointed to the spot, acknowledging that nothing was visible anymore. Pyles asked if "ten or eleven months" was enough time for a bloodstain to go away on its own. Valentine didn't know. Did the chief order an analysis of the clothes to determine that the stain was actually a bloodstain? He hadn't.

Pyles also argued that McGee's alleged confession, which he reportedly gave of his own volition, was tainted, because McGee had no counsel present and was terrified about what might happen to him.

"Chief, did you have him handcuffed?" he said.

"Yes, sir."

"And there was about six or eight men around him in the city jail in Hattiesburg?"

"I imagine there were that many."

"And all of you had guns."

"Yes, sir."

Pyles made a motion to exclude the confession, partly on the grounds that McGee "was told in the presence of officers with guns on that it would be best for him to tell the truth."

Collins overruled. Questioned by the prosecution, Valentine described how he had driven McGee to Magnolia Street in Laurel and asked him, "Willie, what was your truck doing on South Magnolia Street?" McGee said he'd had a breakdown in front of a stucco house and that it had taken a while to get it running again.

"Up until that time, Chief, had you said one word to Willie about him raping anybody?"

"Well, I had talked to him on the way up there about where he had been the night before and what he had done," Valentine said. "And after I had talked to him about this truck being broke down, I asked him about going in this house of the Hawkins up there, and then he set there awhile. And after a while he said, Yes, he did go in it, and then as we went up the street, I asked him to show me where the truck was broke down, and . . . he showed me . . . and then I says, 'Willie, show me the house that you went in.' And we went up the street about a block further and he pointed over to the Hawkins home and the one next door and he said, 'One of those two houses right there.'"

"Chief, did he or not tell you then and there that he had committed this rape?"

"He did." Valentine said he'd asked McGee how he got in the house. McGee said he went in the front door, took a right, and entered Mrs. Hawkins's bedroom.

After several other witnesses were heard from, mostly law enforcement officials, the prosecution closed with testimony about McGee's alleged jailbreak in Hinds County and his mental condition. C. M. Herring, the jailer who was beaten up, said he had thought McGee was probably insane—right up until the moment he bashed him on the head with an iron bar. Allen Boutwell, deputy sheriff of Jones County, said he saw McGee react with a smile when Judge Stennis called him to the bench and told him he was transferring the case. A Forrest County deputy sheriff testified that, during his most recent jail stay, McGee knew what was going on around him and recognized his mother when she visited.

"He talked to her in my presence," he said. "While with her, he led a singing session."

"I will ask you whether or not Willie can sing."

"He certainly can. Sang like a full-grown man."

———

When the defense's turn came, Pyles called McGee as his second witness, but McGee didn't budge from his chair. Court officers carried him to the stand, where he crouched and quivered and said nothing.

"The records show we had the sheriff sit him on the stand bodily," Breland explained to Spivak. "He didn't have sense enough to sit up—to put his feet on the stand. We asked him—I asked him several questions. What his name was and such as that. He didn't answer." He was excused without having uttered an intelligible word.

Pyles called only a few other witnesses, among them N. B. Bond, who said McGee was incapable of knowing the difference between right and wrong, and a Hattiesburg-based photographer named Bob

Waller, who took pictures of McGee at the first trial and noticed that
his eyes didn't bulge when the flash went off, which he called "very
abnormal."

Once again, the longest defense testimony came from Bessie Mc-
Gee, who said Willie had been turned down for army service at Camp
Shelby, Mississippi, and Fort Benning, Georgia, "on account of his
head." She said he'd been diagnosed with "'erysipelas' of the brains"
and named a local physician, Dr. Paul Haney, who was giving him
shots.

Asked if she thought Willie was insane, she said, "Well, to my idea
there's something 'nother wrong with him, something ailing him. I
tried to get him to know me in there while ago, and he wouldn't have
anything to say to me."

Pyles asked again: Was he sane or insane?

"To my believing about it, I just believe that his mind ain't—he
ain't at his self. His mind is bad."

Under questioning from the prosecution, she described what she
said to Willie during her jail visits.

Did you talk to him?
  I had prayer with him.
  Had prayer with him?
  And songs.
  Who led the songs?
  He led some and I led some. . . .
  Willie is a good singer, isn't he?
  Yes, sir, he does pretty good.
  And he sang over there in jail, and he sang pretty loud, didn't he?
  Yes, sir.
  *And don't you know he was putting on a bigger show at Laurel
  than he is putting on down here? (No answer.) When he wants to
  talk to you, he could talk to you, couldn't he, Aunty?*
  I don't know, sir. I will be frank about that.

In his summary to the jury, Pyles pleaded for mercy. "We don't ask you to turn Willie loose," he said. "Send Willie to an institution where he can be guided and do useful work. The defense asks that the jury find Willie not guilty by reasons of insanity."

The jury found him guilty, this time staying out eleven minutes instead of two and a half. Collins quickly set a new death date: December 20, 1946.

five

GOD DON'T LIKE UGLY

A s I type this into my computer, 59 years later, my insides begin to
quiver as they did that night when I was 8 years old."

Those words are from an unpublished manuscript called "My
Mother's Voice," which was written by Sandra Hawkins, the second
daughter of Troy and Willette Hawkins and the woman I'd communicated with through Mary Mostert for so many months.

Sandra showed it to me in the fall of 2006, when my wife and I
visited her and her husband, Brad, at their home in Louisiana. More
than a year had passed since I met her for the first time, in Jackson
in the spring of 2005. Since then, we'd kept in contact—writing each
other directly, no more go-betweens—while I went ahead with my
research. In the summer of 2006, I finished a book proposal, which
Sandra and Dorothy were aware of, since I'd fact-checked everything
I said about them or their parents. (I did the same with the McGees.)
They were cooperating, but with a condition that showed how uncer-
tain they still were about all this: They said I couldn't use their real
names in the proposal. Thus, the three sisters were rechristened Amy,
Sarah, and Helen.

In August 2006, I e-mailed Sandra, telling her the project was on
and repeating what I'd said before: that it didn't matter what anybody
thought they knew about the case, because I was starting from scratch
anyway. If they had a story to tell, they should tell it now, before it
was too late. I wasn't in this to take sides, push a political view, or set
them up to be humiliated. I promised to listen with an open mind and
honestly relate what they had to say.

This time, she agreed, sending back an e-mail that was brief and
informal, with a serious personal note at the end. "My parents were
devoted to one another and I have never experienced a more loving

couple," she said. "I would be happy to try to help you bring them to life as real people who were dishonored."

In spite of the progress, everything still seemed a little touch-and-go. At the end of the Louisiana visit, Sandra gave me a printout of "My Mother's Voice." But soon after I got back to New Mexico, she had second thoughts and asked me to mail it to her. I did, and I didn't pull any cute moves like keeping a photocopy. Then she sent it back, apologizing for being so jumpy.

———

None of that seemed particularly strange. The three sisters, Ann, Sandra, and Dorothy, made up the only advocacy group in the world that existed to defend the memory of the often demonized Willette Hawkins, and it had been a lonely vigil. Journalists weren't invited into the discussion because journalists were the problem—to the Hawkins sisters, it was their sloppiness and mendacity, coupled with the misinformation pumped out by the Communist Party and Bella Abzug, that had defamed their mother. For nearly sixty years, right up until the time they decided to talk to me, they'd only spoken about the McGee case among family and with a few close friends.

Of the three sisters, Sandra had been the most active about researching the story, with Dorothy in there too. Ann, they told me, tended to stay in the background—for a long time, I didn't even ask to speak to her—but she was interested enough to keep an ear open for updates. For most of her adult life, Sandra steered clear of the subject herself. Though it never completely left her mind as she went off to college in 1955, got married, and started a family, she had no desire to muck around in old newspaper clips. Why go through it?

That changed in 2004, when she saw the documentary about Beah Richards. As she and her relatives started trolling the Web, they ran into a stack of information that, to them, was false and libelous. McGee had been proved innocent. Mrs. Hawkins had been unmasked as a liar. The entire city of Laurel had known about the relationship for years, but the truth was covered up.

They'd done research on the case before. Back in the early 1990s, when Sandra and Dorothy were in Jackson doing family genealogy work, they looked at some of the McGee material at the Mississippi State archives. Now Sandra really plunged in, just like Bridgette and Tracey, but with one advantage—since she was closer to Mississippi, it was easier for her to do primary research.

Sandra took trips to Jackson, Laurel, and Hattiesburg, where she wasn't shy about marching into places and asking for what she wanted. But more often than not she came away frustrated. The case was complicated and confusing, important records were missing, and almost all the participants were dead. The circuit court in Laurel only had scraps, and there was nothing in Hattiesburg. The archives had a complete transcript of the third trial, but it didn't come close to answering all her questions. The "affair" wasn't even mentioned in there. At what point did it come up?

In 2004, Sandra decided to write down what she could remember from the morning of November 2, 1945, and in her rendition there was no doubt about one thing: Her mother was a rape victim, period. She was brutalized in her bed by a drunk who crawled through a window and slithered into her room like a snake. Echoing the trial testimony delivered three different times by her parents, Sandra wrote that she and Ann were in the bedroom next to the bedroom where Willette had settled down with the baby. Their father was asleep at the back of the house. Sandra was asleep too, but she recalled waking up to a scene of chaos and terror.

The house was pitch black. My mother was screaming and running . . . with my father running after her and calling after her, trying to catch up with her.

Shortly, there were policemen scurrying about with flashlights. Sirens droning; patrol lights flashing; men shouting; Mother crying in the distance. Ann and I were gotten up and were taken outside. . . .

What had happened? A man had come into our house and attacked our mother while our baby sister was in bed with her. What did he do? As an eight year old, I couldn't understand what could

have gone on. I later learned he held a knife on her and said he
would kill her and the baby if she made a sound. He said he would
slit their throats. . . .

Could an eight-year-old remember such things? I think so, and it's
only fair to reverse the question: If they happened, would they be
easy to forget? Sandra believes Willie McGee was the man who invaded their home, and that the horrors he brought were real, devastat-
ing, and permanent.

"That one night changed many individuals' lives," she wrote. "I
became the 'caretaker' of a baby sister. I took it upon myself to nour-
ish her, play with her, watch over her. When I go to bed at night, 59
years later, I pull the cover up to my chin and have slept like that
since 8 years of age. In all those years, I have never slept without the
protection and comfort of blankets, even in the summer.

"We were forever marked with fear. Through the years, if I
heard an unusual sound at night, I would become paralyzed with
fear. . . . I have slept with a light on all night so shadows wouldn't
frighten me."

═══

Earlier that day, Sandra had greeted Susan and me at the front door to
her home, an airy suburban layout with a circular driveway, stately
old trees, a pool, and a large backyard that swept down a grassy bank
to a lake.

It was a beautiful place earned through a lifetime of hard work.
Sandra met Brad when they were both students at Mississippi Southern in the 1950s. She never graduated. Her college costs became too
much of a drain on her parents, so she dropped out after a few se-
mesters, moved to New Orleans to find a job, and later married Brad,
who went to dental school at Loyola. In 1960, they moved to the
town we were in now—Sandra asked that I not give its name—to
set up his practice. Neither had any connection to the area. That was
part of the idea.

Inside, we sat around a small living-room table that was covered with papers and folders, reminding me of the setup at Bridgette's home in Las Vegas. Brad, who'd had health problems recently, stationed himself on a couch nearby, with an ear cocked for what we were saying, speaking up occasionally—like Harold had done—while we talked and compared notes.

Sandra's pile of paper overlapped with Bridgette's, but Sandra had more primary documents, including a complete transcript of the third trial and a large stack of papers from the FBI file on the case, labeled WILLIE MCGEE, which was first obtained by a Maryland historian, Dr. Al-Tony Gilmore, back in the 1970s. She had a photocopy of a tiny old black-and-white photograph of the house at 435 South Magnolia, which showed the side window the intruder supposedly crawled through. She also pulled out a hand-drawn map of the interior, to show me who was where.

The house was a simple, white-clapboard structure with a low pitched roof and a chimney on the north side, toward the front. It was longer than wide and had a floor plan that relied on connected rooms instead of a standard hallway. On the front left was the room where Willette and the baby were together that night, their bed tucked into a corner on what would have been the room's left side as you faced the street. Lined up behind it was the second bedroom, a bathroom and a small square of hall, and a third bedroom. On the right side, front to back, ran the living room, dining room, and kitchen. In the very back, and as wide as the house, was a screened-in porch with a wooden lower half.

The whole thing came to around a thousand square feet and was nothing fancy: a warren of low-ceilinged rooms, simple furniture, and polished pine floors. This part of Magnolia Street was a solidly middle-class wedge between the white and black parts of town. Laurel's white upper crust lived in the shady streets and avenues north of the courthouse, about a mile away from there.

The floor plan was important relative to something the CRC stressed many times: its claim that Troy Hawkins was sleeping in the "next room" when the rape occurred.

But that isn't what Troy said in court. He testified that he went to sleep in the back bedroom after helping Willette with the baby. Unless Willette and Troy were both lying—which the defense, during appeals, claimed they were—he wasn't in the next room, or even close. He was two rooms, three walls, and twenty-five feet away, making it much more believable that he could sleep through the assault.

It upset Sandra that such a basic detail had been distorted. If people wanted to attack her father's testimony, why didn't they start with what he'd said?

"What had happened, my dad was working at the post office, and he was on the late shift," she said. "And he came in very late that night, maybe eleven, and he took a turn trying to get the baby quiet and didn't succeed. Mother took the baby back and had a bottle. He had heated the bottle for the baby and they were trying to get her, you know, get her happy, and finally she quieted down."

Sandra said the front shades to Willette's bedroom window, which faced the street at a northwesterly angle, were raised a few inches that night. As she understood the story, the intruder drove by that morning, heading south, saw a light on, saw a woman, pulled over, and came back to the house on foot. He went around to the back side and broke the electrical line to the house. Then he came around to the side of the home facing northeast, toward the front, and crawled through a window next to the brick chimney's exterior, which he used as a boost to get himself up and in.

———

I stared at the picture of the house. Was the window big enough for a man to crawl through? Looked like it. I kept staring, scribbling notes on the diagram until Susan reminded me that it wasn't mine to write on. Sandra laughed and said it was OK; she had copies.

Granted, I was more obsessed than the average person, but there was something hypnotic about that picture and diagram. They were all that remained from the site of a small-town crime that, improbably, became famous around the world.

Sandra, Susan, and I spent a few minutes going over the floor plan before I turned to more general questions about the love-affair story. If I understood Sandra's position, she thought the defense invented it as a way to get McGee off, correct?

"I absolutely do," she said, her Southern accent brisk with conviction. "I think Bella Abzug and her attorneys made up the whole thing."

That's exactly what you'd expect a loyal daughter to say, but Sandra brought up points that couldn't be explained away easily. One was that, for at least part of the time the affair was supposed to be roaring along, the Hawkinses weren't living in Laurel—a fact that Willette had mentioned in passing the first time she testified. Troy took a wartime job in Evansville, Indiana, starting sometime in 1942, at Servel Industries, a plant that made airplane parts. Sandra hadn't been able to work out the exact dates, but she felt sure she entered first grade in Evansville in January 1943. Dorothy was born there on February 24, 1944. Sandra's memory was that the family returned to Laurel in November 1944, when her father went back to his old job with the U.S. Postal Service, where he'd worked until 1941. She and Ann both said the family didn't have a car for the first year or so they were back. And all three daughters insisted that their mother never learned to drive. Later, two people who were not part of the family told me the same thing.

All of which clashes with how the affair story usually goes. In the written account McGee gave to Dixon Pyles in 1946, he said it started in August 1944. In affidavits given by Rosalee and Willie in 1950 and 1951, Mrs. Hawkins was clearly described as being a driver. She had a car parked nearby when she accosted them both on the streets of Laurel one night. She drove to a gas station once and left McGee a love note. She picked him up at night and drove him to a graveyard.

Did Sandra have the paperwork to back up her Indiana timetable? Some of it, though she'd experienced the usual frustrations of tracking down such things. The Indiana school records didn't exist anymore, and she hadn't been able to find out when Troy returned to his post-office job. However, the Laurel records indicated that she'd been in school there during part of the final six-week term in 1944.

The move back to Laurel also tied in with another important issue: Mrs. Hawkins's sickly physical condition, which was mentioned during the trials.

"We came back to Laurel because she was not really well," Sandra said. "She was *very* frail. A few weeks after she'd given birth to my oldest sister, she had an appendectomy, and the appendix ruptured and they didn't think she would live. And so my aunt took the baby— my Aunt LaVera, who was always there for us. My mother was down for like six weeks—a long time. And she was always very, very frail, very thin, always trying to gain weight. She was about five-eight, and if she weighed 115, that was really good."

We talked about the emotional fallout from the case. It was terrible all around, Sandra said, though it was a fixed part of Hawkins family history that Willette, ill though she was, had been mentally healthy prior to November 2, 1945. Afterward, it was like a switch had been flipped. She became a semi-reclusive chain-smoker who suffered migraines, couldn't sleep, couldn't keep food down, and was sometimes plagued by nightmares that caused her to wake up screaming.

Sandra said her father never stopped loving her mother and never gave up hope that she would recover. He moved the family to a country place west of Laurel in 1952, where Willette tried to pitch in with farmwork that neither of them was much good at.

"He tried to farm, but he didn't know how to farm," Sandra said of her dad. "I have to tell you this—everything he did, *she* did. When they built the house, she hammered as big as he hammered. Even though she was frail, she was thin, she got up there on that roof with him."

Sandra said her mother always refused to see a psychiatrist, and that the only medical attention she got was counterproductive. "The doctors would give her all these tips on trying to sleep. They gave her sleeping pills. Then they said the thing for you to do is drink beer at night. That might relax you."

"And they were trying to get her to gain weight," Brad called from the couch, referring to the beer.

"Then they tried to . . . uh, they told her to take a drink of bourbon to, you know. Anyway, she became addicted to alcohol."

I didn't know if she meant in the immediate aftermath of the assault or over the long haul. "So she was an alcoholic?" I asked.

Sandra didn't think so. She and her sisters were sure their mother had experienced post-traumatic stress disorder, which is very common among victims of rape. If she sometimes drank too much, it was a way of dealing with that.

"And this whole thing ruined her life?" I asked.

"It ruined her life. Not only . . . everybody's."

I was already aware of what sparked Sandra's interest in the case, but there had to be a deeper drive to keep her going. Brad, along with one of her two sons, had questioned whether it was smart to get into something like this so late in life. Aside from family members, almost nobody knew this aspect of Sandra's story. In this town, where she lived for forty-six years, she had confided in only two friends.

"Nobody talks about it but family," she said. "My son just recently. . . . I told him you were coming, and he said, 'Are you sure you want to revisit this?' I think Brad's probably of the same mind."

"But it's like you've been revisiting it anyway," Susan said. "You've been compelled to keep revisiting it."

Sandra nodded and said, "Her voice needs to be heard before I die."

Of all the characters in the McGee story, nobody has gotten rougher handling from journalists and historians than Mrs. Hawkins, including all those white males—policemen, sheriffs, jailers, prosecutors, jury members, judges, and politicians—who put McGee through the wringer, abusing him physically and mentally and sending him to the electric chair without so much as a blink of regret.

Others have come in for criticism, certainly, but Mrs. Hawkins has endured as the starring rogue. The *Daily Worker* set the tone, comparing her to Potiphar's wife and calling McGee "a slave in the kingdom of jimcrow." In 1951, a day after the execution, the paper published a front-page article that declared, "Willie McGee was murdered because the white woman who had forced an illicit affair upon him for more than four years suddenly shouted 'rape' after the whole town discovered the story." Mrs. Hawkins sued over this passage, but that part of the story was barely covered.

Meanwhile, if you search online and in libraries today, you'll find the essence of the *Daily Worker*'s charge amplified all over the place. In one Web biography of Bella Abzug, readers are told that McGee was "ludicrously charged with rape by a white, 'married' Southern slut who had him intercoursing her for years. When married Willie finally refused to continue the regularly-scheduled performances, she falsely yelled 'rape!'" In a 1979 paper titled *Rape, Racism, and the White Women's Movement*, a writer named Alison Edwards said that McGee's accuser, "Wilametta Hawkins," was "a woman whom people in Laurel, Black and white, all knew had been having an affair with McGee for a long time."

Similar examples turn up in several nonfiction books. Gerald Horne's history of the CRC, *Communist Front?*, treats McGee's affair allegation as proven and asserts that, during the second trial, "Mrs. Willett Hawkins" made "passes at the district attorney throughout . . . given the nature of the charges, this should have impeached her credibility irrevocably in a normal trial, but did not here."

In *A Fine Old Conflict*, Jessica Mitford's 1977 memoir, she wrote that McGee was convicted "despite persuasive evidence that his accuser had long been his mistress." Hazel Rowley's 2001 biography of novelist Richard Wright, a Mississippi native who took an interest in the case from his expatriate's home in Paris, served up an inaccurate detail about how Troy Hawkins learned the truth: "[Mrs. Hawkins's] husband, a traveling salesman, had come back early, and it was then that the white woman accused McGee of rape." Putting a different spin on the same moment, Phillip Dray's *At the Hands of Persons Unknown* says that when McGee "finally broke with Mrs. Hawkins in early 1945 . . . Troy Hawkins learned of the affair. After a ferocious spat between husband and wife that spilled out into the street in front of their house, Mrs. Hawkins called the police and said she had been raped by a black man with kinky hair."

If Mrs. Hawkins did everything people say she did, she deserves the attacks. She was a figure of such ruthless, efficient command-and-control that she somehow accomplished all of the following: started the affair to satisfy her own desires, kept it going against the will of the man she'd targeted, and channeled an entire city's anger onto him once they were caught. Her husband went along quietly because, presumably, he couldn't bear the shame of being cuckolded by a black man, so their elaborate fiction was his only way out.

Law enforcement officials went along because . . . well, that part was harder to figure. If the "whole town" knew the truth, how did Mrs. Hawkins manage to persuade police, prosecutors, and judges to engage in a conspiracy to make her look like the victim instead of the predator? The best explanation I could come up with was a variation on Senator Bilbo's *Take Your Choice* theme: White men of the South believed it was literally impossible for a white woman to have sex with a black man by choice. If Laurel officials were that deluded, then perhaps they would have done anything and everything to protect Mrs. Hawkins's reputation.

Through the years, there's been only one prominent dissenter about Mrs. Hawkins: Susan Brownmiller, the feminist, rape expert, and author. In a chapter from *Against Our Will* called "A Question of Race," Brownmiller focused on lynching and legal lynching cases that involved charges of interracial sex and rape, with a lengthy examination of the McGee case. She interviewed Abzug in person in 1973, pressing her about the question of proof. How did Bella know the affair really happened?

"I placed my own investigators in town," she told me one afternoon in her office. "The affair . . . was common knowledge among blacks and whites." Then why hadn't she put McGee or his wife on the stand? "No jury was going to believe it. Challenging the word of a white woman just wasn't done. The strategy was to depend on a lack of concrete evidence. Nobody believed you could win an interracial rape case in a Southern court. You could only win on appeal."

To Brownmiller, there was reasonable doubt in both directions. "Willametta Hawkins never wavered," she wrote. "She had been raped, she said, but she could not identify her assailant. For this she was vilified and harassed by leftists who smeared her in print as an oversexed and vengeful white witch." She noted that McGee never wavered, either, though on this point she made a small factual error. She was under the impression that he "kept his silence to the end" regarding the affair. In fact, he had plenty to say about it, insisting to reporters on his dying day that it had happened.

Brownmiller's take was worthy of serious consideration, but it got lost in a flurry of controversy caused by her analysis, in the same chapter, of the Emmett Till case, a 1955 lynching that shocked people all across the nation and around the world. Till was a fourteen-year-old African-American boy from Chicago who was visiting relatives near the Delta town of Money, Mississippi. Showing off to some other black kids one August day, he allegedly "wolf whistled" at a white female storekeeper named Carolyn Bryant. Bryant's husband, Roy, and his half-brother, J. W. Milam, heard about it, kidnapped Till from his uncle's home that night, beat him, shot him, and threw him into a muddy river with a seventy-five-pound cotton-gin pulley tied to his neck. Both men were acquitted by an all-white jury, and though they later confessed everything to a journalist, they were never retried.

Brownmiller condemned the killers, but as she pondered Till's wolf whistle, she also saw a youth who—in a foolish attempt to impress his friends—made a gesture that Bryant might well have seen as threatening.

"We are rightly aghast that a whistle could be cause for murder but we must also accept that Emmett Till and J. W. Millam [sic] shared something in common," she wrote. "*They both understood* that the whistle was no small tweet of hubba-hubba. . . ." Rather, "it was a deliberate insult just short of physical assault, a last reminder to Carolyn Bryant that this black boy, Till, had in mind to possess her."

That's quite a leap: Till was a kid whose whistle (assuming there was one) should have earned him, at most, harsh words from his uncle. Inevitably, there was a backlash. In her 1981 book, *Women, Race & Class*, Angela Davis—the famous Black Panther turned profes-

sor—said that Brownmiller's "provocative distortion of such historical cases as the Scottsboro Nine, Willie McGee and Emmett Till are
designed to dissipate any sympathy for Black men who are victims of
fraudulent rape charges." The more nuanced part of Brownmiller's
stance—that Mrs. Hawkins's whiteness wasn't, by itself, proof that
she'd lied about McGee—got lost in the din.

———

As I studied the McGee case, I started over with basic questions about
the affair. If, as Abzug said, it wasn't brought up during the circuit-
court trials, when was it publicly discussed for the first time? And
when was it proved?

The books and articles I already had—along with new ones I found,
including a legal analysis published in the *Journal of Mississippi History* by a pre-law student named Craig Zaim—didn't hold the answer,
and I never saw anything that qualified as proof that Mrs. Hawkins
was lying. Somewhere, somehow, it simply became accepted that she
was, and this got cloned when writer B came along and used writer
A as a source. The sources weren't always quoted accurately either.
For example, in a 1992 book called *In Spite of Innocence*, a study of
wrongful executions, Michael L. Radelet, Hugo Adam Bedau, and
Constance E. Putnam listed McGee as someone who could be considered officially exonerated. But one of their main sources for that was
Carl Rowan, who wasn't sure McGee was innocent.

The newspaper clips I had were far from complete, but I assumed
I would eventually find that the affair story debuted in the *Daily
Worker*. That was correct, but I was surprised to learn that this didn't
happen until very late in the game: in early March 1951, when both
the *Daily Worker* and a Bay Area paper called the *People's Weekly
World* ran stories about it.

The other interesting thing was that both papers attacked Mrs.
Hawkins long before the affair story entered the picture, but from
different angles. For several years, the *Daily Worker*'s charge was
that her account of the rape simply sounded like hogwash—they just
couldn't yet say why—and so they assumed she was lying.

In a story published on December 12, 1945, soon after the first trial, McGee was already being described as the "Negro victim" of "a one-day 'trial' for 'rape.'" By early 1946, a National Federation for Constitutional Liberties press release labeled "Two Minute Justice" served up what would become the standard line for casting doubt on Mrs. Hawkins's testimony.

"Thirteen witnesses, including [McGee]'s alleged victim, appeared against him," it said. "Their story was that he had entered the woman's home at night, assaulted her while at her side in the bed was her small child, and in the next room her husband slept. It was not shown why any of the thirteen witnesses made no attempt to stop the assault. It was not shown either why the woman herself did not cry out or her child, and thus awaken her nearby husband."

That summary raised one nonissue—witnesses like Tal Porter, George Walker, and Paul Britton weren't in a position to "stop" anything—and introduced two inaccuracies. Troy wasn't in the next room, and Mrs. Hawkins did explain why she didn't cry out: The attacker said he would kill her child if she made a sound.

Even so, the language of this release lived on, and the *Daily Worker* forged it into a boilerplate dismissal of Mrs. Hawkins's story. "The allegedly 'raped' woman, Mrs. Troy Hawkins, was asleep with a child in her bed . . . when the 'attack' was supposed to have occurred," said a story from May 1950. "Her husband and other children were asleep in the next room. Neither the child in bed with her, nor her husband or other children, woke up during the alleged 'rape.'"

———

Whatever doubts Brad had about Sandra's sleuthing, he was supportive, and he didn't moan (at least not in front of me) when I suggested that she rendezvous with us in Laurel in a few days, to do some research and an interview. (She'd told me about an important living source, a man named Leroy Jensen who was a teenager living next door on the night of the crime.) Sandra was up for it, which meant Brad would be drafted for a road trip he hadn't planned on. Before we left, Sandra phoned Dorothy, who said she would take a day off from work and meet us in Laurel.

A couple of days later, Susan and I headed toward Laurel from Jackson, making a side trip en route to the town of Collins, the seat of Covington County, where Eliza Jane Payton was from. Bridgette had told me that Eliza Jane divorced Willie at some point, but she didn't have details or documents. I guessed that, if the paperwork existed, it would be in Collins—and so it was, filed under "Magee." The papers said she'd divorced him in 1946, by which time he was in jail. The main cause given was abandonment. McGee had left his family in 1942.

Early that afternoon, we all met up at a sandwich shop in downtown Laurel and headed over to Jensen's house, with Brad veering off to do something else. Jensen lived in the nicest part of the city, where all the big old houses and mansions were, though his place was a modest bungalow. He met us at the door and ushered us into his living room, where everybody perched on antique furniture and pulled out tape recorders and notebooks. Jensen was seventy-seven, blocky and strong, with a full head of brushy white hair that was as thick as a teenager's. Apparently, he'd been quite a heartthrob in the 1940s— Sandra and Dorothy made this clear with a giggle or two before we went inside—and he was still an impressive-looking man. Only now he looked like a retired judge.

The Jensens lived in the next house north on Magnolia Street, number 429. They weren't native Southerners. They were of Scandinavian descent, and they'd made their living in the creamery business in other states before relocating to Mississippi. In 1940, after Jensen's dad sold off an operation in Texas, he moved his family to Laurel to take over a plant that had failed.

Jensen had a good memory, and he told stories in a way that showed it off, with frequent asides on things like railroad deeds and now-demolished hospitals and bank buildings. "My dad was a buttermaker by trade," he said. "When we came to Laurel, there was an old creamery here that was built in nineteen . . . thirty . . . four or five, somewhere in that area. By the Daniels family. The name of it was

Dan-Dee Dairy Products. D-a-n, hyphen, capital D, e-e. They operated three years and went bankrupt."

Leroy was eleven when the Jensens came to Laurel. By late 1945, at sixteen, his standard routine involved getting up at 3 a.m. to get dressed in time to work for his father before school. That's why he was up and about on the morning of November 2.

He emphasized that he didn't see Willie McGee or anybody else who might have been a rapist. But he did see Mrs. Hawkins come screaming out of the house. It would have been hard to miss, he said, because the structures were very close together.

"I was in the back bedroom, my mom and dad was in the middle bedroom," he said. "And my sister was . . . was she home? Or was she still in nurse training? She was still in nurse training. My mother had woke me up to go on the milk truck, and, as I was dressing, I heard this god-awful scream, and I looked out the window, and . . ." He stopped and looked at the Hawkins sisters. "Does this bother y'all?"

"Not one bit," Sandra said.

"And their mother came running across the yard, naked, to the back door of our house, and I hollered at my mother. She went and let her in, and she was just completely, you know, wrecked. And my mother put her in my bed and covered her. After that, things kind of settled down. My mother got hold of Dr. Beech, who was a doctor at the Masonite Hospital back then. He came to the house and sedated her.

"I left . . . oh, I guess after an hour. I left and went to work. And then, to finish the story as I knew it, I wasn't pressing, but my mother told me that they took her on to the hospital for an examination and all. But she was"—he pointed at his forehead—"I mean, it's burned right here that she was just *completely* torn up."

"I've never been able to remember," Sandra said. "Did she have any clothes on? Did she have a top on?"

"Naked," Leroy said firmly. "She did not. She was *naked*."

"I'm not sure I would have seen her. I heard her. But what she looked like, I never have been able to . . . I never knew—"

"I remember it like it was yesterday. I ran in and told my mother that she was at the back door. I did not know what had happened. I went to the front of the house rather than, you know, than being back there and seeing her."

"Right," I said. "And you were the first person to see her in that condition?"

"When she came across the yard, and when my mother went to the back door and got her, and put her in my bed, that's when I saw her. I saw her come across the yard."

"And I'm sure you heard her," Sandra said.

"Oh, gosh, yes. She was screaming."

That was all he remembered, but it gave me plenty to think about. Either Jensen was sitting there lying or Mrs. Hawkins did come screaming out of the house. I didn't think he was lying. Whatever took place and whoever did it, something terrible happened to her that night.

———

"Did you ever hear the story that Mrs. Hawkins was having an affair with Willie McGee?"

That was me two days later, back in Laurel, by myself this time. I was interviewing a nice old lady I'd just met, asking what might be called my default question, since every interview tended to come around to it sooner or later.

"All that was lies," she said emphatically.

"You don't think she was having an affair with McGee?"

"No, I don't."

"And that's because. . . . It didn't seem like something he would do?"

"I just think it's a lie. Mister, you don't know how folks *do* lie. I don't think Willie McGee had an affair with her. I don't think he been over to her house, tell you the truth about it."

"You think he got framed?"

"Framed because he's a black. And that was the only black out there that they *could* frame. At that time, anything could happen."

The woman was an eighty-eight-year-old African American named Bertha Mae Crowell, and she was telling me about an unusual theory—one that, to her dismay, I had trouble understanding. In my defense, her solution to the McGee mystery was the most complicated one I'd heard so far. First, Mrs. Crowell firmly believed he was innocent. (No surprise there. Though I didn't talk to everybody in Laurel, I think it's safe to assume that most local blacks who've heard of the case would say the same thing.) But she didn't buy McGee's love-affair story; she thought he made it up to try to save his skin. (This was a big surprise. I'd only heard a few people say that, all of them white.)

The big twist was this: She didn't think there'd been a rape at all. The truth, she said, was that Mrs. Hawkins only thought she'd been raped, because something was wrong with her mind—a mental abnormality that, as Crowell put it, caused her to have "crazy ideas and fits."

In her reckoning, the real story was a tragic blend of delusion and injustice that started with a bad dream. On the night of the alleged rape, Mrs. Hawkins woke up before dawn from a nightmare, convinced that she'd been ravished in her bed by a black intruder. She screamed and told her husband, who, not knowing any better, called the police. Given the setting and circumstances—1940s Mississippi, a terrified white woman, a black rapist apparently on the loose—the police had to find somebody to blame in a hurry. McGee got tagged when he turned up in Hattiesburg and appeared to be on the run.

Which he was, but Crowell said he was running because he'd lost his employer's money in a gambling game, not because he'd raped anybody. He was terrified about what his white boss or the police would do to him. "I think because he gambled away that money, and he was on his way off, they just got him," she said. "That's my idea."

It sounded pretty wild, but Crowell wasn't just some random person with a theory. Assuming she was telling the truth about her own life story—and she seemed every bit as trustworthy as Jensen—she was in a good position to know things about both McGee and Mrs. Hawkins. She said she was inside one of the gambling houses the night before the alleged rape, and that she saw McGee playing poker with a group of men that included her late brother, Elijah Williams. She also said she knew Mrs. Hawkins. Crowell's mother, Mary Williams, used to work as a maid for Mrs. Hawkins's sister, LaVera Hooks. As a result, Crowell, who would have been twenty-seven in late 1945, was sometimes at both households during the day, either helping with chores or simply hanging around.

From the sound of things, her memory was good, though I noticed a point or two where she seemed off. Mainly, though, I was struck by the number of things she got right. Without any prompts from me, she correctly remembered one of the places McGee worked (Bethea Grocery), named the street the Hawkinses lived on, knew that Willette had a family nickname ("Billie"), and recalled how many children she had. Initially she got that number wrong, but she corrected herself.

"She was a pretty woman," she said. "Had two pretty . . . I think she had about three children. Did she have three?"

"Three girls."

"Three girls," she said. "*Pretty* girls."

Her memory of Willette's physical appearance was inaccurate, however. She described her as a "regular-sized lady, a nice-sized lady" with blonde hair. But Willette had dark hair, and she was so thin that you probably wouldn't forget it. All in all, it was a typically puzzling combination. Crowell was giving me an honest account of what she believed to be the truth—I had no doubt about that. But there was static in the transmission. As usual, it was impossible to know exactly what to think.

———

One thing was certain: I'd been lucky to run into her. Only minutes earlier, I was a few streets away from Crowell's house, talking to another black woman, Margaret L. Cooley, who had graduated from Oak Park High School in 1951. Cleveland Payne had given me her name, and I dropped by to ask about life in Laurel in the 1940s and 1950s. She'd heard of McGee, of course, but she didn't know much beyond the standard plotline, so she tried to think of somebody with more direct experiences. Crowell came to mind, and, in typical Laurel fashion—helpful, informal, immediate—she picked up the phone and called her.

"Bertha Mae?" she said. "This is Margaret. I got a man here who wants to know about Willie McGee." Pause. "OK." She turned to me. "She say to come on."

I drove to Bertha Mae's place—a long, narrow house just a few blocks away—knocked on a screen door toward the back, and found her sitting in a big stuffed chair in her living room, amid the usual medicine-bottle clutter of an old person with ailments. She was barefoot and had on a no-frills nightdress; her hair was pulled straight back from a fleshy, friendly, and bright-eyed face.

Crowell was born in 1918—a year when World War I was still going on and nineteen blacks were lynched in Mississippi, including four just up the road in Shubuta—so she'd lived through nearly a century of changes that would have seemed like science fiction to someone back then. She'd been in Laurel most of her life, and during our talk she occasionally detoured into random memories from the past, her needle skipping across the decades without transition.

"Let me tell you something," she said at one point. "When I was a girl, we had an insurance man . . . I will never forget it. The Ku Klux Klan used to parade . . . that was before your time. They used to come down the boulevard with hoods over their head, parading. Mother and I were standing there at a parade one night, and Momma looked down at this man's foot and saw a shoe. And Momma said, 'That's my insurance man!' Come to our house every week collecting a quarter for insurance, and he was the Ku Klux Klan!"

That was before my time, all right—around 1928, I guessed, since she said it happened when she was ten. The Klan of that era was as above ground as the Rotary Club, so a public march in Laurel wasn't hard to visualize. But the image of a black mother and child standing on the curb, taking in the show, stopped me.

"You saw Klansmen marching around this town?"

"They had parades down the boulevard," she said, frowning and peering at me through her goggle-lens eyeglasses. "That's how Momma knowed the shoes!"

"It was OK for black people to be there watching?"

"Sure, you can stand there watching. They ain't going to say anything about you watching. It's a *parade*."

Getting back to McGee, I asked her to talk about the house where the gambling took place. She couldn't remember whose it was, but she recalled being there and seeing McGee and other men, including Elijah Williams, playing poker. She left around 10:00, but Elijah told her later that McGee stayed put all night.

"They gambled till day," she said firmly.

"And Willie lost money?"

"Lost the company money."

"So you think once the police caught him, for stealing that money, they said, 'Let's go ahead and say he raped her'?"

"Yeah, I'm sure they did. They had to put it on somebody."

She remembered being in the family car the next day—along with her brother and "another lady," all en route to Hattiesburg—and seeing McGee on the side of the highway, trying to hitch a ride. They didn't pick him up. Elijah, not eager to be seen since he'd won some of McGee's money, ducked down in the seat.

Crowell didn't testify at any of the trials—nobody asked her to, and if they had, she would have played dumb. In 1945, she could have gotten in serious trouble if she'd tried to go public with her theory about Mrs. Hawkins. Half a century later, it still sounded bizarre. And yet Crowell insisted—repeatedly, impatiently—that what she described was fact.

She said Mrs. Hawkins had a mental problem that showed up during her menstrual period, which took the form of terrifyingly realistic nightmares. "She was crazy when she menstruated," she said. "When she had that menopause that ladies go through, she was nuts.

"My idea is she must have dreamed that he did that. You know, jump and say somebody done something to her or something had happened? She just had nightmares. You ever heard of a talking nightmare? Well, that's what she had. When she laid down to take a nap when she got menopause on." Crowell said she saw this firsthand, during the times she spent around the Hawkins household with her mother.

All through her discussion of this, though, there was a sketchiness that made me wonder if she was conflating events from different time periods. She used *menstrual* and *menopause* interchangeably. She mentioned being "in school" when these events happened, but she couldn't say when it was. She would have been around nineteen by the time Mrs. Hawkins had her first child; so if there was any babysitting going on, Bertha Mae was already out of school.

I squinted at her, concentrating. She squinted back, trying to understand what my problem was.

I asked her to carefully describe what she saw that made her think Mrs. Hawkins had a hysterical reaction when her period occurred.

"Well, she just *had* it. She just . . . I think it was something like a spasm. You ever heard of a spasm? She had something like that, like she was crazy or something."

"Running around, or yelling, or what?"

"Jumping up and . . . when she sleep, maybe wake up and have one of them spells. But, um, she was a good woman. She's just . . . I think she was half nuts to me."

"You were in the house in the daytime or nighttime?"

"The daytime, when she took a nap. Anytime she go to sleep during menopause. They said that when she sleeped, she dreamed."

" 'They' said that?"

"Everybody said she dreamed! I dreams too! But she had nightmares."

We went around and around, but there wasn't much more to say, and for Mrs. Hawkins things came down to a split decision. Crowell thought she was innocent of the charge leveled against her for years: that she cornered McGee into an affair and then ratted him out. But to buy into that, you'd also have to accept that Mrs. Hawkins was crazy, and that she and Mr. Hawkins, who must have realized eventually that she'd dreamed it up, decided to stick with their story, even though it meant sending McGee to an unjust death.

So, in Crowell's reckoning, Mrs. Hawkins was only partially absolved of guilt. During our conversation, she'd said several nice things about her, but that changed sharply toward the end. Crowell told me she believed that both Willette and Troy carried a curse because of McGee's death, and that the way they died was no accident.

"You know, God don't like ugly," she said. "Did you ever notice that? Do you know what happened to Billie Hawkins and her husband?"

I said I did.

"They had a car wreck and got killed," she said, nodding, as if that settled the point. "See? God don't like ugly."

———————

That night, Susan and I paid a visit to Dorothy Hawkins at her home in central Mississippi. Dorothy, unlike Sandra, didn't seem ready for tape recorders or notebooks, so I sat on my hands and we talked. After a while, she invited us over to her kitchen table to take a look at a family photo album, and I finally got to see a picture of Willette Hawkins.

Along with that, there was one other surprise in store. As I flipped through the album, I came to a yellowing, poorly focused picture of a young black woman sitting outside—on the steps of what looked like a back porch—with two blonde-haired little girls leaning against her. A caption scrawled below the picture identified them as "Ann, Sandra, and Bertha Mae."

six

THE MALADY OF
MEDDLER'S ITCH

In the 1940s, the CRC, the NAACP, the *Daily Worker*, and African-American newspapers like the *Pittsburgh Courier*, the *Chicago Defender*, and the *Atlanta World* were often the first or only sources of substantial reporting when an incident like the blinding of Isaac Woodard took place. If these organizations didn't publicize a story, it might go unnoticed, because mainstream newspapers, in and out of the South, still had a tendency to miss, bury, or ignore such events. Even sympathetic papers didn't always know what to do with stories about racially motivated atrocities. There were a lot every year. Did you cover them all? If so, how much?

When in doubt, the *New York Times* would sometimes run a small wire-service dispatch and then not follow up. In July 1946, for example, a black farmer named Leon McAtee was found floating in a lake near Indianola, Mississippi, the victim of a flogging death at the hands of six men who accused him of stealing a saddle. The *Times* reported McAtee's murder on page forty-eight, running a United Press story headlined "Negro Death Laid to Mississippians." Three months later, in a brief follow-up, readers learned that five men, charged with manslaughter, were all acquitted.

For a while, the Woodard case fell through the cracks everywhere. It happened in February 1946, but, amazingly, the NAACP didn't start publicizing it until July. The national office sent out a press release that month, which generated urgent headlines in African-American papers. "Veteran's Eyes Gouged Out by Hate-Crazed Dixie Police," read a *Chicago Defender* story from July 20. "Atrocity Called Dixie's Worst In NAACP Probe."

The *Times* weighed in, but it never found Woodard's story quite as compelling. The editors didn't ignore Woodard, but they did keep the reporting low-key throughout the paper's coverage of his case in 1946 and 1947. This was typified by one of the early stories the *Times* published, a brief A.P. dispatch that ran on page thirty and carried the headline, "Negro Made Blind at Batesburg, S.C."

In various ways, the years after World War II were a time of change on this front. The wave of postwar racial violence was so shocking that it couldn't be put on the back burner completely, and some stories got prominent play from the start, including the Malcom and Dorsey lynchings in Georgia, which the *Times* treated as front-page news.

In late 1946, the *Times*, recognizing that race-based injustice and civil rights were becoming increasingly important, assigned its first full-on Southern correspondent, a reporter based in Chattanooga, Tennessee, named John N. Popham. The idea originated with a transplanted Mississippian, assistant managing editor Turner Catledge. Popham, a native of Fredericksburg, Virginia, was given the daunting task of covering every Southern state from Virginia to Texas behind the wheel of a car he called the Green Hornet—driving 50,000 miles a year and staying with friends and relatives whenever possible, because the *Times* needed to keep his traveling expenses low.

"The result was a free-wheeling sort of reporting, with Mr. Popham driving vast distances from friend to friend," a *Times* obituary writer explained after Popham's death in 1999. "He sent out 100 boxes of New Orleans pralines each year at his own expense, and his . . . network of contacts included old-school connections and distant relatives."

Popham turned up everywhere over the next few years, and he often wrote stories set in Mississippi. He was in Jackson in early 1947 when state officials were busily trying to come up with new ways to prevent blacks from voting in the Democratic primary. He was there in 1948 when the city hosted disgruntled politicians and voters who organized a revolt against the pro–civil rights drift of the national Democratic Party. And he was there when the McGee case started getting noticed nationally in 1950. In fact, Popham's journalism helped make that happen, spreading the word beyond the confines of the far left. Through his reports, the *Times* legitimized McGee in a way that coverage in the *Daily Worker*, by itself, never could have.

———

Another important change in 1946 took place in the heart and mind of the nation's prime political mover, President Harry S. Truman, who surprised everybody by announcing his intention to push for federal civil rights legislation. That was one crusade neither FDR nor Congress had gotten around to.

Off and on for years, Congress had tried and failed to pass a federal anti-lynching bill, which sometimes made it out of the House of Representatives but always died under the weight of Southern filibusters in the Senate. FDR never publicly supported any of these bills, despite pressure from the NAACP and from Eleanor Roosevelt, who threw everything she had into getting him to back one of the best known of them, the Costigan-Wagner bill of 1934.

Costigan-Wagner was introduced after a resurgent year for lynching in 1933—there were at least twenty-eight nationwide, including one just ninety miles east of the White House, in Princess Anne, Maryland. The bill would have given the federal government authority to bring charges against local law enforcement officials who handed prisoners over to lynch mobs, and to sue counties for damages that would be awarded to victims' families.

Southern legislators were opposed, arguing that lynching was a matter for local and state law enforcement to deal with. Yes, there were times when the system failed and men were mobbed, but Southerners claimed that, as the years went by, they would put an end to the problem themselves. Congressmen like Mississippi's William Colmer, who fought against similar bills over the years, also argued that any such measure had to be universally applied. So he introduced a "gangster amendment," which mandated federal intrusion if police in places like New York and Chicago failed to adequately investigate gangland slayings.

With Costigan-Wagner and other bills like it, Eleanor worked closely with Walter White, executive secretary of the NAACP, who knew the subject of lynching as well as anybody, thanks in part to his unusual physical appearance. Originally from Atlanta, White was of mixed-race descent, and he was light-skinned enough that he was usually assumed to be Caucasian. In a 1948 profile, the *New Yorker* described him as "a dapper, pink-cheeked, and polished man of fifty-five who is so non-Negroid in appearance and on such good terms with high-level statesmen that anyone meeting him for the first time at a Washington cocktail party could easily take him for some thoroughly Anglo-Saxon ambassador."

White's features had made it possible for him to work as an on-the-scene lynching investigator for the NAACP, starting in 1918. Over the next seven years, he traveled thousands of miles, risking his life as he gathered information on roughly fifty lynchings and violent race-oriented riots. In 1929, he published *Rope and Faggot*, an influential study of the history and causes of lynching in the United States.

By April 1934, White had reason to hope that Costigan-Wagner could pass. It had been endorsed by prominent officials, clergymen, journalists, and nonpartisan advocacy groups, and his head count indicated that the bill might make it out of the Senate if it were spared the usual Southern windbag offensive and put to a vote. Knowing that a public endorsement or private arm-twisting by FDR might tip the balance, Eleanor Roosevelt arranged a Sunday afternoon meeting in May that included the president, his mother, herself, and White. FDR seemed to take it in stride that his wife and mother were lined up against him on this issue, and White left feeling convinced that he'd swayed him. But the president did nothing, and the bill died yet again. Later, FDR told White that he couldn't risk alienating his Southern power base.

"The Southerners by reason of the seniority rule . . . are chairmen

or occupy strategic places on most of the House and Senate Committees," he said. "If I come out for the anti-lynching bill now, they will
block every bill I ask Congress to pass to keep America from collaps-
ing. I just can't take that risk."

———

The risk was just as great for Truman. He could have lost the presidency in 1948 as a result of flouting the South's will on civil rights,
and for a time it looked like he would. But he decided he had to
move forward, and the bloody events of 1946 were a major reason why. Truman heard about them during face-to-face meetings
with two prominent representatives of the mid-century civil rights
movement.

One was a man he believed he could do business with, Walter
White. The other was Paul Robeson, the famous ex-athlete, actor,
singer, and Communist sympathizer who by then had become one of
the most caustic voices on the left. Truman's meeting with Robeson
was a disaster, producing nothing but tension and ill will, and it solidified boundaries that would be in place four years later, when Truman
was compelled to start responding to public clamor about the McGee
case. By then, Robeson—a CRC member and spokesman—was one of
McGee's top supporters. From Truman's perspective, this meant Mc-
Gee was backed by the wrong kinds of people.

Truman met with White first, on September 19 at the White House,
along with a delegation that included six officials representing labor,
churches, and the African-American press. White wrote about the
meeting in a syndicated column that ran in African-American newspapers, reporting that Truman was visibly stunned when they talked
about Woodard's blinding and the 1946 wave of lynchings.

". . . Truman's face became pale with horror," White wrote. "His voice
trembled with deep emotion as he assured us that steps must be taken immediately to stop this wave of terrorism before it got out of hand."

The next day, in a memo to Attorney General Thomas C. Clark, Truman wrote that his callers "told me about an incident which happened
in South Carolina where a negro Sergeant, who had been discharged

from the Army just three hours, was taken off the bus and not only seriously beaten but his eyes deliberately put out, and that the Mayor of the town had bragged about committing this outrage. . . .

"I know you have been looking into the . . . Georgia lynchings, and also been investigating the one in Louisiana, but I think it is going to take something more than the handling of each individual case after it happens—it is going to require the inauguration of some sort of policy to prevent such happenings."

Four days later, Truman met with Robeson, who was in Washington to lead a protest rally that had been advertised for several weeks in the *Daily Worker*. Conceived by Robeson, the legendary black intellectual W. E. B. DuBois, and a white Washington lawyer named Bartley Crum, the event was billed as "an American crusade to end lynching." Held on September 23, it was timed to take place near the anniversary of the Preliminary Emancipation Proclamation, on September 22.

Truman might have been receptive, but Robeson seemed more interested in grandstanding than communicating. Before coming down from New York, he delivered a speech at Madison Square Garden in which he criticized the president for the federal government's inability or unwillingness to do anything about lynching.

"This swelling wave of lynch murders and mob assaults . . . represents the ultimate limit of bestial brutality to which the enemies of democracy, be they German-Nazis or American Ku Kluxers, are ready to go in imposing their will," Robeson boomed. "Are we going to give our America over to the Eastlands, Rankins and Bilbos? If not, then *stop the lynchers!* What about it, President Truman? Why have you failed to speak out against this evil?"

At the White House, Robeson led a seven-person delegation that included Mrs. Harper Sibley, whose husband was a former president of the U.S. Chamber of Commerce. During their meeting with Truman, the conversation turned prickly in a hurry. "Mrs. Sibley was the first to nettle him," said a report in the *Louisville Courier-Journal*. " 'Discrimination against the Negroes in this country,' she said, 'is just as bad as the racism of Nazi Europe. We're trying people in Nuremberg for war crimes; but if we really consider them guilty, Mr. President, we should consider those in this country who lynch Negroes are equally guilty.' "

Truman said the two situations weren't the same, displaying ignorance about the nature of mob violence when he added, "We realize, and you must realize, that it is [the Nazis'] philosophy which has infected a few people in this country and is largely responsible for lynchings."

Robeson lectured him along the same lines as Sibley, and Truman lectured him back. "You of all people ought to stand behind this country," he snapped. "The United States and Great Britain are the last refuges of freedom in the world." Truman may not have known that Robeson—in tune with long standing Communist Party doctrine—regarded Britain as part of the problem, not the solution, an imperial colonizer that oppressed people all over the planet. After Winston Churchill's famous "Iron Curtain" speech in Fulton, Missouri, on March 5, 1946—where he issued his warnings about postwar Soviet expansionism—Robeson was the lead signatory on a letter that said British imperialism, propped up by financial support from the United States, was a bigger menace than anything the Soviets were up to. He informed Truman that Britain was "the greatest enslaver of human beings in the world."

Faced with a choice between White's centrist calm and Robeson's thunderclaps, Truman assembled an establishment cast of advisers to help frame his race-relations ideas. On December 5, 1946, he created a Committee on Civil Rights, whose members and staff were charged with holding hearings and doing research that would lead to a major presidential statement about race in America. Most of the fifteen-member group were prominent white males from outside the South. There weren't any Communists, of course, or anybody from the far-left wing of the Democratic Party.

Today, a presidential study commission might seem like the tamest solution to any subject, but it wasn't tame back then. Based on the issue of race, Truman found himself with a problem that would influence everything that happened during the election of 1948. Because of his tough-with-the-Soviets line and his tentative moves on civil rights, he now had two sets of dedicated enemies in his own party, coming at him from opposite directions. With the Republicans powering up for their best chance to win the presidency since 1928, it seemed likely that his decision to interfere with the South would mean the end of his career.

Another unfortunate staple of the racial-atrocities beat were incidents in which white men accused of raping black women either weren't indicted or were set free by a white jury, even when they were clearly guilty. For several weeks in late 1944 and early 1945, the *Daily Worker* and African-American newspapers publicized the story of Recy Taylor, a twenty-two-year-old black woman from small-town Alabama who was allegedly gang-raped by half a dozen young white males. A grand jury refused to indict them, giving the *Worker* an irresistible chance to slam everybody involved: the grand jurors, Alabama judges and state officials, and establishment newspapers that failed to report on what had happened.

"The *Daily Worker* and the *Worker* are the only newspapers, aside from the Negro press, which have mentioned this case," one story said. The charge was accurate as far as the *New York Times* and *Washington Post* were concerned. Neither paper covered it.

With their nationwide network of activists and contacts, the CRC and the NAACP didn't miss many of these stories. But in December 1946, just three weeks after McGee's second guilty verdict, something monstrous happened in Laurel that escaped their notice. The *Daily Worker* missed it too. Otherwise, the paper surely would have given the news four-alarm treatment, because there was never a better example of the double standard applied to the punishment of black and white defendants in Mississippi rape cases.

At around 6 p.m. on December 6, 1946, a twenty-four-year-old white male named Laverne Yarbrough showed up at a small grocery store in the Queensburg section of town. The store's owner, F. A. Hendry, didn't know Yarbrough, but he noticed that he had a bottle of whiskey in his back pocket. Then he closed up for the night and drove home. It was already getting dark; Hendry remembered later that he had to turn on his car headlights to see.

Just down the street, two African-American boys—eleven-year-old Billie Earl Jernigan and twelve-year-old Willie Jones—were playing marbles on the pavement when they saw a man walk past them, leading a small black girl by the hand. They didn't know who he was, but the girl, who was five, didn't seem to mind. They noticed that the man was hiding his face with his hat. Then he picked up the girl and took her into a stand of woods, and the boys didn't see them anymore.

Yarbrough allegedly raped the girl in the woods and ran away, leaving her bloody, terrified, and lost. Her mother had sent her out by herself earlier that day to look for an older sister at a neighborhood store. When her parents realized she was missing, they searched until they found her, hours later, walking alone on a side street, apparently the victim of sexual violence. They took her to the Laurel police department, and she was examined by a doctor that night. The doctor later testified that she was bleeding profusely from lacerations that indicated rape. In a second examination, he took a blood sample.

Local police hit the streets to find witnesses and hunt down the rapist. As they soon learned, various people had seen Yarbrough that afternoon and night, including the owner of a taxi company who said he showed up at his garage around 7:00 or 7:30, trying to get a check cashed. The man reported that Yarbrough had bloodstains on his hands, face, and clothes.

He was arrested at 11 p.m. by Laurel patrolman Jeff Montgomery and Deputy Sheriff Dave Shaw, who nabbed him at a roadside restaurant north of town. They took him to the city jail, where Wayne Valentine ordered him to take off his clothes, just as he'd done with McGee in Hattiesburg in 1945. At Yarbrough's trial, which happened in March 1947, Valentine would testify that the clothing was spotted with blood.

Convinced they had the right man, the police cut a few corners as they compiled evidence for a case. Notably, blood-test evidence was never introduced—apparently, for Laurel investigators, the visual link of a bloody girl and blood on Yarbrough's clothing and skin was enough. That night, the two boys, Jernigan and Jones, were brought in to identify the suspect, and the police ran the lineup in a way that any defense attorney would have objected to. First, they told the boys they were going to show them the man who "raped the little girl." Then they took them inside a room where Yarbrough was sitting by himself. At Yarbrough's trial, the boys were asked to describe how the procedure worked.

"They didn't take five or six men and say, 'Here, son, pick one out and tell me if that's the man that did it'?" one defense lawyer asked. "They didn't do that, did they? . . . They just brought one man in there, and they had already told you they had the man that raped the little girl, and they wanted you to come up and identify the man that raped the little girl?" The boys said yes, that's how it had been.

Yarbrough's court-appointed defense attorney was Jack Deavours, a Laurel fixture who had prosecuted the Ouida Keaton case and who would serve as a special prosecutor during Willie McGee's third trial. The rape victim was called to the stand, despite Deavours's objection that she was too young to qualify as a competent witness. With the jury out and the girl standing in front of the witness chair, answering quietly and gesturing, District Attorney Homer Pittman asked, "Where do bad little girls go who tell stories?"

"To the bad man," she said.

"Where do good little girls go?"

"To heaven."

"Apparently frightened, the witness was slow to answer questions propounded by the district attorney," the *Leader-Call* reported, "but under his gentle phrasing of the queries she was led to tell of the evening of the alleged attack, and then pointed at Yarbrough when Pittman asked her to show the jury her attacker."

Deavours objected, noting that Pittman had pointed at Yarbrough three times when the jury was gone, cueing the girl about who "the bad man" was. After being overruled by the judge—McGee's old nemesis, Burkitt Collins—he didn't try to cross-examine her.

Court-watchers figured Deavours would use an insanity defense—records showed that Yarbrough had spent time in mental hospitals—but instead he stressed procedural points, which he later used in an unsuccessful appeal to the Mississippi Supreme Court. The evidence was circumstantial, he argued; it was dark when the boys saw the man and the girl; and the police never got the blood sample looked at. The three child witnesses had been coached and the girl's testimony was vague. All she said was that the man took her into the woods and laid her down.

On the stand, Yarbrough denied committing the rape, after which Deavours asked questions that had only one possible function: to arouse sympathy. "The defendant . . . told the jury that he was an ex-soldier and was at Pearl Harbor when that place was attacked," the *Leader-Call* reported. "He said that immediately following the battle he became highly nervous and was treated for a nervous disorder in several government hospitals before being discharged." Surprisingly, the tactic failed. After deliberating for two hours, an all-white jury found Yarbrough guilty on March 11, 1947. In another break from the usual pattern, the prosecution asked that the jury give him the death penalty.

It's possible this was done for show, but it doesn't sound that way in the trial records and newspaper reports. During his closing argument, County Attorney Albert Easterling clutched his lapels, raised his voice, and delivered a speech demanding that Yarbrough be electrocuted. Pointing at Yarbrough's wife, who was sitting beside him at the defense table with one of their children, Easterling said this family tableau was staged to generate pity that Yarbrough didn't deserve.

"Easterling turned toward the accused man during his plea to hurl scorching and scathing denunciations which reverberated . . . through the courtroom," the *Leader-Call* reported. " 'Oh, yes, Yarbrough,' he thundered, 'you've got your little wife and baby with you today—but where were they on last December 6—where were they when you took that little negro girl into the woods and raped her?' "

The jurors were sufficiently appalled to find Yarbrough guilty, but they would only go so far. Whether they were motivated by doubts about his sanity, a racist belief that a white man should never be executed for raping a black female—even a child—or something else, they opted for a sentence of life in prison. Unlike McGee, Laverne Yarbrough would be spared.

———

In 1947, McGee wasn't on anybody's list of newsmakers. The second-trial verdict was reported in postage-stamp-sized articles here and there, including *PM*, the liberal New York–based paper edited by Ralph Ingersoll and funded by Chicago millionaire Marshall Field III. The *Times* either didn't hear about McGee or wasn't interested, because it didn't publish anything.

He was driven back to jail in Hinds County, and nothing more was heard from him for the next fifteen months. Later, there would be jailhouse letters—written by him and widely publicized by the CRC—but those didn't start arriving until 1948, and there were only a smattering until 1950, when he began to write often. For a long time, his mother, Bessie, was the sole public voice of the case, and what she mainly did was send letters to the CRC, which the group sometimes used in press releases. From her home on Elm Street in Laurel, she politely beseeched them never to forget her boy.

"Just a few lines to let you hear from me," she wrote on December 9, 1946. "[T]his leaves me doing very well at this time and hope that you are the same. My son Willie he is sintuns again to the chair. But he got a apeal and I do want you all to do all you all can for him."

Several months later, in July 1947, she mentioned a new figure in Willie's life, a woman who evidently had been visiting him in jail: "I got a letter from Rosa and she say Willie was Better I sure was glad to hear that." This is the earliest surviving reference I found to the existence of Rosalee McGee in connection with Willie.

Dixon Pyles and Dan Breland filed a notice of appeal ten days after the verdict, but they didn't submit it until August 6, 1947. It was a fat document of 157 pages, a fourth of them summarizing the second-trial testimony, which at times boiled down in a strangely flat way.

WILLIE MCGEE (Tr. Vol. II, P. 417–419)
The appellant was placed on the stand. He was bodily carried
by sheriff's deputies. His head was held down and he had a wild
expression in his eyes. . . . [T]he appellant did not answer a single
question, nor did he make any response except peculiar noises.

Pyles raised six points. The first would turn out to be the most
significant: that McGee was deprived of his Fourteenth Amendment
rights to due process and equal protection because of race-based jury
exclusion. He also pushed the insanity argument; said McGee should
have been granted a change of venue to someplace far away; challenged the legitimacy of his confession; and went into great detail on
the "consent" angle, arguing that Mrs. Hawkins's failure to fight back
meant that the sex was not against her will.

That was a hopeless line of attack, certain to offend any Mississippi judge who looked at it. Here and there, Pyles thought better of a
particular phrase and drew a line through it, as in this passage: "The
record reveals that the prosecutrix is a rather tall woman and at the
time was 32 years old, in full possession of her mental faculties, and of
normal strength." Elsewhere, he pointed out that she was half an inch
taller than her attacker, not mentioning her wispy build.

The state's response was short and simple: Read the transcript. Mrs.
Hawkins submitted to McGee because she'd been overpowered and
threatened with death. "The sordid and revolting details of this crime
will not be set out," wrote Greek L. Rice, Mississippi's assistant attorney general, "but a reading of the testimony of Mrs. Troy C. Hawkins,
prosecutrix . . . fully establishes the crime of rape."

———

In 1947, the case that grabbed the headlines happened 500 miles away
from Laurel—in Greenville, South Carolina, a textile-manufacturing
city in the northern part of the state. It centered on a lynching that,
this time, was not overlooked by major newspapers. The Times treated
it as important news from the start, sending John Popham to cover it
when the accused lynchers went on trial in May.

The Greenville case stood out for a couple of reasons. One was that local law enforcement, aided by state officials and FBI agents, mounted an aggressive investigation that led to multiple arrests, confessions, and indictments. Another was the staggering numbers involved: Thirty-one men eventually went to trial. The defendants were blue-collar Greenville men—almost all of them taxicab drivers—who were accused of seizing, beating, stabbing, and shooting a twenty-four-year-old African-American murder suspect named Willie Earle. It was, and would remain, the largest lynching trial in U.S. history.

The incident started on the night of February 15, 1947, a Saturday, when a middle-aged Yellow Cab driver named Thomas Watson Brown was robbed and stabbed on the job. Company dispatchers said Brown had picked up two "negro fares" that night, and that nothing more was heard from him until he was found around 10 p.m., still alive and lying on a roadside near the town of Liberty. (Brown survived until just before noon on Monday.) Pickens County sheriff Waymond Mauldin said he suspected Earle because investigators found tracks and identifiable heel prints leading from the cab to the spot where Brown lay, and from there to the home of Earle's mother, about a mile from the crime scene. Earle was arrested on Sunday, allegedly in possession of a bloodstained pocketknife.

Whether Earle did it or not quickly became moot. He was taken for safekeeping to the county jail at Pickens, a small town twenty miles west of Greenville. The jail was an old and vulnerable structure manned by a sixty-two-year-old turnkey named J. Ed Gilstrap, who lived there with his wife and daughter. Before dawn on the 17th, a mob of at least three dozen men—most of them traveling in taxis—drove to Pickens and demanded that Gilstrap hand Earle over. He didn't resist, saying later, "They had shotguns and I danced to their music." He said he didn't recognize any members of the lynch party.

Earle's body was found in the country on Monday morning, laid out on frosty ground near a livestock pen. He'd been brutalized before being killed with a shotgun blast to the head. "The tissue of Willie Earle's brain was left hanging on the bushes," said a report in *Time*. "The lynchers went back to Greenville and drank coffee."

The lynching caused a furor in South Carolina and beyond. The state's new governor, Strom Thurmond, a World War II veteran and former judge who'd been in office less than a month, sent a state constable to Greenville County to investigate and issued a statement promising justice. "Such offenses against decency, law and the Democratic way of living will not be tolerated by the law abiding citizens of this state," he said. "Mob rule is against every principle for which we have so recently sacrificed so much, and we expect to combat it with the same determination."

At the White House, Thurmond's action was noted approvingly as a sign that Truman's statements about race were having an effect. "The President may be interested to see how his Civil Rights Committee is taking him off the hot seat," David K. Niles wrote in a memo. "Day before yesterday there was this brutal lynching in South Carolina. They immediately moved in on it."

FBI agents were sent in to aid locals in the roundup and questioning of some 200 suspects and potential sources. Twenty-six men signed confessions, and several identified a man named Roosevelt Carlos Hurd Sr., a forty-five-year-old cab driver, as the person who finished Earle off. He denied it, saying he "heard" guns being fired but didn't have one himself. "When I seen they were going to kill the Negro, I just turned around, because I did not want to see it happen," he said.

Despite the usual complaining about federal involvement in anything, Thurmond got good reviews in many Southern newspapers, though these often carried an antifederal undercurrent that foreshadowed problems at the trial. "The law is on its throne in Greenville County, South Carolina," said an editorial in the *Atlanta Journal*. "Something is being done about a lynching. This fact is worth many thousands of words of argument in Congress against a federal antilynching statute."

The trial started on May 12, drawing reporters from all over the country, including African-American journalists and correspondents with the wire services. *Life* was there. So was the *New Yorker*, which sent Rebecca West, a British writer known for her book *Black Lamb and Grey Falcon*, a classic travelogue about life in the Balkans before World War II. West had seen plenty of rough stuff in her day—she covered the Nuremberg trials for the *New Yorker*—but the Greenville trial got under her skin. During closing arguments at the eight-day proceeding, she listened as defense attorney John Bolt Culbertson flatly stated that Earle got what he deserved. He'd murdered a white man, and whether he died vigilante-style or at the state's hands, he had to go. "Willie Earle is dead," he declared, "and I wish more like him was dead."

"There was a delighted, giggling, almost coquettish response from the defendants and some of the spectators," West wrote. ". . . A more disgusting incident could not have happened in any court of law in any time."

The judge, a former Washington and Lee football player named James Robert Martin Jr., wanted convictions and had good reason to expect them, since so many men had confessed. But the defense lawyers planted the idea that the confessions were unethically procured with "Trojan horse" trickery by the FBI agents, many of whom were Southerners. (Supposedly, they'd told the defendants they would never be convicted by a white jury, so why not talk?) Martin ruled that each man's confession could be used against him but not against the other defendants as part of a conspiracy charge. He dismissed the charges against some defendants and reduced the charges against others, leaving the total on trial for murder or conspiracy at twenty-eight.

Since nobody denied that Earle had been lynched, the defense's case rested on appealing to the jury's belief that the killing was justified. Culbertson, a labor lawyer who was known locally for his relatively liberal views, drove this home during a closing argument that compared Earle to a rabid dog. "You might shoot a mad dog and be prosecuted, but if a mad dog were loose in my community, I'd shoot the dog and let them prosecute me," he said. His colleague Thomas Wofford played on local resentments about the FBI's role and the presence of "northern press."

Popham wrote that the defense lawyers pulled out all the stops in their emotional appeals, making references to "King Solomon's wisdom, the Book of Deuteronomy, tortures of the Middle Ages, Civil War devastation of Southern homes, the atomic bomb, and Northern publications and radio commentators" to support their argument that the accused were the victims of what one lawyer called "the incurable malady of meddler's itch."

When it came time to release the jury, Judge Martin ordered them to remove such thoughts from their minds. The trial was about illegal punishment administered by a mob. They were not to let "any so-called racial issue to enter into your deliberations."

The jury came back after five hours and handed over their verdict: not guilty for all twenty-eight defendants, on ninety-six counts of murder, conspiracy, and accessory before and after the fact. With a light rain hitting the courtroom windows and black spectators looking down glumly from a segregated balcony, Judge Martin turned to the jurors, told them their service was over, and walked out. "As the roll-call of acquittal was completed," a United Press reporter wrote, "Hurd . . . jumped on a chair and shouted, 'Justice has been done—I feel the best I ever felt in my life.' "

President Truman had a bad case of meddler's itch himself, even though 1947 wasn't a good time to start picking fights. He'd inherited the presidency instead of winning it, the economy was still in a postwar funk, and he was getting raked by critics on both the right and the left as his public opinion numbers plunged. The 1946 congressional elections had been a disaster, with Democrats becoming the minority party in both the House and Senate for the first time since 1928. Politically, he was seen as a lame duck who could easily be defeated in 1948. A popular Republican joke of the time asked, "What would Harry Truman do if he were alive today?"

Despite his weakness, Truman kept making moves that seemed certain to alienate Southerners. On June 29, he gave a major speech on civil rights at the Lincoln Memorial, appearing alongside Eleanor Roosevelt and Walter White before delegates to the annual conference of the NAACP. Speaking to a mostly black crowd of roughly 10,000 in the same setting that Martin Luther King Jr. would use sixteen years later, he made a promise to act.

"I should like to talk to you briefly about civil rights and human freedom," he began. "It is my deep conviction that we have reached a turning point in the long history of our country's efforts to guarantee freedom and equality to all our citizens. Recent events in the United States and abroad have made us realize that it is more important today than ever before to insure that all Americans enjoy these rights.

"When I say all Americans," he added, "I mean all Americans."

The speech didn't get into specifics, but those followed in early 1948, after the October 1947 release of *To Secure These Rights*, a landmark document detailing the injustices facing black Americans. In it, Truman asked for several legislative remedies that were poison pills for Southern congressmen, including abolition of the poll tax, anti-lynching legislation, and the creation of a permanent federal civil rights commission.

The report's brief section on lynching described the murders of Willie Earle, John Jones, and the Malcoms and Dorseys. "[L]ynching is the ultimate threat by which his inferior status is driven home to the Negro," it said. "As a terrorist device, it reinforces all the other disabilities placed upon him. The threat of lynching always hangs over the head of the southern Negro; the knowledge that a misinterpreted word or action can lead to his death is a dreadful burden."

The Southern backlash was instantaneous. "Forty-nine South Carolina legislators denounced this program last week as 'repugnant,'" the *Times* reported. "In a similar criticism, Senator James O. Eastland of Mississippi proposed that the Solid South withhold all its electoral votes to make possible the election of a 'distinguished southerner.'"

The fight was on, and it would cause a huge rift in the Democratic Party: the Dixiecrat revolt. One of its chief architects was a man who played a defining role in the McGee case, Mississippi governor Fielding Wright, who would eventually stand as Strom Thurmond's running mate on the States' Rights Party ticket that challenged Truman in 1948. In mid-February, after Truman delivered a speech about his legislative goals, Wright began mobilizing support for some kind of organized political response. At a conference of Mississippi Democrats held in Jackson on February 12, 1948—which 4,000 people attended—he and others passed a resolution that said Truman's civil rights proposals violated everything held dear by "true white Jeffersonian Democrats."

"Unless we repudiate such action we shall stultify ourselves," he said. "On us should be the stigma of sacrificing principle for paltry gains, of choosing power and losing self respect, of seeking the end, no matter the means. That course we denounce."

———

Without Fielding Wright, there might not have been a Dixiecrat revolt, and his place at the front of a guerrilla political movement was a surprise. Up until the late 1940s, his career had been about as beige as they come.

Wright was born in 1895 in Rolling Fork, Mississippi, a small Delta town forty-five miles north of Vicksburg. He attended the University of Alabama for two years starting in 1912 and then went back home to "read the law," working at a small-town firm—with an interruption for overseas duty in World War I—until 1927, when he ran for state senate. When that term ended he won a seat in the state house, where he rose to the position of speaker by 1936. He left government in 1940 to join a Vicksburg law firm and came back to win a race for lieutenant governor in 1943.

He became governor after Thomas Bailey died of cancer in November 1946, and he won a term in his own right the next year, positioning himself as a low-key bureaucrat. His campaign literature provided lengthy lists of the useful things he'd done—"Helped provide School Lunch Program . . . Pushed financing of Statewide Forestry Fire Protection Program . . ."—and he looked the part: a genial, distinguished-looking man with graying hair and horn-rimmed glasses.

But Wright also had a hard edge, and on a separate issue—law and order as it applied to black defendants—he had already proved himself to be a stern judge, a fact that didn't bode well for McGee. During his first, partial term as governor, he had been confronted with an emotional appeal in a capital punishment case that involved two African-American fifteen-year-olds, Charles Trudell and James Lewis, who were scheduled to die for the murder of their employer, a white sawmill operator named Harry McKey. Blanche Meiers, a middle-aged mother of eight from Oakland, California, mounted a personal crusade to save their lives, and in January 1947 she traveled by train to plead with Wright in person, an uphill quest that was covered as a human-interest story all over the country. Meiers said she was dying of "an incurable disease" and that saving the boys would be her "one last good deed before I meet my God."

Normally, such meddling would have been greeted with scorn in Jackson newspapers, but Mrs. Meiers was hard to dislike. The *Jackson Daily News* ran a picture of her extending her arms for a Jewish-mother hug, under the headline PLEADS FOR NEGRO YOUTHS. The tone of the coverage was that she was well-meaning but misguided.

Wright agreed to see her, but before she arrived he traveled to the boys' jail cell in Woodville, a tiny southwest Mississippi town near the Louisiana border. There, he said, they gave him a full confession and "glibly told of other crimes they had planned." Though Wright's mind was already closed to Mrs. Meiers's words, he treated her with courtesy, and she reciprocated by praising his fairness. "Withhold your criticism of the governor of Mississippi," she said. "He is a good man—the law is wrong."

Local newspapers praised Wright for behaving like a gentleman while standing firm. "That was what Mississippians would have expected of any Mississippi governor," said a *Clarion-Ledger* editorial. ". . . [W]e . . . congratulate His Excellency on his good judgment as well as his inherent instincts and manner."

As promised, Wright didn't relent. Trudell and Lewis were both electrocuted in July.

Prior to the Mississippi gubernatorial primary in the summer of 1947, Wright presented his case to voters at the Neshoba County Fair—a traditional proving ground for Mississippi politicians—not bothering to pretend he was a speaker in the grand tradition of Bilbo.

"He doesn't get angry," the *Memphis Press-Scimitar* reported, sounding disappointed. "He doesn't rave and rant. He is not a flow-ery old-time orator. Wright simply stands before the people and talks quietly, telling them in simple terms what he has done and what he proposes to recommend. . . ." Still, he threw off a few sparks. Late in the speech, without saying quite who he meant, Wright laid down a general warning to anybody—Truman Democrats, liberals, Commu-nists—who would presume to interfere with Mississippi's way of life.

"It is not necessary for me to call your attention to the crusade go-ing on in certain sections deliberately planned and designed to place our state in a false light and hold us up to scorn," he said. ". . . Certain pressure groups who do not approve of our philosophy and some who hate us because of our strong advancement in our economic condition are exerting every means to bring disunity, discord, and strife. . . . I have been battling these outside meddlers during my service as acting governor and since I became governor."

Wright won easily, and his inaugural speech in early 1948 followed Truman's 1948 State of the Union address by two weeks. Truman talked about civil rights again, so Wright made that one of his themes, denouncing the president's civil rights committee and the likely "vi-cious effect" of its proposals. "Those of you who read and studied the report recognize in it a further and, I might say, the most dangerous step toward the destruction of these traditions and customs so vital to our way of life, particularly in our Southland," he said. Mississip-pians had been good Democrats "when no other section stayed with that banner," but their continued loyalty was not guaranteed. This legislation would end it.

Wright moved quickly. In early February, John Popham was on hand in Wakulla Springs, Florida, to hear him urge fellow members of the Southern Governor's Conference to start thinking about a formal break with the Democrats. By the end of the month, the first Jackson meeting had been held; another was scheduled for May. On the eve of that one—a bigger affair that attracted delegates from other Southern states, including Strom Thurmond—Wright delivered a statewide radio address in which he told Mississippi's black population to stop dreaming hopeless dreams: Segregation would never end.

"If any of you have become so deluded as to want to enter our white schools, patronize our hotels and cafes, enjoy social equality with the whites," he said, "then kindness and true sympathy requires me to advise you to make your home in some state other than Mississippi."

———

As if Truman didn't have enough to worry about in the summer of 1948, he also faced strong opposition on the left, led by Henry Wallace, FDR's longtime secretary of agriculture and his vice president during World War II. With FDR's blessing, Wallace was dumped from the 1944 Democratic ticket in favor of Truman. He served as Truman's secretary of commerce but was fired in September 1946, because his public statements on such issues as the Soviet Union, the British Empire, and atomic secrecy were well to the left of the Truman Doctrine, which the president had laid out in a March 12, 1947, speech that called for the United States to support governments around the world that were fighting Communist encroachment.

Later that year, in a September 12 speech at Madison Square Garden called "The Way to Peace," Wallace counseled against a postwar military alliance with Britain, said that only the United Nations should be trusted with atomic bombs, and argued that an overly aggressive stance against Soviet Russia was a mistake. " 'Getting tough' never bought anything real and lasting—whether for schoolyard bullies or businessmen or world powers," he said. "The tougher we get, the tougher the Russians will get."

For good measure, he brought up the 1946 lynchings in Monroe, Georgia, saying that Americans needed to solve their own problems of "prejudice, hatred, fear, and ignorance of certain races" before they could hope to set an example for the world.

Secretary of State James F. Byrnes was furious that Wallace had sounded off about foreign policy, as was Truman. "He is a pacifist one hundred percent," he wrote of Wallace in his diary. "He wants to disband our armed forces, give Russia our atomic secrets and trust a bunch of adventurers in the Kremlin Politboro. . . . The Reds, phonies and the 'parlor pinks' seem to be banded together and are becoming a national danger."

Wallace resigned under pressure on September 20, and Truman had another full-fledged rival to contend with. By the winter of 1947, Wallace was the declared presidential candidate of the new Progressive Party, a group that would have lasting significance to the McGee case. In 1950 and 1951, when the case broke out and started to become well known, it didn't happen solely because of the Communist Party and the CRC. The groundswell of support for McGee, which seemed to come out of nowhere, also occurred because Wallace people rallied around, seeing McGee as a cause that could bring a new level of mainstream attention to the emerging issue of civil rights.

seven

THE ODDS AGAINST
SMILING JOHNNY

In early 1948, McGee won a second reversal from the Mississippi Supreme Court, which led to a third circuit-court trial within weeks. This time, the state judges reversed the decision only grudgingly, in response to a U.S. Supreme Court ruling that was announced on December 8, 1947, when Thurgood Marshall and the NAACP won a unanimous decision in *Patton v. Mississippi*.

The case's central issue was the same one Dixon Pyles raised in his appeal of McGee's second conviction: exclusion of blacks from jury lists, grand juries, and trial juries, in violation of the Fourteenth Amendment's equal protection requirement. *Patton* was filed first, so it reached the U.S. Supreme Court when the Mississippi Supreme Court was still considering McGee's appeal.

Eddie "Buster" Patton was a young black man from Meridian who was accused of killing fifty-three-year-old J. L. Meadows, the white owner of a roadhouse. Meadows was found dead behind a counter on the morning of February 11, 1946, the victim of a blunt-instrument beating that left bruises and cuts all over his head, face, and body. Patton, who'd worked for him at one time, was arrested and questioned for eight hours. He confessed, though the prosecution decided not to use his admission of guilt, apparently anticipating a challenge over whether it had been beaten out of him. The case consisted of circumstantial evidence gained during the confession and physical evidence in the form of footprints, found outside the nightclub, that allegedly matched Patton's shoes. The trial lasted only a day; Patton was found guilty in eighteen minutes and sentenced to death.

The grand jury and trial jury were all white and all male. The county, Lauderdale, was at least 35 percent African-American, but there hadn't been a black on a nonfederal jury there for as long as anyone could remember. Just as Pyles later did, Patton's lawyer, a local named Lonnie Broadway, put officials on the stand who admitted as much, testifying vaguely about two or three unnamed blacks who might have been placed on jury lists in the past but didn't serve.

The Mississippi Supreme Court rejected Patton's appeal, saying the problem wasn't exclusion but a shortage of blacks who met the voter standards spelled out under Mississippi law—among them, the ability to pay a poll tax and to read and interpret sections of the state constitution. The justices knew that those rules, in place since 1890, were there to deny blacks their voting rights, but they pretended to believe the system was run fairly, resulting in a natural mathematical imbalance that explained why none was ever selected.

To support this, the Mississippi judges skipped any analysis of the rigged voting laws and made the scarcity of black voters their starting point. Based on testimony at Patton's trial, they estimated that roughly a dozen blacks would qualify as potential jurors. Comparing that with the larger number of qualified whites (roughly 5,000), the justices concluded that this translated to "about one-fourth of one per cent negro jurors," a ratio of −400 to 1. They imagined a hypothetical case in which county officials called in men for a jury pool of one hundred. Given the imbalanced ratio, they said, the presence of even one black juror would have been statistically unfair to his white counterparts.

"[T]he sheriff, had he brought in a negro, would have had to discriminate against white jurors, not against negroes—he could not be expected to bring in one-fourth of one negro," the opinion said.

The U.S. Supreme Court had ruled as far back as 1880 that jury exclusion based on race was unconstitutional. There was no blanket way to enforce this in the South, but over the years the Court had reversed cases in which glaring violations occurred. With *Patton*, it served notice that Mississippi's number games weren't convincing, and that, by definition, unbroken decades of all-white juries "created a very strong showing that . . . Negroes were systematically excluded . . . because of

race." They dismissed the state court's logic with an especially scorn-
ful word: "unwisdom."

Patton didn't magically end Mississippi jury exclusion, but it
couldn't be ignored in the short term. Two months later, on February 9,
1948, the Mississippi Supreme Court, citing Patton, reversed McGee's
second conviction in a 4–2 ruling. The majority's terse opinion wasn't
nearly as long as a heated dissent by Justice Harvey McGehee, who
insisted again that, as long as there were so few qualified black voters,
it was unreasonable to expect that many or any would be chosen during the blind selection process required by law.

This series of events earned McGee his first mention in the New
York Times, because Patton meant that his third trial would, one way
or another, require the presence of blacks on a jury. Three local black
men—Claude Arrington, Dr. T. J. Barnes, and T. D. Brown—were selected for the eighteen-man grand jury that indicted McGee on February 18, 1948.

Their presence was a modern milestone, and the Laurel Leader-Call
gave them front-page coverage on February 17, complete with a photograph and a headline that said, "Jones County Makes History." Black
jurors had served in Mississippi during and after Reconstruction, but
the McGee jurors were reported to be the first placed on a Mississippi
circuit-court panel of any kind in the twentieth century.

The trickier question was where, exactly, their names had come
from. They were drawn from an all-white list that had been created
months before the Patton decision. And yet, suddenly, there they were,
in an instant turnaround that wasn't easy to explain. "It is considered
unusual that the names of three negroes were drawn from the jury
box," the Jackson Daily News reported on February 16, "since there is
such a small percentage of negroes qualified for jury service. . . ."

It seemed more than unusual, and a question presented itself: Had
the grand-jury process been tampered with? If so, how and why?

Somebody other than Dixon Pyles would have to figure that out, because he dropped the case. Any interest he had in McGee as a cause

was outweighed by the negatives of getting in deeper. In an interview years later, he called it a simple cost-benefit question, saying "the pressure on was so great that I wanted a good deal more money than the people who were backing Willie McGee wanted to pay."

Pyles didn't elaborate, but he faced two obvious problems: anti-McGee sentiment in Mississippi and anti-Red rumblings in Washington. By this point, it was part of the public record that he'd been working with the CRC, a group that the House Un-American Activities Committee had attacked in early 1947, just nine months after it was formed, as a Communist front.

"Having adopted a line of militant skullduggery against the United States with the close of World War II," the report began, "the Communist Party has set up the Civil Rights Congress for the purpose of protecting those of its members who run afoul of the law."

McGee wasn't discussed. At the time, HUAC was more interested in the CRC's support of people like Gerhart Eisler, a New York–based Communist, originally from Germany, who was accused of being a Soviet spy. But Pyles's name appeared on a list of CRC expenditures at the end, which showed that he'd received $1,750 in legal fees and expenses. For what, it didn't say. And though this was just a fine-print mention, it probably would have been noticed by one of the most vocal HUAC members: John Rankin, a wild-eyed Democrat who had represented northeast Mississippi's First Congressional District since 1921.

Having Rankin on your tail wasn't something any Mississippi lawyer would want. Like Bilbo, he was a racist and anti-Semite who held grudges and loved fights. He was especially vehement on the subject of Communism, which he seemed to think was a Jewish conspiracy of ancient lineage. "Communism is older than Christianity," he declared on the House floor in 1945. "It is the curse of the ages. It hounded and persecuted the Saviour during his earthly ministry, inspired his crucifixion, derided him in his dying agony, and then gambled for his garments at the foot of the cross."

Pyles's departure was a serious problem for the CRC, and Bella Abzug made her first trip to Mississippi to persuade him to stick with the case. Abzug discussed this journey in a series of oral-history interviews she did in 1995 and 1996 with Columbia University, where she graduated from law school in 1944. She didn't say when she first got involved with McGee or when she went south, but it appears she came into the case at the suggestion of Abraham Isserman, a CRC lawyer she knew from the New York chapter of the National Lawyers Guild—an organization that often defended left-wing clients under attack by state and federal governments—and that she'd worked on the drafting of McGee's second appeal. Her Mississippi trip must have happened around the second week of February 1947, after the Supreme Court's reversal and before the third trial.

During this trip, Abzug met with Pyles in Jackson, failed to change his mind, and then drove to Laurel alone to ask the local district attorney for the names of qualified defense lawyers. Whoever she spoke with—she didn't give a name—told her there wasn't a person in town who would help her, so she hustled back to Jackson to try her luck there. Pyles, alarmed, told her he'd been getting calls "all day long that there's this white, woman lawyer traveling to Laurel. . . . It's a wonder you're back safe."

"Well, here's where I am," Abzug said. "Can you help me get a lawyer?"

"No. I don't know anybody who would take this on."

Abzug decided to find her man the old-fashioned way, by walking around downtown Jackson, knocking on doors. "I literally went from building to building where lawyers were housed," she said. ". . . Most people weren't in the least interest[ed]. In fact, they thought I was a crazy person."

She finally succeeded thanks to a tip she'd gotten from a brother-in-law who had told her about a young, Jewish Mississippi attorney and army veteran named Alvin N. London. A dapper, dark-haired Hattiesburg native, London was a recent graduate of the Ole Miss law school. His office was on North Congress Street, just a few blocks from Pyles's building. Abzug went in and told him she needed to assemble

a new courtroom team for Willie McGee—immediately. As she recalled:

> He said, "I have some guy I think would do it." I said, "What
> about you?" He said, "Well, I could work with him, but I'm not
> really a trial lawyer." His name was Poole, and Poole was a hard-
> drinking, swearing young man who had lost a leg, I guess it was
> in World War II. He was a very big drinker and Southern kind
> of personality, almost stereotypically, and I got these two guys in-
> volved in the case. That meant that I'd have to spend a great deal
> of time with them, in detail, because they didn't know much about
> anything, to be truthful. So I retained them and I went back to New
> York, and I kept telling them what kinds of actions we would have
> to take.

Most people know Abzug from her heyday in the 1970s as a
congresswoman and feminist. When she served in the U.S. House of
Representatives between 1971 and 1977, she was in her fifties, and
it was then that her iconic look became familiar all over the world:
floppy hats, sacklike print dresses, and a broad, angular-featured face
that could appear joyful or menacing, depending on what she was
worked up about.

But Abzug was only twenty-six in early 1948, a young labor lawyer
who had been a member of the New York Bar for less than a year. She
dressed differently then, wearing fitted dresses and suits, gloves, and
smaller, pinned-on hats—the standard workplace getup for women of
that era, designed to increase her chances of being taken seriously in
the male domains of union halls and law offices.

She looked different too. The Slavic features Bella inherited from
her parents—first-generation immigrants from Russia named Emanuel
and Esther Savitzky—were softer in her youth. "I was all Oriental and
gorgeous then," she told *New York* magazine in a 1977 profile. "I wore
a size eleven." She was kidding around, but it was true: One friend
told an interviewer that young Bella looked like Shirley MacLaine in
The Apartment. After her college graduation, she briefly held a job

modeling fashion turbans in a display window at Macy's. Stalking around downtown Jackson, she must have cut a surprisingly exotic figure.

———

One thing that didn't change, from earliest youth on, was her get-out-of-my-way personality. Born Bella Savitzky on July 24, 1920— the same year women got the vote—she grew up in the Bronx, in a financially strained but happy household supported by her father's endless hours of work at a Hell's Kitchen butcher shop he owned, the Live and Let Live Meat Market. Emanuel died when Bella was thirteen. Her other important role models were Esther—an "all mother" figure, she said, who supported her in everything she wanted to do—and her grandfather, an ancient and loving Orthodox Jew named Wolf Tanklevsky, who used to babysit Bella and take her to synagogue.

"[H]e would be very proud of the fact that I could read Hebrew and he would show me off to all his cronies," she recalled. "But the minute the services started I was placed in a segregated area, because in our religion women and men are separated by what we call a *mechitza*, which is a curtain. Many people have suggested that it was in those early days, behind the curtain, that I probably first got my ideas of feminism. . . ."

Bella was a gifted talker, and, naturally enough, she became a student leader. At Hunter College—then the all-women's campus of New York's City College system, which she attended from 1938 to 1942— she was elected student-council president in her junior year. The late 1930s to early 1940s were turbulent times on New York campuses, and her role involved a mix of corsage-and-tea activity (helping organize the Hunter College "Biennial Carnival") and serious, often radical, undergraduate politics.

Bella was active in the American Student Union, an organization formed in 1935 as a merger of existing groups for students who were Socialists or Communist sympathizers. She said she was neither, even though she was "recruited" by everybody from the Socialists to the

Stalinists. She described herself as a nonaligned progressive with healthy doubts about the American way.

"Certainly it was clear to me that our own system had never been that great," she said. ". . . I thought socialism was an interesting philosophy that should play itself out, if it could happen. I was never a Russophile . . . although I've been accused of being that, historically, all the time. People are always saying that, because I took certain progressive positions, which may or may not have coincided with positions the Soviet Union took."

Among Bella's stances on issues of the day: She supported the anti-Fascist Loyalists in the Spanish Civil War; opposed aid to Great Britain before the U.S. entry into World War II (at the time, many left-leaning students were more concerned about British imperialism than Nazi aggression); and spoke out against the Rapp-Coudert Committee, a long-running attempt by New York State to find and crush "subversive activities" in New York schools and colleges. Bella was also part of a huge ASU contingent that went to Washington in early 1940 to voice opposition to any American involvement in the war.

One controversial issue from those months was the Soviet Union's invasion of Finland, which happened in late 1939, three months after Hitler and Stalin shocked the world by signing a nonaggression pact. On this, Bella was in tune with the party line pushed by American Communists: strong support for the Soviets, on the grounds that conquering Finland provided an essential buffer against potential invasion from the anti-Communist West. A popular party slogan about Britain's and Finland's plight was "The Yanks Are Not Coming," and in late February 1940 Bella proposed the creation of "The Yanks Are Not Coming" clubs on the Hunter campus.

"[T]he youth of America cannot be misled by fine slogans and stimulating horror stories," she was quoted saying in the student newspaper, the *Hunter Bulletin*. ". . . We [demand] that all loans to Finland and money for rearmament be used to alleviate the misery of the unemployed in America, and to extend NYA, WPA, housing and Social Security programs."

Bella got her first taste of bad press when a pair of *New York Post* reporters wrote about Hunter in March 1941, saying that her political stands branded her as "a campus pink."

"Among those who have generally followed the Communist line in her college activities is Bella Savitzky, 20," the story said, alongside a picture of Bella smiling and banging a gavel. ". . . Bella denies that she belongs to the Communist party; she admits that she is anti-British, but says that is because she is a Zionist."

Bella denounced the article in a signed comment on the front page of the *Bulletin*. "Any statements as to my political opinions were pure fabrications," she wrote. "Any implications as to communist affiliations or leanings are completely unfounded." Half a century later, she was still irritated by that article, calling it "a bunch of half-baked, half-truthful ideas about me. . . ."

After college, Bella visited an aunt in Miami, where she met her future husband, Martin Abzug, an aspiring writer from New York who published two novels before going into finance. They married in 1944. She went to law school at Columbia between 1942 and 1944, which, by definition, made her a pioneer. There were only a handful of women in her class; Harvard didn't graduate its first female law students until 1953. Compared with Bella's glowing memories of life at Hunter, law school sounded unpleasant: a prolonged exposure to the attributes she resented in many men.

"The faculty . . . did not treat us well," she said. "They were condescending . . . they were scoffing, and they did not make it easy for us to function in law school." Once again, though, she excelled. She became an editor on the *Columbia Law Review*, an experience she remembered as "a form of torture" that, nonetheless, was "good training in research" and "how to write a good brief."

After law school, Abzug took a job with a prominent labor-oriented law firm, Pressman, Witt & Cammer, whose partners would all become boldface names in the battles over alleged Communist subversion that unfolded after the war. Harold Cammer was a founder of the National Lawyers Guild, which had been labeled a Communist front by Congress and the Justice Department. Nathan Witt was a former secretary of the National Labor Relations Board. During the 1948–1949 hearings and trial of Alger Hiss—the State Department official accused by former Communist spy Whittaker Chambers of having passed secret information to Russia during the Roosevelt administration—Witt was accused of conspiring with Hiss. Best known of them all was Lee Pressman, who had briefly been a Communist when he worked for the Department of Agriculture in 1934, but who publicly recanted that part of his past in 1950. During subpoenaed testimony before HUAC, Pressman corroborated Chambers's claim that a Communist cell had existed inside the Agriculture Department.

Abzug seemed to hate Pressman, who embodied everything that annoyed her: arrogance, condescension toward women, and personal disloyalty. "I never liked the guy," she said. "Never, ever. I thought he was arrogant, I thought he was self-centered. . . . He went before the Un-American Activities Committee and accused his dear friends, whom I worked for . . . of having been in a Communist cell with him. He was a traitor. People never talked to him after that, and they stopped bragging about him. But I knew him for what he was: crap. Absolute crap. Listen. You can tell in a man's attitude toward you. He treated me like I was a piece of nothing."

—————

For different reasons, Abzug wasn't very impressed with John Poole, the young lawyer she hired to run the defense at McGee's third trial. In her oral history, she dismissed him as an alcoholic who was out of his depth and "fancied himself as a person who could argue a big, important issue like this. . . ." Only with Alvin London's help, she said, was she able to get him to "think clearly" about what he had to do.

She was right that Poole had a drinking problem—it's mentioned in an FBI report from 1950—but her assessment seems far too harsh, and it overlooks traits that these unlikely partners had in common. Like Abzug, Poole was smart, hardworking, and energetic. More important in this instance: He was headstrong enough to do the job. By 1948, not many lawyers were willing to take on the risky, thankless chore of defending Willie McGee. Abzug wouldn't. She said it was out of the question for her to try the case herself, because, as a "white, Jewish woman lawyer from New York," she wouldn't have had a chance.

The assignment wasn't any easier for Poole and London. The fact that they were Southern males wasn't an advantage, because they were perceived as traitors to their own culture. They were even younger than Abzug—Poole was twenty-five, London only twenty-three—and they had almost no experience. They were handling divorces and wills when Abzug invited them to take on a challenge that must have seemed nearly impossible. London, who was interviewed in 1952 by Spivak, the investigator representing the *Daily Worker*, frankly admitted that, if he had it to do all over again, he wouldn't.

"It was quite an experience," he said. "It was one of those things I would give a great deal if I had never been in."

Poole's full name was John Riley Poole Jr. He grew up in Jackson, where he attended Central High School and Millsaps College, just like Dixon Pyles. As Abzug correctly recalled, he was missing a leg, but this wasn't from a war injury. He lost it in a 1936 train-hopping accident that happened in Dallas, Texas, when Poole was only sixteen. He and a friend had run away from home and were heading to California—a fact that says a lot about Poole's youthful personality, which was sometimes too adventurous for his own good.

Poole grew up on a street in the Bailey Avenue neighborhood, in what was then north Jackson, in a small house about a half mile from the downtown rail yards. His father, John Sr., worked for the Illinois Central. Poole had six brothers and sisters, some of whom were already grown and gone when his mother, Ada, died in 1936. A sister named Mildred took care of the family, keeping house and proselytizing for Sister Aimee Semple McPherson's Church of the Foursquare Gospel, the Los Angeles–based evangelistic crusade that had been growing steadily since its founding in 1927. Poole was almost drawn in himself. Though he rejected religion as an adult, he was a devoted Bible student back then, and for a while he dabbled with the idea of becoming a Foursquare minister.

Poole had a wilder side, running around with a group of neighborhood guys who called themselves the Bailey Avenue Gang. They weren't a "gang" in the modern sense—though Poole said later that they were "a pretty tough bunch," with some of them winding up in reform school—and it's unclear why Poole decided to raise the bar on his misbehavior and hop a freight to California. He talked about the accident that cost him a leg to a Jackson newspaperman roughly a year and a half after it happened, but never wrote anything in depth himself. His three daughters, Beverly, Carolyn, and Donna, only remember fragments of what their parents told them about it.

Poole told the Jackson reporter that he and two friends decided to head for California one summer, getting as far as Dallas before they decided to turn back. He was groggy when one of his friends told him a freight train was coming. "When I hopped to my feet, I saw it was going too fast," Poole said, "but it seemed like something just made me try for it anyhow. I guess I was still half asleep. I didn't quite get a good hold on the rungs when I grabbed, just enough to jerk me off my feet. It threw me under the boxcar."

Poole's right leg went under the steel wheels and was nearly severed below the knee. His friends carried him to the train station. From there, Poole was rushed off to a hospital, where his leg was amputated, and where he stayed for several weeks. He later said the incident straightened him out for good, and it was during that period that he vowed to get serious about schoolwork, because he'd decided he wanted to become a lawyer.

By the time he was seventeen, in 1939, Poole had also bounced back enough to compete in the ring as an amateur boxer. That year, he was profiled in the *Memphis Commercial Appeal*, in an article headlined "Odds Against Smiling Johnny Bother Him Not One Little Bit." It told the story of how young "Johnny Poole" had thwarted his disability to become a capable lightweight fighter. A captioned photo ("Laughs Off Handicap") showed him looking boyish and all-American—big ears, huge smile, handsome eyes, and a cowlick—dressed in the long cotton boxing trunks he wore to hide his wooden leg.

As the article explained, Poole was determined to compete in a sport, and the basic leg movements of boxing—shuffling, hopping, planting weight—were feasible on his artificial limb. "Despite the unsteady foot work," the *Commercial Appeal* said, "Johnny hits hard. . . . Two good limbs would make him even more powerful with his punches."

When you look at Poole's youth, a consistent theme is this desire to keep striving. During his years at Millsaps, which he attended from 1941 to 1944, he was a joiner—manically so. Among other activities, he took part in the debate club (serving as president), the Millsaps Singers (tenor), the International Relation Club, the Empyreans (a social club), and Pi Kappa Delta (for speech-competition students).

In 1944, he ran for student-body president, using his crowded list of extracurricular activities as its own selling point. "LEADERSHIP MERITS LEADERSHIP," his campaign literature said. "LOOK AT THE RECORD. John has proved that he is an efficient leader. He is president of the PRE-LAW CLUB, president of the DEBATE CLUB, and president of the ECONOMICS CLUB. Under his guidance, these clubs have taken on new life."

Poole lost the race, and the 1944 Millsaps yearbook hinted at a price to his overactivity. He was mentioned in an article about campus big shots, but it was noted that he'd "resigned all of his offices in the honoraries in order to study."

In the summer of 1947, just after Poole's graduation from Ole Miss law school, he ran for office again, taking the bold step of entering the Democratic primary for a seat in the Mississippi House of Representatives. He lost, but that wasn't really the point. Emmett Owens, a friend of Poole's who knew him during the Bailey Avenue days, says he ran for the publicity, as a way of announcing himself as a new face in town.

His decision to defend McGee probably had multiple motives. Owens says he needed money, like Pyles, but his independent streak must have been part of it. "My dad was not a follower," says his daughter Beverly, a longtime Jackson lawyer who was born just four months before Poole took the McGee case. If it was attention he wanted, he got it: Defending McGee eventually made him famous (and infamous) all over the state. But his youngest daughter, Donna, a professionally licensed counselor who lives in Springfield, Missouri, doesn't believe he did it just for the notoriety. For the past few years, she's been work-

ing on a memoir about her father; in her manuscript, she argues that
Poole's decision to defend McGee involved fundamental beliefs.

"Dad must have sensed the danger ahead of time," she writes, "so
his reasons for taking the case—with the chance of his practice being
endangered with a pregnant wife and a toddler at home—must have
been inspired by more than mere adventure. . . . He had told me in
later years, regarding his practice, that he wanted to try to give the
black man in Mississippi the full advantage of his rights under the
law. He felt an obligation to his lawyer's oath to serve anyone impar-
tially, and I suppose then, in seeing the extreme exigency of Willie
McGee, he had set his reasonableness aside."

━━━

Judging by outward appearances, the first and third McGee trials
were quite different. The 1945 edition was held with armed troops in
the courtroom and the threat of lynching in the air. It was one-sided,
simple, and quick—the transcript is only eighty-five pages long.

The third trial happened without the military presence, lasted
several days, and produced a transcript totaling 910 pages. Most of
the extra verbiage came during pretrial arguments over matters like
venue, jury selection, and public attitudes toward McGee, issues that
both sides knew would come up if the case was appealed again. It had
been sent back twice on procedural grounds, so the challenge for the
state wasn't just to get a guilty verdict, but to keep it. To do that, the
prosecution had to anticipate and neutralize any irregularities that
might cause trouble down the line.

The state's three-man prosecution team—locals all, and all more
experienced than Poole and London—was led by Paul Swartzfager Sr.,
the new district attorney, a commanding, hefty thirty-nine-year-old
army veteran who had been elected the previous summer after promising to take the McGee case to a swift conclusion. Working with him
were the county prosecutor, E. K. Collins, and Jack Deavours, who
had been hired as a special prosecutor by the Hawkins family.

Swartzfager died in 2000, but according to his son Jon, a lawyer based in Laurel, people in town let him know that anything less than lasting victory was unacceptable. Jon was only seven in 1948, but he says he remembers his father being summoned to the local VFW hall by a group of men—he doesn't know who they were—who drove the point home.

"They wanted him to bust his butt to get a conviction," Jon told me. "But then also to guarantee that the Supreme Court wasn't going to reverse it, and to guarantee that he would get the death penalty to stick, and guarantee that Willie McGee would be executed. Well, my dad could guarantee all that, but truth of the fact is he couldn't control what the Supreme Court was going to do."

What could be controlled was how Laurel came off in the written record. Mob atmosphere? There wasn't one. During early testimony, the courtroom was only partially full, and Swartzfager claimed that people in Laurel were, believe it or not, bored with McGee. On the stand, Laurel mayor Carroll Gartin testified to a distinct "lack of conversation or discussion" about the case. Thomas Gibbons, publisher of the *Leader-Call*, admitted that he personally thought McGee was guilty but said the public mood was as fair as you'd find anywhere. "[P]eople think justice ought to be done, but I haven't heard anybody blowing their tops on account of it," he said.

The courtroom would fill up once the trial started, but to counter this image of disinterest, the defense needed to produce witnesses who would testify that the public did care, and that there was rampant prejudice against McGee. Poole worked hard to find them, with help from a third lawyer, Jackson-based Clarence Holland, and Tennessee-based CRC investigator Laurent Frantz. But he wasn't playing on a level field, thanks to the rapid pace set by Judge Collins, who presided for the third time and who, from the outset, seemed to function as an adjunct member of the prosecution.

The verdict of the second trial had been reversed on February 9. Poole and London signed up late in the evening on the 17th. The new indictment was issued on the 18th, and Collins scheduled the case for the 20th, refusing the defense's request for a delay. By the 26th,

Thursday of the following week, pretrial procedures were under way. The trial opened on March 3, a Wednesday. The whole thing ended three days later, on Saturday night.

The defense's first move was to ask for a continuance. London put Poole on the stand so he could list the obstacles he'd faced while preparing. Because of his existing caseload in Jackson, he said, and because everything was happening so fast, he'd been unable to read the entire record from the first and second trials. He'd only had about fifteen minutes alone with McGee. He was trying to find new witnesses—he'd driven all over Laurel and Jones County talking to people—but he'd run into a wall of hostility and silence.

"I have talked with lawyers in Laurel," Poole said, "one of whom said this to me: 'You have done the craziest thing you could ever do by taking this case.' "

Poole's statements backfired, giving Swartzfager easy targets during his questioning. Was Poole too busy to prepare? Tough. He shouldn't have taken the job. He felt threatened in Laurel? Maybe he was panicking because he was green. "Now, whether the lawyer was ribbing you, or whether he was serious about the matter, nothing has happened to you, has there?" Swartzfager asked. Poole said it hadn't, but he insisted the threat was real. He added, quietly, that two lawyers had told him this, not just one.

Swartzfager told him to speak up. "What was that, Mr. Poole?"

"I merely said there was another lawyer who told me that also."

Swartzfager still couldn't hear him.

"There was another member of the bar of the Second Judicial District of Jones County, Mississippi, that told me that also."

At that, Deavours—who'd obviously heard every word—interrupted with a wisecrack. "You can't put too much confidence in these lawyers," he said.

"Well, they used to scare me too when I started out," Swartzfager joked.

Later, Poole's inexperience showed when he went on too long about the single exception he'd found to the code of silence: a white woman in her late fifties named Mrs. O. A. McMullan, who reportedly told Poole, "The lawyers themselves should be shot for having anything to do with this case, for defending the old rascal. He is guilty and everybody knows it."

Poole wanted to put Mrs. McMullan on the stand but she was said to be ill. He wanted a stay until she was fit to testify, and to that end he called in her physician, a Dr. C. H. Ramsey, who said she was suffering from coronary thrombosis and was "never" going to get better. Poole kept after him, asking if it would be possible to bring her to court "in a wheel chair."

"In what?"

"In a wheel chair."

"Well, she would have to be carried up."

"That's what I mean. That would be possible?"

"Well . . . the strain, the exertion, the excitement, just being a witness might cause her to have a relapse, in other words, a new attack."

This was a bad image to conjure up: an old lady clutching her chest as she's dragged into court on behalf of an accused black rapist. Things got worse when Clarence Holland took the stand and Swartzfager made him admit that Mrs. McMullan was his aunt. The only reason Poole "interviewed" her was that Holland was obliged to pay her a visit while he was in town. They'd gone to see her in the middle of what Holland sheepishly described as a bridge party and tea.

Poole's search for new witnesses wasn't a complete bust: He found a woman who was never called during the third trial, but who would be important to the case later. Her name was Hettie Johnson, and she had come up in the first trial, when she was mentioned as a resident of one of the houses McGee had gambled in. According to Poole, he'd learned that she had new information that would provide a solid alibi for McGee. He didn't say what it was, just that she and her husband, William, had been difficult to locate, so he needed more time.

"They are Negro witnesses, and I have found now that they are residing in Florida," Poole said. "They were residing in Laurel up until—until not long ago, and I got their addresses in Florida, and it took me some time to do that."

Collins wasn't about to let him reel them in. After sustaining various objections by Swartzfager, he shut down this line of inquiry, saying, "The Court doesn't think the testimony in this case shows any cause for continuance whatever."

———

Poole and London were on firmer ground with the issue of jury selection. They alleged that the state had engaged in chicanery by planting the three blacks who served on the grand jury. How did it work? And why did it happen?

To Poole, the answers were obvious. The state needed black jurors to satisfy *Patton*. The challenge was to have them while simultaneously nullifying their presence. The way to do it was to put them on the eighteen-man grand jury, whose members didn't have to vote unanimously to indict McGee. The trial jury, in contrast, would have to vote 12–0 to convict.

Poole and London questioned various circuit-court and county officials, including E. T. Orso, a Jones County supervisor who, during the second trial, had told Dixon Pyles that he was unaware of any blacks ever being picked for a jury in his district. Now he claimed he'd been pulling their names for years, without "any discrimination at all."

Poole asked Orso to walk him through the Jones County voter statistics, which were similar to the Lauderdale numbers cited in *Patton*: 5,500 qualified whites, 45 qualified blacks. The most recent Jones County jury list had been drawn up in April 1947. Orso said he put the names of "six or seven" blacks on it. The total pool numbered 264 jurors, with 257 of them white.

Poole held up a copy of the list, explaining that the names were typed in three separate blocks. The first group, 42 names in all, was arranged alphabetically in three columns. Below that was a second group labeled OTHERS. Also alphabetical, it contained 187 names.

And below that, beneath a hand-drawn line, sat a third group of

35 names that weren't alphabetized. The three black grand jurors—Barnes, Brown, and Arrington—were at the end of the list. Poole asked Orso "to explain why the names of the jurors have been listed alphabetically up until the last page, and at the middle of that page they are not named alphabetically."

Swartzfager objected. Judge Collins told Poole to clarify what he was getting at.

"We are alleging . . . that the names have been arbitrarily placed on the jury list as well as being arbitrarily placed on the grand jury."

Collins didn't care for that. "Now, gentlemen," he said to Poole and London, "when you say arbitrarily placed. . . . You would have to allege how they were arbitrarily placed on there, and introduce testimony to support that allegation."

Deavours got angry. "I would like to ask whether he means . . . that the Clerk or somebody has been tampering with the Minutes, and that these names have been added to the list since it was made?"

"That is what I am trying to bring out," Poole said.

"All right," Deavours said, gesturing toward Orso, "why don't you ask him if he has been tampering with the jury list?"

Orso didn't wait to be asked. "Is that what you mean to infer, sir?"

"Yes, sir."

"Well, sir, you are just wrong. There hasn't been anything done to the list since last April."

Right then, Poole started losing ground, because he didn't have any witnesses—such as a documents expert—who were prepared to testify that they could confirm physical evidence of tampering. Lacking that, it was his theory against the word of every judicial official in Jones County. He pressed on anyway, asking Orso why all the names of potential black jurors were conveniently placed at the end.

"I don't know," he said.

"But you did know that they were Negroes, did you not?"

"Yes, sir."

"You did know that you placed them on the jury list, didn't you?"

"Yes, sir."

"Well, don't you know why . . . they were the last ones placed on the list?"

That caused a burst of objections; as before, Collins responded by shutting down the exchange. "The Court holds that all this is immaterial as to where and on what position the names of any jurors appear on the list," he said. "The Board of Supervisors has a right to put the names anywhere he wants to in making the list."

———

Direct testimony began on Friday morning, with the prosecution laying out a slightly expanded version of the same case it had presented twice before. Once again, Willette and Troy led off by describing the terrors of that night in November 1945, while other witnesses—Bill Barnes, George Walker, Paul Britton, and so on—made it seem plausible that McGee was on Magnolia Street when the crime occurred. Mrs. Hawkins's next-door neighbor, Mrs. John Jensen—who hadn't testified at the first trial—said that Willette turned up that night at the back of her house right around a quarter to five, hysterical, screaming, and wearing only a "small halter." Jensen said she took her inside and wrapped her in a sheet, which got stained with her menstrual blood.

When Mrs. Hawkins took the stand, journalists and spectators were cleared, and a question hung in the air: How far would the defense go in cross-examining her? Lawyers on both sides would have known that Pyles, in his appeal to the Mississippi Supreme Court, had spent many pages arguing that her failure to scream or to resist McGee constituted consent.

For Pyles, the key was the phrasing she used in her first-trial testimony.

"The prosecutrix testified that . . . she stated or thought, 'Well, if that is all, I can take it,'" he wrote. "She admits that she was not afraid for herself, but that if she resisted she would awake the children.

"From her own testimony," Pyles went on, "it appears that she valued the sleep of her children more than her virtue. A further careful scrutiny . . . leaves a strong inference that she consented to the sexual act."

What most people didn't know was that McGee had told Poole—just as he'd told Pyles—that Mrs. Hawkins seduced him, though with Poole he didn't mention the "double indemnity" plot. In Poole's 1952 interview with Spivak, he said he'd heard McGee's affair story and had even looked into it, but only in a "scanty" way that didn't lead to any corroboration. Later, based on things he'd heard from a source in Laurel, he decided he didn't believe it—at least, that's what he told Spivak. Poole said that, after the trial was over, he paid a visit to a highway patrolman who'd been friendly to him, to ask for an honest account of what he knew about Mrs. Hawkins's private life.

"I told him that . . . I'd just like to talk to him privately and that I didn't want any lies," Poole said. ". . . He said that he went with [Willette] prior to the time she got married. At that time, he did think she was not the type girl that would do it."

"That would do what?" Spivak asked.

"That would go out and commit adultery."

"[W]omen don't run around committing adultery and advertising it."

"He is the type of fellow that would get anything in his hands he could find," Poole said.

"He was, eh?"

"Frankly, I don't believe he [was] trying to cover up this thing at all."

———

Not a word of this came up during the trial. Questioned by Deavours, Mrs. Hawkins told her story again, and he asked what she did to resist. "I begged him not to do anything," she said. "I pleaded with him and I pushed him, and he was so big and rough, he was just a brute and there was nothing I could do."

"Did he make any threats towards you?"

"He said, 'I will cut your throat. Don't make any noise, I will cut your throat.' . . . The baby kept whimpering and he said, 'Keep that damned brat quiet or I will cut her head open' or something to that effect, and during that time I was calling Troy, and every time I said anything he would shut me up . . . and he told me what he came for, and he said he was going to do it and me dead or alive, and the only reason in the world I took such things was for my family. You know, mother instinct is something."

She went on to say that she never consented but was overpowered by a man whom she described as "a brutal beast" and "a monster." There wasn't anything she could do to fight back, she said, but she would have submitted anyway if that had been necessary to save the lives of her family. "I would have taken anything in preference to having anything happen to my little girls," she said.

When Poole's turn came, he established that Mrs. Hawkins couldn't identify the rapist, because it was too dark to see his face.

"I never saw him," she agreed.

"All you know is that he was a big monster of a Negro, that was what you thought?"

"He was a Negro, and he was a beast."

"And he was a big old Negro, and as you termed it a while ago, a monster—"

Deavours objected. She said she hadn't seen his face; there was no need to belabor it. Poole moved on, having made a point that wouldn't do him much good with a white jury. At five feet seven inches, McGee was no "monster." But he was young, muscular, and black, which was all the jurors needed to hear. Besides, whatever size he was, a physically fit male would have seemed monstrous enough to a ninety-two-pound woman with a baby in her arms.

Trial transcripts can make for stark reading, because there's no descriptive language about a witness's tone of voice or physical reactions. In the case of Mrs. Hawkins, however, it's evident that she became terribly upset during her time on the stand. Poole and London talked about this toward the end of the trial, arguing that the prosecution had tried to prejudice the jury by putting her in a side room after she'd stepped down, so they could hear her sobbing. London called her "very much upset, almost hysterical" and said she started crying toward the close of Poole's questioning. As the transcript shows, Poole pushed her in a way that would have angered local spectators.

At one point, after Mrs. Hawkins described the moment when she realized that the man crawling toward her on the floor was an intruder, Poole asked whether she'd screamed when she "first knew it wasn't Troy." She'd already stated that, in her groggy state, she thought the person on the floor was her husband. By the time she realized he wasn't, the attacker was on top of her, using his strength to pin her down and threatening to kill her.

"[D]id you or not testify on one of the previous trials, 'Well, if that is all you want I can take it?'"

"You mean that I said that to the Negro?"

"Yes."

"I didn't say it to the Negro. I might have testified I said it, but at the time I was just thinking that."

Poole started reading testimony from the earlier transcript, and right then he must have realized he'd made a mistake. At the first trial, Mrs. Hawkins had clearly said, "I thought, 'Well, if that's all I can take it. . . .'"

Swartzfager pounced. "She said she thought that and that is exactly what her response was to this question, that she didn't say it, [but] . . . thought it."

At this, Mrs. Hawkins posed a question to Poole: "Do you have a wife?" He nodded. "That's all I want to know."

"Yes, I do," he said, "and as a matter of fact I realize that the crime is awful, especially when perpetrated as this one is alleged to have been perpetrated, so I approach you, not with the attitude of embarrassing you at all, and I hope you understand that."

Mrs. Hawkins didn't seem soothed. She undermined Poole further by testifying that, contrary to the attacker's orders, she had made a sound. "I cried out," she said. "I don't know how loud I screamed."

Poole questioned her closely about the distance between bedrooms in the house, the volume of her cry, and how it was possible that neither her husband nor her two other children woke up.

"Listen, some day your wife . . . this might happen to her and if it does you can ask her all those foolish questions," she said. "What did she do? How loud did she call? What did she say?"

Toward the end, questioned again by the prosecution, Mrs. Hawkins stated that her memories of that night weren't always clear. But why would anybody expect them to be?

"[So] much happened, and so fast, and the first of December I came up here, and I don't know how much dope I had taken," she said. "I stayed in the hospital a week or two, and I was so frightened, I was frightened out of my wits, I had a terrible shock, and I don't want to live, I don't want to live. [W]hen I go places people look at me and say, 'That's the woman that negro man raped,' and I can hear them say it."

Deavours finished by asking, "You have told the truth, haven't you?"

"I have told the truth," she said, "and I think the truth is bad enough."

———

The prosecution's case had the same strengths and weaknesses as always: The circumstantial case was fairly persuasive, but nobody could identify McGee by sight and there was no physical evidence—unless you counted the bloody boxer shorts with no blood on them, which were pulled out of mothballs and displayed again.

Swartzfager tried to offset this with extensive testimony about McGee's two confessions, the one he delivered verbally on the way back from Hattiesburg, and the one he signed in the Hinds County jail. Half a dozen Hattiesburg and Laurel law enforcement officials took the stand, among them Hattiesburg patrolman Hugh Herring, who, with patrolman E. C. Harris, made the arrest on November 3, 1945; Hattiesburg Police Chief M. M. Little; Laurel Police Chief Wayne Valentine; Laurel policeman Jeff Montgomery; and Luther Hill, who was the Jones County sheriff at the time of McGee's arrest.

They presented a united front, saying that McGee had acted like a man with something to hide, and that he'd confessed to the rape without being coerced.

During this round of questions, for the first time, Poole and London started sounding as if they had something up their sleeves. London asked Herring if McGee had been cursed at, hit, or threatened with hanging before confessing. "No, sir, we don't have no gallows there," he said.

This feeling that something new was coming also pervaded Poole's questioning of Valentine and Montgomery, who described the investigation of the crime scene and the circumstances of McGee's confession.

Valentine said that when the police bulletin came from Hattiesburg, he drove over with Montgomery and highway patrolman Jack Anderson. There, McGee voluntarily submitted to a search that revealed the bloody underwear. On the way back to Laurel, he confessed to the rape under routine questioning.

London cross-examined, and he seemed especially interested in the details of the confession. "Now, chief, on the way back to Laurel, did you tell him where you were taking him?"

"Yes, I told him I was bringing him back to Laurel."

"Did you tell him what you were going to do with him up there?"

"Well, I told him I was going to bring him back to jail."

"Did you, while you were driving towards Laurel, tell him . . . that if he would confess, that you would take him to the Jackson jail instead of Laurel jail?"

"No, I did not."

Poole kept it up with Montgomery, asking, "[E]ven if you had made some threats to Willie McGee, you would be somewhat embarrassed to admit it on the stand, wouldn't you?"

Deavours objected. "You talk about deliberately and determinedly trying to insult an officer of the law, and officers of this court," he said. "I never saw a more deliberate attempt at it."

"Your honor, I am not," Poole said.

"You just asked an officer of the law, 'In order to save this case you get up here and swear a lie.' "

Collins rejected the question as improper, but Deavours kept fuming. "If you have no respect for yourself," he said, "you ought to have some for the officers."

———

In fact, Poole and London did think the officers were lying. After the prosecution rested, they called just one witness, Luther Hill, and then told Collins they wanted to put Willie McGee on the stand, for the limited purpose of examining whether the confession story, as described by prosecution witnesses, was admissible. Collins agreed, the jury was cleared, and McGee was brought in.

Finally, after more than two years in which he'd said nothing at all in a public setting, the man at the center of everything walked to the stand and took a seat. With Poole asking the questions, McGee gave answers that sounded perfectly rational. Except that they described a parallel world where every fact was different, and where he'd been subjected to incredible violence.

"State your name, please."

"Willie McGee."

"You are the defendant in this case?"

"I am."

"Willie, there is some testimony given that you made a voluntary confession to the crime charged against you—"

"It wasn't voluntary," he said.

McGee went on from there, saying he'd been beaten viciously from the moment he was arrested in Hattiesburg—by the officers who collared him; inside the Hattiesburg jail; in the highway patrol car on the ride back to Laurel; and repeatedly in Jackson, after he was transferred to the Hinds County jail.

In McGee's version, he was minding his own business in Hattiesburg, about to head for the bus station to return to Laurel, when "two officers run up and grabbed me. I turned around and said, 'What you all want?', and they said, 'What's your name?', and by the time I got

'Willie' out, he hit me. Mr. Hugh Herring hit me in the face there on the street, and he said, 'You done ravished a white woman in Laurel,' and he said, 'You son of a bitch, we gonna break you negroes up that gone in the army from coming back here and raping White women.' And I said, 'I ain't been in no army,' and he took me back—"

"Willie, we want you to tell what happened in the automobile that you rode in to Laurel," Poole said.

"Well, they got me. . . . You mean on the way from Hattiesburg up here to Laurel?"

"Yes."

"They taken me out of the jail and started on the way up here with me, and just as we got in the heart of town, Mr. Wayne told me, 'If you know what's good for you, there's two roads leading out of here. One leads to Jackson and one leads to Laurel, and the White people in Laurel would be mighty glad to get ahold of you. Fact of the business, all they want is to get their hands on you. [I]f you know what's good for you, you better tell me you done it, so I can take you on to Jackson.' And I said, 'I didn't do it.'"

McGee said that, while they beat him, the officers mentioned Howard Wash, the 1942 lynching victim. "Were you actually in fear of being lynched?" Poole said.

"Yes, sir."

"Willie, did they inform you of any rights you had to have a lawyer?"

"They ain't told me nothing, but just kept punching and hitting me in the face and in the side."

McGee said he was beaten repeatedly with a "slapjack"—"Every time I looked around it was a lick"—but that it was the lynching threat that finally broke his will. "[T]hat's when I told him I did it," he said. "[T]hen he said, 'Now, will you tell the sheriff the same thing when you get up there?' If you don't . . . he said, 'Nigger, it will be too bad for you.'"

———

After McGee stepped down, the state started calling witnesses back to contradict his story. One after another, they denied abusing him.

"I was so kind and courteous to that negro that I even gave him ciga-rettes every time I went there," said Albert Easterling, the man who took down McGee's written confession at the Hinds County jail. "I'll tell you, here's what you've got here. He is a smart negro, he writes as pretty a hand as you do, and I imagine he has been instructed by somebody to tell you these lies."

Later, McGee was put on the stand once more, again with the jury absent. When asked about the written confession, which he admitted to signing, he told Deavours that he did so only after two weeks of ad-ditional beatings and confinement in a "hot box," which he described as a cell "where they put you and sweat you nearly 'bout to death."

As he put it further along in the questioning, "[Y]ou stay in that hot box, you sign anything."

Collins supported the law officers on both the oral and written con-fessions, saying of McGee's testimony, "I believe this is just a prefab-ricated story and I don't believe a word of it." The written confession was read into the record.

Late in the day on Saturday, the whole trial began to go off the rails. On pages 909–910 of the transcript, it appears to come to an abrupt halt before it's officially over. There's a routine exchange be-tween London and Collins, followed by boilerplate language from the court reporter, followed by . . . nothing.

What happened? What happened was that Poole and London be-came frightened for their lives and fled the courtroom—and Lau-rel—before delivering their closing arguments. Years later, Poole told Spivak that he was tipped off on Saturday afternoon by a highway pa-trolman. "[He] came up to me and said, 'Poole, I just want to tell you that a group of fellows over there are after you. Be on your toes. Just watch out. They're not so much—they're not after London so much as you. So watch yourself.'"

Poole was aware of the story that Troy Hawkins had brought a pistol into the courtroom at the second trial. During a recess, he went back to his hotel, stretched out on his bed, and thought about his predicament.

"[I] looked over the situation and realized what happened to Dixon," he told Spivak. "What a situation they were in, and then a group of fellows after me. They're a pretty vicious crowd down there. No friends. I got scared. We go back, report all these facts to the judge. We tell the judge we're not going to argue to the jury."

Poole asked the sheriff for a safe escort as he got ready to leave Laurel, but he refused. The sheriff did, however, show Poole and London a back exit from the courthouse, via the catwalk. And with that, the boys from Jackson exercised their last and best strategic maneuver: They jumped in their car and got the hell out of town.

eight

A RUMPUS OF REDS

When McGee's third trial ended—with another death sen- tence—he was taken back to the Hinds County jail for a sec- ond long period of limbo. The first execution date, April 9, 1948, was stayed when Poole and London filed notice that they would appeal to the Mississippi Supreme Court. But that appeal wasn't submitted for another eleven months.

There were differences between this lull and the one that followed McGee's second trial in 1946. Now that McGee had testified in circuit court, his days as a man of silence were over. He started sending let- ters to CRC officials in New York, who released them for use in the *Daily Worker* and in CRC press releases and fund-raising letters.

Dozens of these letters survive in the CRC's archived papers. Probably because the jailers inspected them before they went out, their content often consisted of simple expressions of gratitude. Many are undated. The first with a clear time stamp is from April 20, 1948. It was addressed to Joseph Cadden, a CRC staffer who had sent McGee a letter and a small amount of money.

"I dont No hardly what to say," McGee wrote. "[F]or one thing I do really aprechate it and I prays that some day to meet some of the many friends that have been so nice to me. . . . [I] do believe from the depths of my heart that you all are doing your best for me your kind- ness shall never be forgotten."

Before long, though, Willie and Bessie both started sounding wor- ried. The CRC had brought Bessie up to New York after the third trial to give speeches about her son, the case, and the CRC, but after she got back to Laurel she stopped hearing from them.

In a June 1948 letter to Abraham Isserman, she wrote, "My Dear Counsel. . . . This leave me not feeling well at all. I been sick ever since

I left from up there. I am sorry I did not get to see you before I left to come home, but I do want you to write me at once and let me know what about Willie's trial. . . . Will you please don't stop working for Willie. He ask me to writ you all and tell you all to do all you all can for him, so I will close looking to hear from you soon."

Isserman wrote back, telling her the appeal was under way, but the McGees weren't mollified. In a letter written in August, Willie expressed two worries: Some of his mail was being withheld by the jailers, and he was in the dark about what his lawyers were doing, because they never came by.

"[I] wont to see my lawyer and i can't get them to come to see me," he said. "[T]hey been to see me one time since i been back over here. would you please write them and have them to come to see me." Just over a month later, nothing had changed, and he became insistent: "I want you all to have *My Lawyers to come over here*. . . . I have sent for them and cant get no results at all."

The CRC hadn't abandoned McGee. As Isserman said, Poole was working on the state appeal, which didn't require the defendant's input since it didn't involve trial-court preparation. Poole checked in with Isserman in late April, updating him about the appeal and a side development: He and London had decided to sue the *Jackson Daily News* for libel.

On March 10, 1948, the paper had run an editorial thrashing them both for representing McGee. Called "One Defense Cut Off," the item was primarily a diatribe about an accused black murderer named Arthur Moore, a sixteen-year-old who had reportedly confessed to killing an insurance collector named J. L. Dean. With an eye on the third McGee trial, which had wrapped up on March 6, the editorial complained that, no doubt, Moore would be the beneficiary of similar interference from up north. "It is now quite in order for the National Association for the Protection of Colored People and the Civil Rights Congress to hire some lousy and conscienceless lawyers to defend this red-handed murderer, as they are now doing in the Willie McGee case in Laurel," it said.

"Undoubtedly," Poole told Isserman, "you can well understand the effect of such an editorial, in view of the prejudice of the South on racial matters." Soon he filed a $100,000 suit in the federal district court in Jackson. It would prove to have serious consequences down the road.

———

The CRC had problems of its own, including politically motivated legal attacks against its leadership, which grew out of HUAC's 1947 report labeling the group a Communist front. In April 1948, CRC chairman George Marshall was found guilty of contempt of Congress for refusing to provide HUAC with records from one of the CRC's precursor groups, the National Federation for Constitutional Liberties. A federal judge in Washington, D.C., later sentenced him to three months in jail.

Isserman had his hands full too. In addition to the McGee case, he was about to become embroiled in a huge federal trial involving officials of the Communist Party USA. In July 1948, at the federal district court in Manhattan's Foley Square, prosecutors indicted twelve top-tier party leaders under the Smith Act, a measure from 1940 that made it unlawful to advocate forceful overthrow of the U.S. government. The indictments were short on specifics, but federal officials promised to unravel a sprawling conspiracy by men dedicated to "destroying the Government of the United States by force and violence."

Unlike the McGee case, the Smith Act trial was a national story from the moment it began, with a July 20 roundup at the Communist Party offices on East Twelfth Street in New York. "Six FBI men walked quietly into . . . the ninth floor of Communist headquarters," the *Times* reported in a front-page piece. "[The agents] showed their badges and merely said, 'You are under arrest.'"

Among the six were William Z. Foster, chairman of the Communist Party USA and a grand old man of American radicalism; general secretary Eugene Dennis; Jack Stachel, a national board member of the party; and John Williamson, also a board member. Others were arrested in the next few days, including *Daily Worker* editor John Gates and Gus Hall, the party chairman in Ohio. Southerners undoubtedly noticed that two of the twelve defendants were black: New York City councilman Benjamin Davis and national board member Henry Winston. To them, this supported the view—frequently voiced by commentators in the South—that calls for civil rights were nothing more than the leading edge of a Communist plot.

The CRC put up $35,000 in bail for the twelve, and CRC- and party-affiliated attorneys were involved in their defense from then on. Abraham Unger, whose firm, Unger and Friedman, later defended the *Daily Worker* in the libel case brought by Mrs. Hawkins, represented the original six during their indictment on the 20th. Isserman became part of a defense team that included attorneys Harry Sacher, George W. Crockett Jr., Richard Gladstein, and Louis McCabe. The trial didn't get fully under way until March 1949, but everybody could see that it was a case with immense stakes, whether one sympathized with the Communists or not.

"The recent indictment . . . confronts us with a problem whose perplexity is matched only by its gravity," Columbia University history professor Henry Steele Commager wrote in the *Times*. "For it involves far more than the fate of the Communist party alone. . . . It involves the problem of dissent and nonconformity in our politics. It involves the preservation of constitutional rights of free speech, press and petition, and of political organization by minority groups." Commager didn't doubt that American Communists desired revolutionary change—"If they deny this charge, they are self-confessed frauds"—but he opposed the case on constitutional grounds. The twelve were being pursued for advocating a set of ideas. They hadn't been caught in a concrete plot to overthrow the government. But under the Smith Act, their ideas were the plot.

For Communists, CRC members, and civil libertarians, the indictments seemed like a blatant political move by the Truman administration, designed to discredit anybody on the left—including Henry Wallace and his running mate, Idaho senator Glen H. Taylor—who stood in the way of his supposed desire to start a war with the Soviet Union. In a press release, the National Committee of the Communist Party went characteristically overboard, calling the charges an "American version of the Reichstag Fire."

"Terrified of the growing support for the Wallace-Taylor ticket," the statement said, "the Democratic high command is seeking to brand the new party as 'criminal' because among the opponents of Wall Street's two old parties and their candidates are the Communists, who also join with all other progressives in supporting the new people's anti-war party."

That summer, Republicans were feeling giddy about the Thurmond and Wallace insurgencies, because they seemed to ensure a victory in November by their candidate, Thomas Dewey. It didn't pan out, so it's easy to forget how bad it looked for Truman at the time—and for how long. The *Chicago Daily Tribune* ("DEWEY DEFEATS TRUMAN") wasn't the only organization to miss the call. Pollsters blew it too, as did the *Washington Post* and *New York Times*. Two days before the election in November, a front-page *Times* story stated that Dewey would win easily, 345 electoral votes to 105.

On Election Day, there was enough doubt about Dewey—not to mention Thurmond and Wallace—to make voters return to a familiar face. The final count was 303 electoral votes for Truman, 189 for Dewey, 39 for Thurmond, and none for Wallace. Wallace had hoped to do much better; there had been talk of him attracting between 3 and 5 million votes. He got 1.15 million, far short of Truman's 24-million-plus. And though Wallace was on the ballot in three times as many states as Thurmond, who ran a regional candidacy based on resistance to civil rights legislation, Thurmond beat him in total vote count by more than 18,000.

What explained the weak showing? Communism, as much as anything. Wallace wasn't a Communist—he saw himself as the defender of what was left of New Deal liberalism—but his campaign attracted enthusiastic backing from Communist Party members like Foster and Dennis, as well as from controversial party supporters like Paul Robeson.

This uneasy relationship had been building for a while. There wasn't a Communist presidential candidate in 1948, so people on the far left needed somewhere to go. At the 1947 May Day parade in New

York, party members, enthralled with a recent Wallace speech critical of the Truman Doctrine, marched along beneath a fifty-foot-tall image of their new mainstream hero, complete with a huge text block of his words.

Wallace knew that Communist support would hurt more than it helped, and while he publicly denounced Red-baiting by the Truman administration, he tried to maintain safe separation. As his biographers John C. Culver and John Hyde point out, he made attempts to "distance himself from U.S. Communist Party members, saying the few he had met 'sounded kind of pathetic, like poor, lonesome souls.'" Communists also tried to convey that their dalliance with Wallace had limits. Foster declared in one speech that Wallace's Progressive Party, with its deluded belief that capitalism could somehow be saved, "is in no sense a Communist Party . . . we Communists have many points of difference with it and we do not hesitate to express them."

Still, it didn't help that Wallace supporters often made extreme statements. In an April 1948 speech at Columbia, the novelist Howard Fast—later the author of *Spartacus*, and both a Wallace man and a Communist Party member—denounced Truman and his crew as "obscene, hideous people who can sign a death warrant that will murder 50,000,000 people without a thought." Foster, testifying before a Senate Judiciary subcommittee in May, said that in any war between the United States and the Soviet Union, he could not fight against the U.S.S.R.

The result in some quarters was a rugged referendum on whether Wallace—who had been an extremely capable public servant in his prime—was an idiot, a paid agent of Stalin, or both. In his 1948 book, *Henry Wallace: The Man and the Myth*, literary critic Dwight Macdonald wrote that Wallace's apologies for Stalinism came about because "a large power-mass like the Soviet Union exercises a tremendous gravitational pull on an erratic comet like Henry Wallace. In the past year, this pull has become so powerful—or the resistance has been so weakened—that Wallace's Comet appears to have become a satellite of the larger body."

Wallace never got involved in the McGee case—he left public life before it took off—but many of his followers did, providing Progressive Party support for McGee in 1950 and 1951 that was just as important as his Communist Party backing. Bella Abzug's partner during the 1951 appeals process was John M. Coe, a former state senator and highly experienced lawyer based in Pensacola, Florida, who had volunteered to help coordinate Wallace's Florida campaign. Sidney Ordower, a Chicagoan who came to Mississippi in 1950 as part of a delegation seeking a gubernatorial pardon for McGee, ran for the U.S. House of Representatives as a Wallace man in Illinois.

These people weren't Communists, but they weren't Truman Democrats either. They were hard-left liberals whose views on issues like civil rights put them far ahead of the curve in 1948. Doomed though Wallace was as a candidate, he inspired them and thousands of others, not least by his quixotic decision to take his campaign into the hostile territory of the South in the summer of 1948.

Wallace had no business campaigning in the South—he won only 225 votes in Mississippi and 154 in South Carolina—but he wanted to make a statement. So, in late August and early September, he scheduled a seven-state tour of Virginia, North Carolina, Alabama, Mississippi, Louisiana, Arkansas, and Tennessee, with all his appearances scheduled to take place before desegregated audiences, in defiance of local custom and law.

There was trouble at many of his stops. Prior to a Wallace rally in Durham, North Carolina, a scuffle broke out in the crowd and one Wallace supporter was stabbed (though not fatally) on his arms and back. During a four-town speaking tour the next day, Wallace was pelted with eggs, tomatoes, peach pits, and cries of "Hey, Communist" and "Hey, nigger lover." In Hickory, North Carolina, the *New York Times* reported, "The barrage was so heavy that for the first time Mr. Wallace quit his talk abruptly and paraphrased a passage from Scripture for his tormentors.

" 'As Jesus Christ told his disciples,' he said, 'when you enter a town that will not hear you willingly, then shake the dust of that town from your feet and go elsewhere. . . .' "

By the time Wallace got to Mississippi, violence seemed likely, but it didn't happen, despite provocative editorials in local newspapers. The *Jackson Daily News* warned that Wallace's only purpose was to "spread the doctrine of Communism and promote racial antagonism and strife. Therefore, by all the principles and traditions the South holds dear, Henry Wallace is a public enemy."

Neither Governor Wright nor Wallace seemed eager for trouble. Wallace stopped in Jackson only long enough to file a slate of electors and criticize Wright in a radio speech, saying he substituted "prejudice for reason" on racial matters. Wright provided him with a highway-patrol escort to his most important appearance during this leg of the trip: the Mississippi River town of Vicksburg, about as Deep South as it got. Vicksburg had been the target of the greatest siege campaign of the Civil War, which ended when General Ulysses S. Grant conquered it on July 4, 1863. Until 1945, the town ignored the Fourth of July.

Unexpectedly, not a single egg, fist, or peach pit was thrown, partly because Wright had publicly asked Mississippians to treat Wallace with respect. Wallace spoke outside the Vicksburg courthouse to an unsegregated crowd of 200. Before he took the mike, twenty-nine-year-old folk singer Pete Seeger—who accompanied Wallace during his Southern tour—suggested that everybody join together and sing a song.

"A sullen looking youth snapped out, 'Dixie,'" a *Washington Post* reporter wrote. "To his astonishment, Seeger went into Dixie. He knew every word of it, and played and sang it with gusto.

"The would-be heckler was furious, and began muttering. Police Chief [L. C.] Hicks moved alongside and told him to sit down and keep quiet. He did."

———

In the McGee case, the other crucial development in the summer of 1948 was the emergence of William L. Patterson as the head of the CRC. Patterson was an African-American lawyer and Communist who, by then, had already put in more than twenty years as an organizer, civil rights theoretician, and student of Marxist-Leninist theory and tactics, which he learned during lengthy stays in Russia that took place from 1927 to 1930 and again from 1934 to 1937. While there, he married a Russian woman with whom he had two daughters, but his Russian family couldn't come with him when he returned to the United States in 1937. Patterson took over the CRC at fifty-seven, after George Marshall's imprisonment, moving to New York from Chicago in July and bringing a level of energy and drive that altered the CRC's trajectory. His credo was that action in courtrooms had to be matched by mass political protests, a tactic he'd learned through his involvement with the two most famous left-wing causes of the 1920s and 1930s: the murder trial of Sacco and Vanzetti and the capital rape trials of the Scottsboro Boys. As Patterson explained in his 1971 autobiography, *The Man Who Cried Genocide*, his experiences working on these and other cases left him with little faith in the American legal system's ability to provide justice to politically unpopular or racially oppressed defendants. The outcomes were rigged, he wrote, especially in the South, where it was futile for "a Black American to rely solely on U.S. laws—administered and manipulated by racists— as liberating instruments."

This didn't mean abandoning the law as a tool. After all, much of what the CRC did involved criminal-defense work. But it did mean that public protest was as important as courtroom tactics. Writing about the CRC's various causes during the postwar years—it was active in several legal fights on behalf of allegedly railroaded black defendants, as was the NAACP—Patterson said, "It was proved beyond doubt that mass indignation and protest action had to be mobilized in overwhelming degree to make any dent at all in the solid front of blind bigotry. Such demonstrations do not guarantee a people's justice, but without them the hope is slim indeed."

Patterson's path to the helm of the CRC had been long, colorful, and complicated. As he recounted in *The Man Who Cried Genocide*, he was the son of a former slave, Mary Galt, who was born on a Virginia plantation in 1850, and whose mother was the offspring of the white plantation owner and a slave with whom he sired three children.

Before the Civil War started, the owner sent his "Black family" west to San Francisco, when Mary was ten. She grew up, married a man who later died, and sometime in the late 1880s married James

Edward Patterson, a native of the British West Indies who had been a seaman. William Patterson wasn't certain about his birth date—he believed it was August 27, 1891—nor did he know his father well. James became a Seventh-day Adventist, going away frequently on missionary trips in other countries.

These experiences—along with physical abuse he suffered at his father's hands—left Patterson bitter against both his father and religion. In a biographical statement written for Communist Party officials in 1939, which the FBI later obtained for the 5,000-page file it kept on Patterson, he wrote, "My early family life was one of poverty. My father was a fanatical [S]eventh Day Adventist. He had been a steward on the Pacific Mail Steamship lines but [quit] and gave everything he had to the church. . . . The religious atmosphere was tense, training strict."

Patterson graduated from high school in 1911, when he was twenty years old, enrolled at Berkeley, dropped out, worked for a while, and in 1915 started taking law classes at the University of California, San Francisco. He got his first exposure to Marxism when he walked into a Bay Area bookstore that sold publications like the *Masses* and the *Messenger*. The ideas clicked, and for the rest of his life Patterson never lost faith that Communism was the way out for black Americans, a liberating force for a people who, he believed, had been subjected to organized genocide. In a speech written a few months after the end of World War II, he said, "What the Jew is to Germany, the Negro is to Fascist-minded Americans. The Soviet Union is the friend of all oppressed people. We must seek great changes in the system we now have. I speak as a Communist and I [say] that my party will be in the forefront of the battle."

Patterson finished law school at twenty-seven and explored the idea of moving to Liberia, the West African nation colonized in the nineteenth century by former American slaves. He got as far as England before changing his mind and coming back, this time settling in New York. He found a room in Harlem, where he met his first wife, Minnie Summer, and Eslanda Cardozo Goode, who would later marry Paul Robeson. Through Summer, Patterson met Robeson in 1920, when Robeson was still studying law at Columbia.

By then, Robeson was already on a rapid rise to fame. At Rutgers, where he graduated in 1919, he was a four-sport athlete and a first-team All-American in football. He also sang, acted, debated, and excelled academically—he was elected to Phi Beta Kappa as a junior, delivered his class's commencement speech, and wrote a senior thesis called "The Fourteenth Amendment, the Sleeping Giant of the American Constitution," which, according to his biographer Martin Bauml Duberman, "proceeded to interpret it in a way that prefigured the eventual use of that amendment as a civil-rights weapon."

Patterson was further along the path to radicalism than Robeson, who spent most of the 1920s and 1930s performing in such Broadway and Hollywood productions as *The Emperor Jones*, *Show Boat*, and *Othello*. Robeson didn't become openly political until the late 1930s, when he supported the anti-Fascist side during the Spanish Civil War.

For Patterson, the catalyst was the case of Nicola Sacco and Bartolomeo Vanzetti, Italian-born workers and anarchists who were sentenced to death in 1921 after being convicted of killing two payroll escorts, Alessandro Berardelli and Frederick Parmenter, during an armed robbery in South Braintree, Massachusetts. The debate about their guilt or innocence—which goes on still—was hopelessly tangled up with their politics. They were members of the Galleanists, an Italian-American anarchist group whose followers were suspected in a string of bombings that occurred after the end of World War I. In June 1919, anarchists were accused of setting off bombs in eight U.S. cities, including one at the Washington, D.C., home of Attorney General A. Mitchell Palmer. The Palmer device went off prematurely, killing the bomber and sending body parts flying across a residential block of R Street in Northwest Washington. Palmer's neighbor, Assistant Secretary of the Navy Franklin D. Roosevelt, found human remains on his steps the next morning.

Such episodes spurred a massive federal crackdown on suspected anarchists and Communists that became known as the Palmer Raids. In November 1919, Justice Department agents, armed with deportation warrants, rounded up hundreds of people in cities all over the country, often basing their arrests on extremely flimsy evidence. In

December, nearly 250 people with suspected anarchist, Socialist, or Communist ties were shipped to the Soviet Union on an old troop transport ship called the *Buford*, which was popularly known as "the Soviet Ark." By early 1920, the raids had led to the arrest of some 10,000 suspects and the creation of a new General Intelligence Division in the Justice Department. The man in charge of collecting names was J. Edgar Hoover, then just twenty-four.

In the eyes of their supporters, Sacco and Vanzetti faced execution only because they held unpopular views and were foreign born. Many people at the time—not all of them radicals—believed that the trial judge, Webster Thayer, was so clearly biased that a retrial should have been automatic. Among those supporting a second look were establishment fixtures like Harvard Law School professor (and future Supreme Court justice) Felix Frankfurter, who wrote an influential 1927 article about the case in the *Atlantic Monthly*. Frankfurter dissected a 25,000-word opinion by Thayer—in which Thayer denied Sacco and Vanzetti a retrial based on new evidence—calling it "a farrago of misquotations, misrepresentations, suppressions, and mutilations."

Patterson came to the case late, participating in public protests that occurred on the eve of the execution. On August 22, 1927, he was arrested during a march in front of the Massachusetts statehouse, an incident that was described later in Upton Sinclair's *Boston*, a "documentary novel" about the case published in 1928.

"There was John Dos Passos, faithful son of Harvard," Sinclair wrote, ". . . and William Patterson, a Negro lawyer from New York, running the greatest risk of any of them, with his black face not to be disguised. Just up Beacon Street was the Shaw Monument, with figures in perennial bronze, of unmistakable Negro boys in uniform, led by a young Boston blue-blood on horseback; no doubt Patterson had looked at this, and drawn courage from it."

Patterson was chased by a mounted trooper and arrested by a policeman who said, "Well, this is the first time I ever see a nigger bastard that was a communist." For him, the experience was a one-way push into a life of protest battles, dangerous dissent, and front-line involvement in numerous historic fights over civil rights and civil liberties.

"I had come back to New York as from a university—but a people's university," he wrote of his Boston baptism. "I would follow another road of struggle. My law career had come to an end."

———

The cause that really shaped Patterson was Scottsboro, a multi-defendant interracial rape case in rural Alabama that became a world-wide news story starting in 1931. He wasn't on the margins that time. During the early years of this historic legal battle, which dragged on through most of the 1930s and into the 1940s, Patterson was in charge of a group called International Labor Defense (ILD), a forerunner of the CRC. The ILD organized much of the Scottsboro defense effort, which was aimed at saving the lives of a group of young African-American males who faced execution on a dubious rape charge.

All the tactics employed in Scottsboro—inside courtrooms, on the streets, and in news media—would be used again by Patterson during the later years of the McGee case, and it's easy to see why: In Scotts-boro, ultimately, they worked. Against the odds, and with significant effort from people who had no connection to (or affection for) the ILD, all of the Scottsboro Boys were saved from death. But there were im-portant differences between the two cases, and as McGee's defenders would learn, it didn't always work to apply the same tactics, espe-cially during the anti-Communist fervor of the Cold War.

The Scottsboro story began on March 25, 1931, when nine men and boys—ranging in age from thirteen to twenty—were arrested after hopping a Chattanooga-to-Memphis freight train that dipped south out of Tennessee on its way west. In the northeastern Alabama town of Stevenson that afternoon, a station master was startled by the ap-pearance of several white hobos who said they'd been thrown off the train after losing a fight with a "bunch of negroes."

The station master called ahead to the town of Scottsboro, but the train had already passed through. By the time it reached Paint Rock, twenty miles to the west, law enforcement officials had been noti-fied and a posse was waiting. At first, the nine were suspected only of vagrancy and assault, but the stakes changed with the discovery that two female freight-hoppers were also on board: young white women in overalls and caps named Victoria Price and Ruby Bates. Price told a deputy sheriff they'd been gang-raped by the blacks. The men were immediately taken to jail in Scottsboro, the county seat, where a lynch mob started to form once word got around. Alabama's governor dispatched twenty-five National Guardsmen, but the night's chilly weather was probably more of a factor in the crowd's decision to break up and go home.

Just as in the first McGee trial, the indictments happened fast, and the suspects were assigned second-rate lawyers. The cases were split up, with the first two defendants, Clarence Norris and Charlie Weems, going before a jury together on April 6. The atmosphere at the Jackson County Courthouse was predictably tense. Inside, the courtroom was packed with locals who wanted to see guilty verdicts and death sentences come quickly. Outside, thousands of people had gathered to take in the show, and by necessity there were armed troops everywhere.

Norris and Weems were represented by an elderly local named Milo C. Moody and a Chattanooga, Tennessee, lawyer, Stephen R. Roddy, who appeared to be drunk in court. The state's star witness was Victoria Price, who testified that she and Bates were in an open gondola car with seven white men when a dozen blacks leaped over the side and beat up the whites, ejecting all but one. Price said two of the intruders were waving pistols and that they all had knives. She claimed that Norris came up to her and said, "Are you going to put out?" After that, she said, six men raped her.

As historian Dan T. Carter explained in his 1969 book, *Scottsboro*—a classic history of the case—Price's testimony was controversial from the start. Two doctors testified who had examined the women within ninety minutes of the alleged rape. Dr. R. R. Bridges said that, based on semen samples he'd taken, it appeared that both women had had intercourse sometime prior to his examination, but he couldn't say when, and he said there was no sign of genital bruising or tearing that would indicate sexual assault. "She was not lacerated at all," he said of Price. "She was not bloody, neither was the other girl." A second doctor, Marvin Lynch, concurred: "There was nothing to indicate any violence about the vagina."

Bates testified the next day, agreeing with Price but giving different details. "Victoria gave a colorful description of a desperate struggle with guns blazing, a pistol-whipping, and ending with the white boys leaving in an effort to save their lives," Carter wrote, while Bates described only verbal arguments and a minor scuffle.

Even before the first-trial jury had left the courtroom, the second trial began—this time, of a defendant who would become the best-known Scottsboro Boy, eighteen-year-old Haywood Patterson. Price testified again, as did Bates. Right after Bates stepped down in the Patterson case, the judge, Alfred E. Hawkins, was told that the jury in the Norris and Weems trial had reached a verdict. The Patterson jury was taken into a side room while the decision was read: guilty, with punishment fixed at death. Outside, the crowd greeted the news with a cheer, and it was obvious that the Patterson jury had heard the noise. This would come up when the case was appealed, but, for the moment, the verdicts just kept coming. Patterson was found guilty the next day, April 8. Five other defendants—Ozie Powell, Olen Montgomery, Eugene Williams, Andrew Wright, and Willie Roberson—were convicted on the 9th. A mistrial was declared in the case of Leroy Wright, who was only thirteen, because the jurors couldn't decide whether his youth warranted a sentence of life in prison instead of death.

Judge Hawkins sentenced the eight men to die by electrocution at Montgomery's Kilby Prison on July 10, but the case would go on much longer than that. As the first trials drew to a close, both the ILD and the Communist Party made public statements denouncing the proceedings as a sham, and letting Hawkins know that capable reinforcements were on the way to save the defendants' lives.

———

After the first trials, the ILD entered into a struggle for control of the cases with the NAACP, which, though slow in responding to the arrests, indicated a strong desire to represent the Scottsboro nine going forward. The ILD prevailed, partly through old-fashioned persistence. Organization lawyers hurried south to line up local legal help, interview the defendants in jail, and nail down the cooperation of their parents.

But the ILD sometimes played dirty, and the NAACP's mistrust of Communist legal-defense groups started with Scottsboro. On April 15, 1931, the *Daily Worker* went on the attack, claiming that the NAACP's sluggish reaction time proved that its leaders were "traitors to the Negro masses and betrayers of the Negro liberation struggle."

In late 1932, after the Alabama Supreme Court upheld the first-trial verdicts, the U.S. Supreme Court agreed to hear arguments in the case. In *Powell v. Alabama*, a landmark decision issued on November 7, the Court ruled that the defendants had been denied adequate representation, because the trial was rushed and unfair. "It is perfectly apparent that the proceedings from beginning to end took place in an atmosphere of tense, hostile and excited pubic sentiment," the opinion said. "During the entire time, the defendants were closely confined or were under military guard." Appointment of counsel happened so close to the time of the trial, the Court added, that it amounted to "denial of effective and substantial aid in that regard."

As preparations got under way for new trials, the responsibility for picking a new lawyer fell to Patterson, who had taken over as leader of the ILD in September 1932. He hired a New Yorker named Samuel Leibowitz, a top defense specialist who was known for winning murder cases. Because of his clout and independent means, Leibowitz was able to take the case and keep control of it, something that wouldn't be possible for Bella Abzug when she represented McGee. He let the ILD know he was in charge, and that he would quit if their public statements and protest actions caused him any problems. With some exceptions, he got his way.

Not surprisingly, the ILD's presence—and Leibowitz himself—angered people in Alabama, who didn't like the idea of Northerners, Communists, or Jews coming in to interfere. During Leibowitz's first courtroom defense—of Haywood Patterson in April 1933—his arguments so antagonized whites in the town of Decatur, that when Patterson was put on trial a second time, rumors started spreading about a lynch mob. National Guardsmen had infiltrated a meeting where some 200 men talked about killing the defendants and running Leibowitz out of town. The new trial judge, James E. Horton, stopped the trial to deliver an angry speech about mob action.

"Men who would join in anything that would cause the death of these Negroes not only are murderers, but cowardly murderers," he said. "The soldiers and the Sheriff's men are expected to defend these prisoners with their lives. Any man who defies them may expect to forfeit his life."

Leibowitz had advantages that McGee lawyers like Pyles and Poole later lacked. One was Judge Horton, who put his career on the line to run a fair courtroom. Another was time: Almost five months passed between the U.S. Supreme Court's reversal and the second trial, giving Leibowitz ample opportunity to hunt for new witnesses.

He found some, and he used them to dramatic effect. Leibowitz took dead aim at the credibility of Victoria Price, attempting to prove that she'd fabricated the rape story because she was worried about getting arrested for vagrancy. One new witness, a hobo named Lester Carter, said he and Ruby Bates had had sex two nights before the alleged rape, near a vagrants' camp outside Huntsville, Alabama. A few feet away from them, he said, amid a tangle of honeysuckle bushes, Price was doing the same thing with a man named Jack Tiller. As Leibowitz explained to the jury, Price and Tiller had a past—they'd been arrested in Huntsville in January 1931 on an adultery charge.

Leibowitz's biggest surprise was the appearance of Bates, this time as a defense witness. Bates recanted her previous testimony, saying she hadn't been raped and hadn't seen a rape. During her time on the stand, Price was brought in to identify her, visibly angry that Bates was changing her story.

Bates's testimony had elements that backfired, however, thanks to clumsy handling by the ILD. She said that, since her disappearance from Alabama in late February 1933, she'd been in New York, where she'd experienced a religious conversion with help from a pastor. Prosecutors said the ILD had arranged her trip north and had bought expensive new clothes for her, which left the jury wondering if she'd been bought off.

During cross-examination and closing arguments, prosecutors also insinuated that Bates was a Communist dupe. Wade Wright, a county attorney, called Lester Carter "Mr. Carterinsky." Pointing at the defense table, where Leibowitz sat with an ILD attorney named Brodsky, he urged the jury to "show them that Alabama justice cannot be bought and sold with Jew money from New York." The jury complied. On April 9, Patterson was found guilty a second time and sentenced to death.

There would be other ILD missteps: The most serious came in October 1934, when two ILD attorneys were caught taking part in a scheme to bribe Price to change her testimony. For all his skill and preparation, Leibowitz never won a jury verdict in the Scottsboro cases, and Price never stopped insisting that she'd been raped, so there was no neat resolution. Patterson was tried a third time, in November, after Judge Horton shocked everybody by setting aside his conviction, based on his belief that the evidence didn't justify a guilty verdict. Horton was replaced by a different judge, and Patterson was found guilty a third time. But Leibowitz set the stage for another appeal, focusing on the same issue that Pyles and Poole would later raise in the second and third McGee trials: race-based jury exclusion.

The details were similar to what Poole would present in Laurel fifteen years later. During the trial before Judge Horton, Leibowitz had questioned county officials about why there were never any black jurors. He resumed this interrogation before the new judge, who ordered that the jury lists from Jackson County be brought in. Officials started reading names into the record, calling out the race of potential jurors as they went. For several hours, every name was white. Late in the day, the Jackson County circuit clerk read out the name of Hugh Sanford, who was black.

So? Leibowitz suspected that Sanford's name had been added after the lists were first created. He brought in a handwriting expert who said that most or all of the names of black jurors had been inked in after the fact. The judge denied a motion to quash the jury, but Leibowitz had a winning issue for appeal. He argued the case himself before the U.S. Supreme Court in February 1935, a proceeding at which the justices took the unusual step of examining the physical evidence themselves.

On April 1, in *Norris v. Alabama*, the Court reversed guilty verdicts for Haywood Patterson and Clarence Norris on the grounds of jury exclusion. Even then, the Scottsboro mess persisted. There were more trials and more guilty verdicts, but by 1937, a combination of time, fatigue, and growing doubt saved the defendants' lives. Four were freed in July. The other five were given long sentences and sent off to prison. Between 1944 and 1947, everybody but Patterson was released, though Andrew Wright wound up back in jail for parole violations. Patterson made the news again in July 1948, when he successfully escaped from Kilby Prison. He disappeared, but he would be heard from again.

———

Poole and London presented McGee's third state appeal in late January 1949, focusing on jury exclusion, venue, McGee's testimony about his coerced confession, the hurry-up trial pace set by Judge Collins, and the consent argument, which they handled more carefully than Pyles had. Mrs. Hawkins, they pointed out, had said herself that she stopped struggling in order to protect the lives of her children. It was a selfless sacrifice. But it still constituted consent, because the court had ruled in a previous case that a rape victim had to keep struggling until the act was consummated.

The judges ruled on April 11, dismissing all five claims and heaping special scorn on the consent argument. "Absence of resistance on account of fear caused by an assailant does not prevent [an] attack from being rape," they wrote.

Reading between the lines, they detected an even more offensive argument. "The implication of consent here implies a rendezvous between appellant and his victim," they said. "This cannot be true because in his statement to the officers . . . appellant said he stopped his truck and entered the home, when he saw a woman lying on the bed. . . . This revolting insinuation, in other words, finds no proof in support thereof, reflected by the record."

The judges' use of "rendezvous" shows that they thought Poole was implying that prearranged sex had occurred. But he didn't say that, as he explained in a follow-up appeal filed after the court's initial ruling. "[A]ppellant [argues] that the State failed to prove that the resistance persisted until the act was consummated—not that appellant and the prosecutrix had previously planned the act," he said. This distinction mattered, because it clarified something that got muddied as the years went by: Poole never claimed that McGee and Mrs. Hawkins had an affair. He left the case before that became part of the defense's story. Even so, more than any other lawyer, he would suffer professionally when backlash against this line of attack took shape in Mississippi.

The judges, unmoved, set a new death date: June 3, 1949. When the time arrived, the CRC asked the U.S. Supreme Court for a stay, a move they planned to follow with a formal request for full review of the case. But the Court denied the stay request on the afternoon of June 2— without comment—and in Laurel, preparations immediately began for carrying out the electrocution on schedule. McGee survived that day not because of meddling from Communists or Northern judges. He was spared through the efforts of John Poole, Alvin London, and a Mississippi Supreme Court judge named W. G. Roberds.

In one sense, what happened was a routine paperwork matter. By law, the state supreme court had to grant a stay once Poole's appeal was signed and filed. The hard part was finding a judge to deal with it. In his interview with Spivak, London maintained that the judges "made it their business not to be available" that afternoon. The execution was halted with under five hours to go. McGee even ate what was supposed to be his last meal.

June 2 was a Thursday. McGee was taken from Hinds County to Jones at 4 p.m., in the custody of Sheriff Steve Brogan. A *Laurel*

Leader-Call reporter, on hand to document McGee's final hours, heard him pronounce himself ready to die, saying, "I'm not afraid. I've made my peace with the Lord. I'm not afraid of anything man can do."

He was visited in the Laurel jail by Bessie, her sister, and three black ministers—tellingly, there was no mention of a wife being there. He ate at 5:30 p.m.: steak, fries, salad, and iced tea, which he'd requested to be "extra sweet." He spent the next hour and a half writing letters, including a thank you to Sheriff Brogan for treating him decently. "I hope to meet you in heaven," he said.

At 6 p.m., a "galvanized iron truck" containing the state's portable electric chair pulled up and parked outside the courthouse. The chair and its switchboard were set up in the second-floor courtroom. The state's executioner revved up the motor at around 8 p.m., testing to make sure the generator was ready to deliver its load. Though the executioner didn't know it yet, by that time the whole thing had already been called off. At around 8:30 p.m., McGee was on his way back to Jackson.

What happened? Poole found his judge. London said Poole learned that Roberds was out playing golf. He tracked him down on the course, hobbling over grass fairways, and got him to sign the papers on the spot. According to London—there's no other source for this— Roberds not only scribbled in his name but opined that he thought there was something fishy about the case.

"This was about six or seven o'clock in the evening," London said, "and the Judge said, 'Well, thank goodness you got here' or words to that effect and said, 'I never did believe this fellow was guilty any-how.' . . ."

Reportedly, Brogan declined to accept the stay order by tele-phone, so Poole had to race toward Laurel by car. The CRC quickly issued a dramatic press release ("EXECUTION OF FRAMED NEGRO VET HALTED BY LAST MINUTE ACTION") that said that Poole and an armed acquaintance had met Brogan on the highway, where he scanned the documents by headlight, releasing his prisoner once he'd read the order. McGee was back in the Hinds County jail by 10:30, visibly shaken and trembling. He told a reporter that "faith in God was the only thing that saved me."

———

McGee's U.S. Supreme Court appeal, filed on August 8, 1949, was submitted by two left-wing lawyers from New York, Samuel Rosenwein and Arthur G. Silverman. Rosenwein had been involved in the Hollywood Ten hearings in 1947, in which HUAC probed alleged Communist infiltration of the film industry. Silverman was a member of the National Lawyers Guild.

Their appeal opened with twelve pages of case recap, followed by five specific claims: that McGee's confession was coerced, violating the Fourteenth Amendment's guarantee of due process; that there was "not a scintilla of competent evidence" other than the controversial confession; that there had been systematic jury exclusion in the selection of the grand and trial juries; that local "prejudice, hostility, and hysteria" warranted a change of venue; and that McGee was denied effective assistance of counsel because the trial was rushed and his lawyers felt threatened. The appeal relied nearly as much on sociology and history as on case law, citing such works as Gunnar Myrdal's *An American Dilemma* (the Swedish economist's seminal 1944 study of the effects of racial prejudice and discrimination) and the Truman administration document *To Secure These Rights*.

Every one of the appeal's legal issues had come up in cases heard previously by the Court, including *Brown v. Mississippi*—a 1936 decision that reversed three Mississippi murder-case convictions that had relied on violently coerced confessions—*Powell v. Alabama, Patton v. Mississippi*, and *Norris v. Alabama*. Each of those cases was cited, with the exception of *Norris*, the Scottsboro case that involved jury exclusion. It's unclear why *Norris* was left out, but it may be because Poole had neglected a step that Leibowitz had seen to: introducing physical evidence to prove that tampering had occurred with the Jones County jury lists. In any event, Rosenwein and Silverman only

put forward the general idea that it was impossible to believe Mississippi officials had suddenly decided to allow black grand jurors without some kind of trickery in play.

The consent argument wasn't discussed—that was a state issue—
but the justices were made aware of it by their clerks, who dismissed
it. Rosenwein and Silverman instead emphasized McGee's ordeal after his arrest, appealing to common-sense skepticism about the state's
claim that he'd confessed freely. He hadn't been advised of his right
to an attorney, they pointed out. He was packed away for thirty days
in the Hinds County jail, lacking any contact with a friend or lawyer, while getting repeated visits from "at least a dozen state officials,
prosecutors, sheriffs, jailers, police officers," as well as from McGee's
former boss, Horace McRae, and Troy Hawkins, the husband of his
accuser.

"The only possible purpose for bringing the husband of the alleged victim to the petitioner was to frighten and intimidate him,"
the appeal said. Nonetheless, "the State's position appears to be that
the period of detention merely afforded the petitioner a quiet period
wherein he could freely meditate upon his past and confess his 'sins'
calmly and with good cheer."

To see the lie in that, they argued, all you had to do was look
at McGee before and after his incarceration. Before, he was "employed as the driver of a motor vehicle, apparently physically able
to carry on strenuous work." After, he was "incapacitated, in a state
of nervous collapse and fright bordering on dementia." Citing language from the Court's 1945 opinion in a case called *Screws v. United
States*, which concerned a Georgia prisoner who had been beaten to
death by a local sheriff, Rosenwein and Silverman tried to position
McGee as a man who was being murdered by the system—slowly
but surely.

"He has had the forms of a trial; in reality, he had had no trial at all.
As the late Justice Murphy stated: 'He has been deprived of the right
to life itself. That right belonged to him not because he was a Negro or
a member of any particular race or creed. That right was his because
he was an American citizen, because he was a human being.' "

"The late Justice Murphy" was Associate Justice Frank Murphy, a liberal jurist from Michigan. Citing his dissent in *Screws* was something of an emotional plea, because Murphy had died just three weeks before McGee's appeal was filed. But there was a logical point to it. In *Screws*, Murphy was the most passionate advocate for a position that, at the time, was out in front of where many federal judges were willing to go. Namely, that if a state failed to prosecute the kind of crime at the heart of *Screws*—a race-based murder committed by local officials acting under the authority of state government—the federal government had the right, and the obligation, to pursue justice using federal statutes.

The *Screws* case originated in southwest Georgia's Baker County. In January 1943, Sheriff M. Claude Screws arrested a young African-American man named Robert Hall on a trumped-up charge of stealing a car tire. Screws and two other lawmen, Frank Jones and Jim Bob Kelly, then beat him to death outside the county courthouse, with fists and an iron bar. The real motive for all this was a pistol belonging to Hall: Screws had confiscated it, and Hall had started legal proceedings to get it back.

A local grand jury failed to indict the men, so the U.S. Attorney General's office stepped in. The government charged Screws and his accomplices with violating Hall's civil rights, basing this on language from a Reconstruction-era statute that prohibited officials from impeding constitutionally protected rights "under color of any law," be it federal, state, or local. A jury found them guilty and they were sentenced to three years in prison. After a federal appeals court upheld, the state of Georgia filed an appeal with the U.S. Supreme Court, which agreed to hear the case.

The decision was complicated and it centered, in part, on the question of whether the Justice Department had overreached by bringing its indictment, in effect using an archaic federal law to bypass Congress and give the government the anti-lynching power over states that legislators had always refused to pass. Three justices, including Felix Frankfurter, said that it had. "The only issue is whether Georgia alone has the power and duty to punish," they wrote, "or whether this patently local crime can be made the basis of a federal prosecution." Murphy disagreed, writing that Screws had unquestionably "deprived Robert Hall of his life without due process."

Four judges, including Hugo Black and William O. Douglas, recognized the right of the federal government to intervene in such a case, but they voted to reverse this one on a technicality involving jury instructions. Today, *Screws* is cited as a precedent that helped open the way to a broader application of Fourteenth Amendment protections in civil rights cases. But the more immediate result was an injustice: Screws, Kelley, and Jones were tried again and acquitted.

———

In its response to McGee's appeal, the state of Mississippi took aim at the defense's two most promising arguments: jury exclusion and coercion. In a short brief, Attorney General Greek L. Rice argued that *Patton*'s requirement had been fulfilled by the presence of blacks on McGee's third-trial grand jury. On the coercion charge, the state's argument was simple: The Supreme Court had upheld the idea that state officials had a right to extract confessions as long as this was done without "methods of cruelty." Rice didn't address Rosenwein and Silverman's detailed account of what McGee said had been done to him—instead, he passed over it completely, merely implying that the confession was obtained legally. Given that, he argued, there was no Fourteenth Amendment issue. The Bill of Rights was enacted to protect individuals against the federal government, not against the states. It didn't apply to state prosecutions unless the state used illegal methods, as had happened in *Brown v. Mississippi*.

But suppose Mississippi officials were lying and McGee had been tortured? Or that Poole was right when he said the black grand jurors were planted? The justices must have considered these possibilities, because they were discussed in a circulating memo written by Murray L. Schwartz, a law clerk for Chief Justice Fred Vinson during the 1949 term.

Because of the large volume of appeals to the Court, clerks like Schwartz were—and still are—assigned to read the case record, look at the briefs filed by both sides, and write a memo that summarizes the facts and possible grounds for review. The justices considered petitions in regular meetings that were held in secret, and they didn't release details about their conversations. For the McGee appeal, the only evidence about what went through their minds is a look at what went into them: Schwartz's ten-page memo, along with a shorter memo by Warren Christopher, a clerk for William O. Douglas who later became secretary of state under President Bill Clinton.

Schwartz reviewed McGee's five claims in order, starting with jury exclusion. He explained that, after *Patton*, Mississippi officials said they would obey the law regarding jury selection. He reminded them that voter-registration patterns hadn't changed, so it was reasonable to ask if states like Mississippi were "making a good faith effort to conform to *Patton*, or whether they are ignoring that holding or devising means to evade it." This was hard to answer, because the trial judge had stopped Poole's attempt to explore this question in court. "It is difficult to evaluate . . . without a close reading of the record," he said, "and even then the answer does not come readily."

That statement was echoed throughout Schwartz's memo: To settle the questions raised by McGee, the Court would have to conduct its own investigation of disputed facts, in effect retrying the case. Did McGee deserve a change of venue? The state said no, that passions had cooled and, as the Mississippi Supreme Court put it, there was no "latent terrorism in the atmosphere of this trial."

McGee's lawyers said they were physically threatened and fled. Had it happened? "[I]t is difficult to imagine what kind of strategy other than a threat of violence would have influenced a defense attorney in a criminal case to fail to make a closing argument," Schwartz wrote, adding, "Again this would seem to be a factual question which would be extremely difficult for this Court to resolve."

With McGee's alleged confessions, the disagreement was sharp: McGee said he was beaten up; the police said he wasn't. "Assuming the veracity of the police," Schwartz wrote, ". . . the determination of the issue depends upon facts which are perhaps available only after a long and close study of the record, plus additional testimony."

Wrapping up, he reviewed the case in a big-picture way. An African-American man was on trial for rape in Mississippi. The first trial was reversed because of a mob atmosphere. The second because of jury issues. All-white juries had sentenced McGee to death three times, and the defense alleged misconduct.

"On the other side appears the testimony of all the good citizens of Miss . . . to the effect that after deliberate consideration of all his contentions, petitioner had a fair trial," he wrote. "And there is much to sustain this argument, if only it can believed that a fair trial under these circumstances can be had in Mississippi."

——

The Smith Act trial started in January 1949, minus one defendant—William Z. Foster, whose case was separated because he was ill. In his opening statement, U.S. attorney John F. X. McGohey said he would demonstrate that the goal of any Communist group in a democratic nation was, by definition, overthrow, whatever its leaders said in public. Opposition to capitalist democracies was fundamental to the teachings of Marx and Lenin, and in the United States, change could only come through conspiracy, because voters would never choose Communism at the ballot box. "Remember [the] phrase, Marxism-Leninism," he said dramatically. "You will hear it frequently throughout the trial."

The trial lasted seven months from jury selection to verdict, ending on October 14, 1949. The defendants, fully aware that the deck was stacked against them, used the courtroom as a protest forum, often answering questions with rambling rants against U.S. policies, "FBI stoolpigeons," and the presiding judge, Harold Medina. Early on, Medina warned the defendants and their lawyers that he wouldn't stand for courtroom "rumpuses" aimed at undermining his authority, but his threat never really stopped the flow of abuse.

Medina was also impatient with more reasonable arguments. In June, he ruled out a stack of anecdotal and journalistic evidence that the defense hoped to introduce, designed to demonstrate that American Communists often worked for social justice in the same way that any progressive political group would, as embodied by groups like the CRC. "Judge Medina said the trial would continue for 'years and years' if he admitted in evidence all the speeches, articles, statements and other documents offered to show the defendants had engaged in nonrevolutionary activities to help veterans, youth, workers, Negroes, Jews and other groups with grievances," the *Times* reported.

As promised, the government presented an extended lecture about the perils of American Communism, and the sheer volume of testimony was incredible. Toward the end, the *Times* ran the numbers and estimated that the jury of four men and eight women sat through 158 trial days and 5 million words. The transcript, not counting pretrial challenges and motions, came to 15,000 pages.

McGohey delivered anecdotal evidence heavy on perceived perils and light on tangible proof of a conspiracy. Waving basic texts like Joseph Stalin's *The Fundamentals of Leninism*, he and other prosecutors argued that American Communism had made a radical turn in April 1945, when French Marxist Jacques Duclos attacked the leadership of Earl Browder, the general secretary of the American Party at the time. During the war, Browder had tried to rebrand Communism, dissolving the Communist Party and replacing it with the Communist Political Association, a more mainstream political movement that, under the slogan "Communism is 20th Century Americanism," recommended such heresies as labor-management cooperation. Browder was ousted in 1945 in favor of harder-line types like Foster and Dennis.

That was the dreary gist of the case, though from day to day the trial featured dramatic moments that brought it to life. Benjamin Davis, called in July, gave a good accounting of why a black American might be drawn to the Communist Party in the first place. Davis was from Georgia, where his father was a newspaper publisher, prosperous enough to send Davis to Harvard Law School, from which he graduated in 1928. During the 1930s, he represented Angelo Herndon, a black Georgia Communist who was given a long prison sentence for violating a Reconstruction-era law with a Smith Act–like provision against advocating forceful resistance to state authority. The case went to the U.S. Supreme Court, which overturned Herndon's conviction in 1937.

208] THE EYES OF WILLIE McGEE

"This case was the turning point of my whole life," Davis said. "The judge referred to me and my client as niggers and darkies, and threatened many times to jail me along with my client.

"I was treated in such a way that I could see before me the whole treatment of the Negro people in the South. The fact that I had been luckier than most people in education and income did not shield me from what all Negroes suffered. So I felt if there was anything I could do to fight against this and identify myself fully with my own people and strike a blow against the lynch system, I was determined to do it."

———

As it turned out, the fall of 1949 was a period of turbulence and defeats for the Communist Party and the CRC. In late August and early September, riots broke out at two public concerts featuring Paul Robeson, held on the outskirts of Peekskill, New York, in Westchester County. The concerts were fund-raising benefits for the CRC, and during the second of them, anti-Communist protesters smashed car windows and beat up concertgoers, injuring nearly 150 people. Bella Abzug was there, and she took a rock to the chin that left her with a permanent scar.

On October 10, the Supreme Court, without comment, declined to accept the case of Willie McGee. On the 14th, all eleven Smith Act defendants were found guilty. They were sentenced to prison terms, as were some of their lawyers—including Abraham Isserman—after Judge Medina found them guilty of contempt. McGee, of course, faced death, and by the summer of 1950, the Mississippi Supreme Court had set yet another date for his execution: July 27, 1950.

Left: Willie McGee. The picture is undated, but the street clothes indicate that it was taken at the time of his arrest in November 1945. *Below*: Troy and Willette Hawkins in Hattiesburg, Mississippi, late 1942. Troy is catching a bus to his wartime job at the Servel plant in Evansville, Indiana.

Top to bottom: Two-year-old Dorothy Hawkins, who was in bed with her mother on the night of November 2, 1945; Bertha Mae Crowell (*center*) with Ann and Sandra Hawkins (*right*), late 1942; Leroy Jensen, a next-door neighbor who was sixteen on the night of the alleged rape and saw Mrs. Hawkins run out of her house.

Top: Troops outside the Laurel jail during McGee's first trial in December 1945. *Bottom*: The Jones County Courthouse in 1950, seen from the north. The catwalk on the building's east side was used to transfer prisoners from the Laurel jail.

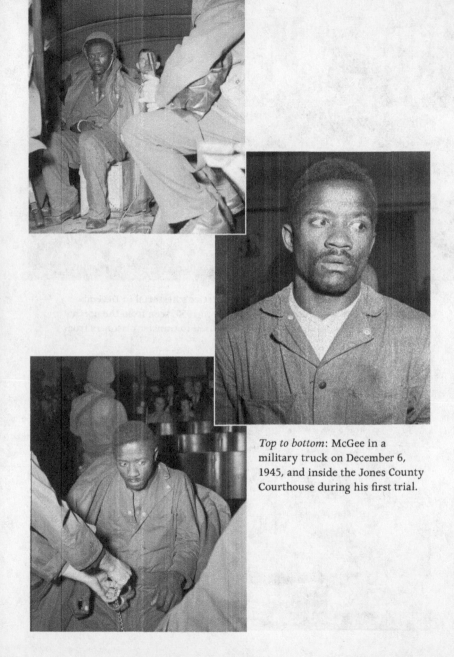

Top to bottom: McGee in a
military truck on December 6,
1945, and inside the Jones County
Courthouse during his first trial.

Top: Dixon Pyles in the mid-1940s. Right: Mississippi senator Theodore Bilbo in 1947. Bottom: Louis E. Burnham, who investigated the case after McGee's first trial.

Top: President Harry S. Truman, Eleanor Roosevelt, and NAACP executive secretary Walter White at the Lincoln Memorial prior to Truman's 1947 speech on civil rights. Bottom: Army veteran Isaac Woodard Jr., whose police-brutality blinding in South Carolina prompted Truman to act.

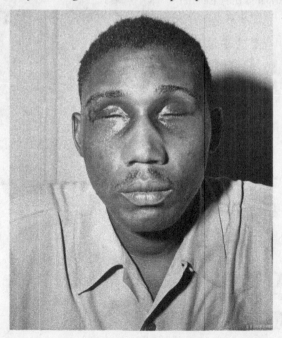

Top: Presidential candidate Henry Wallace in 1948, at the Philadelphia convention of the Progressive Party. *Bottom*: Mississippi governor Fielding Wright, who ran for vice president on the segregationist States' Rights ticket.

Right: Bella Abzug as a young lawyer in New York. *Below, left to right*: John Poole and Alvin London, who represented McGee at his third trial.

Right: Rosalee McGee in New York with Paul Robeson (*left*) and George Marshall, who first identified the McGee case as a cause worth pursuing. *Bottom left*: *New York Times* reporter John N. Popham. *Bottom right*: CRC head William L. Patterson.

Top: Rosalee McGee in 1950 or 1951. *Bottom*: Willie McGee inside the Hinds County jail.

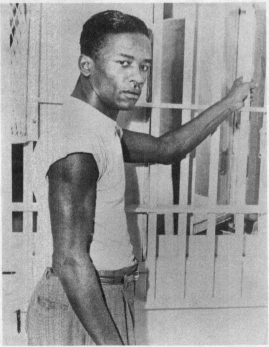

Delegates at the July 1950 clemency hearing in Jackson, Mississippi. *Clockwise from top left*: CRC spokesman Aubrey Grossman; Frank Stoll, a veteran from Madison, Wisconsin; Winifred Feise, a New Orleans–based member of the CRC; and Sidney Ordower, a veteran from Chicago and a Progressive Party candidate for the U.S. House of Representatives.

Top: William Faulkner during the 1949 premiere of *Intruder in the Dust*. *Right*: Jessica Mitford, who traveled from Oakland to Jackson in March 1951 as part of a "White Women's Delegation" organized by the CRC.

Top: Marchers at the April 1951 "Save Willie McGee" rally in Chicago. *Bottom*: Protesters at the Lincoln Memorial, May 6, 1951. Abe Cohen (*hands outstretched*) was an ex-marine and union man from Brooklyn.

Right: McGee inside the Hinds County jail on the afternoon before his execution. *Bottom*: Street protesters in May 1951.

Top: State officials unload Mississippi's portable electric chair outside the Jones County Courthouse on the night of May 7, 1951. *Bottom*: Spectators outside the building, looking up for a sign that the execution has taken place.

Top: Willette Hawkins in 1951 with her mother, Drucilla Darnell, and her youngest daughter, Dorothy. *Bottom*: Hawkins in New York in 1955, with her lawyers at the Foley Square federal courthouse, celebrating victory in her libel suit against the *Daily Worker*.

nine

COUNTRY GIRL

A lvin London dropped out of the McGee case after the Mississippi Supreme Court granted its stay of execution on June 3, 1949. But in 1952, when he talked to Spivak, he still had unfinished business on his mind: The CRC hadn't paid him for the hurry-up work he and Poole did after the U.S. Supreme Court turned them down.

"[T]hey called up and said, 'Just do anything. Just do whatever you can,'" he said. "And we worked around here right up until ten or eleven o'clock that night, and finally got a stay. We did just about everything and almost the impossible . . . and they refused to pay." London said that, without them, the story would have ended that night. The investigator shrugged. He sympathized, but he had nothing to do with the CRC.

Poole stayed involved, and though it was a while before he did any more McGee work, he had McGee-related business to attend to that year. The libel suit he'd started against the *Jackson Daily News* was still a going concern, though London dropped out of it. Poole had filed it in April 1948, at first trying to have it heard in Delaware, where the *Jackson Daily News* was incorporated. Frederick Sullens, owner and chief firebrand of the *Jackson Daily News*, successfully countersued to have that attempt blocked, so the case wound up at the federal court in Jackson. Things got under way in the spring of 1949, when the opposing sides started taking depositions and filing briefs.

Poole was entering dangerous territory. Sullens was the kind of man who fought back, so it was no surprise that his defense lawyers paved the way for a counterattack. Poole was questioned in Jackson by local attorneys Thomas Watkins and H. V. Watkins, who tried to establish that he knew perfectly well that the CRC was a group with Communist ties. Poole hunkered down, acting as if he were be-

ing grilled by HUAC itself, clamming up or claiming ignorance about
most of what they wanted to know.

"What kind of organization is the Congress of Civil Rights?" he
was asked.

"I don't know."

"Do you know where their principal offices are?"

"No, I don't."

"Do you know whether or not they maintain an office or representative in the State of Mississippi?"

"No, I don't."

"Do you know the purpose of the organization?"

"No, I don't."

His memory lapse was almost total: Poole said he only recalled the
last name of the out-of-state attorney who hired him ("Abzug"), that
he didn't know where she lived, and that he'd conferred with her
only once.

He was also pressed about the issue of Mrs. Hawkins's consent to
the rape. Poole had been clear on that, but the Watkinses, like the
Mississippi Supreme Court, seemed to think he had something darker
in mind. Tom Watkins may have heard rumors about the affair story
when he worked with Dixon Pyles before the second trial, because he
indicated a general awareness that an unacceptable theory was floating around.

"Did you or not," Poole was asked, "on one or more occasions prior
to, during, and after said trial make the statement that you had proof
of the fact that the prosecutrix had had previous relations with Willie
McGee?"

"No," Poole said. "I never would have made a statement to the effect I had absolute proof to that effect. But I did, in reviewing the
woman's testimony . . . argue the same question that Forrest Jackson
argued and that Dixon Pyles and Dan Breland argued, that because of
some of the woman's own testimony it would indicate that there might
not have been a lack of consent."

Neither of these attacks had staying power. Poole wasn't a Communist and he hadn't defamed Mrs. Hawkins. But Sullens's lawyers

revealed another strategy, one that was easy to overlook but would ultimately prove fruitful: They started asking detailed questions about Poole's dealings with small-fry clients, for whom he had handled routine matters like divorces and injury claims. Several years would pass before it became clear what that was all about.

When I set out to start answering basic questions about Rosalee McGee—who she was, where she came from, where she went—I discovered that it wasn't going to be easy, and that the methods I used to find the Hawkins and McGee families wouldn't work in her case.

I wrote another letter to the *People's World*, but this time there was no magic call from someone with the answer. Over time, I tracked down sons and daughters of people affiliated with the defense— including Bella Abzug's youngest daughter, Liz, a lawyer based in New York; Dr. MaryLouise Patterson, a pediatrician also living there; and Margaret A. Burnham, a lawyer and professor based at Northeastern University in Boston. None of them knew what became of Rosalee.

The trickiest part was that the name Rosalee McGee was, most likely, an alias. I doubted that she and McGee were ever legally married, since his divorce from Eliza Jane Payton didn't happen until he was already in jail. For a while, Rosalee was a prominent person—her name appeared in scores of newspaper articles between 1949 and 1951—but once the case was over, she dropped out of sight. Judging by a couple of old newspaper stories I had, it looked as if she'd stayed involved with the CRC. In a 1955 *New York Times* story, she turned up, alongside William Patterson, at a federal hearing on whether the CRC should be required to register as a Communist-front organization under the Internal Security Act. She refused to answer a question from a Justice Department attorney on the grounds that it would "intimidate me." Patterson stepped in to say she meant "incriminate."

Still, the material I had offered small hints here and there. A *Jackson Daily News* story from June 7, 1950, referred to Rosalee as "Rosie Lee Gilmore McGee," which made me wonder if Gilmore was her maiden name. And Jessica Mitford's papers on the McGee case, which are kept at Ohio State, contained an old newspaper profile about Rosalee that yielded another useful clue. It was datelined Detroit, and it featured biographical information I hadn't seen anywhere else.

"She is a Negro woman," the story said. "Her name is Rosalee McGee. She is 28 years old. She was married when she was 13. She is the daughter of Henry and Nancy Safford. They were poor farmers in Lexington, Miss. They had 10 children who worked, with their parents, on the tiny farm, from dawn till dark to keep body and soul together."

I sent the names to a friend from Vanderbilt, E. Thomas Wood, a journalist who does genealogical research as a hobby. He guessed that the name was really Saffold, which he said was more common in that part of Mississippi than Safford. He sent me a page from the 1930 Census that looked as if it might be about the right family. Just below the names Henry and Nancy Saffold was the name Rosetta. The record said she was eleven years old in 1930, which meant she was born around 1919. That sounded right, but it wasn't an exact match: Rosetta isn't the same as Rosalee. Was it really the same woman?

———

While I looked for Rosalee leads, I tried to get somewhere with that other great mystery: the connection between Bertha Mae Crowell and the Hawkins family. The picture Dorothy Hawkins had shown me in September 2006 was definitely a shot of the person I'd interviewed—I'd taken a digital snapshot of Bertha Mae, and the resemblance between her younger and older selves was easy to see. A few months later, I proposed the next logical step to Sandra, Dorothy, and Bertha Mae: that we all get together, compare notes, and see what we could figure out. Everybody agreed.

By then, Bertha Mae had temporarily moved to Mesquite, Texas, where she was staying with her daughter and son-in-law for an extended period. It was up to us to do the traveling, so, one weekend in December, Sandra, Dorothy, and I all got ourselves to Mesquite. On Saturday morning, we met in the lobby of my hotel, climbed into the car, and took off to pay our visit. Sandra brought one of her sons, who was curious to see what happened but asked that I not use his name.

When we got to the right address—a nice house on a typical suburban street—I knocked on the front door. There was no answer, and I had a queasy feeling that Bertha Mae had either forgotten the appointment or decided she didn't want to go through with it.

In fact, she was in there by herself doing a jigsaw puzzle—her daughter was off at her church, and her son-in-law was out also—so it took her a minute to walk to the door. Dressed in a bathrobe, she flashed her big smile and took us into a living room, where we sat around on chairs and couches and began our rather strange conversation.

After the opening pleasantries, Dorothy pulled out her photo album and opened it to the old picture of Bertha Mae, Ann, and Sandra. Nobody was sure where it had been taken, but it was dated as being from 1942. Dorothy thought it might have been taken at her aunt's house in Laurel. Bertha Mae had no idea.

"How old do you think you are in that picture?" Sandra said.

"I don't know," she said. "I must be in my twenties, don't you think? Probably my twenties, because I'm eighty-eight now. How old are these children?"

"I *think* I was five," Sandra said.

"Well, I'm eighty-eight now."

"I'm going to be seventy in March. I'm sixty-nine. So that—"

"So I'm eighteen years older than you."

"That's pretty much what I figured."

If the picture was taken in 1942, Bertha Mae would have been twenty-three or twenty-four. As she'd told me previously, her mother worked for Willette's sister, LaVera Hooks, who lived with her husband at thirteenth Street in Laurel before they moved to Hattiesburg. Bertha Mae said she used to hang around with her mother while she worked. As the Hawkins sisters were aware, she had also told me that she was sometimes at their house on South Magnolia.

"Do you mean hanging around Aunt LaVera's house on Thirteenth, or our house on South Magnolia?" Dorothy asked.

"I go to Billie house too," she said. "I used to go to Billie house

all the time on South Magnolia. I knew everybody on that street."
She named a couple of South Magnolia residents she'd known; they
matched names of neighbors whom the Hawkins sisters remembered.

We were going in circles about houses and neighbors and dates
when Bertha Mae changed the subject in her sudden way. "But you
know what, I don't . . . I don't believe Billie was raped," she said. "I
never would believe she was raped, because the night they say that
boy raped her, he gambled all night long with my brother."

I'd told Sandra and Dorothy about Bertha Mae's "nightmare theory" a while ago—I didn't want to set them up for a shock. They
weren't shocked because they didn't believe it. Their view was that
Mrs. Hawkins's mental problems were triggered by the rape, and that
before then she was perfectly normal. I was curious to see if either
of these different takes on reality, aired at the same time in the same
room, would change anybody's mind.

Nothing changed on either side. Bertha Mae was sure she had it
right, and the daughters were sure they had it right. I didn't know who
was right—I still don't, though my gut feeling is that it's very hard to
believe the whole case happened simply because of a bad dream that
persisted as a giant misunderstanding.

I was just as interested to see how the women related to each other
because they were emblematic of a divide about the case that I encountered every time I went to Laurel. Black people, whether they
had their facts straight or not, tended to think McGee was innocent,
that he was yet another victim of a pattern of injustice and cruelty
that was a shared part of their histories. McGee had lost his life, like
so many others, so it was only natural for them to gravitate toward
explanations that put him in the most favorable light. White people
did something similar. Their understanding of the case was usually a
mix of fact and myth too, and though they didn't deny that Jim Crow
courts were often unjust, they wanted to believe that, in this instance,
McGee had gotten a fair trial and the system had worked.

It was an irreconcilable difference influenced by race and background. What impressed me about Bertha Mae, Sandra, and Dorothy
was that they managed to talk about the case, disagree completely,

and still enjoy getting a chance to see each other again. There was a lot of mutual affection and laughter in that room, along with inconclusive memories, head-shaking, and puzzled frowns.

"Do you remember telling me that you saw Mrs. Hawkins inside her house, waking up from a nightmare?" I asked Bertha Mae at one point.

"Yeah, she would wake up from nightmares."

"Tell me about it. What did you see?"

"I can't remember all that. I just remember Billie had nightmares, just like me."

"I thought you actually observed her one day, waking up terrified."

"Yeah, I been to her house when she woke up and have a nightmare. Like she's dreaming, and then she tell me her dream."

Before long, she repeated her theory about the rape. "I believe she dreamed," she said firmly. "I don't believe it happened."

"I have a question," Sandra cut in. "If you don't think it really happened, why do you think our lights and telephone would have been not working?"

"I don't know. I just don't know. But I really don't believe the lady . . . you couldn't make me believe it."

Sandra said she clearly remembered that "we had no lights. And what mother did was, she ran out screaming. And of course that woke all of us up and we all—"

"Did you *see* him?" Bertha Mae asked.

"No, ma'am."

"All right. Anybody can run out screaming. I can jump up in the air with a nightmare and run out screaming. I really don't believe he raped her."

During the rest of the conversation, we went back and forth between small talk and talk of the crime. Bertha Mae didn't budge: She knew what she knew. When challenged on this, her fallback position was that, unless somebody saw Willie McGee running away from the scene with their own eyes, she would never believe it.

The Hawkins sisters didn't budge either. After we left, we went to lunch at a local chain and talked about the interview. Sandra's son was impressed that Bertha Mae remembered so much. He didn't say what he thought about her nightmare notions.

Sandra did, rejecting them without any apparent feelings of doubt. Referring to her mother, she said, "Bertha Mae has confused the time element. Mother did, she would wake up in the night screaming and running. . . . But I really think Bertha Mae has confused the time."

On the Rosalee front, a breakthrough came when I went to the Library of Congress in early 2007 and finally got a look at the archived materials of the CRC, which weren't available in New Mexico. That's when I found out that the papers contained dozens of letters written by Willie, Bessie, and Rosalee—something that wasn't mentioned in any of the books or clips I had at that point. Among other things, the letters confirmed that Rosalee's maiden name was Saffold.

She wrote at least three dozen times between mid-1949 and 1953. In mid-1949, she announced her existence to the CRC twice—first on May 20 and again on June 18—perhaps because she was on the move and didn't want to risk missing their reply. The first letter was sent from 102 West Church Street in Jackson. The second letter's return address said only "Laurel, Miss." The wording was slightly different in each but the gist was the same: Rosalee was letting the CRC know that she existed, that she was McGee's legal wife, and that she, Willie, and their four children desperately needed help.

"To The Civil Rights Congress," the first one said. "I am the wife of Willie McGee who have been behind iron bars since Nov. 1945. We have four children and no one to help me with them and I have been very quite until he get this last sentence in April. I am a poor colored woman and I need my husband with these four kids to help me haveing to send two away to Neb. and I wont to no will he go to the chair on June 3. Please save him for me."

Like most of Rosalee's letters, this one had a lot of accurate information in it, showing that she knew what was going on. The "last sentence in April" was the Mississippi Supreme Court's decision to uphold McGee's guilty verdict. June 3, 1949, was the new execution date. In this and the second letter, which she mailed to Patterson, she also displayed an awareness of the Laurel rape case involving Laverne Yarbrough and the five-year-old black girl.

"There are many other crimes did and their life wasnt taken even in this same county of Jones I live in," she told Patterson. "Some one but not my race did crime on a 5 year old colored child his life was not taken."

Despite what Rosalee said, the "four kids" weren't with her—they were out west with Eliza Jane Payton. Nor had she ever been a permanent resident of Laurel. But it seemed likely that one or two children were under her wing. She mentioned the possibility of sending two kids off to Nebraska, and she offered to send pictures of McGee, herself, and "our oldest child."

For Rosalee, the pressing issue was money. "Please help my husband to get some other sentence if you can," she wrote. "I don't have any money. I will work to help him save his life. . . . Please let me hear from you all at once."

The letters were written in several different hands—other people must have taken down her words for her, at least sometimes—and she signed her name in many different ways, including Rosalee McGee, Rosalie McGee, Rosie Lee McGee, Rosalee Etta Safford, Rosalie Etta Safford, Rosalie Etta Saffolds, and Rosalee Safford. Over the years, she used three different addresses in Jackson, one in Laurel, and one each in the towns of Durant and Lexington, where she had originally come from.

Once Rosalee got started, she was a diligent correspondent, writing frequently that summer and fall. On July 19, 1949, after McGee's June 3 execution was delayed, she wrote to tell the CRC that McGee was sick and that he was being harassed in jail.

"What I wanted to tell you is the jailer got angery because you wrote him about Willie," she said. "[H]e blew up at Willie and wonted to know how did you all know about it. . . . i told him i didn't know no more about C.R.C. than what was wrote up in the paper."

On September 2, after the first U.S. Supreme Court appeal had been filed, Rosalee sent a letter indicating that neither she nor McGee was quite up to speed on developments. McGee, for example, wanted to know if "Lawyer Poole" was still representing him.

But they definitely understood what it meant when the Court said no in October. "Willie is almost crazy," Rosalee wrote. "[H]e wont to hear from you . . . he did all right until Monday after he read the paper and the U.S. turn him down. Lawyer Poole say he happen heard from you all in some time in fack he told me he was not McGee lawyer any more and there wasn't any more to be done."

Patterson wrote Rosalee and Willie separately, saying, in his stately way, that the fight was still on. "The United States Supreme Court has ruled against Willie, but you must not despair. . . .

"We are not giving up. You must not. The fight for Willie's life will yet be won."

Before long, the CRC realized that Rosalee's letters had value as a tool for generating support and funds, and it started telling her story in press releases. "Ever since the frame-up began in November 1945, Rosalee McGee has been writing in an effort to save her innocent husband's life," said a release from October 31. That wasn't true, and unless CRC officials had forgotten what was in their own files, they should have known McGee wasn't living with a loyal wife when he was arrested. Louis Burnham's report from December 1945 specifically said he was separated.

If Willie and Rosalee didn't meet in 1945, then when did it happen?

The letters didn't say, but there was a clue in statements Rosalee made a few months later, when she told Willie's life story for a series of articles that ran in a left-wing newspaper called the *New York Compass*. Rosalee spun an elaborate tale, saying she was thirteen when they married, and that McGee had rescued her from parents who couldn't do anything to improve her life.

She also mentioned that, when she went to see McGee in the Hinds County jail, she visited a cousin of hers named Marvin Murray, who was on death row for the alleged murder of a jailer in Wiggins, a tiny town an hour south of Laurel. The way Rosalee described it in the *Compass*, she was prevented from visiting McGee at first—only Bessie and his lawyers were allowed in—but because she was able to visit Murray, she caught glimpses. "They let me in to see him and sometimes I can see Willie off in the distance," she said, "and I bring him some clothes with my cousin's clothes, but I can't talk to Willie."

Various appeals to save Murray failed, and he was electrocuted on June 29, 1948. Rosalee said the visitation ban was lifted after Murray's death, though the jailers were sadistic about it, telling her that Willie was next and even sitting her down in the electric chair, with a hood on her head, so she could "see how it felt."

That sounds doubtful—the chair wasn't stored at the Hinds County Courthouse—and I also wonder if Rosalee didn't reverse the chain of events. That is, she may have gone to the jail, at first, for the purpose of visiting her cousin, and that's how she initially met McGee.

———

My contact with McGee's descendants kept up sporadically after I met them in Las Vegas that first time in 2005. Sometimes I'd talk on the phone with Bridgette or Tracey, or I'd e-mail them when I came across information I knew they'd want to hear. I told them about finding Evelyn Smith McDowell—who died in 2006—and Donna Poole Mills. I also sent them transcripts of the first and third trials, sent Bridgette copies of Eliza Jane Payton's marriage license and divorce papers, and told them what I knew about Rosalee McGee's real name.

I hoped we would travel to Mississippi together at some point—all three McGees, Donna, Liz Abzug, and me—but that wasn't looking likely as the months went by. Everybody had jobs, so coordinating a trip like that wasn't going to be easy, especially if Della decided to go.

Halfway through 2007, I had a different idea, which was to invite people to Santa Fe for a sort of reunion and informational swap meet. By that point, there were still a few people on the defense side I hadn't found yet, but the final roster of invitees was pretty complete: Liz, Bridgette, Della, Tracey, Donna, and Todd Pyles. Everybody showed up except Todd, who said yes but then decided he wasn't up for traveling.

They all came out on a weekend in July, arriving at different times. In a conference room of the building where I worked, I'd piled up things from my now-huge collection of McGee case material—five file drawers of clips, press releases, court documents, FBI files, correspondence, taped interviews, and photographs.

There was no plan except to let people meet one another, look at whatever they wanted, and ask questions. All of us had our areas of expertise. Liz has been deeply involved in watching over her mother's legacy and papers (which, unfortunately, contain almost nothing about McGee). Bridgette, Tracey, and Donna were researching books they wanted to write—and they knew the most about their own families. By then I knew a lot about the trials, appeals, and the bigger picture: the political context of civil rights and anti-Communism in the late 1940s and early 1950s, and how that inevitably helped shape the outcome of the case.

Bridgette and Della left Las Vegas by car early on Saturday morning, with Bridgette's husband, Harold, at the wheel. Liz was already in town but wasn't coming in until midday. For a while on Saturday, Donna, Tracey, and I were there by ourselves, pawing through papers and talking. Donna, a kind-hearted brunette, didn't know about the Rosalee-as-imposter angle yet, so that was a surprise to her. Tracey and I were talking about Rosalee when Donna said, "So Rosalee came in the picture—"

"We don't know," said Tracey, who spoke in a measured way and had a wise-looking face that sat under a big cascade of hair. "We don't know who she is."

"Oh, really? But she seems to, like, take over claim of the family."

"Pretty much. That's why we want to know who she is."

I told Donna about Rosetta Saffold and the letters, pointing to a file folder full of them and saying, "She just sort of announced herself to the Civil Rights Congress and said, 'Greetings! I am the wife of Willie McGee—'"

"Yes," Tracey said, "her first letter was to Patterson in 1949."

"I've been trying to figure out if the Civil Rights Congress was aware of the discrepancy," I said, "and I think they probably were, because—"

"I think it's very difficult for them not to be," Tracey said.

As we looked at pictures of Rosalee—a striking woman who seemed right at home in the suits and hats she wore while making public appearances up north—Donna asked why the CRC would go along with such an elaborate deception. Tracey gave what I assumed was the right answer: They were creating a better public image for McGee, a man who had enough problems already.

"They wanted a prettier picture, probably, of Willie," she said. "You know, a married man with children, something to pull for . . . sympathy. That's what I think happened."

Later, though, Tracey made a point I didn't agree with, something that Bridgette brought up when she arrived that afternoon. They both found it hard to believe that a "country girl" like Rosetta could have been plucked out of obscurity, taken north, and repackaged to become a viable public figure.

I didn't find that odd at all. It happened frequently during those old cases, when wives or mothers of imprisoned black men were brought north to testify about life under Jim Crow. It didn't matter if the refugees were rough around the edges; that was part of their authenticity. The CRC had brought Bessie McGee up north, and the same tactic was used during the Scottsboro and Martinsville Seven cases. After Scottsboro Boy Haywood Patterson escaped from Alabama in 1948, he was arrested by FBI agents two years later in Detroit. The CRC mounted a successful attempt to prevent his extradition back to Alabama, after which it deployed him as a public speaker.

Tracey saw it differently. Later, while I was telling Donna about the CRC's efforts to publicize the case and turn McGee into a cause, Tracey said she was grateful they'd done all that, but it made her uneasy. "On the other side of it," she said, "I can't get rid of the feeling that they also manipulated it."

How so? "Well, I'm curious as to what connection there is with Rosalee. And how that came about."

———

Just before this, the rest of the McGees had called from the road: They'd had car trouble, and for a while it looked like they might not make it. In the interim, Liz showed up with her partner, a woman named Erica Foman, coming into the room on a wave of Abzugian energy. I'd sent her the third-trial transcript. She'd never seen it before, and soon after she settled in, I asked for her assessment.

"It was ridiculous!" she said in a New York accent that brought her mother to mind, laughing and waving it off. "Today, they would throw it out at the first hearing."

We talked for a bit, and then I took everybody to a different room, where we watched videotapes of interviews with Dixon Pyles and a black woman from Laurel named Rose McGee. They'd both been interviewed on camera in the 1970s by a British crew that was making a documentary about Jessica Mitford. Copies turned up in Mitford's papers at Ohio State.

As we watched, it was interesting to see how people reacted to Pyles, who, to me, was a familiar Southern type: a smart, loud, old-fashioned lawyer who liked to tell stories and jokes. But he gave Tracey and Liz the creeps, and to them, it seemed evident—as it had to historian Gerald Horne—that Pyles's defense of McGee must have been half-hearted. I found that strange, because I didn't hear Pyles say anything they should have objected to. He even reiterated his opinion that McGee was innocent, saying, "I never believed that he was guilty of rape."

The point isn't that they were wrong or I was right: It's that we had such different reactions to the same information. To me, this pattern was starting to seem like a hidden code that might explain some of the McGee case's persistent mysteries.

By now I had a mountain of facts, but I still didn't know what really happened. Most likely, I never would, and I was beginning to suspect that a similar uncertainty had probably been a burden for almost everybody involved in the case. I didn't think any of the lawyers or judges really knew the truth—much less anyone who read about McGee in newspapers and magazines at the time. But then, as now, people on both the left and right arrived at their passionate opinions based on a mix of information, misinformation, prejudices, and wishful thinking.

The problem with the evidence I had was that you could take any piece of it, hold it up to the light, and interpret it in a way that fit whatever you wanted to believe. Everybody did this, on both sides. Bertha Mae knew McGee was innocent, and there was no telling her otherwise. Mrs. Hawkins's daughters knew he wasn't, and their minds didn't seem open to the possibility that she might have been emotionally imbalanced even before the alleged attack.

The McGees, for their part, were sure Willie was blameless, even though they knew he was a man who had lived on the wild side. Tracey told me once over the phone, "The picture we're getting as we talk to relatives is that Willie was a dog. He was a dog on two legs." But somehow it never occurred to the McGees that he might actually have gotten drunk one night, and, in an act of lust, desperation, or rage, crawled through a window to get his hands on something that white society said he could never possess.

For all I knew, I was doing the same thing, and I thought about this when we watched the Rose McGee interview. Rose, a friendly old woman from Laurel, wasn't related to Willie McGee, but she did have an indirect connection to the case. She was a sister of Hettie Johnson, the woman John Poole had wanted to call at the third trial. She said she'd worked as a maid at various times for Mrs. Hawkins's other sister, Thelma Floyd, for Mrs. Hawkins's mother and aunt, and for Mrs. Hawkins herself. She said Willie's mother had worked for Willette's parents, and that Willette grew up knowing McGee. According to her, their forbidden affair started with this childhood acquaintance. "Billie and Willie," she said, "they began to be friends, and they grew up to be lovers."

Of course, she also said that McGee ran away to Chicago, not Nevada or California, and that his mother's name was Rose. To me, it sounded like another Laurel rumor, and I had trouble believing that Willie and Willette had been sandbox sweethearts. Liz and Tracey found it more convincing, but I had to wonder if they didn't know enough about the case to be adequately confused.

———

Della, Bridgette, and Harold made it to Santa Fe in the early afternoon, but they called and said they were having trouble finding their way into town. I told them to park it where they were—a McDonald's way out on Santa Fe's main commercial drag—and I'd come get them. When I got there, Della was standing outside the vehicle, on blazing blacktop, scowling over the glow of a peppermint blouse. Her mood didn't improve much for the rest of the day.

Part of the problem was simple: She felt bad. Della was old, they'd had a tough drive, and she'd gone from 2,000 feet to 7,000 feet in a few hours, which would give anybody a headache. But she was generally cranky that day, and once we got her situated around the table, she wouldn't talk about much of anything except her irritation with Rosalee McGee.

"OK, there was this lady from Mississippi, had four kids, gave our name, and she was trying to get Social Security for her kids in Mississippi," she explained to Liz and Donna as she looked at a picture of Rosalee that I'd pulled out. "A gentleman that helped us out was a schoolteacher and that's how we got Social Security, through this teacher. That's why I say this woman here is not my mama, and I wished I knowed where she's at because . . . she probably dead now."

Bridgette was less talkative than the first time we'd met, but, like Tracey, she said she didn't think Rosalee was a real country person. "She went on after that to still work for the CRC, right? So I'm thinking this lady was already in politics, and somebody hired her." She didn't believe Bessie McGee wrote the letters attributed to her either. "Somebody wrote those letters for her," she said.

That day, it started to feel as if the McGees and I were heading down separate paths. It seemed obvious that Della, for one, would never be able to believe that I was trustworthy enough to tell her family's story. She also felt, I think, that I was stealing something that belonged to her. Liz mentioned that afternoon that I was working on a book, news that Della took in with a display of suspicious surprise, as if I'd been sneaky about it.

I hadn't been sneaky—I had fact-checked my proposal with Bridgette and notified her promptly when I got a contract, so the book was no secret. But I didn't say anything, trying to imagine how this weekend might look to Della. I'd laid out all these documents, thinking I was being helpful, but to her it probably seemed like a show of force. (*I know more about this now. Let me handle it.*) The McGees weren't financially comfortable in the way the Hawkinses were, and, no doubt, Della hadn't been handed many gifts by life.

Meanwhile, the Willie McGee story seemed to have value, but other people were extracting it. Never mind that the story was so confusing and fragmented and error-filled that it didn't have any real substance until you invested a few thousand hours in it. People had been taking things from Della her entire life. I imagine she saw me as the latest in a long line of plunderers.

Rosalee had a busy spring and summer in 1950, marked by stress, fear, and the start of an exciting new chapter in her life. During this period, she exchanged several letters with Lottie Gordon, a woman in the New York office who ran the CRC's Prisoners Relief Committee. Gordon arranged for Willie to receive Bible tracts and newspapers and for Rosalee to get $5 checks and boxes of clothing. "Please let us know how many children you have, what their ages are, what size clothes they wear, if they have any special interests," Gordon wrote in late February. "We cannot promise much, except that we will do whatever is possible." Rosalee wrote back with the ages and sizes.

in your letter you as me how meny children i have. it is four of them ages 12, 11, 9, 8, three girls 1 boy.

Ablige,
Rosalee

Oldest Girl Wear Dress
14. shoes 6 1/2
next girl [size] 12
shoes 5 1/2
son wear shirts size
10 or 12 shoes 5
Fourth wear 10 or 11
shoes 4 1/2

Why did she bother to pretend? To help McGee, and to survive. For all practical purposes, Willie and Rosalee were a couple by then—they even sent out a Christmas card one year—and they needed to present a unified front as a family under siege. Willie must have worried that the CRC would drop him if they knew he'd abandoned his wife and children in 1942. Meanwhile, Rosalee needed subsistence money, and her association with McGee wasn't helping her job prospects. In early April she wrote:

i work so hard and i be so tied when I get home. you see i had a hard time getting a job in town so i am working in country. i had a good Job i mean what you call good here. soon as the Lady found out i was willie wife she didn't wont me to get of to go see him. she did lots of talk about him i didn't thank was right so i quit and every where i would go seem like she would beat me there. i stop telling my real name. I love my Husband altho some time i don't feel like going but i will have to until he is free again to help me with kids. he cryied sunday when i tol him i had to walk almost two miles to get to my job . . . i told he not to worry i get by. Easter is just another day with me. as long as he is alive and i can see him

*i pray every nits to my father in heaven to please let him come back
to me just one more time.*

That summer produced more evidence that Rosalee had two
children in her custody. In June and July 1950, Gordon made
arrangements with the directors of a summer camp in New York State,
called Kinderland, to send "the McGee children" north sometime during July and August. Kinderland was one of several camps from that
era that served the children of leftists and Communists. The letters
that passed between Lottie and Rosalee leave no doubt: Somebody
was heading north. "I hope that by the time you get this, you also received a large package of clothes which I sent you last week," Gordon
wrote on July 10. "This package has a lot of stuff that the children
will be able to use in camp . . . we will be able to take care of [them]
at the camp for one month."

Another factor in Rosalee's deception may have been ordinary op-
portunism: Her exposure to the CRC gave her a glimpse of a different
world outside of Mississippi, and she wanted to see more of it. In May
1950, the CRC paid for her first trip to New York, where she debuted
as a public figure at a CRC event called the "100 Cases" dinner, which
publicized government attacks on various Communist and left-wing
leaders. On hand were people like William Patterson, Paul Robeson,
and Vito Marcantonio. In a photograph from that night, Rosalee is
standing next to Robeson, staring up and beaming as if she were looking at Zeus.

The *Daily Worker* profiled Rosalee on June 18, telling the inspira-
tional but false story of her life as Mrs. Willie McGee. "Before Mrs.
McGee could come north, she had to place her four children . . . where
they would be safe," the story said. "Two . . . are being cared for by
a sister in Ohio; the other two are with their grandmother. . . . Until
she came north a few weeks ago, Rosalee McGee was working in the
little Mississippi town where she lived with her husband and children
before the KKK state administration of Mississippi reached out against
her family."

On July 11, she spoke in front of 9,000 people at Madison Square Garden; on the 22nd, she appeared at a mass meeting in Harlem. By the 25th, she was in Washington, D.C., with Patterson and others on a failed mission to gain an audience with President Truman. She was back in Jackson in time for the dramatic events that occurred there on July 25 and 26.

During all these comings and goings, did the CRC realize Rosalee wasn't the person it advertised? It should have. By 1950, even Mississippi newspapermen were aware that there were two women in McGee's life. Commenting on Rosalee's New York trip, a *Leader-Call* editorial said, "We have not heard whether Willie's wife and mother are back in Laurel yet. Neither have we heard which wife of Willie the speaker . . . was. Willie has two wives and four children, we understand. One is of long standing and one of war-time date. Whoever she is, we'd say she was getting into bad company."

━━━━━

Late in 2007, I finally made it to Rosalee's part of Mississippi—Holmes County, which contains the towns of Lexington and Durant—armed with my one piece of information: Her name was Rosetta Saffold, and she'd lived there once. That was still all I had.

At times during and after the McGee case, Rosalee left Jackson and went home to stay with her parents, writing letters that featured two different Holmes County return addresses, but these were old and imprecise: mailbox numbers on Rural Route 3 in Lexington and Route 2 in Durant. Before coming to Mississippi, I'd sent letters and photocopies of her picture to a couple dozen people named Saffold, then I'd followed up with a call. Nobody had heard of her, and nobody could suggest anybody who might know.

So, groping, I called a few small-town libraries, asking for the name of anybody who was known to be an African-American genealogy buff. At the library in Kosciusko—the seat of the next county to the east, Attala—a woman gave me a name and number for Katharine Carr Esters, a seventy-nine-year-old who lived in the country north of town. I called her. She was friendly and said I should come see her whenever I was in town. She knew of an elderly white couple who she thought might know about "the Durant Saffolds." When my trip shaped up, I called again, and we set a time.

I drove up from Jackson on a Thursday—about seventy miles—and found my way to Esters's house, but nobody answered when I knocked. She'd told me on the phone that she was a dialysis patient, so I began to imagine the worst—that she'd dropped dead in there and nobody knew it yet. I walked around, ringing the front doorbell, looking for a big picture window to look through, checking the back. There was a private fishing lake out there, complete with a bait-and-tackle shack and a sign that read "Heritage House Mini-Lakes. Entrance fee: $1.50. Catfish & bass: $1.50 pound." Unfortunately, it was closed, so I knew Esters wasn't in there selling bait.

Calling 911 seemed like overkill: For all I knew, she'd simply forgotten and left, and I didn't see anything in the driveway or garage that looked like the family car. I took off and drove to the library, where a woman gave me a number for Esters's niece. I left her a message, telling her about my concerns, and then aimed my car west toward Lexington. The only thing left to do was go to the courthouse and see if I could find anything in the old county records.

About halfway there, my phone rang. It was the niece, telling me that Esters was all right. I'd guessed wrong, but not by much: She'd developed a blood clot in her left arm the day before and had to be driven to Jackson for emergency treatment. She was heading home now and would still be glad to see me if I could come by that night.

When I got to Lexington, I was told at the courthouse that the records I wanted were stored off-site, at a repurposed commercial building down the street. I got set up in there for the familiar marriage-record hunt, but I wasn't optimistic as I started pulling out the old ledgers. I figured I might find a record for Rosalee's parents, Henry and Nancy, but I had no reason to feel sure that Rosetta Saffold had ever been married in Lexington. That was just a hunch. Now that I knew her maiden name was Saffold, not Gilmore, I wondered about the old *Jackson Daily News* story that called her "Rosie Lee Gilmore McGee." Maybe Gilmore was a married name.

I found her parents soon enough: Henry and Nancy were married on January 23, 1916. But as I went through page after page of names, I didn't see Rosetta Saffold or any close variation. And then, in the last ledger, almost at the end of the *S* names, there it was: Rosetta Saffold, spelled "Rossetta" in this instance. On December 13, 1941, she'd married a Lexington man named George Gilmore Jr. He was twenty-five, she was twenty-two. The only other information was a preacher's name (L. B. Benson) and her father's name, Henry. It was definitely her.

———

That night, at the home of Katharine Carr Esters, we sat in her den while she wearily described her health adventures. Her blood clot required a surgical procedure, which she had after her grandson zoomed her down to Jackson. "I have a Lincoln Town Car," she said matter-of-factly, reclining her long, large body on an adjustable bed while she talked. "It's just as comfortable as the ambulance ride to me."

I didn't understand what the procedure involved—she described it as "a reaming, when they cut your skin open and go up in to there." Sadly, she wasn't the only family member with health problems: Her niece's husband, who had cancer and was undergoing chemotherapy, had just lost all his teeth. "He had a tooth the size of an orange because of an infection, and they had to pull every tooth in his head," she said.

Stating the obvious, Esters said that, with all this reaming and pulling going on, she hadn't had time to check on the people she'd told me about, but she would. I told her about the Gilmore-Saffold marriage license, and she said she would most certainly ask around about any Durant- and Lexington-area Gilmores too.

She didn't do any of that—that week or ever—but I didn't mind. As usual, it was more than enough to get a chance to talk to a Mississippi old-timer. Esters had had an amazing life, which she wrote about a few years ago in a self-published memoir called *Jay Bird Creek and My Recollections*. (She sold me a hardcover copy on the spot; it was a bargain at $20.) Once I absorbed enough details about her past, I couldn't help but notice a few similarities between her struggles and those of Rosalee McGee.

Esters was born in 1928 in rural Attala County, in a three-room log cabin that was typical of the houses that country blacks lived in back then. "Rural dwellings for black folk were mostly just rustic huts," she recalled in her book. ". . . Ordinarily just two rooms were heated: the kitchen and the bedroom where parents slept. That room, with an open wood-burning fireplace, doubled as a living room."

Her great-grandfather was a white Civil War veteran named Alfred Carr who'd had a black mistress, Ceeley Johnson, from whom Esters was descended. Her father was a black World War I combat veteran who'd lost a hand in a sawmill accident in 1927. Pushed into share-cropping by the Depression, he refused to work in that dead-end system, so the family lived off a disability pension he received. Esters's mother had arthritis and was bedridden for days at a time, and two of her brothers, including her twin, had died young. As a child, she hauled a lot of water around the house and farm, tended animals, and picked cotton while extracting whatever education she could from second-rate country schools.

She'd learned her alphabet at home, writing on the backs of can and flour sack labels. Later, starting in 1938, she got some of her education at a Presbyterian-affiliated boarding school near West Point, Mississippi. But she didn't graduate: Family financial problems forced her to move north to New Jersey before she finished her senior year. She lived with relatives and earned paychecks that helped with the money crisis back home.

Esters got married there in 1947 to Sam Sanford, a soldier who turned out to be a womanizer. They had two kids together, whom she took care of by herself when he was sent off to Guam. She lived for a few months with his family in Tennessee, in a dilapidated house that she tried to improve with money she earned as a cotton-picker. Her in-laws looked down on that—picking cotton was low-class work—but they changed their minds when she started bringing a lot of money home. "I was able to pull from 400 to 550 pounds a day where most women only pulled from 100 to 150," she wrote. "I was proud of myself and in the end they were all very pleased, too."

Her marriage to Sam ended in the early 1950s, and she settled in Milwaukee, remarrying there and finding jobs with the Urban League and a Veteran's Administration hospital. Because of her precarious financial situation, she placed the two children with her Tennessee in-laws, sending them money for upkeep, and they weren't reunited for several years. In the 1960s, Esters got involved in civil rights politics in Milwaukee. She moved back to Mississippi in 1972, where her experience in community organizing led to appointments on the state mental health and probation and parole boards.

In short, she'd become a local big shot, a status that was compounded by the fact that she was a second cousin of Kosciusko's most famous former citizen, Oprah Winfrey. In 2006, Winfrey presented Kosciusko with a major civic gift, a $5.5-million Boys & Girls Club. Standing next to her at the ribbon-cutting ceremony was none other than Katharine Carr Esters, who had helped organize early meetings between Winfrey and town officials.

In the context of the McGee case, what interested me about Katharine's story was how it related to Rosalee. A major theme of *Jay Bird Creek* is the importance of education, faith, and a work ethic to a person trying to overcome disadvantaged circumstances. But, no doubt, that path didn't work for everybody in Jim Crow Mississippi. If I was reading Rosetta Saffold right, she'd had it very hard herself. Judging by the content and literacy level of her letters, there was no way she'd ever had the chance to go off to a boarding school.

But Rosalee was smart and capable in her own way. With two kids, no skills, and a place at the bottom of the socioeconomic pecking order, she did what she had to do: She hustled.

ten

COMMUNISTS COMING HERE

On February 9, 1950, Wisconsin senator Joseph McCarthy began to make his first national splash, telling an audience in Wheeling, West Virginia, that the State Department was infested with Communist spies. No recording of the speech survived, and people argued forever after about whether McCarthy actually said "I have here in my hand" a list of 205 known infiltrators.

Three days later, in a follow-up speech in Reno, Nevada, he lowered the number to fifty-seven but repeated the theme: America was losing the global conflict with Communism, thanks to enemies within. The Soviet Union was in control of Eastern Europe; China had become the People's Republic on October 1, 1949; and East Germany was established on the 7th. Two weeks before that, on September 23, President Truman announced that "an atomic explosion had occurred within Russia in recent weeks," a preface to the world's learning that the Soviet Union definitely had the bomb.

To McCarthy—and to millions of people who believed in him—that many losses in such a short time couldn't have been an accident. He said the people on his list, all burrowed inside the State Department, were "individuals who would appear to be either card-carrying members or certainly loyal to the Communist Party, but who nevertheless are still helping to shape our foreign policy." These people were like Judas, selling out the United States to its enemies, but they were even more dangerous because they were motivated by ideology, not greed. "One thing to remember in discussing the Communists in our Government is that we are not dealing with spies who get 30 pieces of silver to steal the blueprints of a new weapon," he said. "We are dealing with a far more sinister type of activity because it permits the enemy to guide and shape our policy. . . ." He focused particular wrath on Alger Hiss, the former State Department official who on January 21 had been found guilty of two counts of perjury, one of them for denying that he had ever passed secret government documents to ex-Communist Whittaker Chambers.

Alas, the United States was about to begin dealing, very publicly, with the problem of spies who stole new weapons—a story that began to unfold on February 2, when British theoretical physicist Klaus Fuchs, who worked on the Manhattan Project, was arrested in London and charged with giving A-bomb secrets to the Russians. Over the next few months, it came out that American citizens were involved. David Greenglass, a machinist at Los Alamos who was originally from New York, was arrested in June. July and August saw the arrests of Greenglass's brother-in-law, Julius Rosenberg, and his sister, Ethel, both of whom were eventually executed for conspiracy to commit espionage. Julius's lawyer was Emanuel H. Bloch, a New Yorker who, up until the moment of Julius's arrest, was devoting much of his time to the defense of Willie McGee.

Capping the first half of 1950, on Sunday, June 25, the North Korean army turned a simmering conflict into a hot war when it crossed the Thirty-eighth Parallel and invaded South Korea. The United States would be entangled in combat operations there for the next three years, at an eventual cost of more than 36,000 American lives.

Although there was never a good time for Communists to show up in Jackson, Mississippi, the summer of 1950 was as bad as it got. Nonetheless, that July rapidly moving events—pegged to McGee's July 27 execution date—forced a confrontation between the CRC and city and state authorities.

During 1949 and early 1950, things had changed markedly in terms of public awareness about McGee's situation. Thanks to Patterson's tireless efforts, he was no longer obscure, and his story was now being covered in publications like the *New York Times*, the *Washington Post*, and *Newsweek*. Recognizing this, Patterson decided to build on what the CRC had done during its anti-Bilbo fight in 1946 and 1947. This time, it would send a sizable out-of-state delegation of protesters to Jackson to sound off in hopes of stopping the execution. Once these plans became known, the city bristled in anticipation of a conflict that seemed likely to turn violent. Setting the tone was a legendary local newspaper editor who loved nothing more than a good battle: Frederick Sullens.

"Probably no U.S. editor is quite so tough, colorful, eloquent, prolific and unmindful of editorial niceties as 65-year-old, 185-pound Frederick Sullens of the *Jackson* (Miss.) *Daily News*," *Time* said in a 1943 profile marking the newspaper's fiftieth anniversary. ". . . [F]or 38 of those 50 years [it] has come wet from the presses bristling with Sullens's own pugnacious personality. He is perhaps the only survivor of the old Southern-womanhood-must-be-defended school of journalism, whose exponents backed up their words with their fists and divided all office visitors into two classes: 1) those without horsewhips; 2) those with."

Born in 1877 in Versailles, Missouri, Sullens came to Mississippi in 1897 to cover a murder trial. He didn't like Jackson at first, but he stuck around and took a job at the city's oldest daily, the *Clarion-Ledger*. The place he came to love wasn't much to look at—population 5,000 or so, it was a backwater city with dusty streets and shabby buildings, still smarting from its Civil War days as "Chimneyville," when it was conquered and burned before and after the fall of Vicksburg.

Jackson's natural setting was scenic but buggy. A muddy river, the Pearl, slithered past to the east, where water moccasins wriggled about in dark, soggy woods that you could see from the bluffs downtown. There were yellow fever outbreaks every year from 1897 to 1899, and Sullens caught the disease himself. He also launched an editorial campaign to clean the city up, getting behind a $100,000 sewer system that critics considered a boondoggle.

"You can imagine my surprise and disappointment to discover it was a dingy, dreary-looking country town," Sullens told one interviewer. ". . . I've been here ever since, and, having written millions of words in praise of Jackson, it is now rather safe to draw the conclusion that I like the place. In fact, I love it. Today I'd rather own a magnolia sapling in Jackson than the Empire State Building in New York."

Sullens quit the *Clarion-Ledger* in 1905 after a fight with his publisher, who cut one of his pieces—a theatrical review—in half. ("I tore up the galleys and told him he could take his job and go to hell.") He signed on as city editor of the *Jackson Daily News*; the following year he became editor and later bought the paper. There he reigned for the next half century, focusing mainly on Mississippi matters—especially politics and race—but always with an eye on national and world events.

His style of journalism was personal, vitriolic, biased, often sentimental, and he kept readers well informed about his attachments to Mississippi's natural splendors, Pekingese dogs, and Christmas. (A holiday tradition was Sullens's Christmas Eve editorial, described in his obituary as "lasting literature . . . almost Biblical in its purity.") He could be funny in a Menckenesque way. Once, after reading that President Warren G. Harding liked to pour gravy on his waffles, he wrote, "Henceforth and hereafter suspicion and dread will dog his footsteps. . . ." But too often he wasn't funny at all, ranting about race, Yankees, and Communists in ways that sounded like open incitements to violence.

According to legend, Sullens would get so agitated while writing his front-page column—"The Low Down on the Higher Ups," launched in the 1930s—that he would shed articles of clothing while he typed, ending up nearly naked. "The following item published years ago probably best exemplifies the tenor of his column," *Colliers* said in a 1947 profile. " 'Jim So-and-So (naming a prominent state official) came to my office today. I beat hell out of him, his son, and his dog. If anybody else is looking for trouble, he'll find a well-preserved man in his middle fifties well able to take care of himself.' "

He meant it. It was said that no session of the Mississippi legislature was complete without Sullens getting into a fistfight with an elected official. The most famous scrap happened in 1940, when Sullens was sixty-two, and it grew out of an old feud he had with Mississippi's governor at the time, Paul Johnson Sr. In 1931, Johnson had run unsuccessfully for governor against Martin Sennett Conner (the winner) and Sullens's preferred candidate, Hugh L. White. During the primary campaign, Sullens railed against Johnson so often that Johnson bundled his grievances into a libel suit, which the *Daily News* settled out of court, reportedly paying $18,000. During Johnson's campaign in 1939, he bragged, "I'm still spending that buzzard's money. I'm liable to be spending some more of it too when this campaign is over."

The clash of the titans happened on the evening of May 2, 1940, in the lobby of an upscale downtown hotel called the Walthall, where Sullens lived in a penthouse. Johnson was in the lobby with friends, including one named Major G. W. Buck. Sullens was about to enter an elevator with his dog when the sixty-year-old governor—who was six feet three inches tall and 195 pounds—saw him, rushed past Buck, and smashed the back of Sullens's head with a cane. "He jumped over me so fast I didn't know what was happening until blood was shooting every which way from Sunday," Buck told reporters.

Sullens turned and charged like a speared gorilla. "The editor whirled, knocked away the cane, and pitched the . . . Governor across a chair, smashing it, dropped astride him, landing furious rights and lefts in his face," *Time* reported. "The embattled editor was hauled off, and trumpeting that it was 'a cowardly attempt to assassinate me from the rear,' was rushed to the hospital for scalp stitches. The Governor was put to bed at the Executive Mansion a block away."

Sullens was a Democrat and a white supremacist, of course, but he held some unexpected views. He always hated Bilbo, who struck him as a low-class crook. He loathed Communists ("sneaking Bolsheviki"), but he also disdained the widely popular Ku Klux Klan of the 1920s, writing once that its philosophical basis was little more than "flub-dub." He worshipped Woodrow Wilson, partly because he had served under Wilson's banner as an intelligence officer in Washington during World War I. (This was how Sullens picked up a nickname he cherished: Major.) He despised Herbert Hoover for supposedly being too liberal on race. Three days before the presidential election of 1928, the *Jackson Daily News* published a front-page cartoon showing an apelike black man chasing a terrified white girl off a cliff, with captions that said "Remember her at the polls!" and "Why the South is Democratic."

By the summer of 1950, the Major, at seventy-two, was past his prime, a Santa-bellied figure with thin gray hair plastered down on a bumpy skull. But he was more than ready when the showdown with the CRC took shape. Within days of the Supreme Court's refusal to hear McGee's appeal, the CRC had sent out a call to "members of trade unions, church groups, negro people's organizations and all Americans," asking them to "write and wire Gov. Fielding Wright, Jackson, Miss., asking executive clemency for Willie McGee." The response was impressive: By Wright's own reckoning, he heard from 15,000 people before the summer was over. The weeks leading up to July 27 also saw an ominous flow of court maneuvers, blasphemous Yankee journalism, and rumors about mysterious CRC activity in Laurel and Jackson.

Some of McGee's growing national support was little more than background noise, negated by its own shrillness. In the July 1950 issue of *Music Business* ("The Official Organ of the American Society of Disk Jockeys"), one broadcaster asked his fellow jocks to "boycott . . . or smash" copies of a popular Ella Fitzgerald song called "M.I.S.S.I.S.S.I.P.P.I.," to convey their disgust with the state's treatment of McGee. Though Fitzgerald was black and the song was an ode to the river, not to Mississippi's racial caste system, its popularity was still unacceptable.

"There are some who will say we have no right in mixing up the legal lynching of a man with a song," the writer argued. "In that case perhaps we should overlook the death and maiming of millions of Allied troops and write a love lyric to the melody of 'Deutschland Uber Alles.' . . ."

Some of it had impact. Starting on June 14, the New York–based *Compass* started publishing its multipart McGee series. The articles were important because the *Compass*, unlike the *Daily Worker*, had a place in the mainstream, however tenuous. Its founder, Theodore O. Thackrey, had edited the *New York Post*. He launched the new "liberal

crusading" paper in 1949 with a cash infusion from Mrs. Anita Mc-
Cormick Blaine, a Chicago-based International Harvester heiress who,
like Thackrey, had been a Henry Wallace supporter.

This isn't to say the *Compass* was starchy. Accompanied by urgent
display type ("Wife Tells of Frameup," "The Invisible Bloodstains,"
" 'In Sweatbox You Sign Anything' "), the stories were every bit as
emotional as anything the *Daily Worker* published. They relied on interviews with Rosalee and Bessie McGee to convey the CRC's defense
of McGee as it existed in the summer of 1950. There were no public
allegations about a love affair just yet; those came later. Instead, the
attack was aimed at the implausibility of Mrs. Hawkins's story and
the physical abuse of McGee at the hands of his jailers.

"A white woman says she was 'raped' while her husband and children slept nearby," read an editor's introduction to the stories that
ran on June 15. "She says it was pitch dark and she couldn't see who
attacked her, but that it was a Negro.

"The place is Laurel, Miss., and the white woman's statement results in the arrest of Willie McGee on Nov. 3, 1945. For 33 days, Mc-
Gee is held incommunicado, beaten, starved, tortured. He signs a
confession.

". . . In yesterday's installment, [Mrs. Willie McGee] related
how McGee was arrested and how, after 'confessing,' he was nearly
lynched. THE COMPASS is presenting her story exactly as she related
it, without altering her simple but eloquent language."

Patterson knew the timing was perfect for protest action, and he
alerted CRC chapters about the need to step it up. "The Willie McGee
case is really beginning to boil now," he wrote on July 12 to the Detroit branch. "Harvey McGehee, Chief Justice of the Supreme Court
of Mississippi, has a letter in the [*New York Compass*] for Wednesday,
the 12th. . . . He stated in the letter that he has been bombarded with
telegrams, special delivery and air mail letters urging a new trial for
Willie McGee. Well, this should be only the beginning. They should
be literally deluged with this kind of material."

For Sullens, red-alert time came with the CRC's official mid-July
announcement that activists from ten states would assemble in Jack-

son on July 25 to plead for clemency with Governor Wright. Patterson promised a delegation of seventy-five or so. The Reverend R. H. Harris, an African American who ran the CRC branch in Dallas, upped it, claiming that 1,000 people were on their way and that he was bringing a mixed-race group.

That day, the Major fired his opening volley, an editorial headlined "Communists Coming Here." After brushing off Reverend Harris's rhetoric as "gross exaggeration by a loose-lipped Negro," he wrote, "For sublimated gall, triple-plated audacity, bold insolence and downright arrogance, this proposed invasion of the Capital City of our state by a gang of Communists truly passes all comprehension.

"These invaders are just as much enemies of the United States government as are soldiers fighting under the Communist banner in Korea—fighting with Russian arms and ammunition. . . .

"[I]f any hotel in Jackson furnishes shelter for this motley crew," he closed, ". . . then that hostelry should have the rooms they occupy thoroughly cleansed with the most powerful disinfectants.

"Carbolic acid and concentrated lye, combined with DDT, will hardly be adequate for the purpose."

———

Abzug wasn't happy about the protest plans, seeing them as a drag on her courtroom work. There was often friction between her and the CRC—in her oral history, she referred to the group's members, only half-jokingly, as "lunatics" and "egomaniacs"—and she thought the clemency hearing was bad strategy. She'd seen enough of the South to know that verbal harangues from New York weren't going to help. "It was a very explosive case," she said, "and they didn't give a damn what I thought should happen or how it should happen, even though I broke my neck to put it together, in a very hard way."

William Patterson had his own complaints, once writing of Abzug, "She knew her law. She was, however, strong-willed and egotistical." The tension points to an important reality about McGee's defense: For better or worse, two people were in charge. Lacking Samuel Leibowitz's experience and clout, Abzug wasn't able to dictate terms about the wise use of protest machinery. Patterson, with his long history as a street fighter, figured he knew best when to twist the knobs.

For Abzug, Emanuel Bloch, and John Poole, the courtroom challenge was immediate and daunting: saving McGee from electrocution on the 27th. Having been rejected by the U.S. Supreme Court, Abzug tried an unusual legal strategy, filing a petition for a writ of *error coram nobis*.

In a legal context, the phrase means "the error before us." It refers to a rarely used plea, derived from English common law, in which a lawyer asks that a case be reopened on the grounds that significant mistakes occurred during earlier trials and judgments, usually owing to incompetence, fraud, or suppressed evidence. Sacco and Vanzetti's lawyers filed a *coram nobis* plea in 1927, but the Supreme Judicial Court of Massachusetts rejected it, calling the doctrine "obsolete." It was used during long-after-the-fact appeals in cases involving Alger Hiss's perjury conviction, Watergate burglar Frank Sturgis, and Japanese internment during World War II. But in 1950 *coram nobis* wasn't recognized in federal procedures, a position that remained in place until 1954.

In the McGee petition, filed in the Jones County Circuit Court on July 21, his lawyers argued that virtually everything about the first three trials was a sham. They recapped the familiar list of problems: the mob atmosphere, the all-white juries, the third-trial rush job, the coerced confession, and the threat of violence that prompted Poole and London to leave town. They didn't spell out the affair allegation, but they hinted at it, saying that prosecutors had used "perjured testimony as to the essential charge of rape. . . ." This testimony "was submitted by the complaining witness with the knowledge that it was false and that she was not raped by the defendant. . . ."

The meaning of that was murky. Was this Dixon Pyles's old argument that Mrs. Hawkins's "failure to resist" amounted to legal consent? Or was it something new?

A story in the *Laurel Leader-Call* tried to read the tea leaves, saying the argument was thought to be based on McGee's claim that he'd worked as a yardman in the Hawkins's neighborhood, and on his assertion that he "met and knew the ravished woman long before the night of the rape." But that too was unclear.

Paul Swartzfager's answer, filed the next day, denied all the major claims, including things that were obviously true—one being that the case generated angry emotions among the Laurel public. It had, and on the 21st—when Poole and Bloch traveled to Laurel to submit the petition's paperwork—it did again.

In subsequent sworn statements, Poole and Bloch said they tried to file their petition at the Jones County Courthouse just before noon, after coming down from Jackson by car. The circuit clerk said they would have to deliver it themselves to Judge Collins, who was sitting on the bench in Hattiesburg. They made the trip, weren't able to find Collins, and drove back, getting additional runarounds in Laurel. Poole finally reached Collins by phone at his home, and the judge set a time for argument on the petition: 9 a.m. the next day.

According to Poole, as he and Bloch left the courthouse, he was approached and attacked by Troy Hawkins. "He was very angry when he saw me and called me 'a dirty son of a bitch,'" Poole said. "Almost simultaneously he lunged at me in a threatening manner, but I was able to side step him. He then swung with his right hand at my face and I successfully ducked this blow."

Poole climbed into the car with Bloch and tried to drive away. Hawkins got in his car too, and to Poole this was a sign that he intended to "follow me and cause trouble." Poole and Bloch got out of their car and tried to get assistance from Laurel officials, including Mayor Carroll Gartin, who refused them. Poole said Gartin was hostile, telling him "he would not believe me on a stack of bibles," and that Poole was on his own.

Eventually, Poole and Bloch made it out of town. Back in Jackson, they conferred with Abzug and decided it wasn't safe to return. Poole called Collins on the morning of the 22nd, asking that the hearing be moved out of Laurel. Collins said no.

Poole then called Governor Wright, who agreed to an impromptu hearing on whether Poole deserved state protection in Laurel. Poole, Bloch, and Abzug met with Wright and other officials, asking for a state escort. They were denied again, and they didn't go back to Laurel the next day.

In Laurel, Collins dismissed the petition for "lack of prosecution," and a Jones County judge named B. Frank Carter swore out a statement saying that Poole was lying, that he'd seen Poole and Hawkins cross paths at the courthouse and nothing happened. Back in Jackson, Laurel officials countered with an aggressive play of their own. Gartin, Swartzfager, Albert Easterling, and E. K. Collins filed a petition with the Mississippi State Bar Association to have Poole disbarred for consorting with "subversive and Communistic elements."

———

Jackson had gotten a paint job since Sullens took his first doubtful look in 1897. By 1950 it was a rapidly growing city with a metropolitan-area population of 142,000. The influx came mainly from in-state immigration and the baby boom, as people of both races left farms and small towns to benefit from an expanding urban economy. In an early 1950s report in the *Memphis Commercial Appeal*, Jackson-based reporter Kenneth Toler assessed the growth with pride, harking back to the Civil War ransacking as he wrote, "The chimneys of destruction . . . have become the smokestacks of a new industrial empire."

That was a stretch. Jackson never became an industrial center on the order of Memphis or New Orleans, but there had been significant development, which Toler illustrated with upbeat statistics: Retail spending had quadrupled since 1940; several new hospitals and schools were under construction; and "195 diversified industries [are] now operating in the manufacture of about 300 different products."

Downtown Jackson was an attractive, orderly grid bordered by State Street to the east and Mill Street to the west. Pascagoula Street to the south and High Street to the north formed a rough rectangle that contained most of the city's hotels, public buildings, churches, and stores. Much more so than today, central Jackson in 1950 hummed with businesses. On Capitol Street alone—the half-mile-

244] THE EYES OF WILLIE McGEE

long main commercial drag, which ran east to west past the antebellum governor's mansion—there were five movie theaters, more than a dozen places to eat, and at least eighty clothing and jewelry stores.

Two blocks north of the mansion stood the state capitol building—called the "New Capitol" to distinguish it from the Greek Revival "Old Capitol" that it had replaced in 1903. Its architectural style was similar to that of the U.S. Capitol, scaled to about half the size. One of its most striking features is a central interior dome that rises to 180 feet, its arches illuminated by hundreds of fat, round lightbulbs that cast a warm glow on plaque-mounted depictions of "Blind Justice."

Elsewhere downtown, rising over everything, were several landmark office buildings and hotels, including the eighteen-story Tower Building (an art deco structure renamed the Standard Life Building in 1952); and "Jackson's first skyscraper," the ten-story Lamar Life building, completed in 1925 and built under the watch of Christian Welty, an insurance company executive and the father of Eudora Welty. The most notable hotels were the Edwards, the Heidelberg, the Robert E. Lee, and the Walthall—each with at least 200 rooms. Blocky buildings that jutted above low-slung downtown stores, they were emblems of a time when every city worth its salt had central lodgings that functioned as one-stop business and leisure depots. Heidelberg stationery from that era boasted of "Night club dancing and broadcasting in the sky . . . South's most beautiful ladies' lounge, see the mural . . . Garage capacity 500 cars, none other like it."

"An asset to . . . Jackson, the Hotel Heidelberg offers the finest in hotel convention facilities and hospitality and comfort to its guests," said the author of *The Story of Jackson*, a civic history published in 1951. "The entire organization reflects the true hospitable spirit of the city. . . ."

It was all strictly segregated, of course. Only a few blocks from the New Capitol, west and northwest, stood a separate district of relatively plain—and sometimes ramshackle—residences, businesses, and churches. Its namesake thoroughfare, Farish Street, was the main artery of African-American life in Jackson. Between 1948 and 1951, Rosalee McGee lived at three different addresses in the Farish Street neighborhood, which was also home to Percy Greene's weekly news-paper, the *Jackson Advocate*.

Greene had been involved in the CRC's anti-Bilbo campaign in 1946 and was still serving as the go-between for its dealings with Rosalee. (She reconnected with him right after her return from Washington.) But he seemed to be losing his taste for the McGee cause, at least pub-licly. Greene was no radical to begin with—he was the go-slow type, closer in spirit to Booker T. Washington than William Patterson—and he was rattled by the coming of the CRC because its Communist ties were politically dangerous. In an *Advocate* editorial published a few days before the clemency hearing, he held out a stiff arm for all to see, writing that the CRC "is not going to do any good for the case of Willie McGee, and it would be just as well if all the delegates planning to come to Mississippi would stay at home."

————

July 25, a Tuesday, was a bright, hot, humid day in Jackson, with a possibility of afternoon thunderstorms and a 100 percent chance of midday shouting. City officials were flexing as if an army of Visigoths were coming. Police Chief Joel D. Holden canceled all vacations and days off, while American Legion posts in Jackson and Laurel pledged to help maintain order against any "subversive and communist indi-viduals." Governor Wright issued a statement letting the CRC dele-gates know they'd better behave. He dismissed their pleas in advance as "lies and propaganda."

Amid the drumbeats, there were even rumors of Ku Klux Klan activity, which was unusual. The Klan was a national force in the 1920s, and it would be important again in the 1960s. But in 1950 it was a marginal outfit, treated as a joke by Mississippi journalists. On July 17, 1950, an A.P. story outlined a Klan power struggle going on in Jackson between Dr. Lycurgus Spinks, a "white-maned" eccentric who ran for governor in 1947, and Thomas J. Flowers, a retired New York policeman originally from Mississippi. In late May, Spinks held a small rally at his "white frame 'Imperial Palace'" on the outskirts of Jackson—"the first Klan extravaganza here in the memory of veteran newsmen," the story said—but it was a weak display. Policemen told Spinks he couldn't burn a cross on his lawn, so he didn't. Among the spectators was a "Negro boy [who] watched wide-eyed without being molested."

The FBI wasn't so sure the Klan was irrelevant. Throughout the five-day period bracketing the 25th, as the situation in Jackson shifted from unruly to dangerous, agents and informants circulated throughout the city, taking notes, hanging out in government buildings and hotel lobbies, and writing reports. The Bureau's file on the McGee case contains dozens of revealing pages about the events that ensued, including a detailed, unsigned summary document that says the FBI believed local Klansmen were responsible. Whether these were Spinks men, Flowers men, or unaffiliated freelancers remains unknown. After all these years, the names of any alleged Klansmen are still blacked out.

━━━

As it happened, Reverend Harris's thousand-man army never materialized. The CRC had negotiated with Governor Wright, who agreed to grant an audience to a manageably sized group, numbering around a dozen, which consisted of liberal Democrats, former Wallace supporters, and even a Communist or two—though nobody advertised that affiliation. Behind the scenes, there were a few black CRC members in Jackson that week, but everybody who appeared before Wright was white, including the delegation's leader, CRC attorney Aubrey Grossman.

There were several women, among them the most prominent delegate, Dr. Gene Weltfish, a Columbia University anthropologist who had studied under the late Franz Boas, an early proponent of the scientific view that no race was inherently inferior. Weltfish's research specialties were the customs and languages of Indian tribes like the Pawnee, but she became well known for a 1943 pamphlet called *The Races of Mankind*, which she co-wrote with her Columbia colleague Ruth Benedict. Using plain language to describe contemporary research into human traits like skin color, cranial shape, and intelligence scores, *Races* championed Boas's egalitarian racial views against the backdrop of World War II, at a time when America's stance on race was painfully contorted—given that the government was condemning Hitler even as it sent a segregated army to fight him.

"All races of man are shoulder to shoulder," the pamphlet said. "Our armed forces are in North Africa with its Negro, Berber, and Near-East peoples. They are in India. They are in China. They are in the Solomons with its dark-skinned, 'strong'-haired Melanesians. Our neighbors now are peoples of all the races of the earth."

Races was supposed to be a unifying propaganda tool, countering Nazi superman theories, but American race theories killed its chances of becoming a government publication. Both the USO and the army decided against distributing the pamphlet, because Southern congressmen raised so much hell over some of its contents.

The problem was Benedict and Weltfish's argument about intelligence, which they said was influenced more by opportunity than by skin color. Citing 1917 test results from black and white soldiers in the American Expeditionary Force, they pointed out that blacks from New York, Illinois, and Ohio outscored whites from Mississippi, Kentucky, and Arkansas. This happened, they said, because the Northern blacks in the sample generally had better access to education. They tried to put it delicately—"Negroes with better luck after they were born got higher scores than Whites with less luck"—but this still infuriated powerful Southern legislators like Kentucky's Andrew J. May, chair of the House Committee on Military Affairs.

The clemency delegation's rank and file also included less prominent people who were picked because they were young, idealistic, and clean-cut. Frank Stoll was a former bomber pilot, originally from Oshkosh, Wisconsin, who had flown some forty-five combat missions in the South Pacific. He and his wife, Anne, met in Chicago after the war and fell in with a group of progressives centered at the University of Wisconsin, among them Lorraine Hansberry, the African-American poet and dramatist who would later write *A Raisin in the Sun*. Sidney Ordower was a veteran from Chicago who had fought in Normandy, where he won a purple heart as an infantry captain. Among his interests, Ordower was a gospel music lover; he became a Chicago fixture in later years by hosting a TV program called *Jubilee Showcase*.

Some of the delegates were fated for Red Scare conflicts with the federal government as the 1950s ground on. In 1952, Weltfish was attacked for stating publicly that the United States was using germ warfare in Korea, which echoed the propaganda of the Soviet Union. That year, she told a Senate subcommittee that all she'd done was hand out a statement from a Canadian peace activist who had made the charge, but she refused to answer questions about whether she agreed with this claim or had ever been a Communist. Columbia's trustees weren't pleased. Though they denied that politics were a factor, they terminated her contract as a lecturer in 1953.

Another woman in the group was Winifred Feise, who still had clear memories of the clemency hearing when I interviewed her by phone in 2005. Feise was a former New Yorker who, at the time of the hearing, was living in New Orleans with her husband, Richard Feise. They'd moved there when Richard took a wartime job with Higgins Industries, builder of PT boats and the Higgins boat, a landing craft used on D-day. Both had been involved in leftist politics since college, and both would wind up on the government's watch list of suspected subversives. In New Orleans, they got to know activists like Oakley Johnson, an English instructor who'd been fired from New York's City College because of his left-wing political beliefs, and James A. Dombrowski, who was director of the Southern Conference for Human Welfare, an interracial progressive group.

Up until the summer of 1950, Winifred Feise hadn't paid much attention to the McGee case. But the CRC needed bodies in the field, so she signed up. Before going to Jackson for the hearing, she'd been part of a small group that went to Laurel from New Orleans to knock on doors and ask questions about Mrs. Hawkins. These visits were noticed, and the visitors' movements were reported in Laurel and Jackson newspapers. On July 14 the *Laurel Leader-Call* published sketchy details about "two men and two women" who turned up in the Magnolia Street neighborhood looking for evidence that McGee had done yard work on the Hawkins's block. A man named F. S. Ford said the strangers were told repeatedly that McGee was a truck driver, not a yard man, but they persisted. As the story suggestively put it, "The men who accompanied the two women remained in a high-powered and expensive automobile as the contacts were made at the doors of the homes within the crime vicinity."

Winifred was in that group, and she remembered knocking on the door of the Hawkins's next-door neighbor, the Jensens. While the men talked to Mrs. Jensen, Winifred carefully studied the driveway between the Jensen and Hawkins homes. It was her understanding that Mrs. Jensen had testified that she saw McGee run down this driveway during his escape.

That's not quite right, but Winifred seemed certain that this was part of the prosecution's case. "The whole story was made up anyway," she told me. "These two, this woman and McGee, had known each other since they were kids playing on the tracks and stuff. At least that's the story we had. He had an affair with her. Nobody ever denied that. It was not a rape."

———

On the morning of the clemency hearing, Feise came up by train from New Orleans, arriving with another woman, Martha Wheeler, at the Illinois Central Depot, a sturdy brick building on Mill Street, in the shadow of the Hotel Edwards. Walking east into the heart of downtown, she was armored against the day in a sundress and wide-brimmed straw hat.

"We put on our gloves and our hats and knew that we had to behave and be good," she recalled. "The few blacks who were on the street saw us coming and nodded or blinked or let us make eye contact to let us know that they knew we were there. It was an absolutely eerie and amazing sensation and experience."

When the women got to their hotel, the Heidelberg, a surprise was waiting. Feise assumed the meeting would take place in some nondescript state office building, but she was told Governor Wright had decided on a fancier setting—the house of representatives chamber in the New Capitol. The hearing was going to be a public show.

Some 150 to 200 people assembled in the house chamber at 11 a.m. Roughly 25 CRC members were on hand, 10 of them serving as official delegates, but only 4 men and 2 women ended up speaking. Abzug wasn't there. She'd done her part the day before, when she, along with Poole and Bloch, argued the *error coram nobis* petition before the Mississippi Supreme Court. Chief Justice Harvey McGehee turned it down on the morning of the 25th, by which time Abzug was already in Washington, preparing to ask for a last-minute stay of execution from the U.S. Supreme Court. McGehee said the defense was offering no new evidence for its claim that Mrs. Hawkins had perjured herself. He called the charge "wholly unsupported by any proof other than that the petitioner himself had sworn to such general allegation."

Along with local and regional reporters, the Northern press was represented by John Popham of the *New York Times*, Stephen Fischer of the *Compass*, and Harry Raymond of the *Daily Worker*. A *Jackson Daily News* photograph taken that morning showed Raymond, with a sly look on his face, walking into the house chamber—next to Governor Wright, Chief Justice McGehee, Attorney General John Kyle, and Colonel T. B. Birdsong, the state commissioner of public safety.

A caption identified Raymond as a reporter for "the Daily Worker of New York, a Communist publication," but that didn't quite cover it. In fact, he was exactly the kind of person Fred Sullens was so worried about: an old-school Communist agitator, one who used journalism the same way Sullens did—as a tool for advancing his political beliefs, often at the expense of accuracy. Raymond's real name was Harold J. Lightcap. During his long career on the left he'd done time for violent rioting in Union Square (he was arrested in 1930 along with Communist leader William Z. Foster), had reportedly served prior sentences for burglary and auto theft, and had been married to a radical labor organizer from Russia, Rose Nelson (aka Rose Lightcap), who was indicted in 1950 on a trumped-up charge of conspiracy to overthrow the U.S. government. As a *Daily Worker* reporter, Raymond was tireless and fearless, a hard-drinking man who'd covered everything from the race riots in Columbia, Tennessee, to the Willie Earle lynching to the Smith Act trials.

The house chamber was an ornate space with high ceilings, dark furniture, and a color scheme that bathed its inhabitants in soft light. The CRC delegates were seated in big swivel chairs on the front row of the legislators' floor area, facing a lectern with a microphone. Wright and McGehee sat in the second row, interrupting when they felt like it—which was often—through mikes mounted at their desks. Spread out in seats behind the main group, or leaning against walls, were dozens of local spectators, American Legionnaires, and even a reputed Klansman or two—many of them visibly hostile to the visitors from the North.

The hearing lasted just over two hours. Dressed in a wide-lapeled suit, his graying hair slicked down on the sides, Aubrey Grossman led off, starting out calmly but getting frustrated as it became obvious that his arguments weren't doing any good. "[Grossman] delivered the opening address in tempered language," Popham wrote in the *Times*, "but . . . made the closing talk in a shouting voice, and was shaking his finger at Chief Justice Harvey McGehee. . . ."

Both sides contributed to the futility of what took place, but much of the blame goes to Governor Wright, who had no interest in a productive discussion. In essence, the hearing was a strategic (and effective) means of bottling up the opposition while giving the appearance of fair play. He'd managed it so that there were only a handful of CRC delegates in town. Now he had them cooped up in a government building, a setting he controlled, instead of marching around on the streets.

On the CRC's side of the gap, there were two problems. At least one person in the group should have taken the time to read the transcript of the third trial, which was stored right there in the capitol. Judging by the back-and-forth that day, it's apparent that the delegates gleaned their knowledge of the case almost entirely from newspaper stories or, as Winifred Feise had done, from word of mouth. "Some claimed they had read portions of the record," a *Jackson Daily News* story said, "but admitted that what they read was printed either in the leftist newspaper, the Daily Compass, or in Civil Rights publications." The group's skimpy knowledge base left them vulnerable when Wright and McGehee, lawyers both, pounded them about not having their facts straight.

The other problem was the same thing that hobbled Abzug, something that only she or Patterson had the power to change. The CRC kept implying that it had electrifying new evidence proving that Mrs. Hawkins had lied. But they wouldn't say what it was, insisting that the place to do that was inside a courtroom during a fourth trial. Grossman ran into this wall almost immediately.

"Let me make this clear," he said. "We feel positively, definitely, strongly that Willie McGee is innocent. And an innocent man should not die. . . . The evidence, excluding the confession, is meaningless. As time passes, facts will come out to show Willie McGee is innocent."

What facts? He didn't say, so his plea came down to telling hostile state officials that they were cruel and unfair. Grossman threw in a general indictment of Mississippi itself, touching on Jim Crow laws, lynchings and legal lynchings, and the state's racist congressional delegation. He said it was "no accident" that the McGee case happened in the home state of a man like Representative John Rankin, whose ideas were "totally false."

Wright bristled. "I assume that your group came in good faith to present reasons why I should stay the execution of Willie McGee," he said. "You have criticized everything, including the administration of justice in the state of Mississippi. I'm not going to have any more criticisms of our courts, of our customs. Stick to this case!"

It went like that with speaker after speaker. Frank Stoll, the veteran from Wisconsin, said he didn't know all the facts but asked that the state allow a new trial anyway, one "where there isn't a mob yelling outside."

Ordower also admitted he hadn't read the transcript, but said that basic knowledge of the trial was enough to show any thinking person that the evidence was inadequate.

McGehee peppered him with questions about the trial, touching on fine-point details like the break-in method used by the rapist and the location of the parked grocery truck. Ordower replied that everything introduced by the prosecution was "very circumstantial evidence." He happened to be right, unless you counted the confession, which McGehee certainly did. He reminded Ordower that it was, after all, his court that had recognized the confession's legitimacy. Did Ordower not understand that it was judges who decide whether a confession was free and voluntary?

During her turn, Weltfish tried an anthropological argument, which came off as condescending. She told Wright and McGehee that their "customs and background" made it impossible for them to look rationally at a rape case involving a black man and a white woman. "Your stresses and anxieties don't permit for objectivity," she said.

"It is your opinion that there should be no death penalty for rape?" Wright asked.

Weltfish answered with a question. "Do you know how many places in the world rape is punished by death?"

"I don't, but I'm not interested," Wright said. "I'm interested only in Mississippi law."

"Has a white man ever been condemned to death for rape in this state?"

"I don't know. But it wouldn't make any difference."

Wright also attacked Rosalee McGee's trustworthiness. During his heated exchanges with Feise, he made it clear that he knew Rosalee wasn't Willie's first spouse. He referred to the *Compass* stories as "a pack of lies written by Willie McGee's so-called wife."

"Is she not Willie McGee's wife?" Feise said.

"I don't know which one she is," Wright countered.

Feise got some licks in too, shocking the audience with the audacity of her questions. "It was obvious throughout that Mrs. Feise . . . disturbed Gov. Wright and his supporters most deeply," Fischer wrote in the *Compass*. While some women "turned their heads or hid their faces in handkerchiefs," Feise said she'd given the entire controversy deep consideration—from a woman's perspective. Though she was thin herself, it was her belief that Mrs. Hawkins should have, and could have, fought off the rapist.

"Could I allow myself to be raped in bed with one of my children

254] THE EYES OF WILLIE McGEE

by my side?" she asked. "Just lie there and let myself be raped? If so, it would mean that I permitted it." After the gasps died down, Feise scandalized the crowd again with questions about such topics as Mrs. Hawkins's menstrual period.

When the time came for a final appeal, Grossman collected his thoughts and asked Wright to issue a stay. "I'm saying to you, Governor, unless you have some interest in putting McGee to death immediately, what human hurt can be done to delay it, so people throughout the world will never say you refused to grant a stay when McGee's attorneys assure you they have new evidence to present? I ask only for a stay so the evidence can be presented and the issue proved."

No chance. "The meeting is adjourned," Wright said. Then he got up and left.

As the gathering dispersed, Fischer heard ominous sounds from a spectator: "I never did believe I would see a thing like this in all my life, arguing and shaking fingers at the governor in public." The meeting, he wrote, ended in "an angry and tense atmosphere."

———

The tensions boiled over quickly. The FBI report said that about one hundred people, upset by what they'd just witnessed, followed some of the CRC delegates back to the Heidelberg. Later in the afternoon, a few unnamed delegates were walking through the hotel lobby when an "aged Jacksonian" decided he couldn't take it anymore. He ran up and swatted them with a newspaper.

That was harmless, but by the end of the day on the 26th, three separate episodes of real violence had taken place. One of them, an attack against Aubrey Grossman inside his room at the Heidelberg, could have ended with serious injury or death.

The journalists in town reported these events in tune with their newspapers' tones and political stances. Popham discreetly placed details of the attacks in the bottom half of a *Times* story. The *Jackson Daily News* thought it was all very cute: "Willie McGee Defenders 'Mussed Up' In Three Fist Fight Disturbances," a typical headline said. And both the *Daily Worker* and the *Compass* made it sound as if severed human heads were bouncing off the pavement.

"Jackson streets began to look like violent wards of a madhouse," wrote Harry Raymond, who, understandably, felt threatened by the presence of roving groups of anti-Communist vigilantes. Raymond was staying at the Robert E. Lee. Late in the afternoon of the 25th, he wrote, a friend called and "suggested I get out of my hotel room. He said: 'They are coming up to get you.'

"My friend, a local white man, said he heard a group talking about getting the *Daily Worker* man. He insisted I go with him and stay the night under his roof, leaving my bag and typewriter in the hotel.

"Today I feel deeply indebted to this fine Mississippi citizen."

Raymond's counterpart at the *Compass*, Stephen Fischer, wasn't as lucky. He and a group that included Winifred Feise and Sidney Ordower were at the Illinois Central station around 8:30 p.m. on the 25th, waiting to put the New Orleans women on a southbound train, when they were surrounded by what Fischer described as a band of twenty men, some holding wrenches.

"The train was announced and we filed out and walked up to the platform," Fischer wrote the next day from New Orleans. "As we did, the men closed in, some shouting obscenities, others walking with determined silence. Some were drunk. Some were only 20 years old. Others were about 60. One threw a lighted cigarette which hit me on the cheek. . . .

"About 20 of the crowd ringed me, forced me down the platform and closed in with blows and kicks. I blocked some, but not all. My greatest fear was being tossed under the train or forced off the plat-form."

The women and Ordower were left unharmed. A few minutes into the attack, a policeman showed up, the men scattered, and Fischer and the women got on the train. Fischer was so shaken up that he took his *Compass* credentials and "flushed them to the tracks." He had no doubt that the *Compass* series, along with the various editorial

256] THE EYES OF WILLIE McGEE

incitements in Jackson newspapers, had gotten him singled out for the beating.

Ordower was attacked later that night at the municipal airport, three miles northwest of the city center. He went there with John Poole, who had been in New Orleans working on a plea to the Fifth Circuit Court of Appeals, which failed. Ordower was heading back to Chicago; Poole was on his way to Washington to help with the final appeal to the U.S. Supreme Court.

They traveled by cab from the Heidelberg, and they were met at the airport by what the *Jackson Daily News* described as "eight to ten men dressed in white sport shirts." Ordower was pulled out of the car, beaten, and kicked, and Poole ducked a couple of punches. The police weren't around to stop the assault, but the attackers voluntarily took off after landing a few blows.

Both incidents gave off a similar feel: They were well organized, and the violence was limited by the attackers themselves. Whoever was behind them knew when and where to find the CRC delegates. According to the FBI report, Grossman believed that Jackson police were tipping attackers off about their movements. After midnight on the 26th, Ordower called the U.S. Attorney's office in Jackson to register a complaint along similar lines. Grossman followed up and demanded federal action and arrests. Nothing came of any of it.

———

Grossman's turn came on Wednesday. He was still at the Heidelberg, where his day began with a 9 a.m. visit from an official delegation that included Governor Wright, the Jackson chief of police, and the chief of the state highway patrol. Wright strongly suggested that Grossman get out of town. Grossman told Wright he had legal business to attend to and demanded law enforcement protection while he did his job.

He didn't get any help, and everything changed in a flash that afternoon. In Washington, Justice Harold Burton had spent the morning reading written arguments filed by McGee's attorneys and by the state of Mississippi. Abzug and Poole presented oral arguments in

Burton's chambers starting around noon, opposed by R. O. Arrington, Mississippi's assistant attorney general. Poole argued that the recent violence in Jackson and the intimidation he received in Laurel were proof enough that a new trial was needed.

"[Poole] spoke with emotion as he related, again and again, how tense feelings in Mississippi [are], and how it has grown worse in recent weeks after incitement by the *Jackson Daily News*," wrote the *Compass*'s Katherine Gillman. Abzug went next, arguing again that the defense had new evidence. When presented at a new trial, it would prove that the prosecution had purposely lied about the facts of the case.

Burton listened quietly, taking notes on a legal pad in a precise, tiny script. These show that Abzug and Poole revealed a little more about their new information than they had done in Mississippi. "[Petitioner] . . . claims newly discovered evidence that McGee had previously had relations with the prosecutrix and is not guilty," Burton wrote.

He made the call at 1:05 p.m., Eastern time. "No criticism of the courts of Mississippi [is] intended by the decision I am about to make," he said. "But the ends of justice shall best be served by granting a stay of execution until the request for a writ certiorari is disposed of by this court."

A telegram went out to Mississippi attorney general John Kyle within minutes. In short order, news of the stay made its way around Jackson. Rosalee McGee was with Percy Greene when she heard. She and a couple of CRC people, both white, walked to a cafe and made a phone call to Laurel—probably to Bessie McGee. Later, a policeman came in and warned them that they shouldn't be sitting at the same restaurant table.

That afternoon, Grossman was in his room when he heard a knock on the door. Whoever it was said "Western Union," and he bought it, opening the door to yet another traveling beatdown. "[E]ight men pushed in and immediately started attacking me," he told reporters later. "All but the well-dressed leader were swinging black jacks— police blackjacks." He said he was roughed up for ten minutes ("I was

a bloody mess—bleeding from a half dozen cuts on my head") when
the men stopped of their own accord and left.

———

Who did it? The Jackson papers were in a mood to applaud, not investigate, and the left-wing papers couldn't do anything but howl from
afar. The most detailed information shows up in the FBI report. Whoever compiled it—the agent just calls himself "this writer"—was either personally present for, or had sources at, all the major events that
week. He and his associates gathered newsworthy material that was
never published anywhere.

The agent attended the *coram nobis* hearing before the Mississippi
Supreme Court, summarized the clemency hearing in the capitol
building, and reported on the attacks at the train station and airport. When news broke about the stay, he was moving around on the
streets downtown and inside the Heidelberg lobby. There, he saw unmistakable signs of trouble—and he named names, but they remain
blacked out.

"Throughout the morning and early afternoon . . . [I] observed
——, the head of the Ku Klux Klan in Jackson, Mississippi, accompanied by two or three men, in and out of the Heidelberg Hotel. ——
had also been observed by the writer and —— at both the Supreme
Court hearing . . . and the Governor's hearing. . . .

"At approximately 2 p.m. on July 26, 1950," he went on, "the writer
observed two men, both of whom were strangers, go up to the Desk
Clerk at the Heidelberg Hotel and ask if AUBREY GROSSMAN were registered at the hotel. When told that he was, the men inquired as to
his room number, which they wrote down on a slip of paper, and immediately left."

This agent had a hands-off attitude about the CRC delegation: His
only job was to monitor the activity of suspected Communists. Still, his
attitude at this moment seems awfully cold-blooded. For all he knew,
he had just witnessed the first step in a murder plot. But he chose to
believe what he'd been told by an informant on the 25th: The attacks

were "movie" fights that were probably "staged by the CRC delegates themselves for propaganda purposes."

The agent was at a downtown post office when he heard, at 3:55 p.m., that a woman staying in a room near Grossman's had called the police to report a disturbance. When detectives arrived, they found Grossman staggering around in the hall, "very bloody, waving a table lamp in his hand." Before long, the hotel physician looked him over, after which he was then taken by ambulance to the Baptist Hospital, where he was X-rayed and treated. Cuts over his left eye and on the right side of his head were patched up.

The FBI agent still seemed to think it was a put-on, that Grossman had smeared blood on his face to hype his injuries. But the report indicates otherwise. As Grossman tried to defend himself, he backed into the bathroom for what, as far as he knew, might be his last stand. The agent was told that "there were handprints in blood on the wall" and that the bathroom "was smeared up very much with blood spots on the walls, bathroom fixtures, etc."

As the agent reported, there was one other outbreak of violence that week. Around midnight on Wednesday, a gun battle broke out that involved an attack by Klansmen on a white citizen of Jackson. It happened several miles north of town on a rural route called Pocahontas Road. Neither the local papers nor the FBI figured out who was behind it. The agent's best guess was that the attacks on the CRC delegates spilled over into late-night celebrations, drinking, and a need to find somebody else to rough up.

Leonard R. Walters, a truck driver for a concrete company, told police that, right around midnight, he heard a racket in his front yard—"It sounded like a war out there"—and he looked out through a screen door to see hooded men setting up a cross. They were firing pistols and calling his name, so he yelled back, asking what they wanted. They wanted him to go for a ride. He refused. Suddenly, his neighbor, a carpenter named O. L. Bradley, came charging out of his house, letting the intruders have it with a pump shotgun.

"The outlaws fled through a cornfield," the *Jackson Daily News* reported, "and Bradley then got an old Japanese rifle he had in the house and continued to fire at the fleeing bed-sheeted group."

Bradley felt sure he'd hit somebody. He told law enforcement officials that he saw one man go down before running off. Later, a mechanic named R. L. Sheppard showed up at a Jackson hospital with pellets in his left eye, left hand, forehead, and face. He denied knowing who shot him or why. A car was shot up too.

It seemed likely that Tom Flowers, the rival of Lycurgus Spinks for control of the local Klan, had something to do with all this, since he was a more effective leader. But he assured the *Jackson Daily News* that this was probably the work of an outlaw Klan faction, or of outright imposters. "We don't do business that way," he said.

eleven

A LONG, LOW SONG

In Laurel on July 26, law enforcement officials were able to get McGee safely out of Jones County and back to Hinds—barely. On the 27th, he wrote Patterson from the Hinds County jail, describing his latest trip to the edge.

"They are all hot, mad feelings are running high here," he said. "I was nearly mobbed Wed. when they brought me from Jones Co. jail. Was knocked down. There was a crowd there. We have to run out the jail to the patrol car. They like to get me, just lucky that I jumped in the floor of the back of the car. Was hit several times before the patrol could pull off. I can't explain to you on paper but I was just lucky that through God I am alive today. I was in a serious place Wed. It all happen so suddenly."

McGee wasn't exaggerating. The *Laurel Leader-Call* ran a front-page story, frankly reporting that he was nearly seized and lynched. "His removal from the jail here was the first time that he has actually faced death from mob violence," the story said.

The court order sparing McGee arrived in Laurel at 11:32 a.m., and word got around fast. "Small groups began to assemble within the courthouse vicinity and before 1:00 o'clock more than a hundred men had reach[ed] the area," the *Leader-Call* said. "They were bitter and there was much talk against the Civil Rights Congress and the Communist Party. . . . 'Go to Washington,' one man said, 'and tell them you are a member of the Communist Party and they'll give you the dome to the Capitol.'"

More ominously, two women moved through the crowd in mid-afternoon, expressing "bitterness and anger" that justice wasn't being served.

262] THE EYES OF WILLIE McGEE

The key moment came at 3:45, when Deputy Sheriff Preston Royals went into the jail by himself to fetch McGee. From there, Royals took him to the courthouse by way of the catwalk that connected the two structures on their second floors. With most of the crowd unaware of their position, they went down the courthouse stairs, out the west entrance, and into a state automobile parked on Fifth Avenue. That side of the courthouse wasn't completely empty, though, and McGee was hit by a man's fist as he ran to the car.

"If the blow had knocked the negro to the sidewalk it appears almost certain that he would have died by lynching," the report said.

With the execution stalled, Laurel's leaders channeled the town's anger into a mass meeting held that night, a response to the alien forces that were causing the delays. Some 300 people gathered inside the courthouse to hear speech after speech by businessmen and city officials who wanted to follow the recent example of Birmingham, Alabama, which had passed an ordinance that mandated fines and jail time for anybody who was a known Communist.

"I am not in a speaking mood tonight, I feel so strongly about this situation," said Mayor Carroll Gartin. "As Mayor, I favor an ordinance to keep communists out of Laurel and the state of Mississippi."

"The situation is more serious than you think," said County Prosecutor E. K. Collins. "This is more than just the trial of Willie McGee." He said the stay happened because of foreign pressure on the State Department, and he urged people to write their congressmen and senators.

In Laurel on August 8, speaking to 2,000 people at the civic auditorium, Governor Wright added to the local sense of outrage, excoriating President Truman, hinting that he might run as a States' Rights candidate for president, and calling the CRC delegation "the nastiest group you ever saw."

———

Wright liked to believe McGee's supporters were, to a person, wily Communists with cynical agendas, but it wasn't true. The best evidence for this is the flood of letters, telegrams, and postcards sent to him in the days and weeks before the clemency hearing. They were mailed from all over the United States and several foreign countries, sometimes written in inscrutable languages. One was addressed to "Gowerner Friedling Wright, Jack-On Stan Missisipi U.S.A."

Harvey McGehee got another thousand or so cards and letters himself. Publicly, both men refused to acknowledge that this correspondence had any significance. Nonetheless, Wright—or somebody in his office—took the trouble to save much of what came in. Stored at the state archives in Jackson, the letters fill twenty boxes. If you take a look through any random stack, it's evident that the CRC had succeeded in making McGee's case resonate with a broader audience than Communists and fellow travelers.

Some of the letters were indeed insults from the left. Carl and Anne Braden, Louisville, Kentucky-based leftists who would figure prominently in the McGee case later, opened with this: "Sometimes you people in Mississippi act like you don't have good sense. You are always picking on some poor person who can't defend himself. You make the rest of the world think that all Southerners are a bunch of Hitlers."

But most were appeals from people who wanted Wright to give serious thought to what was about to happen. A disproportionate number came from the New York area, often inspired by the *Compass* stories.

"I have been reading a series of articles on Willie McGee's case, and my blood was deeply chilled, to see how justice was served to him," wrote a Manhattanite named Edgar A. Walker. ". . . The case has absolutely no foundation, nor substantial evidence to prove that McGee raped Mrs. Hawkins. . . . How could a jury accept such an incredible story?"

Addressing his remarks to "Governor Fielding Elliot," Lewis Fulton, another New Yorker, said, "I don't believe in 'Northerners' meddling in the affairs of 'Southerners.' . . . But in the situation confronting *the world* today, no person with any feeling towards the human race can not but feel that a most terrible injustice has been framed up on Willie McGee. . . . Justice must be done! GRANT A STAY OF EXECUTION!"

Some Southerners spoke up too. Emily Miller Danton, a Mississippi native who was the director of the Birmingham Public Library and whose father, Thomas Marshall Miller, had served as Mississippi's attorney general in the late 1800s, wrote, "From what I can learn of the Willie McGee case, this man has been convicted and sentenced on slight evidence, and a confession secured by torture. I beg that you will stay the execution of that sentence until you *personally* are convinced, not only that this man is guilty of the crime charged, but that he has had a fair trial, and has not been convicted because he is a Negro."

A. D. Beittel, president of Alabama's Talladega College, an African-American institution founded after the Civil War, said he'd been in Europe in 1931 and saw how the Scottsboro case was used to "defame the United States by people who were not cordial to our country." The same thing would happen with the McGee case, he warned, this time in Korea and all over Asia. "Since nothing will be gained by the execution . . . and something may be gained by commuting the sentence," he wrote, "I respectfully request you to extend mercy to the prisoner and see that he is not put to death on this doubtful charge."

———

With the CRC delegates gone, Jackson and Laurel slowly quieted down as combatants on both sides applied bandages, declared victory or vowed revenge, and looked ahead to the next round, which would happen at the U.S. Supreme Court. In Washington, Associate Justice Harold Burton got his own bag of letters about the stay, mostly notes of gratitude from McGee supporters. Many seemed to think his decision indicated a personal preference that, this time, the Court do something to give McGee his freedom.

"Being a white woman, and knowing the terrible prejudices against the negroes in the south, I was heart-broken when I thought that a man must go to his death because of the color of his skin," wrote a Bronx woman named Mrs. Ray Dee. "Not being able to do much in his behalf, I was happy to hear that a man of office had at last had the courage to speak out. . . .

"Thank you again for the great democratic action you have taken, and may God bless you."

Burton heard from detractors too, who crudely attacked his judgment and patriotism. "Let me state this question, Sir," wrote A. W. Hendrix, a Mississippi native living in New Orleans. "*If your* wife, or mother, or daughter had been raped by a *nigger*—who *knew* better—how sir, would *you* feel? I have no hesitation in saying you have committed a travesty of justice in your arbitrary action, taken in the case of Willie Magee—an honestly and legally convicted *rapist* of one of our women."

"Hurrah for you and Robeson," said a curt telegram sent by a Texas man named Gordon Allen. "You are without a doubt the number one and two red in the country."

Congressman William Colmer of Mississippi, whose district contained Jones County, denounced the CRC in the *Congressional Record*, along with the " 'do-gooders,' fellow travelers, and left-wing press" who were devoted to "fomenting discord and disunity between the Negroes and the white people of the South."

In the North, the words were flying just as furiously that summer, in part because there had been a victory in another much watched legal-lynching fight: the case of the Martinsville Seven. In that one, which NAACP lawyers were defending, seven young black men in the town of Martinsville, Virginia, had been convicted of the January 8, 1949, gang rape of a thirty-two-year-old white woman named Ruby Floyd. All were sentenced to death, and, as in the McGee case, they'd been kept alive only through state and federal appeals. On July 26—the same day Burton issued his McGee stay—there was an encouraging Martinsville development when the NAACP persuaded a city judge in Richmond, Virginia, to stay the executions while he examined a petition they'd submitted for a writ of habeas corpus.

These two temporary wins, happening so close together, inspired the *Daily Worker* and the *New York Compass* to proclaim that final victory was in sight. "They couldn't get away with their 'legal' murder of Willie McGee and the framed seven Negroes of Martinsville,

266] THE EYES OF WILLIE McGEE

Virginia," a *Daily Worker* editorial said. "No. The world of the KKK lynchers and their rotten judges and governors is not exactly what it used to be when the murder of a n—r, either with or without benefit of a 'jury trial' was just routine."

To the *Worker*, both cases had taken on transcendent significance. They were of a piece with a revolutionary movement against white domination and colonialism that was beginning to sweep the world. "All Asia is aflame as the colored peoples in Malaya, Indo-China, the Philippines, [and] Indonesia act to throw off the 'white supremacy' lynch terror. Africa seethes like a volcano as the black man's anger and revolt mutters like coming lightning and thunder."

In the *Compass*, Ted Thackrey kept his comments closer to home, but he was jubilant too. "It is a late hour and the victory by no means complete—but United States Supreme Court Justice Harold Burton advanced the cause of democracy around the world when he granted a stay of execution to Willie McGee, Negro," he wrote. "Justice Burton's action assures a Supreme Court review this fall of McGee's arrest and conviction. . . .

"His action will have the effect of erasing some of the grave damage already done in the McGee case to our pretensions of a democratic system in which all men are equal before the law. . . ."

It would indeed, assuming the Supreme Court decided to hear the case—a big assumption, since the justices had twice declined to do so. In the interim, as the *Worker* and *Compass* both appeared to forget, the Court's makeup had barely changed.

———

In Mississippi, it was a period of paybacks. One thing the FBI missed during its July surveillance was that a black maid at the Heidelberg, a woman named Raberthe Hanks, had put herself at personal risk to protect Aubrey Grossman from the beating he received—and then lost her job as a result. Nobody knew about this at the time, including Grossman, but in early 1952 he got a letter from Hanks, who described what had happened.

"I am a poor Negro woman who was working at the hotel where you was beat up in the year 1950," she wrote. "I was fired because I would not turn over to the manager of the hotel . . . the key [to give] the leader of the gang that beat you. He has not been fired. But I can't get a job anywhere in Mississippi." Hanks said she'd moved to the Delta looking for work—no luck—and had come back to Jackson, where she tracked down Rosalee McGee to tell her story. She hinted that perhaps she, like Rosalee, could travel north to speak before crowds. "[I]f can do any good, please notify me at the above address for I am willing to come to New York but I has no money," she said.

As for McGee, the July disturbances prompted his jailers to retaliate by cutting off his visitation rights. Rosalee wrote Patterson about this on August 1, 1950.

> Well I feel very bad today because I can't even visit Willie now. And I know he needs some clothes and cigarettes. . . . They got him in the death cell with two white men. One of the Negro trustees slip out and told me what the jailer said about me and I told Mr. Greene and he told me not to go over there.
>
> The jailer said if I ever come over there, he was going say something to me so he could beat hell out of me and lock me up. He said if it had not been for me, the CRC never would have come down here and that he was going to keep me and my mother-in-law out his jail. . . .
>
> Everybody tell me you should leave here, but I feel with McGee here my job is not done and if I began to run, I can't fight. And if I die about the truth, I won't feel hurt at all. . . .
>
> Mr. Patterson, I want each and every one to know that I do thank them for helping me and I am going to fight until all Americans are free from Jim crow system. I have learned that Willie's life is not the only one that is in danger. And I am going to fight not for one but for all. We never know who may be next.

Rosalee wrote frequently in the weeks ahead as her situation deteriorated. On August 22, she reported that she was broke, having worked "only five days since I been back" to Mississippi from her

Northern trip, and that she'd been bedridden with pains in her side. The CRC lost track of her in September, but she wrote several times in October, saying she'd been out of town dealing with the September 19 death of "my oldest sister."

Rosalee didn't name the sister or say where she went to be with her, but she mentioned that this woman had looked after her children when she was away on her CRC travels. Seeing shadows, she speculated that her sister might have been murdered to interfere with her CRC work. "[T]hey say the Doctor kill her so [my children] wouldn't have no place to stay when I am away. The Doctor gave her shot and cort a stroke. . . ."

Rosalee also had a problem with Percy Greene, publisher of the *Jackson Advocate*, whose support of McGee apparently ended with the July incidents. She described her conflicts with him in several letters, but they boiled down to two things: She accused Greene of withholding money the CRC had sent to her through him, and she said he was harassing her about the foolishness of staying involved with Communists.

On October 24, she wrote, "I went to see Mr. Greene, to the one I thought was my friend and I hate to say this but he turn me out so cold I was just like a lost sheep from the fold. But I want you all to no that I didn't get the money and I am not going to do what he told me. Commie or whatever the peoples was, I know that save my husband life."

It's hard to separate fact from fiction in these letters—there's another one in this period by Gracie Lee McGee, supposedly mailed from Laurel. But, overall, there's a consistency to the tone and details. Rosalee was having a hard time getting by: She still appeared to be taking care of real children, and she still believed in McGee and the CRC's larger mission.

"I was working at two places but one of the lady wanted me to work all day for one dollar and a half and some old clothes," she said in one letter. ". . . I'm not going to be a dog for no one when Willie have been facing death for 1,829 days. . . . I don't have dime but I am willing to suffer and wait for Willie."

McGee started sending letters again in August, usually to Lottie Gordon, thanking her for the CRC's support and the care packages she sent. Months later, when Christmas came around, Gordon arranged to have gifts sent to Willie, Rosalee, and the kids. Rosalee put together a wish list from the four McGee children, and Gordon sent along two winter coats, a football, a cap, and a watch. Willie asked for a modest creature comfort: pajamas.

"I wear a medium size pajama suit," he wrote in late November. "I not a very big man at all." They arrived in time, and he wrote Gordon a thank-you note on December 26. "[T]hey was just right," he said, "and I like them."

———

Another person who suffered setbacks that summer was John Poole. His conduct in the McGee case had angered powerful people in Mississippi, and they started coming after him in a way that left no doubt they were in it for the long haul.

The opening move was the disbarment action filed on July 22 by various Laurel officials. Their petition to the Mississippi Bar Association charged that Poole was unfit to practice because he was "aligned with and employed by subversive and communistic elements." They also alleged unscrupulous conduct for making false charges and filing false motions. Here, they were referring to Poole's claim at the third trial that the prosecution had tampered with the grand-jury selection process, and to the unacceptable manner, in their view, in which he'd pursued the question of whether Mrs. Hawkins had "consented" to the rape.

Dixon Pyles had poked the same sore spots—why hadn't he been attacked? There were two main reasons. First, Pyles got out of the case before people paid much attention, while Poole was in the thick of it at the worst possible times: during the third trial and the CRC's "invasion." In addition, Poole's libel suit—which eventually went to trial before a federal jury in Jackson—guaranteed the long-term wrath of people like Fred Sullens.

The libel trial happened prior to the CRC protests, in late June 1950.

It wasn't transcribed and it received little coverage—even in Jackson newspapers—but it was a full-blown proceeding, complete with testimony that took up two and a half days. Jurors heard from Sullens, from Laurel officials like Judge Collins, and from fifteen character witnesses who spoke up for Poole. He had sixty-five supporters lined up, but the presiding judge, Sidney Mize, called that number "undue" and told his lawyers to pare it down.

Poole was kept on the defensive throughout—the trial was really about him, after all. Under oath, he admitted to taking money from the CRC but said he was working for a client, not an ideology, and that his right to do so should be unquestioned. "I just took their money to defend a man and I would take yours," he told Tom Watkins. "I think it is entirely two different things, if I take money to go out and try to overthrow the government, and another thing, to defend a man."

Poole was attacked for questioning the grand-jury process and for smearing Mrs. Hawkins. When Sullens took the stand, he said that, for these and other reasons, he proudly stood by his editorial. "Clarifying his meaning, he said he meant by 'lousy' not that Poole was 'lice-infested' but was 'sub-standard or below par,'" the *Jackson Daily News* said in its story about the trial. "Regarding the word 'conscienceless,' he said that any lawyer 'who would willfully besmirch the name of a woman who had been through dire tragedy' is 'conscienceless.'

"'I meant that then, and I mean it now,' he declared."

For Poole, the problem—as always—was the jury: a panel of white men whose attitudes about race, women, and Communism were the same as those of McGee's trial jurors. After deliberating for four hours, they ruled on June 29 that no libel had occurred.

The next day, in a triumphant *Jackson Daily News* front-page story, Sullens said the victory was not his alone. "The invasion of Southern courts by Northern interventionists bent on saving the lives of proven Negro rapists was repudiated here . . . by a Federal Court jury," the article began. ". . . The jury in effect . . . backed the right of the Jackson Daily News to continue to interpret the news fearlessly and courageously."

The loss was a crushing blow to Poole, a young lawyer who, according to a federal judge and jury, had been proved to be "lousy and conscienceless." This, coupled with the fallout from the CRC's Jackson protests, made him finally decide he'd had enough. On August 16, he withdrew as McGee's lawyer, distancing himself from the CRC in a statement released to the press.

"I am not a member of the Civil Rights Congress, and I am not associated with it in any manner whatever," he said. "As a matter of fact, I strongly object to the actions of its members when they were in Jackson."

Unfortunately, Poole was past the point where he could just walk away. In Laurel, Albert Easterling called his statement a transparent act of appeasement, saying, "He is in direct peril as a result of his own acts and with more zeal and fervor we shall press our charges against him." As it turned out, Fred Sullens wasn't finished with him either.

———

William Patterson was heading for legal problems himself, ones that would torment him for years. At issue was the oft-argued question of whether an organization like the CRC, a politically active nonprofit with Communist members, had a right to keep its records private. Committees like HUAC had long used Congress's power to punish people for contempt—with penalties ranging from fines to jail time, all duly litigated in federal courts—as a tool to pry information from suspect organizations or to put their leaders in jail.

On August 3 and 4, Patterson was called before the House Select Committee on Lobbying Activities, which ordered him to hand over CRC records, including the names of people who contributed to the group. He refused. In the process, he made a Georgia congressman so angry that their exchanges nearly ended in a brawl.

During Patterson's second day as a witness, he maintained that the committee's harassment was keeping him from doing his real job: defending the civil rights of people like Willie McGee and Rosa Lee Ingram, a black woman from Georgia who was serving a life sentence, along with two of her sons, for the 1947 killing of a white man named

John Stratford. Ingram said Stratford had tried to molest her and that one of her sons struck him in self-defense. As Patterson knew, all three were originally sentenced to death, and during his testimony he denounced the case as a legal lynching. This angered Henderson Lanham, a sixty-one-year-old congressman from Rome, Georgia, who was the committee's acting chairman. He said the state of Georgia had never lynched anybody and called Patterson a liar.

"The state of Georgia tried to lynch nine men in the Scottsboro case," Patterson shot back. "Georgia is a state of lynchers." He misspoke—as he certainly knew, Scottsboro happened in Alabama. But he'd made his point, which he stood by. "A black man has no rights that a white man is bound to respect in Georgia," he said.

"You're a liar," Lanham said. "If any state is fair to niggers, it's Georgia."

Patterson stared at him a moment, seething, and then said, "You're a liar too."

That did it for Lanham. Shouting "Black son of a bitch!" he jumped out of his chair and ran toward Patterson with his fists clenched. Two capitol policemen stopped him and dragged him back to the committee-room dais, where, according to a report in the *New York Compass*, "he paced back and forth repeating the epithet four more times. . . ."

The *Compass* story was accompanied by a Ted Thackrey editorial that apologized for quoting the congressman's foul language before reminding readers, in a somber tone, what this incident exposed: American fascism at its worst. "Have the apostles of Hitler become so bold that no lover of democracy is left in the House with sufficient courage and decency to denounce them when their acts are clear and indulged in as House officials?"

Apparently so: Lanham was never penalized. Months later he wisecracked that, if he had it to do over again, he would have called Patterson a Communist SOB instead. Patterson was cited for contempt of Congress in late August. In November, he was indicted in federal district court in Washington. For the rest of the time that Patterson worked to keep Willie McGee alive, he would also have to fight to keep himself out of jail.

———

The bomb that never dropped during the Jackson invasion—which Abzug hinted at when she pleaded before Justice Burton—was an affidavit by Rosalee McGee, which had been put to paper in Washington on July 25. As sworn statements go, it's a strange one, since large portions of it can't be true. The central premise is that Rosalee was married to Willie—living in Laurel and helping raise their four children—during the crucial years in the early 1940s when, according to this version, his affair with Mrs. Hawkins got going. But Rosalee was living in the Lexington and Durant areas at that time, married, for however long, to George Gilmore Jr.

Still, just because she was lying doesn't rule out the possibility that the affidavit contained elements of truth. Willie could have told Rosalee a true account of what had happened to him—and how his ex-wife played into it—asking Rosalee to swear to the story in Eliza Jane's place. But that's the best possible interpretation for the deception. The worst is that he dragged her into a lie because it was his only chance of survival.

As for the CRC, it's hard to imagine they didn't have some inkling the story was suspicious, but there's no way to know. Whatever files Abzug and Poole kept on the case have not survived, and there's nothing in the CRC papers about it. In the FBI file on McGee, buried in a July 25 report from the Washington, D.C., field office, there's one hint that Abzug was worried about Rosalee's veracity. An informant told the Bureau that McGee's lawyers had presented a copy of Rosalee's affidavit to U.S. attorney general J. Howard McGrath and Democratic National Committee chairman William M. Boyle Jr., "with the threat that it would be published unless they take some action on it." But the informant also said Abzug was "fearful of publishing affidavit in present form for fear it may contain inaccuracies as to dates and places."

That could mean almost anything, though. Abzug may have merely thought the document needed basic fact-checking. Still, it would be a long time before the CRC went public with it: not until March 1951. From then on, even though the affidavit was full of false statements, McGee supporters would treat it as proof that Mrs. Hawkins had lied.

The story Rosalee told began "back in 1936 and 1937," when she said McGee and Troy Hawkins were both working at the Masonite plant in Laurel. This led to McGee's getting hired to do yard work and housecleaning at the Hawkins home.

"As far as I can remember, starting at least back in 1942, before Willie went into the Army, Mrs. Hawkins used to come to our house and ask for Willie," Rosalee said. "The first time she came, she asked me where Willie was. I told her Willie wasn't home and asked her what she wanted. She told me she wanted him to work in her yard.

"That night I asked Willie, 'What she want?' So he tell me, 'Next time she come, tell her to go away. She don't want me to work in no yard.'"

Willie's departure for the army solved the problem until 1943, when he came back to Laurel and resumed married life with Rosalee. But Mrs. Hawkins quickly swooped in. Willie and Rosalee were walking home from the movies one night, around 10:30, when she came out of an alley and tried to force Willie to get in her car.

"I got so mad I said, 'What's that!'" Rosalee said. "And I started to pull him away.

"And Willie himself he told her, 'Go 'way. This is my wife. I'm with my wife.'

"So she says to Willie out loud, 'Don't fool with no Negro whores.'"

Willie told Rosalee everything that night. How the affair had started and why he was powerless to end it. How Mrs. Hawkins was threatening to expose him to harm if he didn't do what she wanted.

"Down South, you tell a woman like that no, and she'll cry rape anyway," Rosalee said. "So what else could Willie do." His first impulse was to gather his family and leave town, but "we didn't have no money for Willie and me and the four children, all of us to go away. So Willie went away to California by himself."

Rosalee didn't say how long he was gone. When he came back, homesick, the affair started again. Rosalee's account said nothing about why Willie went to the Hawkins home on the night of the alleged rape—presumably, it was just another date—but she said it was common knowledge that Troy and Willette "had a big argument" that night and that Troy was seen "chasing her right out into the street at five o'clock in the morning—they say her husband was about ready to kill her that night.

"So I guess to save herself from her husband," Rosalee concluded, "she figured she would say she was raped and get Willie lynched."

———

Abzug filed McGee's latest Supreme Court appeal on November 22, 1950, but even at this critical moment she didn't mention Rosalee's dramatic claims. In hindsight, that seems like a tactical blunder. But at the time, and in the context of what Abzug was asking the Court to do, it made sense.

The goal was to get a reversal of Harvey McGehee's refusal to grant a writ of *error coram nobis*, leading to a new jury trial where the evidence would, at last, be presented. As any lawyer knew, it wasn't the Supreme Court's job to retry a case based on new evidence, so Abzug decided it would suffice to describe the allegations in general terms while explaining why she'd thought it necessary to follow the same strategy with the Mississippi Supreme Court. Thus, the appeal said that any sex Mrs. Hawkins had with McGee was "voluntary," and that she'd lied on the stand. But it didn't fill in the blanks, which reporters and Supreme Court clerks couldn't help but notice.

The *Clarion Ledger* said of the brief: "It is charged, without proof so far, that false testimony was presented against the Negro." Louis Lautier, a Washington-based writer with the National Negro Publishers Association, gave Abzug's argument careful scrutiny for an article distributed to African-American newspapers, and he seemed to guess what was left out—and what would come later. "Attorneys for Willie McGee . . . hint strongly in a petition for a review of the case that the prosecutrix was not ravished," he wrote. ". . . [McGee] charges that the State knew the prosecutrix lied when she testified that the alleged 'sexual intercourse' which took place November 2, 1945, constituted an act of rape."

Supreme Court clerk Murray L. Schwartz, writing again for Chief Justice Vinson in an undated circulating memo, wrote, "[I]t should be pointed out that it now appears to be petitioner's argument that the intercourse from which the rape charge arises took place voluntarily on the part of the prosecutrix. . . ." As Schwartz explained, the Mississippi Supreme Court had denied the writ because the defense failed to present witnesses and evidence supporting its claims. In Abzug's appeal to the U.S. Supreme Court, she said there was a good reason for that: If she'd used her witnesses in front of McGehee, there would have been so much community hostility against them that they wouldn't have dared testify again.

"If [Willie McGee] had attempted to produce them at a preliminary hearing in the Mississippi Supreme Court, their identity would have become known and popular passion would have restrained them from testifying at the full hearing," Schwartz wrote.

As he noted, there were other claims in the appeal—Abzug argued that McGee had been denied equal protection because of the "gross imbalance between death sentences received by white men and Negroes for rape" and that the prosecution lied about how his confession was obtained—but the *coram nobis* claim was the central pillar.

It wasn't convincing to Schwartz, however, who recommended that the Court again deny the appeal. It bothered him that the defense was asking the justices to accept it on faith that the new evidence, whatever it was, warranted a fourth trial.

"[I]t seems to me that . . . it was incumbent upon petitioner to indicate to the Miss. Supreme Court, and indeed to this Court, what his evidence is, to warrant the holding of a trial on the issues," he wrote. ". . . Whatever doubts there may be as to the validity of this conviction, I do not see how it can be said that the failure to hold a hearing on the allegations of the petition was a denial of a federal right."

John G. Burnett, a clerk for William O. Douglas, agreed. "It seems doubtful to me that it would be appropriate for this Court to reverse and direct issuance of the writ solely on the basis of unsupported allegations," he wrote in a memo dated January 11, 1951. "It may be true that community passions are at such a level that it would be justifiable not to present witnesses at these proceedings. But, absent evidence, the state court would seem in the best position to take judicial notice of such facts and excuse the failure to present witnesses."

Four days later, the Court declined to hear the case, and the optimism of 1950 instantly became the despair of 1951. In Jackson, Fred Sullens beat his chest. In a January 17 *Jackson Daily News* editorial called "No More Interference," he talked about McGee's lawyers in the same insulting terms that had prompted Poole's libel suit. "This should end the matter," he wrote, ". . . from now on any lousy, conscienceless lawyer who seeks to defeat the ends of justice in the Willie McGee case should be branded as a public enemy and treated as such."

As word spread among McGee's supporters, the seriousness of this setback was unmistakable. The *Daily Worker* was eloquent that day, publishing an editorial that mourned the outcome but promised victory down the road.

"These judges fear the freedom-seeking, 14,000,000 Negro people trampled on inside the U.S. by the 'white supremacy' system," it said. "The judges are a part of that system. They work to uphold it. . . .

"When they crush the liberties of the Negro victims, they also crush the liberties of the entire nation. Lincoln knew that this was the battle-line. We must know it, and act on that knowledge."

In Mississippi, Bessie McGee wrote the CRC from Laurel, plaintively asking, what now? "My hart is hurt after I saw what I did in the paper about Willie," she said. "I aint been well at all. I rote Bella and I sent her Friday paper about [this] and I just want to no what are you all going to [do] now."

For several days, the CRC was unable to find Rosalee to let her know. Aubrey Grossman wanted her to come north again, to take part in public protests over the McGee and Martinsville Seven cases. She turned up in late January, writing three letters in quick succession, explaining that she'd taken the children to Lexington because they were upset by the bad news and saying that, yes, she would be glad to travel wherever they wanted her to go.

"I was dead broke until i got to Jackson and found the money order from Lottie," she wrote on the 24th. "[Y]ou ask me bout going to va. yes i will go where ever you wont me to go."

She didn't make that trip, however, and she couldn't have done much good if she had. The Martinsville Seven were dead within two weeks.

———

Since taking over the CRC, Patterson had vigorously pursued his "mass defense" strategy in the McGee case and had been successful at bringing attention to a story that was overlooked before he came along. If he'd had his way, the CRC would have used the same tactics with several high-profile cases from that era, but there was a problem. The NAACP had control of many of them—including the trials of Rosa Lee Ingram and the Martinsville Seven—and its officials never relented about treating the CRC as a pariah organization.

Patterson's public reaction to this was confusion and hurt feelings. The CRC and NAACP were working for the same thing—racial justice—so why couldn't they work together? But the NAACP may have been right to mistrust his intentions. In 1947, an FBI informant reported on Patterson's attendance at a meeting of Communist Party leaders in New York. One issue was Communist strategy in relation to the NAACP, and Patterson said it had been decided that the goal was to infiltrate the older, larger group at the leadership level.

"Informant stated that he learned from Subject [Patterson] that the strategy of the Party would not be to attempt to completely capture the NAACP but merely to guide its policies by electing Communists to the executive board of that organization," said an FBI report from late 1947. "The same informant advised that on August 30, 1947 he had attended a meeting of the Negro Commission of the Communist Party and that Subject had presided as chairman. At this meeting it was decided that the Communist Party would send their people into the NAACP and prepare to put up a struggle to place trade union members on the NAACP executive board."

The Martinsville Seven case, which came to an end in early February 1951, is a good example of how the NAACP kept the CRC at bay. Early on, Patterson had attempted to get a CRC loyalist attached to the case, announcing in June 1949 that the group would provide a lawyer who would request a new trial for one of the convicted men, Francis DeSales Grayson. But Martin A. Martin, the NAACP's chief lawyer for the Martinsville cases, announced that any association between the two organizations was out of the question. "Our firm and the NAACP cannot at this time be associated in any way with any organization which has been declared subversive by the United States Attorney General," he said.

Cooperation wouldn't have worked anyway, since the groups had opposite views of the best strategy. Martinsville was different from the McGee case in one key respect: Many people, including people who wanted to save the defendants' lives, believed that at least some of the men had raped Ruby Floyd—a conclusion later shared by criminal justice professor Eric W. Rise in his 1995 book, *The Martinsville Seven: Race, Rape, and Capital Punishment*. During its appeals, the NAACP didn't argue the question of guilt or innocence; instead it argued that the men hadn't received a proper trial or fair sentancing. In a letter to the *Nation* written after the case ended, NAACP lawyers explained, "The question of their guilt or innocence was not raised by us, for under the law a person is presumed to be innocent until proved guilty beyond all reasonable doubt after having had a fair trial. The NAACP has maintained that these men did not get a fair trial and that therefore the presumption of their innocence remains."

Patterson treated Martinsville as another sham rape charge. "The alleged victim was well known to be a prostitute as well as a mentally retarded person, and there was no evidence that a rape had taken place," he wrote in *The Man Who Cried Genocide*. As in the McGee campaign, however, that claim wasn't proven—it was only asserted, and in Ruby Floyd's case, it seems especially doubtful that the CRC had it right.

Floyd was a Jehovah's Witness who often sold used clothing and vegetables in black neighborhoods. According to her story, she was out trying to collect an unpaid debt on some clothing—accompanied by an eleven-year-old African-American boy named Charlie Martin—when they came across a group of four young black males gathered near a stretch of railroad tracks. When they passed by again after finishing their errand, Floyd said, she was dragged into a stand of woods and raped, first by the four men who originally spotted her, and later by three more who came along when they heard about what was going on. That evening, according to Rise, she turned up at the door of a woman named Mary Wade, "clad only in her shirt, sweater, and a torn slip." She had scratched arms, tangled hair, and, said Wade, "her thighs were rubbed red-like."

There were other witnesses as well. Charlie Martin testified that he saw four of the men attack her. Josephine Grayson—the wife of defendant Francis DeSales Grayson—was walking along the tracks with another woman when Floyd staggered out of the woods, fell into her arms, and begged for help. She didn't get any, and Floyd was shortly dragged back into the woods by a defendant named Joe Henry Hampton.

After all the men were found guilty in April and May 1949, the NAACP's lawyers tried a variety of appeals—including a failed appeal to the U.S. Supreme Court, based on Virginia's discriminatory application of the death penalty for rape. As Rise explained in *The Martinsville Seven*, Martin A. Martin drew on various studies to press this claim, including one that showed that "93 percent of the men executed for rape in thirteen southern states between 1938 and 1948 were black." In early 1951, however, the Court declined to take the case. The same arguments were also used, without success, in McGee's appeals.

Shut out of the courtrooms, the CRC made its contribution in the streets. In late January, it helped organize a "mass pilgrimage" designed to persuade Governor John S. Battle or President Truman to stop the executions. In Washington, CRC-affiliated writers like Dashiell Hammett and Howard Fast took part in a "death vigil" in front of the White House. The picketing went on for several days, around the clock, and was carried out in frigid temperatures. Patterson was there, escorting Mrs. Grayson and her children.

The protests had no effect. On Friday, February 2, defendants Joe Henry Hampton, Booker T. Millner, Howard Lee Hairston, and Frank Hairston Jr. were electrocuted in Richmond. On Monday the 5th, they were followed by James Hairston, John Clabon Taylor, and Francis DeSales Grayson. Among the public mourners was a 900-person mixed-race group in Richmond, who carried floral wreaths to the state capitol. There were vigils in Philadelphia, Boston, Chicago, Los Angeles, and Harlem.

The *Daily Worker* mixed its words of mourning with turbulent imagery ("From their funeral pyre shot up a flame so high it was seen around the world"), while *Time*, offended by the Communists' use of the case for propaganda, reflexively sneered: "The Communist calliope swung into high. . . . Moscow trotted out its tame intellects. . . . The radio of the Chinese People's Government broadcast an appeal to stay 'this barbaric sentence.' "

In those days, events like this often inspired protest poetry, and the bard of the Martinsville case was a man named Walter Lowenfels, a *Daily Worker* contributor who wrote a haunting piece called "The Martinsville Chant." Lowenfels was moved by the sight of Mrs. Grayson, trudging back and forth on the picket line.

Singing her long, low song to its final end in silence
as she marched on the vigil the last day in front of the
White House lawn
and her eyes tightened closer and her dark face settled like
an Aztec mask
and her body drooped lower and the last sound
parted from her like the living heart ripped warm out
of the living sacrifice in the temple stones of America.

Reviewing the case in the *New Leader*, writer Henry Lee Moon criticized the CRC for sullying the protest efforts but was more offended by mainstream journalism, which gave surprisingly little coverage to the case. "If there were not a deliberate conspiracy to suppress the story there was certainly widespread unconcern over it, as though the sacrifice of seven lives for a single crime which involved no loss of life were an everyday occurrence," he wrote. He called it a "ghastly spectacle" that could only encourage anti-American sentiment abroad. "Not only the Communists," he said, "but millions of others must ask why the death penalty for rape is reserved exclusively for Negroes."

On February 3, 1951, McGee signed an affidavit before the Hinds County chancery clerk that gave his account of what had happened between him and Mrs. Hawkins, and it would color every event from then on. He'd told the story privately to his trial lawyers in 1946 and 1948, but this version was simpler because it was stripped of two dramatic plot elements: There was no mention of McGee's impregnating Mrs. Hawkins and not a word about their alleged scheme to murder Troy.

McGee either forgot these details (which seems impossible), dropped them because they weren't true or because he was afraid he'd be lynched, or dropped them because his lawyers told him he had to. In any event, the "double indemnity" plotline was gone. It was replaced by a more conventional tale of a lust-driven affair that came to an end when McGee, as he told it, was caught by Troy Hawkins and framed to save Willette's reputation.

The 1946 version was much longer and featured a different timetable about when the affair started. It began with McGee's account of his life story, in which he listed various jobs he'd held up through 1941. The years between 1941 and 1944 were largely skipped, but he said the affair started in August 1944. He didn't mention doing household or yard work prior to then for the Hawkins family.

He said Mrs. Hawkins had flirted with him once when he offered to carry something for her, but that the affair didn't commence until she invited him inside her home one day to wash windows and wax floors, seducing him in a bedroom.

In 1951's compressed version, McGee only mentioned working at Masonite, saying he was there "in the late nineteen thirties" and that, during this period, he started doing house and yard chores for various white people in Laurel, including Troy Hawkins, who had worked at Masonite at the same time. He didn't say when the affair began, only that Mrs. Hawkins made sexual overtures while he was inside the house, and that he returned frequently for more encounters. McGee feared the consequences, so "I went to California about the year 1944 because I knew what was happening would one way or another come out and get me killed."

Thus, the new version had McGee running away from the affair in the same year that, in the old version, it started. Later—McGee didn't say when—he came back, and Mrs. Hawkins "renewed the acquaintance." She would turn up at his house looking for him, which made his wife suspicious. He alluded to the same incident that Rosalee had described in her statement from July 25, 1950, in which Mrs. Hawkins harassed them on the streets one night. That story was absent from his 1946 account.

The most interesting new detail concerned what allegedly happened when Troy discovered the truth. In 1946, McGee said he had gone to the Hawkins home on the Thursday night before the alleged rape, had sex with Willette, and backed out of the murder plot. Now, in 1951, McGee said that "the night before the night on which they claim I raped her"—which meant Wednesday, October 31—"I went by the house about 10:30 or a little later to get some money from her. While I was there Mr. Hawkins unexpectedly came in and I was in the house although I was not at the time doing anything wrong and Mr. Hawkins said angrily, 'What in the God Damn Hell does this mean,' and he grabbed me and I shoved him back and I ran out of the door. That night I came to the house on foot. The following night when they claim I raped her, I had the truck but I did not go to Mr. Hawkin's [sic] house or anywhere near it."

McGee's implication was that Troy and Willette decided to hoax the rape and frame him, to cover up their shame and get revenge. The statement concluded with McGee explaining why he hadn't told this story before. He said he had but that his lawyer, John Poole, "told me that if I said anything about it I'd get both him and myself killed."

twelve

BARE-LEGGED WOMEN

On February 5, the Mississippi Supreme Court set a new execution date for McGee: March 20, 1951. Bella Abzug and John Coe were already working on new federal appeals, and this time they included details of the affair, making McGee's bombshell story part of the package from then on.

The claim started showing up in left-wing newspapers just before Abzug and Coe presented it in court. The *Daily Worker* mentioned it first, on February 25, summarizing what McGee had said and adding something that wasn't in his statement: the charge that Mrs. Hawkins "threatened to cry rape and place him at the mercy of the lynch mob if he didn't agree to the relationship."

That language was from CRC press materials, which appear to have taken details from both Rosalee's and Willie's statements and, in the process, added a few new twists. The *Daily People's World* used the same information in a story published on March 2, which claimed, "The relationship was well known in the community, thus moving white supremacists to press feverishly for McGee's death."

Abzug and Coe presented their new material on March 5, when they filed a petition for habeas corpus with Judge Sidney Mize, who heard them at the federal district court in Vicksburg. Their summary contained more precise dates than McGee's affidavit. They said Willie and Troy first started working together at Masonite in either 1936 or 1937 and that, "[b]eginning about the year 1941," McGee began doing odd jobs for the Hawkins family. The affair started a year later and continued with only two interruptions: during McGee's army service in "1942 or 3 and by a later period of residence in California after he was discharged from the Army." During all this time, they said, the Hawkins family lived at 435 South Magnolia Street in Laurel.

That was wrong—the Hawkinses were in Indiana for part of that time—but what is more interesting is how messy the affair story was becoming. Already, it was a blend of two different stories by McGee, a fabricated story by Rosalee, the lawyers' input, and new flourishes supplied by Communist journalists like Harry Raymond.

A month before, in February, Raymond had written a CRC- and Communist Party–sponsored pamphlet called *Save Willie McGee*, which based its arguments on the old claims used at the clemency hearing in 1950. There was no mention of an affair back then, and the pamphlet did nothing more than hint at it, relating a rumor that Troy and Willette had had a fight on the night of the rape. Henceforth, the *Daily Worker* would write about the affair as if it were an established fact. Not only had it happened, the paper would argue, it had been widely known in Laurel for years.

There was one other thing in the mix—a second alibi. Abzug and Coe had a new affidavit in hand, taken on March 4 from Florida-based Hettie Johnson. Her story was that McGee was at her house all through the night of the rape, drinking and gambling. She said her husband and some other men had a game going across the street that migrated to her house around 11:00. McGee and Bill Barnes were part of the group, and Johnson recalled hearing McGee say he was "going to take a chance with some of the company's money."

Johnson got sleepy and lay down, but she was in a sufficiently "wakeful state" to feel sure that the game kept going and that McGee stayed put. Around daylight an argument broke out, with Johnson's husband threatening to hit McGee over the head with a pistol. McGee lost his temper because he'd gambled away Laurel Wholesale Grocery cash that wasn't his to lose.

"Willie said he had messed up the boss man's money and he would have to go to his wife and get some," Johnson said. He left in the company truck, accidentally hitting another man's truck with enough force that "a small piece was knocked off of the body of Willie's truck, which lay in the street the next day."

Johnson said she'd been prepared to tell this story at the first trial and was subpoenaed, but with the trial in progress she was taken aside at the courthouse and threatened for having allowed gambling and bootleg whiskey in her home. Her details sounded specific: Wayne Valentine served the subpoena, she said, and at the courthouse she was "taken into a little room where there were some soldiers and two policemen or deputy sheriff's [*sic*] with guns, and some gentleman who was acting for the state. . . ."

The affidavit contained one other notable detail. Johnson said she was working at the time as a maid for "Mrs. Delia Lennon"—the correct spelling was Leonard—who was Mrs. Hawkins's aunt, and that she went to work at her home at 7:30 on the morning after the rape.

"[W]hen she got there," the statement said, ". . . Mrs. Lennon said that something awful had happened that night to 'Bill,' as Mrs. Wiletta Hawkins was known, and Mrs. Lennon said that a 'nigger' had come into her house and raped her." Johnson asked her how they knew the rapist was black. Leonard said Willette had felt his hair. She added that "Mrs. Hawkins might have had a nightmare, and 'she was hoping that that was what it was,' because she did not see how Mrs. Hawkins could have been raped with her husband and children in the next room."

Taken together, the new information was tantalizing and confusing. Johnson's statement could have been checked out—starting with the damaged truck and Mrs. Leonard's comments. But it was also puzzling, because it took McGee's alibi in two directions. He was innocent because, yes, he was regularly having sex with Mrs. Hawkins inside her home, at her insistence. He was also innocent because he wasn't there the night she was raped.

Mize didn't linger over the mysteries. He rejected all of them, saying the defense lawyers should have presented any new evidence at the third trial. He refused to grant a stay to permit time for further appeals, so Abzug and Coe hurriedly moved their petition up the line, going first to the Fifth Circuit, which also said no, and next, on March 15, lodging an appeal for a stay with the U.S. Supreme Court.

———

In her 1977 book, *A Fine Old Conflict*, British-born writer Jessica Mitford tells the story of her adventurous involvement with the McGee case during these months, in a chapter called "Mississippi."

It starts with a cross-country road trip that she and three other CRC-sponsored women made in March from Oakland, California, to Jackson, where they went door to door trying to solicit public support for McGee—usually with dim results. It climaxes with the group, whose members called themselves the White Women's Delegation, trying one last tactic on its way out of the state: On March 20, they dropped in unannounced at Rowan Oak, William Faulkner's stately home in Oxford—a small, historic university town in north Mississippi. Their goal was to convince the great man, who four months earlier had won the Nobel Prize, to issue a statement on McGee's behalf.

"We asked a gangling, snaggle-toothed white boy for directions to Faulkner's house," Mitford recalled in the book, a memoir of her fifteen years as a Communist Party member. " 'Down the road a piece, past the weepin' willa tree,' was his response, which I took as augury of our arrival in authentic Faulkner country."

There aren't any pictures of this meeting, but judging by photos taken around the time of the trip, the women would have dressed up. Rowan Oak, now owned and maintained by the University of Mississippi, is a large white Greek Revival house with a distinctive entrance: a brick walkway leading through an alley of tall cedar trees to a columned portico. After tapping over the bricks, the women rang or knocked and Faulkner himself invited them in. Mitford doesn't say where they sat, but he probably took them into a parlor that opened up to the right, or to a library on the left, which contained simple white bookshelves he'd built by hand.

Wrapped in a velvet smoking jacket, the silver-haired novelist spoke in what Mitford called "convoluted paragraphs . . . of murky eloquence" about his belief that McGee was innocent. "I was desperately trying to take down everything he said in my notebook, and frequently got lost as he expatiated on his favorite themes: sex, race, and violence," she wrote. "The Willie McGee case, compounded of all three, was a subject he seemed to savor with much relish; it could have been the central episode in one of his short stories."

They left after two hours, and then Mitford called William Patterson in New York to tell him about the interview. Patterson was excited—Faulkner's opinions would make news—but he told Mitford she had to get him to sign a release, so he couldn't deny his own words later. Mitford trooped back to Rowan Oak and found Faulkner, who was doing horse-stable chores with a black employee. Standing there in manure-splashed hip boots, he scanned and initialed a statement Mitford had written, then supposedly mumbled, "I think McGee and the woman should *both* be destroyed."

"Oh *don't* let's put that in," Mitford said, scurrying off to her car.

Whether it happened like that is debatable. The "snaggle-toothed white boy" sounds contrived, as if Mitford took a wrong turn onto Tobacco Road, and "Mississippi" is written in a style that blends fact with manufactured comedy, which Mitford sometimes did during her long career as a humorous memoirist and muckraking journalist. The interview was real, though, and the story got picked up in newspapers. Faulkner wasn't quoted directly. He had asked Mitford to paraphrase what he said, and she honored that. But what she got was juicy enough.

> *Oxford, Mississippi—William Faulkner, 1950 Nobel Prize winner for literature, whose novels on Mississippi life are world-famous, has expressed his belief that Willie McGee, Mississippi negro worker awaiting execution on a false rape conviction, is innocent and should be freed. . . .*
>
> *Explaining that he did not for a moment doubt McGee's innocence, Faulkner agreed that new evidence proving perjury by the woman who charged McGee with "rape" was also true.*

Mitford published an account of the interview a few days later in the *Daily People's World*, writing that Faulkner "said the McGee case was an outrage and that it was good we had come. He said Southerners would listen to us where they wouldn't listen to men."

What she didn't mention was that Faulkner started backing off almost immediately. An editor at the *Memphis Commercial Appeal* who saw the press release called Faulkner's longtime friend Phil "Moon" Mullen, an Oxford newspaperman, to tell him it sounded like trouble. Mullen went out to see Faulkner, who, after listening to Mullen's assessment of the likely fallout, pointed at his typewriter and said, "Sit down and write what you think I should say." In a follow-up release, Faulkner retreated a bit but stood by his stance that McGee's life should be spared.

"I do not want Willie McGee to be executed, because it will make him a martyr and create a long lasting stink in my native state," he wrote. "If the crime of which he is accused was not one of force and violence, and I do not think it was proved that, then the penalty in this state or in any other similar case should not be death."

Predictably, there was a backlash in Mississippi. On March 28 in Laurel, District Attorney Paul Swartzfager, who had known Faulkner during his school days in Oxford, labeled the comments "so untrue as to make the blood of any red-blooded American boil." Faulkner had either been "seduced by his own fictitious imaginations or has aligned himself with the Communists."

In a letter to a friend two days later, Faulkner moaned that he'd been bewitched. "Those people, all women, knocked on my front door without warning, no telephones in advance or anything," he wrote. "They told me who they were, and I should have known their commie bosses wanted only a chance to use me, since I don't think any of them really give a damn about McGee. . . .

"I was wrong, I spoke out of turn. Was stupid, since my opinions could not change things, besides, they were private opinions which I had no intention of airing to anyone, since, as I told the people, I knew too little about the facts of the matter to go on record. I have learned a lesson, though."

———

Actually, Faulkner had learned this lesson before and would learn it again. For a writer whose themes weren't overtly political, he had a knack for getting in hot water by sounding off about subjects like Willie McGee, the Attala County massacre, and, a few years later, the lynching of Emmett Till.

His fame was double-edged. It gave him international standing as a wise man and an oracle, but it put him in a hopeless position when race was on the table. If he spoke up, most Mississippians expected him to inform the rest of the world that the existing system—segregation, white supremacy, and enforcement of the social order through any means necessary, including violence—was justified. Northerners sometimes assumed, wrongly, that he was "progressive" in the way a Henry Wallace supporter would have recognized, so they were disappointed when he sounded more Mississippi than Manhattan.

Politically, Faulkner was a Southern Democrat from a genteel, slightly threadbare background. This meant he wasn't a Snopes, the kind of man likely to turn up cheering at a Bilbo rally. But it also meant he wasn't comfortable with federal civil rights legislation, lectures from Northern intellectuals and politicians, or Communist Party anything. Faulkner once joked that left-wing literary colleagues of his day, describing how they perceived his politics, assigned him the label "Gothic fascist."

In any event, it usually worked better when he expressed his sweeping ideas about history and race in fiction instead of commentary. In 1956, in a widely publicized Q & A with a newsmagazine called the *Reporter*, he said he opposed both locally enforced segregation and federally enforced integration. So what was he for? His preferred path was a "middle road" that involved changing things at a slow, safe pace set by the South. Moving too fast would cause bloodshed and revolt, he predicted, adding, "[I]f it came to fighting I'd fight for Mississippi against the United States, even if it meant going out into the street and shooting Negroes." This caused as much trouble up north as his McGee comments had in the South. He tried to make it go away by insisting, lamely, that he'd been "grossly misquoted."

When Faulkner wrote about the interplay of crime, accusation, and rumor that could lead to a lynching or a legal lynching—which he did in the 1931 short story "Dry September" and the 1948 novel *Intruder in the Dust*—he didn't have to look far for background material. Though Oxford wasn't among the worst lynching towns in

292] THE EYES OF WILLIE McGEE

Mississippi, lynchings had happened there, and Faulkner would have known about a couple of them.

When he was ten, an accused murderer named Nelson, or Nelse, Patton was killed by local vigilantes who chased off the sheriff, knocked holes through walls of the Oxford jail, shot Patton, scalped him, and hanged him on the courthouse lawn. In 1935, murder-trial defendant Ellwood Higginbotham—whose jury, in the opinion of some townspeople, was taking too long to reach the desired guilty verdict—was taken from jail, driven out of town, shot, and hanged. "[T]he black put up a strong fight, but was subdued by the mob and a well-rope looped over his head," the *Clarion-Ledger* reported. "In the struggle the negro managed to get the noose in his mouth and fought so strongly that the mob finally took a tire tool to get the rope loose from his jaws."

When Faulkner addressed lynching as a theme, he was, true to form, tugged in two directions. "Dry September," which appeared in the January 1931 edition of *Scribner's Magazine*, tells the story of an innocent man, Will Mayes, who gets lynched because of a false rumor that he sexually assaulted a white spinster named Minnie Cooper. For dramatic reasons—and perhaps for taste reasons—Faulkner shied away from depicting the lynching itself. Readers were shown the events leading up to it and the aftermath, but not the killing, so the story delivered tension in place of horror. Nonetheless, the political message was clear: Lynching was wrong, it sometimes led to the death of innocent men, and its continued existence was a curse on the land.

So said Faulkner the artist. The next month, Faulkner the opiner wrote a letter about lynching to the editor of the *Commercial Appeal*, and he sounded like a different person. Headlined "Mobs Sometimes Right," it was a response to an earlier letter from a black man named W. H. James, a resident of Starkville, Mississippi, who had written to express his general gratitude to women of Mississippi who had joined a Southern anti-lynching advocacy group. "The good women felt that something needed to be done," he wrote. ". . . I feel that we have some friends who will protect us against the crime which has been perpetrated against so many of us without even a possible chance to prove our innocence or guilt."

For some reason, this irritated Faulkner, who wrote a long reply arguing that, while mob justice was wrong, he had never heard, "outside of a novel or a story," of a lynching victim who had "a record beyond reproach." He failed to mention that he had just published a short story starring such a man.

"It just happens that we—mobber and mobbee—live in this age," he concluded. "We will muddle through, and die in our beds, the deserving and the fortunate among us. Of course, with the population what it is, there are some of us that won't. Some will die rich, and some will die on cross-ties soaked with gasoline, to make a holiday. But there is one curious thing about mobs. Like our juries, they have a way of being right."

———

Seventeen years later, Faulkner published his grand statement on the subject: *Intruder in the Dust*, the story of Lucas Beauchamp, an innocent black man accused of murdering a rural white named Vinson Gowrie, whose relatives were known to be violent and vengeful. Lucas is not only blameless, he's clever enough to control his own fate by convincing two white people to perform dangerous detective work that proves his innocence.

From the get-go, Faulkner meant for *Intruder in the Dust* to be read as both an artistic and a political statement. "The story is a mystery-murder though the theme is more [the] relationship between Negro and white," he said in a letter to a book agent, ". . . the premise being that the white people in the south, before the North or the govt. or anyone else, owe and must pay a responsibility to the Negro."

For all its literary trappings, the novel was partly a defense of the "middle road." When Lucas is arrested and taken to jail in downtown Jefferson (Faulkner's fictional version of Oxford), lynch talk is already in the air. Lucas calls out to the book's other central figure, a white sixteen-year-old named Charles "Chick" Mallison Jr., that he needs help from Chick's Uncle Gavin, a local lawyer. By this point, we know from a flashback that Lucas and the boy have met before. On a winter day four years earlier, Chick had fallen through creek ice while rabbit hunting. Lucas warmed him up inside his cabin, refusing to accept money and leaving Chick with the gnawing sense of being indebted to a black man.

Gavin and Chick go see Lucas in jail. Gavin doesn't believe Lucas is innocent—he assumes he'll lose the case and hopes, at best, to save his life. After Gavin leaves, Chick goes back inside and Lucas calls in the old debt, asking him to help prove the truth by digging up Gowrie's body, to show that he was shot with a different handgun than the .41 Colt that Lucas owns. In a passage loaded with meaning about the future sources of change, Chick ponders why Lucas would ask him to do such a thing—rather than his uncle or the sheriff—and recalls an earlier episode involving an old black man who chose to trust him with a secret instead of a white adult. "Young folks and womens, they ain't cluttered," the man had said. "They can listen. But a middle-year man like your paw and your uncle, they can't listen. They ain't got time."

After that comes a far-fetched series of events. Chick, along with a black teenage friend named Aleck Sander and an old woman named Eunice Habersham, ventures into the dark heart of Gowrie country at night to exhume Vinson's corpse. They find another man's body, unmistakable evidence that something is wrong. Various twists and turns follow, and by the end Lucas is exonerated and freed.

Surprising things—even a few heroic things—happened during the long, sorry history of lynching, but there was never a story with this combination of Huck Finn plot elements. Why did Faulkner stray so far from reality? One obvious and positive reason was to create a black character who wasn't merely a victim. But as New Yorker literary critic Edmund Wilson noticed in his 1948 review, there was a reactionary theme under the surface.

"The book contains a kind of counterblast to the anti-lynching bill and to the civil-rights plank in the Democratic platform," he wrote. In a long speech by Gavin, Wilson detected what he took to be Faulkner's position on civil rights: Southerners themselves, white and black, would solve their problems in time. But if the white South were pushed too hard, blacks would be thrown, in Gavin's words, "not merely into injustice but into grief and agony, and violence, too, by forcing on us laws based on the idea that man's injustice to man can be abolished overnight by police."

Unlike most of Faulkner's novels, *Intruder in the Dust* was well-suited to the big screen, and MGM bought the rights. It was filmed on location in Oxford in 1949, during a much-covered springtime shoot that employed a number of locals as actors and extras. The movie, which premiered in Oxford in October of that year, was hailed for its realistic depiction of Southern race relations. But it wasn't realistic—it was a fantasy about what ought to have been. MGM filtered out the novel's voice and complexity to emphasize the detective story and the overall sense of heroism.

Of course, a realistic depiction of lynching wouldn't have gotten made in 1949. Whatever its faults, *Intruder in the Dust* was a daring project because it addressed the subject on any level. For its part, Oxford became the setting of a unique sociological experiment: How would its white citizens react to a story that depicted their town as the source of mob passion?

"Admittedly, there was much concern about the public relations problem of bringing negro actors into this small Southern city to make a motion picture of the South's racial problems," the *Oxford Eagle* reported. John Popham called it a "ticklish situation" in a *New York Times* story.

They reacted pretty well, partly because they caught the Hollywood bug. MGM met them more than halfway by observing all the written and unwritten race codes. Juano Hernandez, a Puerto Rican actor who played Lucas, stayed at the home of a local black undertaker and said nice things about greens and fatback. When MGM thanked Oxford's officials, merchants, and extras in a full-page *Oxford Eagle* ad, it segregated the names by race.

So, as breakthroughs go, this one was limited. But man-on-the-street interviews after the premiere showed that the movie inspire serious reflection among some of Oxford's citizens.

"It's a shocking story, but definitely a true picture of Southern attitudes," said Jack Odom, a former Ole Miss football player who had a speaking role as a truck driver. "A lot of people I talked to didn't know what to make of it. . . . I was that way myself, but after I got home and thought about it, I began to realize that it is a true story of a misunderstanding and of how the colored people are treated. The ending is left up to the audience. People are running away, and the audience has to decide whether they're running away from the negro after he was proved innocent or whether they were running away from themselves or the truth." Odom's take? "They were running away from themselves."

———

Jessica Mitford was living in the Bay Area, working and writing under the name Decca Treuhaft, when the CRC put out its latest call to action about McGee in early 1951. The name she went by then was a combination of her childhood nickname, Decca, and the last name from her second marriage, to labor lawyer Robert Treuhaft. At the time, she was a housewife and Communist Party activist, not a professional writer yet. Her breakthrough books—*Daughters and Rebels*, a memoir of her aristocratic upbringing in England, and *The American Way of Death*, an exposé of the U.S. funeral industry—were still a decade off.

During the climax of the McGee case, Mitford was running the Oakland CRC office. As she recalled in *A Fine Old Conflict*, she opened the mail one day to find an urgent McGee appeal from New York, asking chapter members to send money, organize local actions, and provide volunteers who would travel to Mississippi to protest in person. By design, the participants would all be white women, a dramatic way to show Southerners that the very people they hoped to "protect" were disgusted by what Mississippi was about to do.

"[A] White Women's Delegation sounded to me like a marvelous idea," Mitford wrote. ". . . I was determined to be part of this great conclave."

For the most part, Mitford describes the experience as a romp— thrilling adventure" and "a welcome breather from diapers and 1sework"—but it took real courage to do what she did. She was thirty-three in early 1951, the mother of three young children. Back then, just getting to Mississippi by car from California was a challenge. Setting out on March 5, she and the three other CRC delegates—Louise Hopson and Billie Wachter, both Berkeley housewives, and Evelyn Frieden, a union shop steward in the Bay Area—drove all the way to Jackson, with stops for meetings and canvassing en route.

They covered more than 2,600 miles on the old U.S. highway system, and they had no idea what might happen at the end of the road. They were going to Jackson as card-carrying CRC troublemakers, at a time when anti-McGee feelings were more intense than ever. Eight months earlier, in the summer of 1950, McGee's CRC supporters had been severely beaten. For Mitford and her crew, jail time was a strong likelihood, and worse things were possible.

Mitford handled the challenge with a brand of energy and drive that was a product of her unique background and her status as a breakaway rebel—not just from middle-class convention, but from her own family. Born in 1917, in Gloucestershire, England, to David Freeman Mitford, a British lord, and Sydney Bowles, the daughter of a member of Parliament, Jessica was one of the famous Mitford sisters, women whose glamour, achievements, and political escapades mesmerized and appalled the British public throughout the 1930s, 1940s, and 1950s.

Two of the sisters, Pam and Deborah, led fairly conventional upper-crust lives. The oldest daughter, Nancy, born in 1904, was a fiction writer best known for *The Pursuit of Love* (1945) and *Love in a Cold Climate* (1949), novels that took her family's quirks and spun them into comedy with an edge. At the center was the blustering figure of Matthew Radlett, a terrapin-hided xenophobe inspired by David. On the walls of the family estate, Matthew proudly displayed a trenching tool he had used to slaughter "the Hun" during hand-to-hand combat in World War I. To amuse himself, he liked to chase his daughters through the woods with hounds.

The real David wasn't this crusty, and though he was far to the right politically, he was never a big fan of Adolf Hitler. But two of his daughters, Diana and Unity, were great admirers of the Nazi leader, becoming infamous prior to World War II because of their public embrace of fascism. They were exposed to fascist ideas in the 1930s, at a time when figures like Hitler and Mussolini were seen by some upper-class Brits as an acceptable bulwark against the great threat from the east: Soviet Communism.

Their youthful dabblings became more serious in early 1935, when Unity was in Munich having lunch at an outdoor restaurant called the Osteria Bavaria. She was on hand hoping to be noticed by Hitler—who, as she knew, ate there regularly—and it worked. He spotted her one day and had an aide invite her to his table, initiating a friend-ship that continued until the outbreak of the war. British and Ameri-can newspapers never got tired of reporting that Hitler once called blonde-haired Unity "the most perfect Nordic beauty in the world."

Diana was already married when she met Sir Oswald Mosley, the head of the British Union of Fascists, a right-wing political party founded in 1932. They started an affair, left their spouses, and were married in a private ceremony in 1936 that took place at the home of Nazi propaganda minister Joseph Goebbels. Looking on with a fa-therly smile was Hitler himself. Their political activities continued, and during the spring and summer of 1940, they were arrested sepa-rately in England and locked up until 1943.

Unity made it into Hitler's inner circle and seemed to be in love with him, though her biographer, David Pryce-Jones, concluded that there probably wasn't a sexual relationship. There's no question she understood what Nazism was all about. She fantasized that Germany and Britain would unite against the Soviet Union, and she hinted that she might do something drastic if the two countries went to war. After Poland fell, word trickled out of Germany that Unity had fallen "mys-teriously ill." Her condition remained unknown for months, even af-ter her parents succeeded in bringing her back to England in January 1940. "One report was that she had been shot after a violent quarrel with Herr Hitler, who once gave her a specially made swastika badge," the New York Times reported. "Another was that she had been found poisoned in Munich."

In fact, she had put a pistol to her head and pulled the trigger. The bullet entered her brain and lodged at the back of her skull, but she'd somehow survived. Disfigured, partially paralyzed, and mentally impaired, she was later taken to the west coast of Scotland and lived out her days at a family property on Inch Kenneth Island, among villagers who generally treated her with kindness, as someone who had suffered enough. After her death from meningitis in 1948, an obituary writer called her "a lonely figure who spent most of her time walking the windswept moors with her spaniels."

⸻

With so much to rebel against, Jessica made the most of it. She was the sixth of the seven Mitford children—there was also a brother, Tom, who died in 1945, fighting against the Japanese in Burma—and she served notice early that she would blaze her own trail. At eleven, she started socking away money in a "running away account." As a teenager, she augmented her homeschooling curriculum with self-education about issues like poverty, privilege, and economic injustice.

"I became an ardent reader of the left-wing press, and even grudgingly used up a little of my Running Away Money to send for books and pamphlets explaining socialism," she wrote in *A Fine Old Conflict*. ". . . When Boud [Unity's nickname] became a Fascist, I declared myself a Communist. Thus by the time she was eighteen and I fifteen, we had chosen up opposite sides in the central conflict of our day."

At first the spat was almost funny, but the gulf became real as they marched off in different directions. Jessica had a precocious younger cousin named Esmond Romilly, a nephew of Winston Churchill's who, by 1935, was publishing a left-wing student magazine called *Out of Bounds*. Newspapers loved writing about Churchill's "red nephew," and Jessica developed a crush on him before they met. When the Spanish Civil War started in 1936, Esmond joined the International Brigades that formed to fight the fascist-backed troops of General Francisco Franco. He saw combat, and though he wasn't wounded, he came down with a severe case of dysentery that got him shipped back to England.

Esmond and Jessica met in early 1937, during a country-house weekend. They hit it off, and he agreed to her suggestion that the run away to Spain, where he would work as a war correspondent. They eloped to Bilbao, and the Mitford family had yet another news-making daughter on their hands. British foreign secretary Anthony Eden used his influence to track them down, but there was no bringing them back.

"The story, with considerable embellishment, made headlines in all the papers, and many European ones, for weeks," Mary S. Lovell wrote in *The Sisters*, one of several books about the Mitford clan. " 'Another Mitford Anarchist,' 'Consul Chases Peer's Daughter,' 'Mixed Up Mitford Girls Still Confusing Europe.' " Unable to marry in Spain because of legal pressure applied by Jessica's father, they made it official on May 18 in Bayonne, France, with both their mothers present and Esmond shaking a fist at conventionality. "Threats of imprisonment make no difference," he said in a press release. "We both regard marriage mainly as a convenience. . . ."

The couple spent the next few years in Britain, Corsica, and the United States, combining a life of social activism and scraping by. They moved to America in early 1939, living at various times in New York, Miami, and Washington, D.C., while plugging away at odd jobs like bartending, saleswork, and freelance writing. In 1940, they co-wrote a series of *Washington Post* articles that repackaged their experiences as the escapades of two love-struck kids. In pictures that accompanied the articles, Esmond was dark, cheerful, and handsome; Jessica brown-haired, round-faced, and pretty.

"[Their] background is not the sort to produce the usual stodgy comments of the 'British Visitors Find America Wonderful' school," the *Post* said in an introduction. "Instead, the . . . forthcoming stories need only musical scoring to make them a latter day Gilbert and Sullivan operetta."

Esmond joined the Royal Canadian Air Force in the summer of 1940, became a combat aviator, and was killed in late 1941 during a bombing flight. By then, Jessica was living in Alexandria, Virginia, with her ten-month-old daughter, Constancia. In time, she found a government job as a typist at the Office of Price Administration, where she met Robert Treuhaft. She transferred to San Francisco in early 1943 and became involved with the CIO-affiliated United Federal Workers of America, her way back into the realm of politics. Treuhaft followed a few months later, and they married that summer.

Jessica wasn't very active politically in Washington, but there was already an FBI file on her, opened because Unity's and Diana's misadventures had put the Mitfords in the glare. In the FBI's early assessment, the agents didn't see red. They saw red, white, and blue. "She is said to be liberal in her political philosophy and sympathetic with Russian experiment, but loyal to Democratic principles and proud of her connection with United States Government," said an internal report from April 1943.

Not quite. Put off by "[t]he boring and oppressive American preoccupation with material comforts," she felt the old pull of radicalism. In the fall of 1943, Jessica and Bob were secretly invited to join the Communist Party. That same year, she signed up. It didn't take the FBI long to notice. By February 1945, there was a new entry in J. Edgar Hoover's "Confidential Security Index Card File," labeled JESSICA LUCY TREUHAFT . . . COMMUNIST.

Mitford and the Bay Area Three hit the road the same day Abzug and Coe went before Judge Mize. One early stop was Needles, California, where they spent two hours knocking on doors and speaking with local NAACP members and preachers, including an old black minister named J. M. Caddell. (Caddell told them he was raised in Newton, Mississippi, which he called "a good place to be from.") A few people promised to write letters, but the editor of the town newspaper brushed them off, saying, "Not local news."

Mitford filed stories at every stop for the *Daily People's World*, making the best of what she had. Her Needles dispatch began with a brisk, mission-accomplished lead: "This small railroad community of 1,000 persons, located in the heart of the Mojave desert, is going to make its contribution to the nationwide campaign to save the life of

Willie McGee." Parsed, it didn't mean much, but it was in tune with the spirit of the trip: Whatever happened, press on.

The most important stop before Jackson was St. Louis, a rallying point for the CRC's gathering army of white women. But as Mitford soon learned, there would be no army. Aubrey Grossman came out from New York to deliver the disheartening news that only a handful of people were heading south.

" 'Where are the others?' " Mitford asked. "[Grossman], not in the least abashed, explained there *were* no others—we four were the whole delegation, the generals and soldiers of this great nationwide call to action. . . . Nor was there any blueprint, or plan of campaign. . . . We should have to develop our plans on the spot when we arrived in Jackson, and he would do his best to get other women to join us there."

Mitford was exaggerating, but only a little. A group shot taken in St. Louis shows a few other people who made the trip—three women from Chicago and Milwaukee, a white male preacher from New York—and there was a separate group of women who had been deployed from Detroit, Memphis, and other cities.

By any measure, they were an outmanned platoon, bound for Jackson at a tense time, just as word was spreading about McGee's shocking claim of a love affair. On March 12, the *Daily People's World* poured fuel on the fire by publishing a sensational story based on Rosalee McGee's affidavit. Calling the affair and frame-up a "story of sick horror," the paper said Rosalee "stated that Mrs. Willimetta Hawkins, the alleged white victim who claimed she'd never met McGee before, had in fact forced McGee to maintain a reluctant relationship with her dating back to 1942."

The women made it to Jackson in a couple of days and got rooms at the local YWCA. Their routine consisted of door-to-door canvassing, with all precautions taken and proprieties observed. "We drew up strict rules of conduct," Mitford recalled. "[N]ever venture from the Y except in pairs; work from early morning until sunset but never after dark; wear hats, stockings, and white gloves at all times."

Before long, their presence twitched the antenna of Fred Sullens, who decided their numbers were closer to 150 than 15 and took great interest in their most mundane doings. A *Jackson Daily News* story reported on the activities of "two bare-legged Chicago women" who paid a call to "three indignant Jackson housewives." The intruders waved a printed copy of Rosalee's account of the affair and ordered the Jacksonians to read it. "The three women gasped when they read 'Mrs.' McGee's 'filthy' letter," the report said. "One horrified local housewife told the crusaders she knew the Negro woman never wrote that typewritten sheet of lies. . . .

" 'I got so mad at 'em my hair was standing up on end,' " one woman said. "I told them that's just what the Russians were using to stir up trouble in our country."

Jackson mayor Allen Thompson issued a statement denouncing the mysterious callers. "He suggested that homeowners should ask them away and if they persisted in staying the Jackson police department is willing to co-operate," the *Jackson Daily News* reported on March 16. "The action came after a meeting in City Hall Saturday morning attended by the city prosecuting attorney, city attorney, police officials and others."

There was no justifiable reason to interfere with the canvassers. They were talking to people about a court case, which was their right— just as it was the right of homeowners to either listen, laugh, curse, or slam the door. The dialogues must have been strange, though. By and large, the members of the White Women's Delegation didn't know any more about McGee's guilt or innocence than the people they were lecturing. They were pushing a party line, which they accepted without question because they believed in the cause and the political system behind it. Most of their listeners embraced a party line too—Southern orthodoxy on race relations—so it wasn't an easy sell.

Mitford approached the task with characteristic gusto. As she had done in Needles and St. Louis, she kept a careful tally of how the pro-McGee arguments were received:

Hostile (we don't want outsiders, etc.): 12
Listened to us but wouldn't discuss their own opinion: 8
Convinced of McGee's guilt, but willing to listen: 7

At first convinced of his guilt, but changed mind on the basis of
our discussion: 5

Convinced of his innocence, but made no commitment to act: 7

Pledged action, talk to neighbors, write Truman, Gov. Wright: 4

Mitford also collected anecdotes that she used in her reports and,
years later, her book. A female teacher visiting Jackson for a convention told her, "I've always been skeptical about this rape business. I'm
convinced it is almost impossible to rape a woman if she really doesn't
want it." Another woman claimed it was widely known that the CRC
people who were injured in 1950 had beaten themselves up with a
lamp. An anonymous woman told her, "I lived for many years in Laurel, and still have friends there. It is common talk in Laurel about this
relationship between Mrs. Hawkins and Willie McGee."

In her newspaper stories and in *A Fine Old Conflict*, Mitford
attributed the anecdote to the director of the YWCA, who was not
named, but who was described as a narrow-minded Southerner. As
Mitford told it, she kicked the White Women out of the Y once she
realized what they were up to.

Mitford may have taken some literary license with this character: The Y's director at that time was a Canadian named Jean
MacGillivray, who was born on Prince Edward Island, and whose
parents were immigrants from Scotland. Mitford's "Director" uses the
word "Nigras" and talks about traveling to Laurel frequently, where
old friends told her it was common knowledge that the relationship
between McGee and Mrs. Hawkins "had been the talk of the town for
years." This point matters because, for all the door-knocking Mitford
did, "the Director" is the only person she found who said anything
concrete about the affair.

In the end, the bare-legged women did their job and made a statement, but their overall results symbolized the hopelessness of changing
McGee's fate by knocking on doors. One day, Mitford and company
walked into the office of Dr. W. D. Hudgins, pastor of the huge First
Baptist Church in downtown Jackson, an important establishment
bastion. His response didn't show up on her tally sheet, but it was

memorable all the same. "Hudgins," Mitford said, "screamed and ranted at us to get out of the state."

————

What did it all add up to? Nothing you could easily calibrate, but the grassroots activity came to something. As the FBI file on the McGee case shows, CRC chapters all over the United States and its territories—from Philadelphia to South Bend to Denver to Portland to Honolulu—were meeting about McGee during these months, taking small actions that got people thinking and talking. Nationally, the CRC organized a protest vigil in Washington and extensive speaking tours by Rosalee. In March, April, and May, she appeared in several cities, including New York, Detroit, Chicago, Denver, San Francisco, Seattle, Portland, and Los Angeles.

When McGee faced execution in July 1950, one measure of his support was the flood of letters and telegrams sent to Governor Wright. Something similar happened again. On March 15, the day that Supreme Court justice Hugo Black heard stay-of-execution arguments from Abzug, Coe, and Vito Marcantonio, he took the unusual step of publicly berating the American people for sending him so many messages about McGee. He had gotten a five-inch stack of telegrams and letters, and he wanted it understood that he didn't make decisions based on emotional pleas. "I am not compelled to read these and have not and will not," he said. "It is a very bad practice. There is no defense for it except ignorance on the part of the people who did it."

Like Justice Burton, Black kept much of the correspondence, and it's hard to believe he didn't read some of it. One letter came from Newton, Mississippi—J. M. Caddell's old hometown—and it was written by a white out-of-state doctor named Walter D. Jensen, who was there doing federal tuberculosis-eradication work. Dr. Jensen thought McGee was probably guilty and deserved prison time, but not death. He reminded Black that "no white rapist was ever executed in Mississippi" and then walked him through details of a little-reported 1949 case in Houston, Mississippi.

"On the 2nd of July, 1949, a drunken trio, two men and a soldier on leave . . . drove out of town and on a narrow country road caught up with a negro family in a lumber wagon, a man and wife and four children," he wrote. "The negro stopped to let the car pass as the road was very narrow. . . . One of the men got out of the car, and went over and crushed the negro's head with a bumper jack. All they got for that was a supposedly life sentence. They will be out in three or four years. . . .

"I believe in equal justice for all, but Southern justice is mighty hard to swallow. I am sending this letter via Baltimore, through a nephew, for fear that it might be intercepted. *Please do not divulge* my name."

Black's file also contains newspaper clippings about McGee from the *Michigan Daily*, the student newspaper at the University of Michigan. Somebody mailed them as an example of how debate about the case had taken hold at a typical campus, far from Mississippi. The *Daily* covered McGee, or printed letters about him, more than a dozen times in March, April, and May. A campus-based Ad Hoc Student Committee to Save Willie McGee was created in early March to persuade students to send cards and letters to "Washington and Mississippi officials." Rosalee spoke in Ann Arbor that month, at an event the *Daily* described as a "stormy rally." Typical of the divide on many campuses, young progressives squared off against young Republicans, arguing about the merits of the case and the demerits of McGee's Communist defenders.

"[Mark] Sandground accuses the people on campus who are sponsoring the movement to stop the execution of Willy McGee of being 'agitators, rabble-rousers, and plain Communists who are trying to destroy our freedom,' " two students wrote that month. "Why must everyone who believes in sticking up for the underdog be labeled a Communist?"

Unlike Burton, Black didn't leave behind any notes about his decision-making process, but the result was the same: He decided to stop the wheels of execution and take one more look. He ordered a stay on March 15.

Sullens was furious, calling Black a bad lawyer and worse judge in an editorial titled "Justice Again Ravished." Mathew Bernato, a private investigator from Philadelphia, wrote Black directly, saying that McGee was "a three time loser on previous appeals to the Supreme Court." Despite this fact, he said, Black gave in to the very pressure he said he would ignore.

As they had done in 1950, supporters of the stay seemed to think Black's move was a vote of confidence in McGee. "[T]he Civil Rights Congress claims to have new and most important evidence," Howard Selsam, a resident of New York, wrote in a letter to Black. ". . . Is there to be no way in which this evidence can be examined? Are the authorities of Mississippi to be allowed to send McGee to death simply because they *want to* and do not want to examine any new evidence that might prove his innocence?"

Selsam should have known from high-school civics that the Supreme Court didn't conduct trials. The same can't be said of Michael B. Creed, whose handwritten note read, "Mr. Justice Black: Thank you for saving Mr. Willie McGee. I hope he can soon go home to his wife + four children." Michael was eight and a half.

⸻

In 1950 and early 1951, nearly six months passed between Burton's stay and the Supreme Court's refusal to hear McGee's appeal. This time, the process took only eleven days. After hearing arguments on March 20, the Court discussed the case in conference, aided by two clerk memos— one leaning toward taking the case, one leaning against. John G. Burnett, William O. Douglas's clerk, told the justices that "the main question is whether petitioner, through his affidavits, has made out a sufficient case on the charge of knowing use of perjured testimony to warrant a full hearing" by a U.S. District Court. He reviewed the facts and the new evidence: the affidavits from Willie, Rosalee, and Hettie Johnson.

Johnson's story didn't sway him. Apparently unaware that Johnson said she fled Laurel after being threatened, he indicated that the defense should have called her when it had the chance. He was more interested in the allegations made by Rosalee and Willie, which, to his mind, were detailed enough to be compelling, but also to raise a question: Why hadn't the defense found other witnesses to back up their stories?

"The prosecutrix and her husband both testified they had never seen petitioner prior to the alleged rape," he wrote. "If this was perjury as petitioner claims, it would not seem difficult to establish. . . . There should be some record to show that petitioner and the husband worked together. Since petitioner has very active counsel, it is difficult to understand the failure to produce such evidence."

Writing for Chief Justice Vinson, Murray L. Schwartz saw the issues the same way, but the stakes now gave him pause. "One of the difficulties with this case is that it has to deal with highly improbable alternatives," he wrote. The prosecution's version of events had convinced three juries, but it bothered Murray that "[t]he husband and two other children" slept through McGee's break-in and forcible rape.

"On the other hand, it is petitioner's theory that because he had had intercourse with the prosecutrix on other occasions, she made up this rape story to get even with him," he wrote. "But it seems most improbable that she would have picked the night and hour she did, without knowing definitely that he would not be able to show an alibi. . . .

"The disposition of the case is not assisted by the many times it has traversed the courts," he concluded. "Neither is it helped by the facts that the only affidavits on the perjured testimony point are by petitioner and his wife, the most interested parties for his continued living. But this is a capital case, and it would seem that there is merit to petitioner's argument that he is entitled to a full hearing."

The Court didn't agree: On the 26th, it denied certiorari for the fourth time. This didn't mean that McGee's supporters were giving up. April would see new court actions, marching in the streets, and a rising level of clamor about McGee that, more and more, began to spread internationally. But the situation was becoming bleaker by the day. Barring a miracle, Willie McGee was going to die.

thirteen

SORROW NIGHT

I went to Laurel again on Election Day 2007, with a friend I'd made during my visits to Mississippi: a retired judge named W. O. "Chet" Dillard, whom I'd met through Ed King, the civil rights veteran who shared a house with Todd Pyles.

Judge Dillard, who lived in Jackson, was a funny, energetic, old-school gentleman who was generous with his time and knowledge, which was drawn from an amazing stock of life experiences. Born in 1930, he'd grown up in a dirt-poor white family that was driven to the brink by the Depression. In *Clearburning*, a book he wrote in 1992 that combines his life story with commentary about civil rights episodes from the 1960s, he recalled how, at age three, he and two older brothers were sent off to a Baptist orphanage because his father was broke, his mother was seriously ill, and his parents' only choice was to give up the smallest children or watch them starve.

Most of the family was back together by 1936, when Dillard's father relocated to Pachuta—the area where Willie McGee's people were from—to farm as a sharecropper. Dillard lived there through high school, and his family was so bedraggled that he had to endure regular humiliations in grade school.

"My main memories of this time are of the real discrimination and total rejection of the Dillards," he wrote, ". . . . since we were much poorer than anyone else in the community and were continuously harassed, insulted, and abused by adults and other children. . . . There were occasions when an adult, supposedly a friend of mine, would pull down my pants in public to show that I didn't have any underwear."

Dillard made a lot of himself, graduating from Mississippi Southern in 1953, serving as a navy pilot, then earning a law degree from Ole Miss, and later becoming a district attorney in Laurel, the Mississippi commissioner of public safety, an assistant attorney general, and a chancery judge. When he was first setting up in Laurel in 1960, he was assigned to defend a black man named Willie Stokes, who was accused of murdering a white woman who ran a small store, stabbing her with a butcher knife. Dillard said there wasn't much doubt that Stokes was guilty, so the best he could hope for was to save him from the death penalty. He pleaded for mercy, based on Stokes's poor, rugged background and lack of education.

It didn't work. Stokes was executed in 1961 inside a gas chamber at Parchman, the state of Mississippi having retired its electric chair in 1955. For years, Dillard was haunted by a moment toward the end of the trial when Stokes—who was so frightened that he urinated on the floor in the courtroom one day, and who barely spoke to Dillard the entire time—asked him what he thought was going to happen. Dillard told him: No doubt about it, he was going to be found guilty and sentenced to death.

"He thought a long time and finally asked what he could do," Dillard wrote. "Searching my heart and soul, I told him I didn't know of anything he could do except pray about it. I was astounded by his answer, which I remember clearly to this day. He said, 'I don't know how to pray.' He continued, 'I lay in my bunk tossing and turning all night in my cell trying, but no one has ever taught me how to pray, and I just don't know how to do it or what to say.'"

———

I met Dillard early in the morning at the Elite Café, a diner in downtown Jackson where he goes most days for breakfast with a group of retired judges, lawyers, and assorted cronies who make up what's called the Weaver Gore Coffee Club.

Those guys—including Gore himself, a white-haired attorney who is a well-known figure in Jackson legal circles—were in the back of the restaurant, which was long and narrow. I was up front in a green vinyl booth with Dillard, who was dressed in a brown, tweedy jacket, blue shirt, red tie, and a pin that said SALUTE ME I VOTED.

Also present was Dorothy Hawkins, who had come to the city for the day but wouldn't be going to Laurel. I'd invited her because I thought she'd want to hear Dillard's opinion about the third McGee trial. Before coming to Mississippi, I'd sent him the transcript, asking him to make notes and tell me what he thought of the evidence.

He thought McGee was clearly guilty. He mailed me seventeen pages of legal-pad notes explaining why, but the short version went like this: He was sufficiently convinced by the circumstantial evidence—and so unconvinced by McGee's love-affair alibi—that he decided McGee made up the affair to save his neck. One page of notes contained a list called FACTORS CONTRA CONSENSUAL.

1. Time—5:00 am is out of the question—especially since he had been out all night drinking and gambling.
2. NO WAY with young child @ 2 yrs old in bed with her, two daughters in adjoining room with husband in the rear bedroom.
3. All evidence indicates she was having her period and no consensual sex would be arranged at such a time.
4. If consensual no such vulgar language would have been involved. Also in some location where they would not have been recognized.
5. If consensual he would have claimed this in an effort to save his life.
6. He entered and exited through a window; if consensual, would he not have entered through the door?

When I looked at his list, I felt bewilderment, not clarity. The problem is, you can take most of those points and extract opposite conclusions from them. Consider the third one. Suppose Willette and Willie had arranged to meet in her bedroom that night. Now suppose Willette's period hadn't started when they'd set up the date, but that it did start just before he arrived. Could that have been why McGee reportedly told her, "You lied to me"?

Though I no longer put any credence in the affair story—I couldn't get past the huge discrepancies between the two versions McGee delivered—I was still unable to accept that the prosecution presented a case that proved his guilt beyond a doubt. To me, there wasn't enough evidence, then or now, to be sure either way. But, obviously, I thought it was wrong that he died for the crime of rape, given the unequal sentencing practices of the time. On that score, there was no getting around the terrible unfairness of the sentencing, compared with the 1946 Laverne Yarbrough child-rape case.

Before long, Dorothy had to take off, and Dillard and I had to climb into his car and head south, so we said our good-byes. On the way down, rolling along in his smooth-riding Cadillac through towns like Magee and Collins, I brought up yet another rumor you hear about Mrs. Hawkins: that she made a pass at, and possibly had an affair with, Paul Swartzfager.

Dillard didn't know anything about that, but he had trouble imagining Mrs. Hawkins engaging in an affair. "This woman only weighed ninety-two pounds," he said. "You know, a woman that didn't weigh but ninety-two pounds wouldn't be very sexually attractive."

I said that photographs I'd seen made Mrs. Hawkins look almost anorexic. He nodded and said, "I don't see how a ninety-two-pound woman could hardly have all those babies."

———

On Saturday, May 5, 1951, Abzug filed an appeal at the federal district court in Jackson, asking for an injunction against McGee's execution on the grounds that Mississippi's conduct amounted to a violation of his federally protected civil rights. Several hours before this, she and Coe had had an early morning meeting with Governor Wright inside his executive offices in the capitol, where they made a final plea for clemency. This meeting was the end of the line for Coe. In a letter to Abzug written before he went to Jackson for the hearing, he told her he had reserved the right to decide when "my duty was done" in the case. Now, he said apologetically, that time had come.

Both appeals were long shots, since Wright and Sidney Mize, the federal judge who would hear Abzug's plea on Monday, both seemed determined not to allow any more delays. From Abzug's perspective, it didn't help that the CRC had decided, once again, to organize a public protest to coincide with her efforts. The CRC didn't have any choice—it was now or never for such gestures—but Abzug had to spend part of her day dealing with the consequences: the mass arrest of forty-two people, including a large group of out-of-state white women and a smaller group of black male union members from Memphis.

"Without consultation with me . . . they sent down this delegation of . . . people, who immediately got arrested," she recalled. "I was outraged by that, because at that point, who was going to get [McGee] out? I had to . . . and I had to interrupt what I was doing to call up the attorney general and say these people had a right to petition, they had a right of speech, and you had no right to arrest them."

During their meeting with Wright and other state officials, Abzug and Coe touched very gingerly on the affair claim—merely alluding to it as "testimony and evidence [that] has never been heard." Instead they put more emphasis on their lingering doubts about McGee's confession and the racial bias of Mississippi's sentencing practices.

"[L]arge numbers of the citizens of the Nation believe that Willie McGee is not deserving of the punishment which hangs over him," they wrote. "Rightly or wrongly (and we submit rightly) they feel that if he were a white man, he would not be doomed to die."

Wright met every one of Abzug's arguments with counterarguments, questioning the very premise of her plea. Was she asking for clemency because McGee was innocent, or because Mississippi's sentencing for rape seemed unfairly applied?

"We submit that there is some doubt," she said, "and as long as there is doubt we believe there should be clemency."

"Why didn't you take that same line when this case was painted to the world in . . . lies?" he said. Attorney General J. P. Coleman was aggressive too, asking why the defense had ignored the fact that the Hawkinses were living in another state during some of the years the affair supposedly took place. He also said that Masonite's payroll records, which he said he'd had examined, contained no evidence that McGee worked there at the same time as Troy Hawkins.

Coe tried a high-minded approach, telling Wright that he should avoid putting himself in the historical position of Pontius Pilate, which was exactly what would happen if he washed his hands and said, " 'The courts did it, not I.' "

"When I make my decision, I'll assume full responsibility," Wright assured him brusquely.

During the hearing, Laurel mayor Carroll Gartin read a statement demanding an end to the defense's stalling tactics and its attacks on Mrs. Hawkins. "As though she has not already endured enough suffering at [McGee's] bestial hands, his friends now try to cast a stench of dark suspicion about her," he said. "The filth and foulness of such obscenity is a dastard insult to the name and honor of a Laurel wife and mother who . . . is fine and noble and pure."

When Wright announced his decision on Monday, he agreed: There would be no clemency.

———

At around 9:30 a.m. on Saturday, just as this hearing was getting under way, roughly two dozen women gathered at a street corner in front of the capitol, dressed like they were going to play bridge. Jackson police arrived and told them to disperse, but nobody moved. The women's leader was twenty-six-year-old Anne Braden, the Louisville-based leftist who had insulted Governor Wright by mail in the summer of 1950. Now, addressing a dozen highway patrolmen and police, she announced her group's intent: "We're going to the hearing."

"No you're not," said L. C. Hicks, chief of the highway patrol. "You'll have to quit gathering. . . . We've had enough trouble with this case, and we're not going to have any more."

After about ten minutes, the women were arrested—the charge was conspiracy to obstruct justice—and taken to the city jail. Separately, the cops started rounding up blacks, including a group of "well-dressed Negro men" who were seen standing in front of the Robert E. Lee hotel. In all, there were forty-two arrests of people who weren't doing anything but assembling.

Local and national newsmen headed to the jail to find out who they were, even though the police weren't in the mood for a media scrum. Photographers from the *Jackson Daily News* and *Life* had their cameras confiscated temporarily, an action Fred Sullens raised hell about. The women were CRC members or sympathizers who had responded to another clarion call, and they had come from all over the United States—New York, New Jersey, Michigan, California, Tennessee, Kentucky, and South Carolina, among other places—representing church groups, unions, and progressive organizations like the Bronx Women of Peace and the Emma Lazarus Federation of Jewish Women's Clubs. Local reporters wrote about them as if they represented an exotic new species of female.

"One of the most attractive women of the group identified herself as Miss Elaine Parun," the *Jackson Daily News* reported. ". . . 'I represent the Greenwich Village (New York City) chapter of the Civil Rights Congress,' she said. She looked 'Bohemian,' as the Village folks are commonly expected to look."

The hubbub continued for a few hours, while the women sang anti–Jim Crow songs and griped about the jail food, which included boiled turnip greens. "I can't eat that slop," one woman said. "Can we send out for something?" Abzug and Coe made a deal with officials: The women would plead not guilty and be released, with the understanding that they would leave the state immediately. The men were harassed and threatened, but nothing came of it—all of them left town safely, primarily by train.

The weekend's other big protest happened a thousand miles away, in Washington, D.C. On Sunday afternoon, McGee picketers, including William Patterson, marched back and forth in front of the White House. At the Lincoln Memorial, a mixed-race group of union members and war veterans—many of them Communists affiliated with the International Fur and Leather Workers Union—gathered for a larger demonstration and protest vigil. Three groups of a dozen or so men—all wearing white T-shirts that said FREE WILLIE MCGEE over their suits—chained themselves in a circle around the huge support columns at the top of the memorial's steps. "Lincoln freed the slaves," they chanted. "Truman free McGee."

316] THE EYES OF WILLIE McGEE

The novelist Howard Fast, who was there, watched hundreds of people come by to take in the spectacle. "They stood there, and most of them left as they had come, in a curious silence that was threaded through with wonder and doubt," he wrote later. "[O]nly one person, a soldier, asked why all this fuss over one life? Then we walked together into the shrine where Lincoln sits and the boy seemed confused and regretful over what he had said. Another visitor answered the young soldier: 'Sometimes, one life becomes a symbol of a million lives.'"

———

McGee was taken from the Hinds County jail around 6 p.m. on Saturday, for what was supposed to be his last trip to Laurel, but he didn't make it all the way. News of Abzug's civil rights appeal prompted Attorney General Coleman to have him brought back to Hinds County for safekeeping until the matter was resolved.

Details of this aborted trip, reported in Jackson papers, made it obvious that law enforcement officials were worried about a last-minute lynching. The group accompanying McGee was a strong-arm contingent that included Jones County sheriff Steve Brogan; deputies George Oalman, A. R. Tillman, and Tony Parker; and highway patrolmen Bud Gray, Willis Obre, and J. C. Puckett. When they were called back to Hinds, they were in a small town called Raleigh, which was on a roundabout route to Laurel. They were avoiding obvious roads.

That day, reporters and photographers had gotten a quick look at McGee before he was taken away. Clad in the blue shirt of his "pajama suit" and a pair of khaki pants, he responded good-naturedly to sarcasm from Brogan and Oalman. Brogan told McGee he was looking a little thinner than the last time he'd seen him.

"Yessir, I ain't been eating too good here," McGee said. "The food just didn't agree with me."

"I guess they didn't feed you like we did the last time we had you in Laurel," Brogan said. "That meal cost us nearly $4."

"We know how to feed you down in Laurel," Oalman said. "You like 'taters and 'possum, don't you, Willie?" McGee laughed and agreed that he did.

At the same time, McGee served notice that he wasn't going quietly. Asked if he had any additional statement to make, he said, "I ain't got anything to say now, but I'll have plenty to say later on. That is, if you're there then."

During these final days, he started writing his last letters. In one dated May 3, he'd written to Rosalee, who was in Detroit, under the wing of its very active CRC branch. His usual optimism was starting to sound like resignation. "I love you with all my heart do believe me darline," he wrote. "Oh yes honey give my regards to all and remember where ever you be [or] what ever come [or] go I shall always stand by you."

In a note written on Monday, May 7, he became fatalistic. "Dearest Wife: I no you have done everything there is to do and I apraciate you courage," he wrote. "Don't worrie honey take care of the children. . . . I am going away but don't give up the fight you have started. I know you want. I am so glad to no I have some one that will stand by the children. Yours truly husband Willie McGee."

On Monday, while Judge Mize listened to Abzug's arguments—which lasted from 1 to 7 p.m.—McGee spent a couple of hours with reporters, starting in mid-afternoon, when *Life* photographer Robert W. Kelly was allowed time to shoot portraits. After that, McGee sat down in a rocking chair in a hallway of the jail, smoking and giving an unfiltered version of what he still said was the truth about Mrs. Hawkins.

The *Clarion-Ledger* didn't print McGee's statement, which he'd prepared with advice from Abzug. The *Jackson Daily News* did—Sullens's news sense apparently overrode his distaste for McGee's comments. The paper later got sued for this by Mrs. Hawkins, in an action that was eventually dropped.

In his statement, McGee reiterated the details of his February affidavit, saying that Mrs. Hawkins had lured him into an affair and then refused to let him out. "Taking my life doesn't end such things as have been existing, will be existing till the end of the world," he said. "There is a lot more things that causes me not to get a fair decision about this—solely because I am a Negro; this is a white woman. . . .

318] THE EYES OF WILLIE McGEE

"A lot of folks, a lot of men, think they know a woman and don't. They find it hard to believe that Mrs. Hawkins would just hold on and not let the truth be known."

Mize threw out the civil rights claim around 7 p.m. Even before he had ruled officially, McGee was en route to Laurel. Brogan took charge of him at 6:30; they were on the road within ten minutes.

"McGee was visibly nervous but his disposition and speech was not affected," the *Clarion-Ledger* reported. He'd gotten a telegram from Father Divine, a black evangelist based in New York, and he was quietly singing a hymn to himself called "Farther Along," which begins, "Tempted and tried, we're oft made to wonder, why it should be thus, all the day long."

Quickly, the officers took him down the elevator and into a waiting vehicle. "As the car pulled away," the story said, "McGee slumped between two officers on the back seat, holding tight to a cardboard box of personal belongings."

———

For Dillard and me, the first stop in Jones County was the Laurel Country Club, where we'd arranged to meet William Deavours for lunch. Deavours, who was in his late seventies, was the son of Jack Deavours, the prosecutor who worked with Paul Swartzfager Sr. during the third McGee trial. A friend of Dillard's was going to be there too—a local businessman who asked that I not use his name, so I'll call him Warren Tabor.

The club was almost deserted, smelling of cleanser and old wood, and we wandered around randomly until we found the men alone in a side dining room, a silent space with a plush, leaf-print rug. Deavours, a balding, clear-eyed man, was dressed in tan slacks and a blue plaid shirt. Tabor had plenty of hair left, thick limbs, and a cheerful, slightly weary-looking face. He was more of a talker.

It was generous of Deavours to agree to the lunch. I figured he didn't want to be here; like many people affiliated with the prosecution side, he tended to assume that discussions of McGee couldn't lead to anything good. Still, I was disappointed when he said he didn't know much. Dea-vours was twenty-one and serving in the navy when the execution took place, and he said he hadn't ever discussed it at length with his father.

"Was your dad hired by somebody to help on the case?" I asked at one point.

"I don't know how the connection came about," he said genially.

"Do you remember, at the time, if you were aware of the claim that there had been a love affair between McGee and the woman?"

"I never even heard that."

"The whole time? Had you heard of it before I mentioned it?"

"I don't think so."

"Did your father ever talk to you about the case?"

"Sometimes it would come up in the course of a conversation. But as far as discussion of it from start to finish? I don't think he ever did, not with me."

I pulled out a picture of the Lincoln Memorial protesters. Deavours said he had no idea the case had caused so much commotion up north, nor did he care. "If they'd done that around here," he said, "every-body would have had a good laugh over it."

Dillard threw out a lifeline, recalling where he was the night of the execution—something I'd forgotten to ask him. He was a student at Southern that year, a member of the Pike fraternity, and he was hang-ing around with some frat brothers who debated whether they should drive up to Laurel and catch the scene at the courthouse.

"Back in those days, you know, it was public," he said. "But they got to checking, and they said the crowds was such that you couldn't get close to the courthouse. So we laid up there and . . . somebody broadcast the whole thing on the radio. So we laid up there and lis-tened to it like a soap opera, you know."

"*I* was there," Tabor said suddenly. "What impressed me was that big old generator producing the power that run the electric chair."

"They had a mobile electric chair, didn't they?" Deavours said. "That traveled?"

Tabor didn't hear him, so he went on: "And I stood over there in the yard of city hall, across the street from the courthouse, listening to that big generator. 'Course, I was more interested in the crowd than anything else, just to see who was there. Some folks I was amazed to see there, and some I expected to be."

Later, I asked if it was an interesting thing to have witnessed. "I wouldn't call it that," he said very seriously. "I was somewhat ashamed of being there. When I grew up, my dad did his best to have me in the right spot, and I would have debated whether or not he thought that was the proper place to spend any time. I was there with a lot of misgivings.

"But it was public property," he concluded somberly, "and I had every business being there standing if I wanted to."

———

The men remembered it right: The execution was broadcast live, and there was a "traveling" electric chair in use. In 1940, the Mississippi legislature changed the way executions were handled. Up until then, prisoners were hanged in the county where they'd been convicted. The new legislation codified the switch to electrocution, maintaining the tradition of holding executions in counties rather than at the state pen at Parchman. To that end, Mississippi commissioned a Memphis company called TriStates Armature & Electrical Works to build a portable chair.

It was used the first time in October 1940, in the south Mississippi town of Lucedale, to execute an African-American man named Willie Mae Bragg, who had been convicted of murder. The *Clarion-Ledger* ran a picture of Bragg as the current took his life. "At the extreme right are the hands of Executioner Jimmy Thompson at the switch," read a caption. "Note Bragg's hands gripping the chair and his neck bulging in death's throes."

The old chair, minus some of its straps and hardware, is now on display in the lobby of the Mississippi Law Enforcement Officers' Training Academy, a facility ten miles southeast of Jackson. It's a surprisingly simple-looking thing with a flat seat bottom, an upright plank on the backrest, and a notched brace where the backs of a prisoner's calves would fit. What's left of the skull-piece electrode sits on an armrest, a combination of padding and wire cable shaped into a crude circle.

Tabor wasn't inside to see the death scene. Like most people, he was outside with a crowd of spectators whose numbers I've seen estimated at anywhere from 500 to 1,500. Everybody was white and most were adults, but not all. Some people brought their children, and some kids just pedaled in on their bikes. At least one boy climbed a tree for a better look. Most people stood around, but some thought ahead and brought lawn chairs. Bill Minor, a longtime Southern newsman who covered the execution for the *New Orleans Time-Picayune*, told me he remembered being struck by the festive mood he saw outside before going in. "There were children present—it was like a circus atmosphere," he said. "Somebody was selling cold drinks, even."

The crowd clustered between the courthouse's south entrance and city hall, which was across a short street called Yates. The jail was east of the courthouse. In those days, the jail's second floor was connected to the same floor of the courthouse by an enclosed, barred catwalk on the north side of both buildings. When the time came for McGee's last walk, it involved a trip through the catwalk to the courtroom, where the chair was set up. One reporter referred to it as a "bridge of sighs," a phrase Lord Byron made famous in *Childe Harold's Pilgrimage*, which referenced the enclosed Venetian bridge that connected the Palace of the Doges, where sentences were passed, to the prison where executions took place.

Tabor made a sketch showing me what was where. While he did that, Deavours and Dillard talked about the old jail, which was no longer in use. Deavours recalled that it contained a built-in gallows. "When they built that jail next to the courthouse," he said, "all the cells were on the second floor, and as you went up the stairs, you looked up overhead—"

"There was a trap door," Dillard said, nodding.

"Nope," he said. "Well, yeah. But there was a big ring in the ceiling up there where the rope went." Deavours once gave a tour of the courthouse to his middle daughter's Girl Scout troop, which included a quick duck into the jail entrance for a look at the hangman's loop. At the end of the tour, he asked the kids if they had any questions. A girl raised her hand. "Mr. Deavours," she said, "did they ever have any big-time criminals here, like Communists?"

Before long, we got back to McGee. Deavours, Tabor, and Dillard all agreed that, despite the criticisms of Mississippi justice, the system had worked well. Tabor said, "When you have men like John Stennis and J. P. Coleman and Burkitt Collins and the others handling the situation—including Paul Swartzfager, for that matter—you know the average citizen felt like they'd handled that thing all right. And they went on with their work. I mean, it just wasn't something that was daily talk around here."

"When it was over with, as far as people around here were concerned, it was *over*," Deavours said.

Soon the lunch ended, and I got in the car with Dillard. He needed to go by a local bookstore to see about placing a few copies of a new book he'd written, so we took care of that first. The woman who ran the shop perked up when Dillard told her I was researching the McGee case. She said her parents knew the Hawkinses and had taken her to the courthouse on execution night, when she was twelve or so. I asked if she'd ever heard the love-affair story.

"Oh, yeah," she said quickly. "I mean, I was aware of that as a child. I mean, that that was what they were trying to make it look like." I told her many people treated the story as fact. She laughed. It wasn't fact to her.

Dillard and I made the short drive to the courthouse and jail. The catwalk was gone—a renovation years ago joined the structures with a blocky addition. Inside the jail, on the second floor, the old cells were intact, but they and seemingly ever other space were being used to hold records. The place smelled dusty and rusty, and there wasn't much to see.

We gave up, went back outside, and walked to the courthouse. Inside, a young white woman Dillard knew pulled out the keys and let us into the courtroom, which looked about like what I had expected:

dim walls and heavy judicial furniture, darkly stained and varnished. The judge's bench was against the east wall, with counsel tables and spectator benches lined up in front of it. The old balcony for blacks was gone, and the renovation had wiped out the windows and balcony on the south side, which is where the electric chair's power lines had come through.

Dillard had told the woman we were in town doing research about McGee, and as we stood there, she started asking questions.

"Who represented him?" she said. We told her about the three trials and the various lawyers.

"Nobody ever did a psychiatric evaluation on him either," she suddenly declared. I started to tell her about the second trial and N. B. Bond, the psychologist, but she interrupted.

"I *still* think she took advantage of that," she said, "she" being Mrs. Hawkins. "I think she was just using him. They were seeing each other, I think, for sure. I think he was innocent. And just got caught. That's just my opinion."

"Well, that's the story that's widely accepted," I said noncommittally.

"Because a lot of people knew. I mean, her friends knew, people that knew him knew it was going on. And when he got caught she screamed rape. That's just what I'll always believe. And I don't believe his soul's at peace, and I believe he still haunts this place. I don't care what anybody says."

She wasn't kidding about the ghost. A custodian told her she saw a shadow one night in a hallway; other people said they heard voices. For this woman, the really spooky thing was the elevator, whose second-floor door was positioned in the hallway just outside the courtroom. It was an old-timey unit, and to get it to work you had to be inside, pushing the buttons yourself. But sometimes, she said, it went up and down by itself, empty.

She believed McGee's spirit was in there, riding forever because it was restless. "I've heard too many stories about somebody's soul not being at peace," she said, "based on what happened at the death."

The Jackson arrests and the Lincoln Memorial vigil were the climax of McGee's public support, but they weren't all there was to it. Between the Supreme Court's final refusal and McGee's last night, the story transcended the facts of the crime, the trials, the alibis, and the appeals and assumed its final form as an American myth. Carl Rowan got it right when he wrote that McGee went from being a "nobody" to becoming a unique and complicated symbol—part victim, part Communist pawn, part mysterious tangle of disputed realities. Whatever he had or hadn't done, Rowan said, his name would "live a long time—in the minds and consciences of honest people who feel that, guilty or not, he paid too much."

As always, the involvement of Communists crept into everything, and to people like Max Lerner, a liberal columnist for the *New York Post*, this aspect of the case was a deal breaker that prevented it from stirring "the national sense of injustice" in a way that had true mass appeal. The Scottsboro case had it, he wrote, but "the case of Willie McGee . . . seemed to have become the exclusive property of the Communists."

All the same, Lerner had sympathy for the man. "Willie McGee is—or was—a human being," he wrote. "We would be wrong to erase him from our conscience only because the Daily Worker has written his name on every Communist banner. The Russian police-state has its own Willie McGees, millions of them, which is what makes the weeping of the American Communists such a mockery. But America cannot afford to judge the just and unjust by political tags."

Whether McGee's story became as measurably "big" as Scottsboro, there's no denying that it stirred people, and Lerner was wrong that it only captivated the far left. When you look at the acts of ordinary citizens who said and did something in those last weeks—through petitions, letters, poems, speeches, rallies, campus debates, and other tools of dissent—it's obvious that the CRC continued to get through to Americans who had no interest in the Communist agenda.

All over the United States—in Los Angeles, San Francisco, Oakland, Phoenix, Chicago, Detroit, St. Louis, New Orleans, Washington, New York, and other cities—union members, Communists, progressives, liberal Democrats, students, and church groups marched and organized petition- and letter-writing drives. Some of these acts made headlines; some were barely noticed. In a way, the little gestures were more noteworthy than statements by people like Einstein, Faulkner, and Norman Mailer, because they came from anonymous people who had caught the fever of the moment and were acting from their hearts.

In Oakland one day, a team of signature-gatherers was stationed in front of a Sears store when several clerks rushed out, saying, "Let me sign this thing!" After listening to a talk in Los Angeles by Juanita McGee—Willie McGee's California-based sister-in-law—a man named Irving Oppenheim grew so angry that he dialed the governor's mansion in Jackson and somehow got Fielding Wright on the line. He lit into him about sending an innocent man to his death on a phony rape charge.

"Where'd you get your information?" Wright asked.

"From the Civil Rights Congress."

"It's a pack of lies," Wright said. He and Oppenheim traded insults until Wright told him to "go to the devil" and hung up.

A 500-person Times Square rally on April 1 was broken up by mounted police; six people were arrested, including a man named Harvey Bellet, who was charged with trying to kick a patrolman's horse. That same day, Rosalee McGee spoke at the Abyssinian Baptist Church in Harlem, vowing, "I'm going to keep fighting till my blood runs like water." She kept busy throughout the final months, appearing in several cities, including Detroit, Denver, Memphis, San Francisco, Oakland, Seattle, Portland, and Chicago. Her Detroit appearance in March was typical of the stops she made. Anne Shore, a CRC member there, told Patterson that she drew "[c]lose to 1,000 people, a wonderful program and a real demonstration of Negro white unity."

Unions kept things stirred up all through April, organizing events from New York to San Francisco. One of the largest marches happened on April 29 in Chicago, when thousands of CIO-affiliated packinghouse workers turned out for McGee. One was a man named John Polk Allen, a twenty-one-year-old union meatpacker who would become famous himself in the 1990s, when he was the driving force behind the controversial science experiment known as Biosphere 2. Recalling the march nearly fifty years later, Allen teared up as he tried to convey why Willie McGee had such resonance. "It was so outrageous and so different from the Martinsville Seven," he said. "It was one individual, and you could look at his photograph . . . and you knew that a great wrong was being committed."

On April 30, in Phoenix, Vice President Alben Barkley encountered a picket line as he arrived at the local Jackson-Jefferson Day dinner. He ignored everybody there—including a mother and her eight-year-old son who had traveled 115 miles from Tucson to hold up signs.

Of course, not everybody was swept up. One of the ironies of McGee's final weeks was that mainstream African-American newspapers, by and large, turned their backs on him because of the Communist involvement, even after the NAACP relented ever so slightly about McGee in the spring of 1951. In March, Walter White urged chapter members to write or wire Governor Wright and ask for clemency, though they were told to keep in mind that the NAACP was in no sense working with the CRC.

Overall, papers such as the *Chicago Defender* and *Pittsburgh Courier* treated McGee like somebody else's news. The *Defender* didn't write about the execution at all until two weeks after it happened, when it published an editorial blasting both "the Communists and white supremacists" for "making a mockery out of democratic concepts which undergird our republic."

These papers' silence was countered by steady mainstream attention—in the *Times*, *Life*, and so forth—along with wall-to-wall coverage in papers like the *Daily Worker*, *New York Compass*, *Daily People's World*, and the Paul Robeson–affiliated publication *Freedom*, which ran a mid-April extra devoted to the case. Under a banner headline that read, YOU CAN SAVE MY DADDY! the front page featured a sketch of black children holding signs that said, "Pappa was electrocuted for 'rape' " and "Don't lynch our father."

The feedback from outside the United States was also impressive.

Cables came in from Mexico City (Diego Rivera, Frida Kahlo, and others wrote Truman, calling the sentence "monstrous"), the Soviet Union (Dimitri Shostakovich, Anton Chekhov's widow, and others, who informed the supreme court of Mississippi that "mankind shall not forgive those guilty of this terrible infamy"), Ireland, England, and France. In early April, the *Daily People's World* ran a photo of protesters in front of a London movie theater, holding up signs that said, WILLIE MCGEE MUST NOT DIE! Later that month, Mississippi lieutenant governor Sam Lumpkin complained about having to deal with pro-McGee letters and telegrams when Governor Wright was out of the state. "They must have an effective underground to keep up with what's going on," he said, mentioning one letter that came from "30 residents, 19 Cornwall Ardens, London."

President Truman, like every major official who got near the case, received thousands of letters and telegrams, which his staff summarized for him in long daily lists of names and organizations that often began, "The following writers ask for clemency for Willie McGee." On May 2, he was sent an "open letter" signed by ninety-one prominent people, including Uta Hagen, Oscar Hammerstein, Garson Kanin, Norman Mailer, Wallace Stegner, and Sam Wanamaker. May 8 was Truman's birthday, and somebody had cards printed up to remind him of this, which said, "Save this Man, Willie McGee, Mr. President, for a Happier Birthday for You and a Happier America for all."

Frequently, the letters had to be translated, because they were from Europe or Asia. The State Department forwarded this one:

KONING, Miss Annemarie
Voorstraat 27
Delft, The Netherlands

Letter to the President, dated 2/18/51, written in Dutch.

Translator's Summary of Communication

328] THE EYES OF WILLIE McGEE

The writer, a nine-year-old girl, thinks it terrible that the President wants to kill Willy McGee, and she asks that he be released at once. He didn't do anything, and anyone who says he did is lying.

Another was sent by "114 members of the Free German Youth of the District Youth School of Königstein," who demanded that Truman stop and study the facts in "the coming execution of the young American Negro Willie McGhee of Mississippi, who is to be killed this month. He could never have committed the crime he is accused of, since he was proved to have been 45 kilometers away from the scene of the crime when it was committed."

Interest remained especially high in France, where left-wing and Communist papers like *Combat* and *L'Humanité* kept the case in the news every day, and where the execution was front-page fare all over the country. "[T]he scope of the sentiment against racism is indicated by the kinds of letters and protests in response to *Combat*'s appeal," a *Daily Worker* correspondent reported from Paris. "One comes from the secretary general of an independent union of editorial workers; another from 96 students of the young women's junior college in Paris; a third from a group of artists; a fourth from a dozen people in a hospital of the Paris suburb of Garches."

Everybody knew that China and the Soviet Union were tuned in—periodically, Chinese officials sent telegrams or issued statements berating Truman or Wright. On the night of the execution, shortwave-radio operators in Europe and the United States picked up broadcasts from Moscow that blasted the American government for letting McGee die. "The Moscow announcers read the same piece of script at least once an hour from early evening up to 10 or later," the *Memphis Commercial Appeal* reported. "Coupled with the pleas for McGee were bald statements that 15,000,000 Negroes in the United States are now living under a reign of terror because they have . . . taken the lead in supporting the peace aims of USSR and the 'great Stalin.'"

McGee didn't arrive in Laurel until shortly after 10:00. The drive shouldn't have lasted that long, but his escorts once again took a roundabout route. They would have been wary of going all the way until they knew the execution wouldn't be halted again. There were still legal appeals in play.

After Mize's decision, Abzug's colleague Mary Metlay Kaufman— a New York–based lawyer who had worked on the U.S. prosecution team at Nuremberg—asked a federal judge in New Orleans to grant a restraining order until, at their behest, he had reviewed the arguments they'd presented to Mize. He refused. In Washington, Vito Marcantonio placed a call to Presidential Assistant David K. Niles, asking him to persuade Truman to intervene, based on a lengthy clemency plea Abzug had submitted that day—written by her, but styled as if McGee were addressing the president directly. The document called on Truman to live up to the spirit of his 1947 Lincoln Memorial address, recognizing that a Southern court was incapable of giving McGee fair treatment in a case like this. McGee insisted that fear of mob violence had prevented him, for years, from telling the real story.

> To charge as I did under oath, that there was actually no rape and that the prosecution knew it, that the complainant's story was not the truth . . . that far from never having seen me in her life, as she testified, we knew each other intimately over a number of years, would have been beyond the power of someone like myself, imprisoned, terrorized by my jailers, and constantly under fear of lynching. My lawyers took the same attitude, making it plain that to interpose such a defense . . . would be out of the question in Mississippi, and they could not see their way clear to present it in open court.

Marcantonio was told that afternoon that the president wouldn't step in, so the final pleas were aimed at the U.S. Supreme Court. Starting at 6:30, Marcantonio, along with lawyers James T. Wright and Ralph Powe, appealed in turn to William O. Douglas, Hugo Black, and Chief Justice Fred Vinson. At 10:25 p.m., Vinson announced that he wouldn't take action, and that was that. There were no more legal options.

In Laurel, the crowd had reached capacity by 10 p.m. The *Leader-Call*, which published the highest estimate, thought there were as many as 1,500 people on the scene. The west side of the building, on Fifth Avenue, was jammed with parked cars. The courtroom, where the electric chair was set up in late afternoon by state engineer John Laird and executioner C. W. Watson, was off limits to everyone but roughly five dozen officials, spectators, and reporters—all male—who would be allowed to witness the electrocution. Troy Hawkins arrived at around 11:00 and took a seat four rows back in the benches, accompanied by Mrs. Hawkins's brother and two of her brothers-in-law. Mrs. Hawkins and her children were probably out of town, but that's unclear. She had been in Jackson that day for the federal court hearing, but she didn't return to Laurel. According to her daughters, the four of them stayed with a family friend in Birmingham that night.

Neither Rosalee McGee nor Bella Abzug was in Laurel. Rosalee was still in Detroit. Abzug stayed in Jackson with Ernest Goodman, a colleague from the Detroit CRC who had flown in to take the place of John Coe. According to Goodman, who talked about his brief involvement in the case in an oral-history interview, as midnight approached he and Abzug walked together from their hotel to the governor's mansion, having arranged to speak with Wright one last time.

"We went in the side way," he said, "and there we were met by a uniformed butler, black man, of course. We were escorted into the living room, and there in one part of it was a card table. And two couples were sitting there playing bridge. One of them was the governor and his wife and the other was the Attorney General and his wife. And they were waiting for us."

Abzug made her plea, but, inevitably, Wright said no. "Did you ever make an argument to a metal statue of a human being?" Goodman said. "One, however, who was a Mississippi governor, and gracious, lovely, pleasant, and polite? That's what it was like."

One of the photographs from that night shows a portion of the crowd outside the courthouse, looking up in unison. There is no indication of when the picture was taken, but it had to have been before the execution, since the faces still looked expectant. There were smiles and grins all around. More men than women were there—by about 7 to 1— and the men were dressed the way they would for a Saturday night, not a Sunday morning: casual shirts, sports jackets, caps, and hats.

From where these people stood, they wouldn't have been able to see into the courtroom. They were just looking for signs that something was happening, and for that the south side was the best place to be. From there they could see the generator truck, which was parked on a driveway between the jail and courthouse, the second-floor catwalk, and the balcony and south-facing windows.

The old newspaper stories don't agree on how McGee was transferred from the highway patrol vehicle to the jailhouse, but it appears that the authorities used a decoy. Wayne Valentine Jr.—the son of onetime Police Chief Wayne Valentine, who was nineteen at the time and who later became a highway patrolman—told me that lawmen dressed him up like a prisoner, drove to the Yates Street jail entrance, and hustled him inside. If that's true, it fooled Bill Minor's colleague on the *Times-Picayune*, Robert Peters, who reported that the vehicle holding McGee stopped in front of the jail and unloaded him there.

I think the *Laurel Leader-Call* probably had it right. Its lead story said McGee was "hurried through the north door of the courthouse" by a group that included Brogan, Tillman, Oalman, and Jack Anderson. They hustled him up the stairs, through the courtroom and past the electric chair, and through the catwalk and into his cell. He would remain there for nearly two hours, talking to a preacher, smoking a cigar, writing last letters to his mother and Rosalee, and getting his hair clipped. With McGee locked in, an officer informed the south-side crowd that everything would now move forward as planned, so they should settle down and behave. "We have waited a long time for this," he said. "You have been patient. We want no demonstration. Let's everybody be nice."

The radio broadcast originated from Hattiesburg station WFOR, which sent over a crew with a portable transmitter powered by a car battery. The on-air voices were Granville Walters, the station manager and a Mississippian, and Jack Dix, a newsman originally from Minnesota. At around a quarter to twelve, Dix started setting the scene.

"I'm sure that you have heard over both radio stations, WFOR and WAML, that all channels open to Willie McGee to save his life have now been exhausted, and the execution is to take place here this evening," he said. "As far as the crowd is concerned, I think the only thing we can say is that there are many, many people here, milling around the courthouse. Naturally, many rumors have gone around. The *Life* photographer is now climbing up on top of the truck. There are two of them here tonight, and one of them is now climbing up on this big, silver-bodied truck. He's set his camera up there. And now he is following his camera up here, and that's where he is going to sit."

Looking for signs, they paid close attention to three things: the catwalk, various men whom they could see moving around near second-floor windows, and the truck itself. "There's no activity around the truck yet," Dix said. "Naturally, when we hear the motors of the generator of this truck kick off, you'll know that the electrocution is very near indeed." He said that the catwalk, with its "bars and grill-work . . . looks for all the world like one of the entranceways that a circus uses to get lions from . . . their cages into the arena."

Walters took a turn, noting that light and shadows coming through the barred windows of the jail were casting huge images on the east side of the courthouse. "And it certainly presents a very eerie appearance," he said, "when you look over the two-story wall there with the jail bars, the window bars, outlined clearly all up and down the courthouse wall." He also touched on the intense interest in the case ("This event tonight has really, as you well know, created nationwide attention"); his glimpses of people he couldn't identify ("There has also been some gentleman up there, a reporter probably, possibly an A.P. or U.P. man, who has been very busy at the telephone. . . ."); and the whereabouts of McGee.

"Time is rapidly running out for Willie McGee," he said. "And down here, right below us, they are opening the truck, getting it all set, ready to turn it on, so that the juice will be funneled up through these cables that are running from the truck to the chair, and will of course provide the power that will give Willie McGee the execution."

At this point, for the first time, you can hear the generator, which comes through as a steady thrum of white noise. "Those of you who are listening, I could hear the motor of the truck," Dix said. ". . . Let's put our microphone over the rail just a moment and see if you can pick that up. Jim, if you're listening, you might jack our gain up a little bit."

As news accounts of that night make clear, McGee died with dignity, though the *Jackson Daily News* was stingy with its wording, saying McGee walked to his death "[a]lmost bravely, almost defiantly." At around 11:30, a local black barber, Alex Spencer, showed up to cut his hair and shave his head at the base of the skull. McGee gave 55 cents to Reverend T. W. Patterson, a black Laurel preacher who stayed with him to the end, and left $7.25 for his mother. He smoked while the barber worked, and at one point announced, "I got all my business fixed. I'm not worried at all. Willie is ready to go."

They took him over just after midnight, with Patterson reading the Twenty-third Psalm before they left the cell. Outside, Dix had just marked the time—"It's now straight up of twelve o'clock"—when, after about forty-five seconds, he saw a moving mass of people. "I believe that is McGee going in now, there can be no doubt of that," he said. "Because there was a party of perhaps—oh, shucks, there must have been at least a dozen people that passed through that passageway, and they're still going. The county attorney has left the window, the man is still at the telephone, no lights at all on that party as they came through there. So we assume now that it will be just a moment until his execution takes place."

The final preparations went fast. The *Leader-Call* said McGee "took his death seat without being urged or aided and remained calm as attendants fastened leather straps around his abdomen, ankles, and wrists." He didn't make any last-second statements and apparently said only one thing: "Is the Reverend Patterson here?" He was, but McGee couldn't see him while the men strapped him in. "McGee appeared interested in the fastening of the large leather straps to his body, wrists, and ankles," the story said. "His wide eyes flashed several times as he watched the officers go about their grim business."

He was wearing a short-sleeved green shirt, blue trousers, yellow socks, and bedroom slippers. Attendants removed the slippers and placed them on the floor as they adjusted the leg straps. Then, the *Leader-Call* reported, the executioner put a "metal skull-shaped electrode to McGee's head and strapped a wide leather band across his face, covering the eyes, but leaving openings for his nose and mouth."

The first shock, 2,500 volts, was applied at 12:05, only three minutes after McGee was brought in. His hands formed fists as the charge went through him for half a minute. The executioner applied a second jolt, but McGee was probably gone by then. "Twice, yeah," Bill Minor recalled. "And I just have a vague memory that you could smell the odor of scorched flesh, of burnt flesh, in that courtroom."

Two local physicians checked McGee's chest and pronounced him dead at 12:10. He was left there for another fifteen minutes before he was put on a gurney, covered, taken downstairs and through the crowd outside, and placed in a hearse that took him to the funeral home of Pete Christian. "Hundreds lined the sidewalk leading to the south door of the courthouse, as McGee's body, covered with a white sheet, was rolled to a waiting hearse," the *Leader-Call* said. The hearse rolled away, and that was the end. With nothing left to see, the crowd dispersed within minutes.

In Jackson, Abzug said she got the news from a caller at the courthouse who held up a phone, allowing her to hear what she called "the blood-curdling cries" of the spectators. "And then . . . I cried too," she said. "I cried at the notion of the human degradation that could kill a man because of his color, because that's what it was."

Goodman was with her, at a pay phone, and he remembered it the same way. "[W]e had arranged to call a newspaper reporter there. . . . And just as we got him on the phone, we heard the rebel yell, the rebel yell of victory, just so loud we couldn't hear him talking. They had just turned the switch. They'd won another battle. . . . We left immediately."

———

After that, everything else was reaction: Fred Sullens gloating, Paul Robeson predicting the decline and fall of the Western world. Two of the more eloquent statements came from Josephine Baker and McGee himself, whose last letter was cleaned up grammatically by a CRC editor and then sent off to newspapers.

Baker was performing that week at the Fox Theater in Detroit. She paid for Rosalee McGee's plane ticket back to the South—she went to New Orleans—and she also wired money for McGee's burial expenses. Prior to one of her performances, she took a minute to talk to the audience about McGee.

"Today is a tragic one for all American negroes and darker peoples of the world," she said. "The execution of William McGee does not stop with just the death of McGee. It means a part of every American negro died a little with him."

Two weeks later, when *Life* published its story on the case, it had two compelling photographic portraits to choose from. In one, McGee was hanging his head, looking thoroughly defeated. In the other, he was staring straight into the camera, showing a face that was calm, self-assured, even defiant. *Life* ran the first picture, but the second one was more in tune with the spirit of McGee's final letter.

"Dear Rosalee," he said. "They are planning here to kill me and I dont no if you and the people will be able to save me. if I have to die I want you to say goodbye to my mother and the children and all the people who no it is wrong to kill a man because of his color.

"You no I am innocent. tell the people again and again I never did commit this crime. tell them that the real reason they are going to take my life is to Keep the Negro down in the south. they cant do this if you and the children keep on fighting. never forget to tell them why they killed their Daddy.

"I no you won't fail me," he concluded, "tell the people to Keep on fighting."

WHISKEY IN A PAPER SACK

A couple of days after my Laurel trip with Dillard, I went back alone and had a few final conversations. One was with an old African-American man named Gus DeLoach, who in 1951 was living across the street from the Pete Christian funeral home, where McGee's body was kept before it was taken to Pachuta. DeLoach was an army veteran and longtime Masonite employee who became one of the first blacks put in a management job when the company changed with the times in the late 1960s. He remembered McGee, saying he'd worked at Masonite at some point, though he couldn't remember when.

"Willie was a hard worker, and he had a wife and children," he said. "Beyond that, until this happened, he was just a hardworking fellow. Until this came about, I never heard anything irregular about Willie McGee."

DeLoach listened to the execution on the radio and sat on his porch afterward, watching law enforcement officials and mourners come and go. When things settled down and the funeral home emptied out, he went over for a private look. He smiled when I told him about Evelyn Smith McDowell's memory that McGee was "burned black." No, he said, he wasn't burned black. He was just dead.

"Why did you go look at him? Curiosity?"

"Well, yeah, out of curiosity—and he was right next door to me, and he was a friend. Well, I say a friend. We had worked together. And, usually, black people make visits like that, when one has passed on."

Thinking of both McGee and of Dillard's client, Willie Stokes, I asked DeLoach what he thought about while he stood there, and whether he had said a prayer.

"No, I didn't say a prayer, not specifically for him," he said. "But for the conditions of our community, I did."

———

I also spoke with Jon Swartzfager, the youngest son of Paul Swartzfager. There was another son in town—Paul Jr.—but I'd already talked to him years before and gotten nowhere. Like Bill Deavours, he was cordial and smiling, but he told me his father never said much of anything about the case.

Jon was a different kind of guy. I'd spoken to him on the phone beforehand, and he obviously had some things he wanted to say. On Saturday night in Laurel, after dinner with him and his wife, I followed them back to their house. He and I settled down in the den, and Jon told the story of what his father did on the night of the execution.

According to Jon, his dad was a "softhearted, kindhearted man, and I think it really bothered him to know that he played a role in somebody being put to death." That night, Swartzfager drank a few beers before heading off to the courthouse, taking along a .38—in case the execution was stayed again and a riot broke out, Jon said—and "a pint of whiskey in a brown sack." Jon said the whiskey wasn't for his dad, but for McGee. He said his father didn't really know whether McGee was guilty or innocent, and it was tormenting him. And so, operating from a mix of mercy and curiosity, he went to see McGee at the jail and let him have a few drinks, both to ease the pain of what was coming and to loosen his tongue.

"It was probably an hour after Willie started in on the bottle," Jon said, "and he asked him, 'I just want to know one thing. Did you do it?' And McGee said, 'Yessir, I did it, but she was just as guilty as I was.'

"And that crushed my dad," Jon said. "He apparently believed Willie to the extent that he thought, 'Here's a man about to die, what does he have to lose by telling the truth?' And he's inebriated. And he says he didn't rape her but that it was consensual sex."

According to Jon, his father was never the same, especially around Christmas. "He just couldn't stand Christmas and couldn't stand seeing people happy and celebrating and all that, because I think he saw the world as very sad and unfair after that. It was a terrible thing."

———

It was a moving story, and I was grateful that Jon trusted me enough to share it. Unfortunately, it was probably apocryphal. As I subsequently found out, Swartzfager had no apparent sympathy for McGee, and he gladly engaged in grand-jury tampering to help put him in the electric chair, just as John Poole had always said he'd done.

I know this thanks to interviews done years ago by a physician in Mississippi named Luke Lampton, a Jackson native who became interested in the McGee case back in the late 1980s, before he entered medical school. As a young man, Lampton was a precocious history buff—he was using the Mississippi State archives regularly by age twelve—and he'd been doing research on a project about J. P. Coleman, the state attorney general during the last years of the case, when he got sidetracked into a brief obsession with McGee. Many of the main characters were still alive then, and Lampton got busy and interviewed several of them, including Bella Abzug, Jessica Mitford, Dixon Pyles, Hettie Johnson, Leroy Jensen, and Paul Swartzfager.

I found him only by luck: He had written a journal article about Ouida Keeton, and we were exchanging e-mails about that when he asked what I was working on. When I told him, he generously offered to let me listen to his tapes, which I did during my final trip to Mississippi in mid-2009. The interviews were excellent—young Luke was persistent and persuasive in a way that ought to be bottled and sold to journalism schools—and his Swartzfager interview was a revelation. It reminded me, as if I needed reminding again, that people's opinions about the McGee case were inextricably mixed up with what they wanted to be true. Jon, understandably, liked to think his father had acted humanely at a moment of state-sponsored retribution that he had helped bring about.

Maybe he did—I wasn't there—but it didn't sound that way when

Lampton talked to him. Without prompting, Swartzfager crudely boasted that, yes, there had been grand-jury tampering before trial three. Just as Poole claimed, the state put handpicked black men on the panel to satisfy the U.S. Supreme Court's *Patton* mandate, but in a way that wouldn't affect the outcome.

"The first thing I had to do was to get a damn nigger on my grand jury," Swartzfager said. "The truth of the whole matter is . . . we made arrangements . . . and we had two nigger doctors. . . . Dr. Barnes we called 'the clap doctor,' he treated the niggers for clap, gonorrhea. And he was quite all right, old Barnes was."

The way it worked was simple: When the grand jury met and listened to testimony in support of a new indictment, the three blacks were instructed to sit in a corner, mind their own business, and shut up until they were told to raise their hands. In the same interview, Swartzfager made it clear that he didn't know whether McGee had raped Mrs. Hawkins or had consensual sex with her. But it didn't matter to him. Either way, it was his job to put him away.

Hearing confirmation of the jury tampering made me wonder: Would McGee's fate have been any different if the Supreme Court had taken his case and reversed it on jury-selection grounds? Not necessarily. Eddie Patton's "victory" in *Patton v. Mississippi* didn't mean he went free. It just meant that he got another trial. He was found guilty a second time and executed in early 1950.

Still, Supreme Court intervention had helped the Scottsboro Boys, and that was McGee's last, best hope of survival. In the end, there was no getting around the fact that the federal courts had failed McGee, even if he was guilty. With its obvious reluctance to take on what were clearly one-sided trials in Mississippi, the Supreme Court balked at giving McGee the protections guaranteed him by the Constitution. Craig Zaim, in a legal analysis of the case published in the *Journal of Mississippi History*, put it perfectly when he wrote, "The Supreme Court could not reform the Mississippi criminal justice system in 1951 because of its inability to enforce unpopular decisions and its unwillingness to expand the scope of the Fourteenth Amendment. Willie

McGee died a casualty of the battle Mississippi waged to maintain its autonomy against federal power."

⸺

At the same time, federal courts of that era proved to be quite efficient at putting Communists in jail for exercising their constitutional rights. After the McGee case ended, William Patterson spent much of his time in legal battles with the U.S. government, ultimately serving two different ninety-day prison sentences in 1954 for contempt convictions that grew out of his refusal to hand over CRC records.

Patterson was never one to stay idle, and while he was in prison he studied the sociology of his fellow inmates and wrote memorable letters to his wife, Louise, and his daughter, MaryLouise, who was a grade-schooler in 1954 and 1955. Describing prison life, he told her to imagine a school with no yard, no place to play, and no good, clean air.

"Maybe I write too seriously for you," he said. "Now is the time however for you to learn the most serious things of life. . . . Never forget that you are a little Negro girl. Never forget that black men and women have fought for three hundred (300) years to make this a free country. Never forget that the fathers and mothers of the white children with whom you play now fight together with daddy. No color is bad except that color which shows a lack of sunshine and fresh air."

⸺

By the mid-1950s, the civil rights movement was moving rapidly, spurred by dramatic events that set the tone for the historic changes of the late 1950s and 1960s: *Brown v. Board of Education*; the murder of Emmett Till; the Montgomery bus boycott and the rise of Martin Luther King Jr.; the integration of Little Rock Central High School in Arkansas; the arrival of the Freedom Riders in several Southern cities, including Jackson; and the 1963 March on Washington and the legislative revolution that later followed.

These events—and the eventual triumph of the NAACP's core strategy of forcing change by waging constitutional battles in federal courts—made it easy to forget that the Civil Rights Congress had ever existed, which it ceased to do in early 1956, depleted of energy and resources as it fought against attacks from the state of New York and the federal government, both of which accused it of channeling funds to subversive causes.

U.S. Communism also hit rocky times in 1956, when word spread that spring of Nikita Khrushchev's "Secret Speech" to the Twentieth Party Congress on February 24 and 25, in which he denounced Stalin for his mind-boggling brutality and abuses of power. Many American Communists abandoned ship, including Howard Fast and Jessica Mitford. By the time Mitford published *A Fine Old Conflict* in the 1970s, she had repurposed her experiences in a way that sometimes played her discarded ideology for laughs.

As a courtesy to her old boss, Mitford sent Patterson a copy of the book after it came out. He read it, didn't like it, and wrote Mitford a scolding letter, telling her she should have let him see it in manuscript form so he could have corrected its numerous errors. "It is possible to point to many mistakes that the CPUSA has made," he wrote. ". . . But where lies the alternative[?] The class struggle goes through many stages. But would you not agree, Decca, that the struggle must result in the triumph of a socialist world where racism, war and hunger are finally extirpated from human society and mankind achieves freedom not only from nature's vicissitudes but from exploitation of man by man[?]"

Before these various setbacks, Patterson had a last hurrah in late 1951. For years, the CRC, like the Tuskegee Institute, had collected reports and clippings on lynchings, legal lynchings, and other acts of violence and discrimination against black people. Much of the organization's work involved litigating such cases, but there was never enough money and manpower to take them all on.

The group's archiving didn't go to waste, however. In the early 1950s, Patterson came up with an audacious idea: The CRC would produce a book-length compendium of these incidents, to show America and the world the full extent of the racial oppression that was still all too common. It was published in November 1951 under the title *We Charge Genocide*, and its lists of killings, beatings, and judicial abuses went on for page after page after page:

MARCH 24, [1949]
—*Three houses occupied by Negroes in the North Smithfield district of Birmingham, Alabama, were shattered by dynamite.*

APRIL 25, [1950]
—*CORNELIUS LARKIN, 27, of Los Angeles, California, mentally deficient, was shot by police who were allegedly investigating an attempted burglary. Larkin was on his way home when police closed in on him. Excited, he ran and was shot.*

Of course, some of the items could have used additional fact-checking. The McGee case was summarized as if it had been proven beyond question that he was a war veteran, that the love affair happened, and that the state of Mississippi "ordered his death" to hide the truth of the relationship. And the CRC forgot to mention the embarrassing way it had cried "frame-up" after the December 1950 arrest of Scottsboro Boy Haywood Patterson, who killed a man in a Detroit bar fight and was later sent to prison for it.

Still, it was a powerful document overall, and it contained a great deal of unpleasant truth. In 1948, the United Nations adopted a "Convention on the Prevention and Punishment of the Crime of Genocide." Using that as his cue, Patterson positioned *We Charge Genocide* as a vast indictment, saying the United States had committed a "murderous assault" against black citizens. During a speech in Paris to launch the book, he once again compared the American government to Nazi Germany, complete with talk of a U.S. plot for world domination. "It has been demonstrated that the germs of world war are inherent in a racist attack upon the nationals of a country from their own government," he said. "The proof is the course of the Nazi government of [Hitler's] Germany. . . . Thus, this petition is extremely timely for it comes before, not after the deluge."

As Patterson recalled in *The Man Who Cried Genocide*, while in Paris he ran into Dr. Channing Tobias, an NAACP board member who was there as an alternate delegate to the U.N. General Assembly. Patterson dismissed Tobias as a Cold War Uncle Tom. "Our rulers had, since the Civil War, needed a Black spokesman to caution Negro workers against the dangers of trade unionism . . . ," he wrote. "Now [they] needed a Negro like Dr. Tobias to caution Negroes against the dangers of communism."

Tobias, for his part, thought Patterson was blind, and asked him why his speeches failed to mention the genocidal practices of the Soviet Union. Patterson said there weren't any.

———

Among the dignitaries who signed the genocide petition—including such people as W. E. B. DuBois, Louis Burnham, and Paul Robeson—was the familiar name of Rosalee McGee, who stayed loyal to the CRC long after the McGee case ended. Shortly after the execution, the *Pittsburgh Courier*—a middle-of-the-road black newspaper that was sometimes anti-CRC—published a story in which Josephine Baker reportedly blasted the CRC for using McGee "to swindle thousands of Amercians into furthering its despicable plan to conquer the world." Rosalee, who was in New Orleans by then, swore out an affidavit in which she said, "I just don't believe Jo Baker said all those things about the CRC. I am no fool. I know who swindled my husband from me, and who fought to the last minute to save him."

Rosalee had a difficult time of it in 1951, writing frequently from Lexington, where she took care of her sick mother and picked cotton. "I try my best not to worry," she said, "but I look [at the kids] and thank about McGee and I can't help but cry, and the people here make me wont to kill my self telling me we told you they were going to kill Willie. You see it didn't do any good.

"[But] I no it did good. We lost a life but we didn't lose the fight and I be glad when I can get away from all of this. If it wasn't for my poor mother and father I would just walk away. I never get well until I can leave here. I wont so much to be in NY or some where fighting and helping the CRC."

By 1952, Rosalee was desperate to get out of Mississippi. She told the CRC that she was being persecuted by law enforcement officials in Jackson, who allegedly confiscated her mail and showed up at her home with search warrants for bootleg whiskey. She started doing CRC speaking engagements again, in cities like Chicago and New York, and at some point that year she began working as an employee in the CRC's New York office. A subsequent report by the federal government's Subversive Activities Control Board listed her as the head of the National CRC Prisoner's Relief Department, the same job Lottie Gordon had held. In 1955, she turned up as a witness during a Control Board hearing held at the Foley Square courthouse in New York. She was identified as a resident of Brooklyn. Under oath, she described the McGee case to hostile Justice Department lawyers, falsely claiming to have been in the courtroom during his first and third trials.

I don't know how long that job lasted, but I do know that Rosalee never looked back once she got out of Mississippi. In 2008 I finally found a living relative of hers—an old man from Lexington named Jesse James Harris, who is her nephew.

During an interview at Harris's home, an old country place a few miles out of town, he easily identified Rosalee from a picture I showed him, and he cleared up a mystery about her first name. He said Rosalee and Rosetta were both accurate. "We called her Rosalee," he said. "But most people called her Rosetta."

He was sure she had two children, and it was his belief that they were adopted, but on that and a few other details he wasn't really sure. He said she remarried, but he couldn't remember the names of her new husband or the kids—he thought the husband's name might have been Lawrence Allen. He was certain she died in the late 1960s, in Brooklyn, and he said he was present at her funeral. He had no idea where the kids ended up or whether they were still alive.

Harris knew Rosalee was involved with some sort of civil rights organization in New York—he even heard she traveled overseas once—but he knew nothing of her involvement in the Willie McGee case. He nodded and smiled when I told him about it, but, to be honest, I don't think he really believed it was true.

———

Just as Susan Brownmiller said, Willette Hawkins never wavered from her story that she'd been raped. In August 1951, at the federal court in Foley Square, she went after the *Daily Worker* by filing a million-dollar libel suit against its parent company, Freedom of the Press Company, Inc., claiming she'd suffered "indescribable mental and emotional agony, injury and . . . psychological injury" because of the paper's false and malicious claims.

The suit's existence isn't mentioned in any of the books that summarize the McGee case, but Willette persisted with it for years, and the *Daily Worker*, with help from the CRC, invested considerable resources to search for witnesses who could help prove she'd lied. The *Daily Worker*'s investigator, Spivak, never found any. The closest he came was during an interview with her pastor, the Reverend Grayson L. Tucker, who said, after prompting, that he believed it was true that McGee had worked in the Hawkinses' neighborhood and that he knew Troy. But he also said he knew this only because he'd read it in the newspaper. He said he thought McGee committed the crime, calling him "a Negro who I think was just slightly mentally off, especially on the subject of passions."

Spivak wasn't the only person looking: CRC activists with the Detroit branch also tried to find several Detroit-area blacks, originally from Mississippi, who were believed to know something, but that quest came up empty. In the spring of 1952, during procedural back-and-forth about where depositions would be taken, defense lawyer David Freedman asked that Mrs. Hawkins be forced to come to New York for pretrial questioning. Only two people in the world could "bear witness" about the affair, he said: Willette and Willie McGee. McGee was dead, leaving her as "the only person who can be looked to for direct evidence on a crucial issue of the case."

That was a strange argument, considering the old *Daily Worker* line that everybody in Laurel knew of the affair. Rosalee McGee wasn't even mentioned. Somebody must have decided that she no longer qualified as an eyewitness to the events.

After long periods of inactivity, the case was settled out of court on May 5, 1955, with the *Daily Worker* agreeing to pay Mrs. Hawkins $5,000 and publish two retractions, admitting that their allegations against her were not proven. She traveled to New York to finalize the settlement, posing in front of the federal courthouse with her two New York lawyers. On that day, anyway, the years of pain and misery were forgotten: In the picture, she smiled like a newlywed.

———

McGee's defense lawyers went on with their lives without hitting much of a bump: Pyles had a long, successful career; Breland migrated into business; and London went back to Hattiesburg and worked the quieter fields of real-estate law.

Bella Abzug became Bella Abzug, one of the best-known New York political figures of the 1960s and 1970s. When Luke Lampton interviewed her, she had nicer things to say about the Mississippi lawyers she'd worked with, including London and Poole. "Both those guys worked very hard," she said. But the man she admired most was her appeals partner, John Coe. After the case ended, he wrote her to apologize for quitting at the end. In a letter written in June, she more than forgave him.

"I want you to understand that one of the most constructive experiences that came out of the many relationships and facets of the McGee case was my association with you," she wrote. "You must know that your ability, courage and strength can only be likened to an oasis in a desert. Everything that you are in view of your entire background . . . stands out as a might[y] example and symbol of truth and honesty at a time when so little of that kind of thing prevails either North or South, West or East. For me as a young person . . . my contact with you was a rich thing from which I gained much inspiration and courage. As you know, what I lack in eloquence, I make up for in directness, and if my words do not flow smoothly, I think you can feel the heart in them."

———

As for John Poole, he did pay a price. His reward for doing his job honestly was disbarment in the state of Mississippi, a process in which, according to Dixon Pyles, Fred Sullens may have had a hand. Before pressing his libel case in Jackson, Poole tried to sue in Delaware, where the *Jackson Daily News*'s parent company was incorporated. That suit died, Pyles said, because Sullens's lawyers were able to block it on the grounds of *forum non conveniens*, that is, the lack of a convenient forum.

"As a result of the threat," he said, "Fred Sullens hired an investigator and looked into John Poole's background. John Poole was a very able young lawyer. But they found that some of the funds in a small estate which he was handling . . . were not accounted for, so he was promptly disbarred. But about a year later we managed to get him reinstated."

Pyles's timetable was a little off, but the basics were right. Poole's practice had collapsed as a direct result of the McGee case—he even lost his home—and it came out that he'd been convicted of assault in a fight that occurred not long before his libel trial in the summer of 1950. Poole also sometimes held on to small amounts of cash that clients had given him to pay fines, probably using the money as a temporary way to pay family expenses. He voluntarily withdrew from practicing law in March 1953, relocating to Texas for a period of rehabilitation, which he described to the Chancery Court of Hinds County when he faced disbarment proceedings the next year.

"There, respondent quit the drinking of intoxicants, worked very hard, attended church regularly, was attentive to his family . . . and revamped his philosophy of life," his statement said. He was shown no mercy in the short term: He was disbarred in May 1954.

With help from Pyles and other Jackson lawyers, Poole was reinstated and practicing again by 1956. He had a long career in Jackson after that, building a reputation as a top-notch defense lawyer and earning newspaper coverage a few times as a result of yet another of his competitive skills: chess. Poole was an excellent amateur player, winning city and state titles in the 1960s. In 1965, in the town of Magnolia, he played fifteen boards at once during an exhibition, winning thirteen and tying two.

Unfortunately, Poole had a bad habit he never kicked. He was a pack-a-day smoker and eventually developed lung cancer. On November 13, 1980, weary of the pain and hoping to spare his family needless expense, he wrote a letter to his wife and daughters, telling them he loved them and apologizing for what he was about to do. And with that, Smiling Johnny went out his own way, holding a pistol to his head and sending himself into a long and merciful sleep.

Acknowledgments

The Willie McGee case is a painful subject for the people of Laurel, Mississippi, and I didn't know what to expect when I showed up in town several years ago, basically unannounced, and started asking questions about it. What I encountered—there and elsewhere in Mississippi—was a remarkable amount of courtesy and hospitality for which I'll always be grateful. Special thanks to these individuals in Laurel, Jackson, and Lexington, Mississippi, whose knowledge and generosity made it possible for me to understand this complicated historical event: Louis Beverly Jr., William Boyd III, Margaret L. Cooley, Bertha Mae Crowell, Gus DeLoach, Ollie DeLoach, W. O. "Chet" Dillard, Jeannetta Edwards, Jesse James Harris, Raymond L. Horne, Leroy Jensen, Cleaven Jordan, Ed King, Dr. Luke Lampton, Evelyn Smith McDowell, Bill Minor, Emmett Owens, Cleveland Payne, Simmie Roberts, Edward Saffold, and Ann Sanders.

I also received invaluable cooperation from relatives of the men and women who were directly involved in the case. Nearly sixty years after the McGee story ended, it's still a raw memory for many of them, and I appreciate their candor and trust. Thanks to Liz Abzug, Margaret A. Burnham, Mitchel Cohen, Carolyn Poole Ellis, Danny Grossman, Ann Hawkins, Dorothy Hawkins, Sandra Hawkins, Maurice Isserman, Ann London Liberman, Mitch Liberman, Della McGee, Tracey McGee, Donna Poole Mills, Steven Ordower, Dr. MaryLouise Patterson, Beverly D. Poole, John N. Popham IV, Todd Pyles, Bridgette McGee Robinson, Constancia Romilly, Lucile J. Ross, Percy Stanfield Jr., Anne L. Stoll, Courtenay Pyles Stringer, Jon Swartzfager, Susan Boone Vincent, and Wayne Valentine Jr.

Archival materials from this case are scattered all over the United States; without the expertise of research librarians, courthouse employees, and the researchers and writers who came before me, I wouldn't have been able to find my way around. Particular thanks to the staffs of the Mississippi Department of Archives and History; the Library of Congress; the New York Public Library; the National Archives and Records Administration; the Federal Bureau of Investigation's FOIA branch; the Auburn Avenue Research Library; the Manuscript, Archives, and Rare Books Library at Emory University; the Oral History Research Office at Columbia University; the Tamiment Library and Robert F. Wagner Labor Archives at New York University; the Moorland-Spingarn Research Center at Howard University; the Rare Books and Manuscripts library at Ohio State University; the special collections departments at the University of Mississippi, Mississippi State University, the University of Southern Mississippi, and Millsaps College; the Walter P. Reuther Library of Labor and Urban Affairs at Wayne State University; the Harry S. Truman Library and Museum; the Tuskegee Institute; the Lauren Rogers Museum of Art Library; the Laurel Jones County Library; and the county courthouses in Laurel, Hattiesburg, Jackson, and Lexington, Mississippi.

Several friends and colleagues helped by putting in research time on my behalf. Thanks to Jan Cheetham, Claire Crawford, Charles Euchner, Claire Napier Galofaro, James McNally, Michael Roberts, Christopher Solomon, Joe Spring, Tom Tiberio, Laurel Wamsley, and E. Thomas Wood. Thanks also to the writers, experts, and activists who helped me understand the era in which this story took place: Terrie Albano, John Polk Allen, Ace Atkins, Jeanni Atkins, Steve Babson, Leslie Brody, Sarah Hart Brown, Susan Brownmiller, Jerry Dallas, John Egerton, Katharine Carr Esters, Winifred Feise, Al-Tony Gilmore, Hunter Gray, Ernie Lazar, Scott Martelle, Gerald Meyer, Chester M. Morgan, Mary Mostert, Michael Ravnitzky, Ed Sharp, Peter Y. Sussman, Leonard Van Slyke, Christopher Waldrep, and Craig Zaim.

This project wouldn't have gotten off the ground without the encouragement and hard work of my agent, Joe Regal, and my editor, Tim Duggan. Thanks also to the talented people at Regal Literary and HarperCollins who contributed in so many ways: Jonathan Burnham, Bess Reed Currence, Markus Hoffmann, Richard Ljoenes, Allison Lorentzen, Cal Margulis, and Tom McNellis.

My thanks to friends, colleagues, and family members who offered moral support and critical insights as the book took shape: the Cheetham family, Richard Chenoweth, Jon Cohen, Dave Cox, Dianna Delling, Eric Etheridge, Kevin Fedarko, Amy Feitelberg, John Gurley, Tracey Harden, Julia Heard, Ken Heard, Malcolm Heard, Mike Hiestand, Elizabeth Hightower, Rex and Kathy Joyce, Tom Jurkovich, Christopher Keyes, Hannah McCaughey, Scott and Kathleen Morgan, Justin Nyberg, Stephanie Pearson, Scott and Leah Richardson, Jack Shafer, Grayson Schaffer, Nancy Swenton, Andrew Tilin, Mary Turner, Kent Wells, and Brad Wetzler.

Most of all, I thank Jim Leeson, who first told me about Willie McGee and who has offered years of priceless friendship and wisdom, and my wife, Susan, without whose intelligence, encouragement, and love I would have packed it in long ago.

Bibliography

PRIMARY SOURCES

Documents and Manuscripts

Albany, New York
Robert F. Hall Papers, 1928–93. New York State Library.

Atlanta, Georgia
Papers of the Southern Regional Council, news clippings file. Auburn Avenue Research Library on African-American Culture and History.

National Archives and Records Administration, *John R. Poole v. Mississippi Publishers Corporation*. U.S. District Court, Southern District of Mississippi, Jackson Division, Case No. 1324.

John Moreno Coe Papers. Manuscript, Archives, and Rare Book Library, Emory University.

Austin, Texas
Tom C. Clark Papers. Tarlton Law Library, University of Texas School of Law.

Columbus, Ohio
Jessica Mitford Collection. Rare Books and Manuscript Library, Ohio State University.

Detroit, Michigan
Papers of the Michigan Civil Rights Congress. Walter P. Reuther Library of Labor and Urban Affairs, Wayne State University.

Hattiesburg, Mississippi
Mississippi Oral History Project. McCain Library and Archives, University of Southern Mississippi.

William M. Colmer Papers. McCain Library and Archives, University of Southern Mississippi.

Independence, Missouri
Harry S. Truman Papers. Harry S. Truman Library and Museum.

Jackson, Mississippi
Federal Bureau of Investigation, Jackson field office. "Lynching of Howard Wash: Laurel, Mississippi," November 4, 1942.

Millsaps-Wilson Library, Millsaps College.

James P. Coleman Papers. Mississippi Department of Archives and History.

Fielding Wright correspondence. Mississippi Department of Archives and History.

Mississippi Supreme Court case files. Mississippi Department of Archives and History.

Willie McGee subject files; miscellaneous subject files. Mississippi Department of Archives and History.

Miscellaneous subject files. Historic Preservation Division (architecture), Mississippi Department of Archives and History.

Laurel, Mississippi

Jones County Courthouse, *State of Mississippi v. Howard Wash*, Jones County Circuit Court, Case No. 995, October 1942.

Laurel-Jones County Library.

Subject files, Lauren Rogers Museum of Art Library.

Lexington, Kentucky

Stanley F. Reed Papers. William T. Young Library, University of Kentucky.

New York, New York

Bella Abzug interviews, 1995–96. Oral History Research Office, Columbia University Libraries.

Hunter College Archives and Special Collections.

National Archives and Records Administration, *Willett* [sic] *Hawkins v. Freedom of the Press Company, Inc., John Gates, and George Lohr*. U.S. District Court, Southern District of New York, Manhattan Division, Case No. 68–305.

Vito Marcantonio Papers. New York Public Library.

Papers and photographs of the Civil Rights Congress and the Communist Party USA. Schomburg Center for Research in Black Culture, New York Public Library.

Simon W. Gerson Papers. Tamiment Library and Robert F. Wagner Labor Archives, New York University.

Papers of the Southern Negro Youth Congress. Tamiment Library and Robert F. Wagner Labor Archives, New York University.

Northampton, Massachusetts

Mary Metlay Kaufman Papers. Sophia Smith Collection, Smith College Library.

Oberlin, Ohio

Carl T. Rowan Papers. Oberlin College Archives.

Oxford, Mississippi

William Faulkner Papers. J. D. Williams Library, University of Mississippi.

Carroll Gartin Papers. J. D. Williams Library, University of Mississippi.

James O. Eastland Papers. J. D. Williams Library, University of Mississippi.

Starkville, Mississippi
John C. Stennis Papers. Mitchell Memorial Library, Mississippi State University.

Kenneth Toler Papers. Mitchell Memorial Library, Mississippi State University.

Tuskegee, Alabama
Tuskegee Institute news clippings file (microfilm), Series II: Miscellaneous Files, subseries on lynching, 1899–1966, reels 231–34. Tuskegee Institute Archives, Tuskegee University.

Washington, D.C.
Federal Bureau of Investigation. FBI files on Bella Abzug, Aubrey Grossman, Willie McGee, Jessica Mitford, William Patterson, John Poole, and Dixon Pyles.

Hugo L. Black Papers. Library of Congress.

Harold H. Burton Papers. Library of Congress.

William O. Douglas Papers. Library of Congress.

Papers of the Civil Rights Congress (microfilm). Library of Congress.

Papers of the National Association for the Advancement of Colored People. Library of Congress.

William L. Patterson Papers. Moorland-Spingarn Research Center, Howard University.

National Archives and Records Administration. U.S. Supreme Court case files.

Interviews and Correspondence

Liz Abzug
John Polk Allen
Steve Babson
Ralph Boston
William S. Boyd III
Leslie Brody
Susan Brownmiller
Margaret A. Burnham
W. D. Coleman
Margaret L. Cooley
Bertha Mae Crowell
Jerry Dallas
William Deavours
Gus DeLoach
W. O. "Chet" Dillard
Jack Dix
Carolyn Poole Ellis
Katharine Carr Esters
Buddy Evers
Winifred Feise
William C. Gartin Jr.
Jack Gordy

Danny Grossman
Jesse James Harris
Ann Hawkins
Dorothy Hawkins
Sandra Hawkins
David Horowitz
Maurice Isserman
Leroy Jensen
Paul B. Johnson III
Zeb Jones
Cleaven Jordan
Ed King
Jim Leeson
Ann and Mitch Liberman
Evelyn Smith McDowell
Della McGee
Tracey McGee
Bridgette McGee
  Robinson
Lawrence McGurty
Gerald Meyer
Donna Poole Mills

Bill Minor
Chester M. Morgan
Mary Mostert
Steve Ordower
Emmett Owens
Cleveland Payne
Beverly D. Poole
John N. Popham IV
Todd Pyles
Simmie Roberts
Lester Rodney
Constancia Romilly
Lucile J. Ross
James Rundles
Ann Sanders
Marshall L. Small
Anne Stoll
Courtenay Stringer
Peter Y. Sussman
Jon Swartzfager
Paul Swartzfager Jr.
Wayne Valentine Jr.

Newspapers and Periodicals

Arkansas State Press
Atlanta Constitution
Atlanta Daily World
Atlanta Journal
Boston Guardian
Chicago Defender
Clarke County Tribune
Colliers
The Commonweal
Congressional Record
Daily Compass
Daily People's World
Daily Worker
Delta Democrat-Times
Detroit Free Press
Detroit Times
Freedom

Greenville News
Hattiesburg American
Jackson Advocate
Jackson Clarion-Ledger
Jackson Daily News
Laurel Leader-Call
Life
Memphis Commercial
    Appeal
Memphis Press-Scimitar
Meridian Star
Michigan Daily
Mississippi Enterprise
Nation
New Orleans Times-
    Picayune
New Leader

New Republic
Newsweek
New Yorker
New York Post
New York Times
Norfolk Journal and
    Guide
Oxford Eagle
People's Voice
Pittsburgh Courier
Raleigh News & Observer
The Reporter
Saturday Evening Post
Sumter Daily News
Time
Washington Post

Government Publications

President's Committee on Civil Rights. *To Secure These Rights: The Report of the President's Committee on Civil Rights.* Washington: Government Printing Office, 1947.

Reports of the Subversive Activities Control Board, Volume 1. Washington, D.C.: U.S. Government Printing Office, 1966.

United States Senate, Seventy-ninth Congress, Second Session. *Hearings Before the Special Committee to Investigate Senatorial Campaign Expenditures, 1946.* Washington: Government Printing Office, 1947.

United States House of Representatives, Eightieth Congress, First Session. *Report on Civil Rights Congress as a Communist Front Organization.* Washington: Government Printing Office, 1947.

United States Senate, Eighty-fourth Congress, Second Session. *Hearings Before the Subcommittee to Investigate the Administration of the Internal Security Act and Other Internal Security Laws, 1956.* Washington: Government Printing Office, 1956.

Pamphlets, Speeches, and Miscellany

Gerson, Simon. "Tribute to a Workingclass Journalist," eulogy for Harry Raymond. Simon W. Gerson papers, Tamiment Library, NYU.

Hillegas, Jan. "Preliminary List of Mississippi Legal Executions," Revised. Jackson: New Mississippi, Inc., 2001.

Lowenfels, Walter.: "The Martinsville Chant." William Patterson papers, Howard University.

Patterson, William. "We Charge Genocide," speech prepared by William L. Patterson for the General Assembly of the United Nations, Paris, France—December 1951. Patterson papers, Howard University.

Raymond, Harry. *Save Willie McGee*. New York: New Century Publishers, July 1951.

SECONDARY SOURCES

Books

Ackerman, Kenneth D. *Young J. Edgar: Hoover, the Red Scare, and the Assault on Civil Liberties*. New York: Carroll & Graf Publishers, 2007.

Beautiful Jackson In Pictures. Jackson, Mississippi: Hederman Brothers.

Benedict, Ruth. *Race, Science and Politics*. Revised edition, with *The Races of Mankind* by Ruth Benedict and Gene Weltfish. New York: Viking Press, 1945.

Bilbo, Theodore G. *Take Your Choice: Separation or Mongrelization?* Poplarville, Mississippi: Dream House Publishing Company, 1947.

Blotner, Joseph. *Faulkner: A Biography*. Single volume edition. New York: Random House, 1984.

Brown, Sarah Hart. *Standing Against Dragons: Three Southern Lawyers in an Era of Fear*. Baton Rouge: Louisiana State University Press, 1998.

Brownmiller, Susan. *Against Our Will: Men, Women and Rape*. New York: Simon and Schuster, 1975.

Busbee, Westley F., Jr. *Mississippi: A History*. Wheeling, Illinois: Harlan Davidson, Inc., 2005.

Bynum, Victoria E. *The Free State of Jones: Mississippi's Longest Civil War*. Chapel Hill: University of North Carolina Press, 2001.

Carter, Dan T. *Scottsboro: A Tragedy of the American South*. New York: Oxford University Press, 1971.

Chalmers, David M. *Hooded Americanism: The First Century of the Ku Klux Klan, 1865–1965*. New York: Doubleday, 1965.

Cook, Blanche Wiesen. *Eleanor Roosevelt: The Defining Years, Volume Two, 1933–1938*. New York: Penguin Books, 1999.

Crowe, Chris. *Getting Away with Murder: The True Story of the Emmett Till Case*. New York: Phyllis Fogelman Books, 2003.

Culver, John C., and John Hyde.: *American Dreamer: A Life of Henry Wallace*. New York: W. W. Norton, 2000.

Davis, Angela Y. *Women, Race & Class*. New York: Random House, 1981.

De Courcy, Anne. *Diana Mosley: Mitford Beauty, British Fascist, Hitler's Angel*. New York: William Morrow, 2003.

Dillard, W. O. "Chet." *Clearburning: Civil Rights, Civil Wrongs*. Jackson, Mississippi: Lawyer's Publishing Press, 1992.

Dittmer, John. *Local People: The Struggle for Civil Rights in Mississippi*. Urbana: University of Illinois Press, 1994.

Donovan, Robert J. *Tumultuous Years: The Presidency of Harry S. Truman, 1949–1953*. New York: W. W. Norton, 1982.

Dray, Philip. *At the Hands of Persons Unknown: The Lynching of Black America*. New York: Random House, 2002.

Duberman, Martin Bauml. *Paul Robeson*. New York: Ballantine Books, 1989.

Edwards, Alison. *Rape, Racism, and the White Women's Movement: An Answer to Susan Brownmiller*. Chicago: Sojourner Truth Organization, 1979.

Egerton, John. *Speak Now Against the Day: The Generation Before the Civil Rights Movement in the South*. New York: Alfred A. Knopf, 1994.

Esters, Katharine Carr. *Jay Bird Creek and My Recollections*. Kosciusko, Mississippi: Solid Earth, 2005.

Fairclough, Adam. *Race & Democracy: The Civil Rights Struggle in Louisiana, 1915–1972*. Athens: University of Georgia Press, 2008.

Faulkner, William. *Collected Stories of William Faulkner*. New York: Vintage International, 1995.

———. *Intruder in the Dust*. New York: Random House, 1948.

Federal Writers Project, Works Progress Administration. *Mississippi: The WPA Guide to the Magnolia State*. New York: Viking Press, 1938. Jackson: University Press of Mississippi, 1988.

Frederickson, Kari. *The Dixiecrat Revolt and the End of the Solid South, 1932–1968*. Chapel Hill: University of North Carolina Press, 2001.

Gacs, Ute, Aisha Khan, Jerrie McIntyre, and Ruth Weinberg, eds. *Women Anthropologists: Selected Biographies*. Urbana and Chicago: University of Illinois Press, 1989.

Gates, John. *The Story of an American Communist*. New York: Thomas Nelson & Sons, 1958.

Goodman, Walter. *The Committee: The Extraordinary Career of the House Committee on Un-American Activities*. New York: Farrar, Straus and Giroux, 1968.

Green, A. Wigfall. *The Man Bilbo*. Baton Rouge: Louisiana State University Press, 1963.

Honey, Michael Keith. *Black Workers Remember: An Oral History of Segregation, Unionism, and the Freedom Struggle*. Berkeley: University of California Press, 1999.

Horne, Gerald. *Communist Front? The Civil Rights Congress, 1946–1956*. Rutherford, New Jersey: Farleigh Dickinson University Press, 1988.

Janken, Kenneth Robert. *White: The Biography of Walter White, Mr. NAACP*. New York: The New Press, 2003.

Johnston, Erle. *Politics: Mississippi Style*. Forest, Mississippi: Lake Harbor Publishers, 1993.

Lawson, Steven F. *Black Ballots: Voting Rights in the South, 1944–1969*. New York: Columbia University Press, 1976.

Lee, Harper. *To Kill a Mockingbird*. Fortieth anniversary edition. New York: HarperCollins, 1999.

Levine, June, and Gene Gordon. *Tales of Wo-Chi-Ca: Blacks, Whites and Reds at Camp*. San Rafael, California: Avon Springs Press, 2002.

Levine, Suzanne Braun, and Mary Thom. *Bella Abzug: How One Tough Broad from the Bronx Fought Jim Crow and Joe McCarthy, Pissed Off Jimmy Carter, Battled for the Rights of Women and Workers, Rallied Against War and for the Planet, and Shook Up Politics Along the Way*. New York: Farrar, Straus and Giroux, 2007.

Lovell, Mary S. *The Sisters: The Saga of the Mitford Family*. New York: W. W. Norton, 2002.

Matusow, Allen J., ed. *Joseph R. McCarthy*. Englewood Cliffs, New Jersey: Prentice-Hall, 1970.

McCain, William D., and J. F. Hyer. *The Story of Jackson: A History of the Capital of Mississippi, 1821–1951*. 2 vols. Jackson, Mississippi: J. F. Hyer Publishing Company, 1953.

Macdonald, Dwight. *Henry Wallace: The Man and the Myth*. New York: Vanguard Press, 1948.

McCullough, David. *Truman*. New York: Simon & Schuster, 1992.

McMillan, Stokes. *One Night of Madness*. Houston, Texas: Oak Harbor Publishing, 2009.

McMillen, Neil R. *Dark Journey: Black Mississippians in the Age of Jim Crow*. Urbana: University of Illinois Press, 1989.

Meeropol, Michael, ed. *The Rosenberg Letters: A Complete Edition of the Prison Correspondence of Julius and Ethel Rosenberg*. New York: Garland Publishing, 1994.

Meriwether, James B., ed. *Essays, Speeches & Public Letters by William Faulkner*. New York: Random House, 1965.

Meyer, Gerald. *Vito Marcantonio: Radical Politician, 1902–1954*. Albany: State University of New York Press, 1989.

Mitford, Jessica. *A Fine Old Conflict*. New York: Alfred A. Knopf, 1977.

———. *Daughters and Rebels*. Cambridge, Massachusetts: Riverside Press, 1960.

Mitford, Nancy. *The Pursuit of Love & Love in a Cold Climate*. New York: Random House, 1945. Reissue, New York: Vintage Books, 2001.

Morgan, Chester M. *Redneck Liberal: Theodore G. Bilbo and the New Deal*. Baton Rouge: Louisiana State University Press, 1985.

Oshinsky, David M. *A Conspiracy So Immense: The World of Joe McCarthy*. New York: The Free Press, 1983.

Patterson, Haywood, and Earl Conrad. *Scottsboro Boy*. New York: Doubleday, 1950.

Patterson, William L. *The Man Who Cried Genocide: An Autobiography*. New York: International Publishers, 1971.

———, ed. *We Charge Genocide: The Historic Petition to the United Nations for Relief from a Crime of the United States Government Against the Negro People*. New York: Civil Rights Congress, 1951.

Payne, Charles M. *I've Got the Light of Freedom: The Organizing Tradition and the Mississippi Freedom Struggle.* Berkeley: University of California Press, 1995.

Payne, Cleveland. *Laurel: A History of the Black Community, 1882–1962.* Laurel, Mississippi: 1990.

———. *The Oak Park Story: A Cultural History, 1928–1970.* National Oak Park High School Alumni Association, 1988.

Price, David H. *Threatening Anthropology: McCarthyism and the FBI's Surveillance of Activist Anthropologists.* Durham, North Carolina: Duke University Press, 2004.

Pryce-Jones, David. *Unity Mitford: An Enquiry Into Her Life and the Frivolity of Evil.* New York: Dial Press, 1977.

Radelet, Michael L. Hugo Adam Bedau, and Constance E. Putnam. *In Spite of Innocence: Erroneous Convictions in Capital Cases.* Boston: Northeastern University Press, 1992.

Richards, Beah E. *A Black Woman Speaks, and Other Poems.* Sue E. Houchins, Penelope Choy, and Jeanne Joe, eds. Los Angeles: Inner City Press, 1974.

Rise, Eric W. *The Martinsville Seven: Race, Rape, and Capital Punishment.* Charlottesville: University Press of Virginia, 1995.

Roberts, Sam. *The Brother: The Untold Story of the Rosenberg Case.* New York: Random House, 2001.

Rowan, Carl T. *Dream Makers, Dream Breakers: The World of Justice Thurgood Marshall.* New York: Little Brown and Company, 1993.

———. *South of Freedom.* New York: Alfred A. Knopf, 1952.

Rowley, Hazel. *Richard Wright: The Life and Times.* New York: Henry Holt and Company, 2001.

Simon, James F. *The Antagonists: Hugo Black, Felix Frankfurter, and Civil Liberties in Modern America.* New York: Simon & Schuster, 1989.

Sinclair, Upton. *Boston: A Novel.* New York: A. & C. Boni, 1928.

Southern Reporter, Second Series: Cases Argued and Determined in the Courts of Alabama, Florida, Louisiana, Mississippi. St. Paul, Minnesota: West Publishing Company, 1946–51.

Stocking, George W., Jr. *The Shaping of American Anthropology, 1883–1911: A Franz Boas Reader.* New York: Basic Books, 1974.

Street, James. *Tap Roots.* New York: Dial Press, 1942.

Thompson, Julius E. *Lynchings in Mississippi: A History, 1865–1965.* Jefferson, North Carolina: McFarland & Company, 2006.

Topp, Michael M. *The Sacco and Vanzetti Case: A Brief History with Documents.* New York: Palgrave Macmillan, 2005.

Tushnet, Mark V. *Making Civil Rights Law: Thurgood Marshall and the Supreme Court, 1936–1961.* New York: Oxford University Press, 1994.

Urofsky, Melvin I. *Division and Discord: The Supreme Court under Stone and Vinson, 1941–1953*. Columbia: University of South Carolina Press, 1997.

Wagman, Robert J. *The Supreme Court: A Citizen's Guide*. New York: Pharos Books, 1993.

Waldrep, Christopher. *The Many Faces of Judge Lynch: Extralegal Violence and Punishment in America*. New York: Palgrave Macmillan, 2002.

Watson, Bruce. *Sacco and Vanzetti: The Men, the Murders, and the Judgment of Mankind*. New York: Viking Press, 2007.

Welty, Eudora. *One Writer's Beginnings*. Cambridge, Massachusetts: Harvard University Press, 1984.

Wharton, Vernon Lane. *The Negro in Mississippi: 1865–1890*. New York: Harper & Row, 1947.

White, Walter. *A Man Called White: The Autobiography of Walter White*. New York: Viking Press, 1948.

———. *Rope and Faggot: A Biography of Judge Lynch*. Reissue, New York: Arno Press and the New York Times, 1969.

Williams, Juan. *Thurgood Marshall: American Revolutionary*. New York: Times Books, 1998.

Williams, Tennessee. *Orpheus Descending with Battle of Angels*. New York: New Directions, 1958.

Williamson, Joel. *William Faulkner and Southern History*. New York: Oxford University Press, 1993.

Articles

Brenner, Marie. "What Makes Bella Run?" *New York*, June 20, 1977.

Butler, Hilton. "Lynch Law in Action." *New Republic*, July 22, 1931.

Carter, Hodding. " 'The Man' from Mississippi—Bilbo." *New York Times Magazine*, June 30, 1946.

Cogley, John. "Willie McGee." *The Commonweal*, May 25, 1951.

Dallas, Jerry. "Capitol Street, Jackson, Mississippi—Then and Now." http://usads.ms11.net/dallas.html.

Fleegler, Robert L. "Theodore G. Bilbo and the Decline of Public Racism, 1938–1947." *The Journal of Mississippi History*, Spring 2006.

Henderson, Harry, and Sam Shaw. "Bilbo." *Colliers*, July 6, 1946.

Henderson, Harry, and Sam Shaw. "Punch Lines by Sullens." *Colliers*, September 13, 1947.

Hodge, Jo Dent. "The Lumber Industry in Laurel, Mississippi, at the Turn of the Nineteenth Century." *Journal of Mississippi History*, November 1973.

Howe, Russell Warren. "A Talk with William Faulkner." *The Reporter*, March 22, 1956.

Kahn, E. J. "The Frontal Attack." *New Yorker*, September 4, 1948.

Lampton, Lucius. "The Rest of Your Mother: The Story of Eudora Welty, Ouida Keeton, and the 'Legs' Murder." *Journal of the Mississippi State Medical Association*, January 2003.

Lehman, Milton. "Will Bilbo Fool 'Em Again?" *Saturday Evening Post*, June 29, 1946.

Leuchtenburg, William E. "New Faces of 1946." *Smithsonian*, November 2006.

Life, "The End of Willie McGee," May 21, 1951.

Life, "Lynch Trial Makes Southern History," June 2, 1947.

McMillen, Neil, and Noel Polk. "Faulkner on Lynching." *Faulkner Journal* 8:1 (Fall 1992; published Fall 1994), 3–4.

Moon, Henry Lee. "The Martinsville Rape Case." *New Leader*, February 12, 1951.

Mostert, Mary. "Death for Association." *Nation*, May 5, 1951.

Mullen, R. D. "The Great Author, the Great Scholar, and the Small-Town Reporter." *Journal of Mississippi History*, May 1991.

Newsweek, "Bilbo's Successor," November 3, 1947.

Rowan, Carl T. "McGee Was Going to Die." *Stag Magazine*, March 1953.

Rutledge, Wilmuth Saunders. "The John J. Henry-Theodore G. Bilbo Encounter, 1911." *Journal of Mississippi History*, November 1972.

Stuart, Lyle. "Mississippi." *Music Business*, July 1950.

Time, "Communist Calliope," February 12, 1951.

Time, "Gentleman from Georgia," August 14, 1950.

Time, "Justice & the Communists," May 14, 1951.

Time, "The Martinsville Seven," February 12, 1951.

Time, "Pizen Slinger," May 13, 1940.

Time, "Prince of the Peckerwoods," July 1, 1946.

Time, "Southern Scorcher," January 18, 1943.

Time, "Trial by Jury," May 26, 1947.

Time, "Twelve Men," June 2, 1947.

Time, "Vicksburg Surrenders," July 9, 1945.

Valentine, C. Wayne, and Odelle G. McRae. "Unraveling the Ouida Keeton 'Legs' Murder." Ouida Keeton subject file, Rogers.

West, Rebecca. "Opera in Greenville." *New Yorker*, June 14, 1947.

Wilson, Edmund. "William Faulkner's Reply to the Civil-Rights Program." *New Yorker*, October 23, 1948.

Zaim, Craig. "Trial by Ordeal: The Willie McGee Case." *Journal of Mississippi History*, Fall 2003.

Zarnow, Leandra. "Braving Jim Crow to Save Willie McGee: Bella Abzug, the Legal

Left, and Civil Rights Innovation, 1948–1951." *Law & Social Inquiry*, December 2008.

Dissertations and Theses

Hilliard, Elbert Riley. "A Biography of Fielding Wright: Mississippi's Mr. State Rights." Master's thesis, Mississippi State University, 1959.

Key, David Stanton. "Laurel, Mississippi: A Historical Perspective." Master's thesis, East Tennessee State University, 2001.

Randall, Terree. "Democracy's Passion Play: The Lincoln Memorial, Politics, and History as Myth." Ph.D. diss., City University of New York, 2002.

Skates, John Ray, Jr. "A Southern Editor Views the National Scene: Frederick Sullens and the Jackson, Mississippi, *Daily News*." Ph.D. diss., Mississippi State University, 1965.

Notes

ABBREVIATIONS
  CL: Jackson Clarion-Ledger
  Compass: The New York Compass
  CRC: Civil Rights Congress
  DW: The Daily Worker
  JDN: Jackson Daily News
  LLC: Laurel Leader-Call
  LOC: Library of Congress
  MDAH: Mississippi Department of Archives and History
  NAACP: National Association for the Advancement of Colored People
  Rogers: Lauren Rogers Muscum of Art Library
  SRC: Southern Regional Council
  NYT: The New York Times
  WaPo: The Washington Post

EPIGRAPH
sorrow night: Hansberry, *Masses and Mainstream*, July 1951, 19–20.

ONE: THE HOT SEAT
1 **F. Aegerter:** "Mrs. Roosevelt Calls McGee 'Bad Character,'" CRC press release, June 1, 1951. CRC papers.

1 **from obscurity to fame:** See Rowan, *South of Freedom*, "Run! The Red Vampire!," 174–92; Zaim, "Trial by Ordeal: The Willie McGee Case," *Journal of Mississippi History*, Fall 2003, 215–47.

2 **The story began:** *State of Mississippi v. Willie McGee*, December 1945 Special Term, Jones County Courthouse, Laurel, Mississippi; *CL*, *JDN*, *LLC*, December 6–7, 1945.

3 **Hinds County jail:** *CL*, December 14, 1930.

3 **thousands of individuals:** see "15,000 'Free McGee' Pleas Swamp Wright," *Compass*, July 29, 1950.

4 **"Dear Mr. President":** Willie McGee letters, April 30, 1951, CRC papers.

4 **Faulkner:** Meriwether, *Essays, Speeches & Public Letters by William Faulkner*, 211–12; Blotner, *Faulkner*, 539.

4 **Einstein:** "A Letter from Albert Einstein," *NYT* display ad, May 4, 1951.

4 **State Department:** *JDN*, April 25, 1951.

4 **Combat:** Rowan, *South of Freedom*, 191.

5 **Mayella Ewell, Tom Robinson:** Lee, *To Kill a Mockingbird*, 172–77, 190–242, 269–70.

5 **love affair:** Willie McGee's initial account of his alleged relationship with Willette Hawkins appeared in an autobiographical statement he wrote for his first appeals lawyer, Forrest Jackson, which he and others expanded on later. See Dixon Pyles's interview with a *Daily Worker* investigator, CRC papers, 1952; Willie McGee's affidavit, February 3, 1951, Hinds County Courthouse, Jackson, Mississippi, CRC papers; and Rosalee McGee's affidavit, July 25, 1950, MDAH.

6 **"depraved, enslaved, adulterous woman":** References to Mrs. Hawkins were cut from "A Black Woman Speaks" when Beah Richards published a collection of her poetry in 1974. The original version, which she read at a civil rights meeting in 1951, is widely available on the Web. See www.thumperscorer.com/discus/messages/11222/8608.html.

6 **Carol Cutrere:** Williams, *Orpheus Descending*, 27–28.

6 **Roosevelt was no coward:** Cook, *Eleanor Roosevelt: Volume Two, 1933–1938*, 153–54, 177–81; Janken, *White*, 209–11.

7 **China, Soviet Union:** *NYT*, July 27, 1950; see "Execution of M'Gee Blasted by Moscow," Toler Papers, Mississippi State University.

7 **Julius Rosenberg:** Meeropol, *The Rosenberg Letters*, 98.

7 **CRC origins:** "Congress on Civil Rights" invitation; Walter White memo, May 1, 1946; Marian Wynn Perry memo, May 7, 1946, NAACP papers.

8 **"the Communists persuaded":** Eleanor Roosevelt to Roy Wilkins, July 18, 1950; Walter White to Eleanor Roosevelt, July 24, 1950, NAACP papers.

8 **"added suspicions":** Eleanor Roosevelt to Aubrey Grossman, March 14, 1951, CRC papers.

9 **radio broadcast:** "Willie McGee Execution," Jim Leeson audio recording, May 7–8, 1950, University of Southern Mississippi oral history collections.

9 **execution scene:** *CL, JDN, LLC, NYT*, May 8, 1951.

11 **Dray seemed convinced:** Dray, *At the Hands of Persons Unknown*, 397–405.

11 **as did Mitford:** Mitford, *A Fine Old Conflict*, 160–94.

11 **not proven fact:** Brownmiller, *Against Our Will*, 239–45.

11 **Carl Rowan in Laurel:** Rowan, *South of Freedom*, 174–92; Rowan, "McGee was Going to Die," *Stag*, March 1953.

12 **Adolphus and Marjorie McGee:** In *Tales of Wo-Chi-Ca: Blacks, Whites and Reds at Camp*, authors June Levine and Gene Gordon recall these as the names of two McGee children who attended a leftist summer camp in the late 1940s.

13 **Mary Mostert:** author interview, September 2004; Mostert, "Death for Association," *The Nation*, May 5, 1951; Mostert, "Internet Journalism—the Guerilla Warfare Wing in the Media and Propaganda War," July 26, 2003, http://www.renewamerica.com/columns/mostert/030726.

14 **"Willie McGee . . . raped my mother":** Sandra Hawkins e-mail to Mary Mostert, July 17, 2004.

14 **Richard Barrett:** author e-mail to Mary Mostert, September 13, 2004; see Nationalist Web site: http://www.nationalist.org/index.html.

15 **McGee family:** author interview with Tracey McGee, December 2004.

16 **Bridgette and Della:** author interviews, February 2005.

16 **brave CRC spokesperson:** Willie McGee series, *Compass*, June 14–19, 1950.

17 *Life* **story:** "The End of Willie McGee," May 21, 1951, 44–45.

19 **McGee obituary:** *Mississippi Enterprise*, May 19, 1951.

19 **Cleaven Jordan:** author interview, May 2005.

22 **Hawkins obit:** *LLC*, March 27, 1967.

23 **Evelyn Smith McDowell:** author interview, May 2005.

25 **Hawkins sisters:** author interviews, May 2005.

TWO: A MAN WASN'T BORN TO LIVE FOREVER

27 **McGee photograph:** *Time* published this picture on May 14, 1951.

27 **lynching figures, 1890 to 1930:** see Thompson, *Lynchings in Mississippi*, for decade-by-decade comparative figures of state and national totals, 35, 98.

27 **Lang and Green lynching:** *Chicago Defender*, November 7, 1942, March 6, 1943; *Journal and Guide*, October 17, 1942; *Clarke County Tribune*, October 16, 1942; *NYT*, October 13, 1942; *Atlanta Daily World*, October 16, 1942; *DW*, October 27, 1942.

28 **Madison Jones report:** Payne, *I've Got the Light of Freedom*, 14.

28 **Governor Bailey:** Thomas Bailey subject files, MDAH.

28 **Hernando executions:** *NYT*, February 12–13, March 17, 1934; *LLC*, March 16, 1934.

30 **initial arrest:** *LLC*, November 2–3, 1945.

30 **"Willie Magee" arrest:** *LLC*, November 5, 1945.

30 **"Magee" confesses:** *LLC*, November 10, 1945.

30 **trial fast-tracked:** Ibid.

31 **Laurel population:** Laurel City Directory, 1945–46.

31 **Laurel history:** *LLC*, "Chemurgic Trek Edition," March 1939; Hodge, "The Lumber Industry in Laurel, Mississippi, at the Turn of the Nineteenth Century," *Journal of Mississippi History*; Key, "Laurel, Mississippi: A Historical Perspective"; Busbee, *Mississippi: A History*, Bynum, *The Free State of Jones*; Payne, *The Oak Park Story* and *Laurel: A History of the Black Community, 1882–1962*; *Mississippi: The WPA Guide to the Magnolia State*, 222–26; Rogers, subject files.

32 **Davis Knight:** *WaPo*, December 19, 1948; Bynum, *The Free State of Jones*, 1–7.

32 **Pachuta:** see McGee's autobiographical statement in Dixon Pyles's interview with Daily Worker investigator, 1952, CRC papers.

32 **Jasper McGee:** Laurel City Directory, 1922–1923, 1936.

32 **the red line:** Payne, *Laurel: A History of the Black Community*, 67.

32 **"Chemurgic City":** *LLC*, "Chemurgic Trek Edition," March 1939.

33 **Masonite:** subject file, Rogers.

34 **" 'New South' in the heart of the Piney Woods":** Key, "Laurel, Mississippi: A Historical Perspective," 25.

34 **Oak Park Vocational High School:** Payne, *The Oak Park Story*, 7–13.

34 **" 'liberal Laurel' ":** author interview with Ralph Boston, August 2008.

34 **Sam Bowers:** Debra Spencer interview with Sam H. Bowers Jr., October 24, 1983, MDAH.

35 **McGee's arraignment:** *LLC*, December 3, 1945.

35 **Boyd and Koch:** Ibid.; Louis Burnham to George Marshall and Milton Kemnitz, December 26, 1945, CRC papers.

36 **Burkitt Collins:** subject file, Rogers.

36 **"strongest charge":** *LLC*, December 3, 1945.

37 **Ouida Keeton:** Lampton, "The Rest of Your Mother," *Journal of the Mississippi State Medical Association*, January 2003; Valentine, "Unraveling the Ouida Keeton 'Legs' Murder;" trial proceedings, and verdict, Keeton subject file, Rogers.

38 **Eudora Welty:** *Journal of the Mississippi State Medical Association*, January 2003.

39 **Howard Wash arrest and trial:** *State of Mississippi v. Howard Wash*; *Memphis Commercial Appeal*, June 29, 1942; *LLC*, October 17, 1942.

40 **Wash lynching:** FBI report, Jackson field office, "Lynching of Howard Wash: Laurel, Mississippi," November 4, 1942; *NYT*, October 18, 1942; *LLC*, October 17, 1942; *Memphis Commercial Appeal*, October 25, 1942.

40 **Enoc P. Waters:** Waters, "Two Lynched Boys Were Ace Scrap Iron Collectors in Mississippi Town," *Chicago Defender*, March 6, 1943.

41 **Emergency Committee:** *DW*, October 27, 1942.

41 **Paul Johnson Sr.:** *Atlanta Daily World*, October 16, 1942; *LLC*, October 17, 22, 1942; *JDN*, October 20–21, 1942.

42 **Wash investigation and lynching details:** FBI report, Jackson field office, "Lynching of Howard Wash: Laurel, Mississippi," November 4, 1942; *LLC*, October 17, 19–20, 1942.

43 **federal lynching trial:** *Memphis Commercial Appeal*, October 18, 1942; January 13, April 15, 22, 25, 1943.

43 **first trial:** *CL, JDN, LLC*, December 6–7, 1945.

44 **"It becomes our painful duty":** *State of Mississippi v. Willie McGee*, December 1945 Special Term, sanity hearing, 3.

44 **"horse play" and sanity hearing:** Ibid., 5–27.

45 **Willette Hawkins:** *State of Mississippi v. Willie McGee*, December 1945 Special Term, direct testimony, 3–11.

46 **first trial, direct testimony:** Ibid., 12–84.

54 **first trial verdict:** *LLC*, December 7, 1945.

THREE: TAKE YOUR CHOICE

55 **Forrest Jackson background:** subject file, MDAH; author interview with Lucile J. Ross, May 2009.

55 **ran for Senate:** Jackson subject file; "Bilbo's Successor," *Newsweek*, November 3, 1947.

55 **Hall on Jackson:** Carsie A. Hall to Prentice Thomas, October 15, 1942, NAACP papers.

55 **Willie Carter:** Tushnet, *Making Civil Rights Law*, 59.

56 **folded into the mix:** CRC press release, May 22, 1950, Kaufman papers, Smith College; Horne, *Communist Front?*, 13.

56 **Jackson hired:** Louis Burnham to George Marshall and Milton Kemnitz, December 26, 1945, CRC papers.

56 **McGee wanted Wingo:** *State of Mississippi v. Willie McGee*, December 1945 Special Term, 28.

57 **Burnham investigation:** George Marshall to Louis Burnham, December 13, 1945; Burnham to Marshall and Milton Kemnitz, December 26, 1945, CRC papers; author interviews with Margaret A. Burnham.

57 **The Neck, K.C. Bottom:** author interview with Cleveland Payne, November 2007.

58 **Jackson's appeal:** Forrest Jackson to Jones County Circuit Clerk, December 28, 1945; Jackson telegram, January 3, 1946; *LLC*, December 28, 1945.

58 **"Bilboism":** see "Demonology," *NYT*, September 2, 1935, 16.

58 **Robert Taft:** Fleegler, "Theodore G. Bilbo and the Decline of Public Racism, 1938–1947," *Journal of Mississippi History*, Spring 2006; *CL*, April 27, 1946.

58 **"Oust Bilbo" campaign:** Horne, *Communist Front?*, 56; "Unseat Bilbo Campaign Begun by Mississippi Voters," CRC "action bulletin," September 16, 1946, NAACP papers.

58 **fat target:** Bob and Adrienne Claiborne, "Listen, Mr. Bilbo," *People's Songs*, March 1947; *NYT*, November 12, 1947; *DW*, November 11, 1946.

59 **"merchant of hatred":** Lehman, *Saturday Evening Post*, June 29, 1946.

59 **bright spot:** Morgan, *Redneck Liberal*, 16.

59 **Bilbo as orator:** Green, *The Man Bilbo*, 39.

60 **cola bill:** Ibid., 28.

60 **pistol-whipping:** Rutledge, *Journal of Mississippi History*, November 1972, 357–72; *NYT*, July 7, 1911.

60 **Bilbo background:** Green, *The Man Bilbo*, 9–10; Morgan, *Redneck Liberal*, 26; author correspondence with Chester M. Morgan.

60 **Mississippi Democrats:** Morgan, *Redneck Liberal*, 5–14.

60 **Bilbo's rise in Mississippi:** Ibid., 37.

61 **2nd term, college consolidation:** Ibid., 44–45; Green, *The Man Bilbo*, 72–77.

61 **New Deal loyalist:** Morgan, *Redneck Liberal*, 70–77.

61 **meaning of "redneck liberal":** Ibid., 47–48.

61 **Bilbo-Hoover feud:** *NYT*, October 20, 25, 1928; *JDN*, October 20, 1928.

61 **Charley Shepherd:** *JDN*, December 29–31, 1928, January 1, 1929; *CL*, December 29, 1928, January 1, 1929; *Delta Democrat-Times*, December 31, 1928.

63 **"investigate 2,000 people":** *CL*, *NYT*, January 2, 1929.

63 **McGee jailbreak:** *JDN*, February 21, 1946; *CL*, February 22, 1946.

63 **"Jackson doctors":** *CL*, January 18, 1946.

64 **Hinds County Courthouse and jail:** *CL*, December 14, 1930.

64 **1944 jailbreak:** *WaPo*, February 28–29, 1944; *JDN*, February 27–28, 1944.

65 **Gallego and Sorber:** *CL*, September 11, 1954; *NYT*, September 11, 1954; *WaPo*, September 15, 1954.

65 **Sherman Street:** *People's Voice*, January 12, 1946; "Two Minute Justice," undated press release on McGee and Street, CRC papers; Milton Kemnitz to Abraham Isserman, February 14, 1946, CRC papers; *Southern Reporter, Street v. State*, 36138, Volume 26, 2nd series, 678–80.

65 **Charlie Holloway:** *Southern Reporter, Holloway v. State*, 36075, Volume 24, 2nd series, 857–59.

66 **Street, Holloway executions:** Hillegas, "Preliminary List of Mississippi Legal Executions," 2001; Tuskegee news clippings file, reel 233, frame 0479.

66 **lynching statistics:** Thompson, *Lynchings in Mississippi*; Tuskegee news clippings file, reels 231–34.

67 **lynching motives:** Thompson, *Lynchings in Mississippi*, 34.

67 **Southerners take credit:** *Black Dispatch*, January 26, 1952.

67 **lynching total, 1945:** *NYT*, January 1, 1946.

67 **CRC on Tuskegee:** see "Tuskegee Lynch Report Challenged by the Civil Rights Congress," Tuskegee news clippings file, reel 234, frame 0799.

68 **Alonzo Rush:** see Tuskegee news clippings file, reel 233, frame 0594, 1946 totals, ibid., frame 0568.

68 **Attala County massacre:** Tuskegee news clippings file, reel 234; *CL*, December 3, 2006; *Mississippi v. Whitt*, Attala County Circuit Court, 6293, March 1950; *Southern Reporter, Whitt v. State*, 37791, Volume 50, 2nd series, 385–87. *DW*, January 2, 1950; author correspondence with Stokes McMillan.

69 **" 'saved' from extralegal executioners":** *DW*, August 4, 1947.

69 **executions for rape:** see "Rape Executions in USA, 1800–1964," *Critical Criminology Journal*.

70 **"I regret"**: Forrest Jackson to Abraham J. Isserman, February 23, 1946, CRC papers.

70 **first appeal**: Brief for Appellant, *Willie McGee v. State of Mississippi*, Mississippi Supreme Court, 36116, March 28, 1946.

70 **first trial reversed**: *LLC*, June 10, 1946; *McGee v. State*, 36116, June 10, 1946; *Southern Reporter*, Volume 26, 2nd series, 680–84.

71 *Smith v. Allwright*: U.S. Supreme Court, 321 U.S. 649 (1944); Rowan, *Dream Makers, Dream Breakers*, 124–27.

71 **"floodgates of hell"**: Fleegler, *Journal of Mississippi History*, Spring 2006, 9.

72 **"queen of Greater Liberia"**: Ibid., 15.

72 **"Dear Dago"**: Bilbo to Vito Marcantonio, July 24, 1945, Marcantonio papers, New York Public Library; *NYT*, July 13, 24–25, 1945; Green, *The Man Bilbo*, 102.

72 *Take Your Choice*: http://www.churchoftrueisrael.com/tyc/tyc_toc.html.

72 **"distinctly wooly"**: for this passage, Bilbo cited *America's Greatest Problem: The Negro*, by R. W. Shufeldt.

73 *Take Your Choice* sales: *NYT*, March 8, 1947.

73 **"Mississippi is white"**: Henderson and Shaw, *Collier's*, July 6, 1946.

73 **"red-blooded Anglo-Saxon man"**: Etoy Fletcher, *NYT*, June 23, 1946.

74 **Bilbo won**: *NYT*, July 3–4, 1946.

74 **Senate investigates**: *NYT*, July 2, September 7, November 17, 1946.

74 **1946 elections**: *NYT*, November 6, 1946.

74 **black Mississippians in World War II**: Thompson, *Lynchings in Mississippi*, 119.

74 **1,000 Mississippians voted**: *NYT*, July 3, 1946.

74 **1941–1946 lynching statistics**: summary report on lynchings between 1913 and 1952, Tuskegee news clippings file, reel 234; SRC clippings file, "Lynchings 1946."

74 **Isaac Woodard**: NAACP press release, July 11, 1946; "Isaac Woodard Case, 1946," SRC clippings file; *NYT*, August 19, 1946, November 14, 1947; *WaPo*, November 6, 1946.

75 **Orson Welles**: http://www.archive.org/details/1946OrsonWellesCommentaries.

75 **Woody Guthrie**: http://www.folkarchive.de/blind.html.

75 **Columbia riot**: "Columbia, Tennessee" and "Columbia, Tennessee Riot, 1946," SRC clippings file; *NYT*, February 27, March, October 5, 1946; Egerton, *Speak Now Against the Day*, 366–69.

76 **Georgia lynchings**: "Lynching, Monroe, Georgia 1946," SRC clippings file; Tuskegee news clippings file, reel 233; *NYT*, July 27, 31, December 20, 1946; Egerton, *Speak Now Against the Day*, 366–69.

76 **John Jones**: "Lynching—Minden, Louisiana, 1946," SRC clippings file; Tuskegee news clippings file, reel 233; *NYT*, August 16, October 19, 1946; *WaPo*,

November 28, 1946; Fairclough, *Race & Democracy*, 113–18; Egerton, *Speak Now Against the Day*, 369–70.

77 **Max Yergan:** Tuskegee news clippings file, reel 233.

77 **kickbacks:** *NYT*, November 1, 1946.

77 **Bilbo's cancer:** *WaPo*, September 8, November 23, 1946; *New Orleans Times-Picayune*, January 5, 1947.

77 **"Un-seat Bilbo":** Horne, *Communist Front?*, 56; CRC "Action Bulletin," September 16, 1946, CRC papers.

78 **Dashiell Hammett:** *WaPo*, October 14, 1946.

78 **crossed paths:** Lawson, *Black Ballots*, 105.

78 **Bilbo hearings, Jackson:** *CL*, December 3, 5, 1946; *JDN*, December 3, 1946; *WaPo*, December 3, 4, 1946; *NYT*, December 5, 7, 1946; Lawson, *Black Ballots*, 105–15; "Hearing of the Special Committee to Investigate Senatorial Campaign Expenditures," 1946, 79th Congress, 2nd Session, 333–61.

79 **Bilbo hearings, Washington:** *WaPo*, January 3, 5, 1947; *NYT*, December 7, 1946; *JDN*, December 29, 1946, January 3–5, 1947.

79 **He left, by car:** *JDN*, January 5, 1947; *WaPo*, January 6, 1947.

80 **Gerald L. K. Smith:** Green, *The Man Bilbo*, 118.

80 **Bilbo's death:** *NYT*, August 22, 1947; *Black Dispatch*, August 30, 1947.

FOUR: HER JITTERBUG

81 **second trial begins:** *LLC*, October 7–9, 1946; *CL*, October 8, 10, 1946.

81 **stubborn Collins:** *LLC*, October 10, 1946.

81 **"Twenty troopers":** *LLC*, October 7, 1946.

81 **Dixon Pyles:** Pyles interview transcript, Mitford papers, Ohio State; Pyles interviews with Chester M. Morgan, the Mississippi Oral History Program, University of Southern Mississippi, 1983.

81 **Bilbo and labor:** Morgan, *Redneck Liberal*, 76.

82 **. . . and CIO:** *NYT*, May 10, 1946.

82 **thirty minutes:** Pyles interview, Mitford papers; author interviews with Todd Pyles and W. O. Dillard.

83 **Collins steps aside:** Pyles interview, 1952, CRC papers.

83 **Stennis changes venue:** *LLC*, October 16, 1946; *CL*, October 17, 1946.

84 **Spivak and Pyles:** Pyles interview, 1952, CRC papers.

84 **Hawkins libel suit:** *CL*, August 2, 1951; *Willet* [sic] *Hawkins v. Freedom of the Press Company, Inc.*, United States District Court, Southern District, August 1, 1951, National Archives, New York.

86 **"very frightening":** Breland interview, 1952, CRC papers.

86 **McGee's affair story:** Pyles interview, 1952, CRC papers.

90 **Dray and Pyles:** Dray, *At the Hands of Persons Unknown*, 397–405.

91 **"a decent guy":** Bella Abzug interviews, Columbia University.

91 **"theoretical foundation":** Laurent Frantz letter to CRC, September 23, 1946, CRC papers.

91 **racist language:** Horne, *Communist Front?*, 78.

91 **Crafts:** SRC clippings file, "Mississippi Mob—Craft Brothers 1946"; Horne, *Communist Front?*, 196; *NYT*, August 20, 1946.

91 **Truman on Powell:** McCullough, *Truman*, 576.

92 **prepared to shoot:** Breland and Poole interviews with *Daily Worker* investigator, 1952, CRC papers.

92 **Pyles background:** author interviews with Todd Pyles and Courtenay Stringer; Dixon Pyles interviews with Chester M. Morgan, the Mississippi Oral History Program, University of Southern Mississippi, 1983; Pyles interview transcript, Mitford papers, Ohio State; McCain, *The Story of Jackson, Biographical Sketches*, 704; *Mississippi: The WPA Guide to the Magnolia State*; subject file, MDAH; U.S. Army Certificate of Service, December 31, 1945.

93 **Dewey Swor:** *CL*, September 3, 1948.

94 **Hattiesburg:** subject files, MDAH.

94 **the same judge:** after stepping aside in Laurel, Burkitt Collins returned to preside over the case in Hattiesburg. See *LLC*, November 14, 1946.

94 **McGee in Hattiesburg:** *JDN*, October 18, 1946.

95 **"[H]e was crazy":** Breland interview, 1952, CRC papers.

95 **sanity motions:** motions, instructions, and partial testimony from the second trial are contained in the records of Mississippi Supreme Court case 36116, *McGee v. Mississippi*, MDAH.

95 **grand-jury challenge:** *McGee v. Mississippi*, 36116, transcript 3–104.

96 **Scottsboro Boys:** see *Norris v. Alabama*, 294 U.S. 587 (1935); NYT, April 2, 1935.

98 **jury selection:** Ibid.

98 **sentencing guidelines:** Ibid., motions and instructions, 24.

98 **second trial, direct testimony:** *State of Mississippi v. Willie McGee*, case 36411, summary of testimony, Kaufman papers, Smith College; *Hattiesburg American*, *CL*, *JDN*, *LLC*, November 12–14, 1946.

99 **Pyles was aggressive:** *Hattiesburg American*, November 12, 1946.

99 **definition of rape:** Ibid., motions and instructions, 31.

99 **"she didn't holler":** Breland interview, 1952, CRC papers.

102 **McGee placed on stand:** Ibid.; *Hattiesburg American*, November 13, 1946.

102 **Bond, Waller, Bessie McGee:** *State v. McGee* summary, Kaufman papers.

104 **"We don't ask you to turn Willie loose":** *JDN*, November 14, 1946.

104 **McGee convicted:** *Hattiesburg American*, November 14, 1946.

FIVE: GOD DON'T LIKE UGLY

105 **Sandra Hawkins:** Hawkins, "My Mother's Voice," unpublished manuscript; author interviews and correspondence with Ann, Sandra, and Dorothy Hawkins.

109 **FBI file:** in 1977, the FBI released several hundred pages of headquarters documents, labeled "Willie McGee," to historian Al-Tony Gilmore.

109 **"next room":** see, for example, the CRC's "Willie McGee Case Fact Sheet," March 30, 1948, Kaufman papers, Smith College.

111 **Pyles, McGee affidavits:** Pyles interview, 1952, CRC papers; Rosalee McGee affidavit, July 25, 1950; Willie McGee affidavit, February 3, 1951.

113 **Potiphar's wife:** Rowan, *South of Freedom*, 187.

113 **"Willie McGee was murdered":** *DW*, May 9, 1951; *Hawkins v. Freedom of the Press Company, Inc.*

114 **"ludicrously charged with rape":** Abzug profile, Stonewall Veterans' Association, http://www.stonewallvets.org/BellaAbzug.htm.

114 **"Wilametta Hawkins":** Edwards, *Rape, Racism, and the White Women's Movement*, 13.

114 **"Mrs. Willett Hawkins":** Horne, *Communist Front?*, 78–80.

114 **"despite persuasive evidence":** Mitford, *A Fine Old Conflict*, 161.

114 **"traveling salesman":** Rowley, *Richard Wright*, 392.

114 **"ferocious spat":** Dray, *At the Hands of Persons Unknown*, 399.

115 **"A Question of Race":** Brownmiller, *Against Our Will*, 239–45.

116 **Emmett Till:** Crowe, *Getting Away with Murder*, 50–69.

116 **"a deliberate insult":** Brownmiller, *Against Our Will*, 245–48.

117 **"provocative distortion":** Davis, *Women, Race & Class*, 197.

117 **legal analysis:** Zaim, *Journal of Mississippi History*, Fall 2003, 215–47.

117 **McGee exonerated:** Radelet, Bedau, Putnam, *In Spite of Innocence*, 332–33.

117 **first affair stories:** *DW*, February 25, 1951; *Daily People's World*, March 2, 1951; "Fact Sheet On Willie McGee," Kaufman papers.

118 **"one-day 'trial' ":** *DW*, December 12, 1945.

118 **"Two Minute Justice":** draft press release, CRC papers.

118 **boilerplate dismissal:** *DW*, May 28, 1950.

119 **divorce papers:** *Eliza Jane Magee v. Willie Magee* [sic], Covington County Chancery Court, Collins, Mississippi.

119 **Leroy Jensen:** author interview, September 2006.

122 **Bertha Mae Crowell:** author interview, September 2006.

124 **Shubuta lynchings:** *NYT*, December 21, 1918.

124 **1920s Klan:** see Chalmers, *Hooded Americanism*.

SIX: THE MALADY OF MEDDLER'S ITCH

128 **McAtee:** *NYT,* July 31, 1946; *Lexington Advertiser,* August 1, 1946.

128 **Woodard:** *Chicago Defender,* July 20, 1946.

129 **"Negro Made Blind":** *NYT,* August 18, 1946.

129 **postwar violence:** Egerton, *Speak Now Against the Day.* See "Epidemic of Violence," 359–75.

129 **Georgia lynching:** *NYT,* July 27, 1946.

129 **John N. Popham:** *NYT,* February 9, 1947; December 14, 1999; Salisbury, *Without Fear or Favor,* 352–56; author interview with John N. Pophera IV, November 2009.

130 **Costigan-Wagner:** *NYT,* April 10, June 4, December 30, 1934.

130 **1933 lynchings:** Thompson, *Lynchings in Mississippi,* 98.

130 **Princess Anne lynching:** *NYT,* October 19, 1933.

130 **Southern legislators were opposed:** see, for example, " 'Lynchings at Vanishing Point,' Says Dixie Solon; Lauds South," Tuskegee news clippings file, reel 233, frame 0286.

131 **"gangster amendment":** Colmer papers, University of Southern Mississippi.

131 **Walter White's appearance:** Kahn, "The Frontal Attack," *The New Yorker,* September 4, 1948, 28.

131 **lynching investigator:** White, *A Man Called White,* 39–60; Janken, *White,* 29–55.

131 **meeting with FDR:** Cook, *Eleanor Roosevelt: Volume Two, 1933–1938,* 153–54, 177–81; Janken, *White,* 209–11; *NYT,* January 5, June 17, 1934.

132 **Truman, White meeting:** *NYT,* September 20, 1946.

132 **"pale with horror":** "The President Means It," Walter White, February 12, 1948, David K. Niles papers, Truman Library.

132 **Truman on Woodard:** Harry Truman to Thomas C. Clark, September 20, 1946, David K. Niles papers, Truman Library.

133 **"American crusade to end lynching":** *Chicago Daily Tribune,* September 24, 1946; Duberman, *Paul Robeson,* 306.

133 **"swelling wave of lynch murders":** Duberman, *Paul Robeson,* 305.

133 **Truman, Robeson meeting:** *Chicago Daily Tribune,* September 24, 1946; *Louisville Courier-Journal,* September 29, 1946.

134 **"Iron Curtain" speech:** *NYT,* March 6, 1946.

134 **British imperialism:** Duberman, *Paul Robeson,* 304.

134 **Truman appoints committee:** *NYT,* December 6, 1946.

135 **Recy Taylor:** Tuskegee news clippings file, reel 233.

135 **Yarbrough rape case:** *LLC,* March 10–12, 1947; *Yarbrough v. Mississippi,* 1947, Mississippi Supreme Court case files, MDAH. Also see *Southern Reporter,* Volume 32, 2nd series, 436–40.

139 Second trial coverage: *PM*, November 15, 1946.

139 *PM*'s origins: *NYT*, October 18, 1940.

139 "Just a few lines": Bessie McGee letters, CRC papers.

139 "Rosa": Ibid., July 16, 1947.

139 second appeal filed: *CL*, November 16, 1946.

139 second appeal: *McGee v. State*, 36411, August 6, 1947.

140 "sordid and revolting": *McGee v. Mississippi*, reply of appellant, September 12, 1947.

141 Willie Earle lynching: "Willie Earle" subject files, SRC clippings file; Tuskegee news clippings file, reel 233; *NYT*, May 11, 13–15, 17–18, 21–22, 1947; "Trial By Jury," *Time*, May 26, 1947, and "Twelve Men," *Time*, June 2, 1947; West, "Opera in Greenville," *The New Yorker*, June 14, 1947; Egerton, *Speak Now Against the Day*, 371–73.

142 "offenses against decency": *Sumter Daily News*, February 18, 1947, SRC clippings file.

142 "The President may be interested": David K. Niles to Matt Connelly, February 19, 1947, Truman papers, Truman Library.

142 Despite the usual complaining: *Atlanta Journal*, March 7, 1947.

142 *Life*: "Lynch Trial Makes Southern History," *Life*, June 2, 1947, 27.

143 "delighted, giggling": West, "Opera in Greenville," *The New Yorker*, June 14, 1947.

143 "mad dog": Tuskegee news clippings file, reel 233.

143 pulled out all the stops: *NYT*, May 21, 1947.

144 Earle verdict: Tuskegee news clippings file, reel 233; *NYT*, May 22, 1947.

144 1946 elections: "New faces of 1946," *Smithsonian*, November 2006.

144 Lincoln Memorial speech: *NYT*, June 30, 1947.

145 *To Secure These Rights*: *NYT*, February 3, 1948.

145 . . . and text of report: *NYT*, October 30, 1947; President's Committee on Civil Rights. *To Secure These Rights: The Report of the President's Committee on Civil Rights*, Washington: Government Printing Office, 1947, http://www.trumanlibrary.org/civilrights/srights1.htm.

145 'repugnant': *NYT*, February 3, 1948.

146 first Jackson meeting: *NYT*, February 13, 1948; Hillard, *A Biography of Fielding Wright*, 86.

146 Fielding Wright background: Frederickson, *The Dixiecrat Revolt and the End of the Solid South, 1932–1968*; Hilliard, *A Biography of Fielding Wright: Mississippi's Mr. State Rights*; subject files, MDAH.

146 Bailey death: *NYT*, November 3, 1946.

147 Trudell, Lewis, Meiers: *WaPo*, January 2, 1947; *NYT*, January 5, 1947; *JDN*, January 4–6, 9–10, 1947.

147 **Clemency denied, Wright praised:** *CL*, January 12, 1947.

147 **execution:** Hillegas, "Preliminary List of Mississippi Legal Executions," 2001.

148 **"He doesn't get angry":** *Memphis Press-Scimitar* (reprinted in *JDN*, August 3, 1947).

148 **Wright inauguration speech:** *JDN*, January 21, 1948.

148 **governors' meeting:** *WaPo*, February 9, 1948.

148 **Jackson meeting, February:** *NYT*, February 13, 1948.

149 **Jackson meeting, May:** *CL*, May 10–11, 1948.

149 **"If . . . you have become so deluded":** *NYT*, May 10, 1948.

149 **Wallace background:** Culver and Hyde, *American Dreamer*.

149 **Wallace dumped:** *NYT*, July 22, 1944; *American Dreamer*, 353–66.

149 **"The Way to Peace":** "Selected Works of Henry A. Wallace," http://newdeal. feri.org/wallace/haw28.htm; *NYT*, September 13, 1946.

149 **Byrnes:** *NYT*, September 14, 1946.

150 **"a pacifist one hundred percent":** Culver and Hyde, *American Dreamer*, 425.

150 **Wallace dismissed:** *NYT*, September 21, 1946.

150 **Progressive Party candidate:** Culver and Hyde, *American Dreamer*, 456–58.

SEVEN: THE ODDS AGAINST SMILING JOHNNY

151 **U.S. Supreme Court:** *NYT*, December 9, 1947; *Patton v. Mississippi*, 332 U.S. 463 (1947).

151 **Patton case:** *The Meridian Star*, February 28, March 1, 1946; *Patton v. Mississippi*, Mississippi Supreme Court, 36298, 1946; *Southern Reporter, Patton v. State*, 36298, Volume 29, 2nd series, 96–100.

151 **Mississippi Supreme Court:** *McGee v. State*, 36411, February 9, 1948. See *Southern Reporter*, Volume 33, 2nd series, 843–49.

152 **as far back as 1880:** *Strauder v. West Virginia*, 100 U.S. 303 (1880); *Patton v. Mississippi*, 332 U.S. 463 (1947).

153 **McGee reversal and dissent:** *McGee v. Mississippi*, 203 Miss. 592 (1948); *Southern Reporter*, Volume. 33, 1948, 843–49.

153 **McGee indicted:** *JDN*, February 19, 1948.

153 **black grand jurors:** *NYT*, February 10, 17, 1948; *LLC*, February 17, 19, 1948; McMillen, *Dark Journey*, 221–23; Wharton, *The Negro in Mississippi*, 137.

153 **"considered unusual":** *JDN*, February 16, 1948.

153 **Pyles quits:** Pyles interview, Mitford papers, Ohio State.

154 **"Communist front," Eisler:** HUAC, *Report on Civil Rights Congress as a Communist Front Organization*, February 15, 1947; *NYT*, December 12, 1946, February 5, 1947.

154 **Rankin on Communism:** *Congressional Record*, July 18, 1945, 7737.

154 Abzug's first Mississippi trip: Abzug interviews, Columbia.

155 Isserman and Abzug: "Summary of Activities of Abraham J. Isserman in Labor and Civil Rights Matters, 1930–1961," 14. Papers of Maurice Isserman.

155 Alvin London: Abzug interview, Columbia; author interview with Ann London Liberman and Mitch Liberman, August 2008.

156 New York Bar: NYT, May 2, 1948.

156 "all Oriental and gorgeous": "What Makes Bella Run?" New York, June 20, 1977.

156 looked like Shirley MacLaine: Harold Holzer interview in Levine and Thom, Bella Abzug, 77.

157 Macy's: Abzug interviews, Columbia.

157 Abzug background: Ibid.; author interviews with Liz Abzug; Levine and Thom, Bella Abzug; Hunter Bulletin, May 27, 1940; NYT, November 26, 1939.

157 Hunter College: NYT, November 26, 1939, May 23, 1940.

157 American Student Union: Abzug interviews, Columbia; NYT, January 5, 1936, January 10, 1941.

158 issues of the day: Abzug interviews, Columbia; Savitzky, "Armistice Day— and The Last World War," Hunter Bulletin, November 6, 1940.

158 ASU contingent: WaPo, February 11, 1940; Hunter Bulletin, February 26, 1940.

158 "The Yanks Are Not Coming": Hunter Bulletin, February 26, 1940.

159 "a campus pink": New York Post, March 10, 1941.

159 "pure fabrications": Hunter Bulletin, March 25, 1941.

159 Martin Abzug, law school: NYT, September 21, 1970; Abzug interviews, Columbia; Harvard Crimson, May 6, 2003

159 Cammer: NYT, September 17, 1950, October 25, 1995.

159 Witt: NYT, August 4, 1948.

160 Pressman: NYT, August 28–29, 1950.

160 Abzug on Pressman: Abzug interviews, Columbia.

160 Abzug on Poole: Ibid.

160 drinking problem: FBI file, John Poole.

161 "Jewish woman lawyer": Abzug interviews, Columbia.

161 "quite an experience": London interview, 1952, CRC papers.

161 Poole background: author interviews with Donna Poole Mills, Beverly D. Poole, Carolyn Poole Ellis, Buddy Evers, and Emmett Owens.

162 train accident: "Young Johnny Poole Packs Wallop, Will," undated newspaper clipping, Poole family papers; author interview with Emmett Owens.

162 "Smiling Johnny": undated Memphis Commercial Appeal clip, Poole family papers.

163 **Poole at Millsaps:** *Bobashela* (yearbook), 1942–45; *Purple and White* (newspaper), February 4, 1944; Poole family papers.

163 **House race, 1947:** Poole family papers.

164 **"Dad must have sensed the danger":** from "Crossfire," unpublished manuscript by Donna Poole Mills.

164 **third trial:** *State of Mississippi v. Willie McGee*, MDAH; (See Supreme Court case 36411, *McGee v. Mississippi.*) *LLC*, February 26, 28, March 1–6, 8, 1948; *JDN*, February 27–28, March 4–5, 7–8, 1948; *CL*, February 28, 1948.

164 **Deavours:** Poole interview, 1952, CRC papers.

165 **Swartzfager:** author interview with Jon Swartzfager, November 2007.

165 **pretrial testimony:** *State of Mississippi v. Willie McGee*, 16411, 3–501.

170 **direct testimony:** *State of Mississippi v. Willie McGee*, 16411, 502–910.

170 **'If that is all . . . ':** *McGee v. State*, 36411, filed August 6, 1947.

178 **Poole and Spivak:** Poole interview, 1952, CRC papers.

179 **Poole quits:** Ibid.

EIGHT: A RUMPUS OF REDS

180 **third trial appeal:** John Poole to Abraham Isserman, April 26, 1948, CRC papers.

180 **McGee to Cadden:** Willie McGee letters, CRC papers.

181 **"don't stop working for Willie":** Bessie McGee to Abraham Isserman, June 1948, CRC papers.

181 **CRC reply:** Abraham Isserman to Bessie McGee, June 25, 1948.

181 **"come to see me":** Willie McGee letters, August 17, September 29, 1948, CRC papers.

181 **Poole's libel suit:** John Poole to Abraham Isserman, April 26, 1948; *John R. Poole v. Mississippi Publishers Corporation.* U.S. District Court, Southern District of Mississippi, Jackson Division, 1324, National Archives, Atlanta, Georgia.

181 **"One Defense Cut Off":** *JDN*, March 10, 1948.

182 **George Marshall:** *WaPo*, April 22, 1948, May 15, 1948.

182 **Smith Act arrests:** *NYT*, July 21–22, 1948.

183 **trial under way:** *NYT*, March 8, 1949.

183 **"The recent indictment":** Commager, "Should We Outlaw the Communist Party?," *NYT*, August 22, 1948.

183 **"Reichstag fire":** *NYT*, July 21-22, 1948.

184 **Pollsters blew it:** *NYT*, October 31, 1948.

184 **1948 electoral totals:** http://www.uselectionatlas.org/RESULTS/national.php?f=0&year=1948

184 **May Day:** *NYT*, April 18, 1947.

185 "distance himself": Culver and Hyde, *Henry Wallace*, 464–65.

185 "in no sense a Communist party": *NYT*, August 3, 1948.

185 "obscene, hideous people": *NYT*, April 17, 1948.

185 Foster on U.S.-Soviet conflict: *NYT*, May 29, 1948.

185 "erratic comet": Macdonald, *Henry Wallace: The Man and the Myth*, 93.

186 John Coe: *The Worker*, February 22, 1948.

186 Sidney Ordower: author interview with Steven Ordower, March 2005.

186 Southern swing: Culver and Hyde, *American Dreamer*, 493–96; *NYT*, August 30–31, September 1–3, 1948; *WaPo*, August 28, 30–31, September 3, 1948.

187 Vicksburg: "Vicksburg Surrenders," *Time*, July 9, 1945.

187 Wallace in Mississippi: *JDN*, *Vicksburg Evening Post*, September 2, 1948; *NYT*, *WaPo*, September 3, 1948.

187 William L. Patterson: Patterson, *The Man Who Cried Genocide*; William L. Patterson papers, Howard University; FBI file, William Patterson.

188 George Marshall's imprisonment: *DW*, June 1, 1950.

188 "mass indignation": Patterson, *The Man Who Cried Genocide*, 7–13.

189 fanatical father: see ". . . Life History of Party Functionaries," Patterson FBI file.

189 "What the Jew is to Germany": Patterson FBI file, Chicago field office report, December 12, 1945.

190 Robeson's early rise: Duberman, *Robeson*, 19–109.

190 Sacco and Vanzetti: Topp, *The Sacco and Vanzetti Case*, 1–51; Patterson, *The Man Who Cried Genocide*, 75–90; Felix Frankfurter, "The Case of Sacco and Vanzetti," *The Atlantic*, March 1927; *NYT*, August 18, 23–24, 1927.

190 Palmer bombing: *NYT*, June 3, 1919.

190 Palmer Raids: Ackerman, *Young J. Edgar*, 6, 113–23, 155–63, 340.

191 "There was . . . William Patterson": Sinclair, *Boston*, 682–84.

192 "people's university": Patterson, *The Man Who Cried Genocide*, 90.

192 the Scottsboro Boys: Carter, *Scottsboro*; *NYT* and *WaPo* coverage, 1931–35; Patterson and Conrad, *Scottsboro Boy*.

192 arrests and first trials: Carter, *Scottsboro*, 3–50; *NYT*, March 26, April 9–10, 1931.

194 ILD, NAACP: Carter, *Scottsboro*, 51–103; *NYT*, June 21, 28–31, July 6, December 28, 30, 1931.

195 Powell decision: *Powell v. Alabama*, 287 U.S. 45 (1932); *NYT*, March 25–26, April 10, May 17, June 1, October 11, November 8, 1932.

195 Patterson, ILD: Carter, *Scottsboro*; Patterson autobiography, FBI file.

195 Samuel Leibowitz: Carter, *Scottsboro*, 181–82; for an example of Leibowitz's murder cases, see "Frame-Up Charged in Gordon Murder," *NYT*, June 19, 1931.

195 threatens to quit: *NYT*, April 3, 1933.

195 **lynch rumors:** *NYT,* April 6, 1933.

196 **second Scottsboro trials:** Carter, *Scottsboro,* 192–242; *NYT,* March 28, April 6–10, 1933.

196 **Ruby Bates recants:** *NYT,* April 7, 1933.

197 **"Jew money from New York":** *NYT,* April 8, 1933.

197 **Haywood Patterson verdict:** *NYT,* April 10, 1933.

197 **bribery attempt:** *NYT,* October 2, 1934; Carter, *Scottsboro,* 308-309.

197 **Horton voids conviction:** *NYT,* June 23, 1933.

197 **Patterson's third trial:** *NYT,* December 2, 1933.

198 *Norris* **decision:** *NYT,* April 2, 1935; *Norris v. Alabama,* 294 U.S. 587 (1935).

198 **Scottsboro conclusion:** see Patterson and Conrad, *Scottsboro Boy,* "Timetable of Events in the Scottsboro Case," 301–309.

198 **Haywood Patterson's escape:** *NYT,* July 21, 1948.

198 **third Mississippi Supreme Court appeal:** *McGee v. Mississippi,* 36892, January 28, 1949.

198 **. . . and opinion:** *McGee v. Mississippi,* 36892, April 11, 1949. See *Southern Reporter,* Volume 40, 2nd series, 160–72.

199 **Poole's follow-up:** "Suggestion of Error," *McGee v. Mississippi,* 36892.

199 **stay granted:** *LLC,* June 3, 1949.

199 **execution preparations:** Ibid.

200 **Poole and Roberds:** London interview, 1952, CRC papers.

200 **Brogan declined to accept:** CRC press release, June 3, 1949, Kaufman papers; *JDN,* June 3, 1949; *DW,* June 5, 1949.

201 **U.S. Supreme Court appeal:** *Willie McGee v. State of Mississippi,* No. 238, "Petition for Writ of Certiorari," National Archives, Washington, D.C.

201 **Rosenwein and Silverman:** *NYT,* October 20, 1947, December 15, 1955; *Report on the National Lawyers Guild,* HUAC, 1950.

201 *Brown v. Mississippi:* 297 U.S. 278 (1936); *NYT,* February 18, 1936.

202 *Screws v. United States:* 325 U.S. 91 (1945).

203 **Murphy's death:** *NYT,* July 20, 1949.

203 *Screws* **case:** 325 U.S. 91 (1945); *WaPo,* October 8, November 3, 1943, May 10, 1945; Waldrep, *The Many Faces of Judge Lynch,* 170–72.

204 **Mississippi response:** *McGee v. Mississippi,* No. 238, brief of appellee, National Archives, Washington, D.C.

204 **Murray L. Schwartz:** "Faculty Obituary: Murray Schwartz," UCLA School of Law, February 19, 2009; author correspondence with Marshall L. Small.

204 **Supreme Court procedures:** Wagman, *The Supreme Court: A Citizen's Guide,* 8–9.

205 **Christopher memo:** U.S. Supreme Court papers, No. 238, 1949, National Archives, Washington, D.C.

205 **Schwartz memo:** Clark papers, Tarlton Law Library, University of Texas, Austin.

206 **Smith Act trial:** *NYT,* March 8, 22, April 28, June 1, July 8, 12, October 9, 1949.

207 **Browder, Duclos:** *NYT,* May 25, 1945, March 30, 1947, March 22, 1949.

208 **Peekskill riots:** *NYT,* August 28–29, 1949.

208 **Abzug at Peekskill:** author interviews with Liz Abzug.

208 **Supreme Court declines:** *CL,* October 11, 1949.

208 **Smith Act verdict:** *NYT,* October 15, 1949.

208 **new death date:** *DW,* June 13, 1950; Kaufman case timeline, Kaufman papers, Smith College.

NINE: COUNTRY GIRL

209 **London's complaint:** London interview, 1952, CRC papers.

209 **Poole's libel suit:** *John R. Poole v. Mississippi Publishers Corporation,* Southern District of Mississippi, National Archives, Atlanta, Georgia; Dixon Pyles interview transcript, Mitford papers, Ohio State University; *Southern Reporter,* Volume. 44, 2nd series, 467–77.

211 **"intimidate me":** *NYT,* May 3, 1955.

211 **"Rosie Lee Gilmore McGee":** *JDN,* June 7, 1950.

212 **"She is a Negro woman":** "This is the story that Detroit papers were afraid to touch," by William Allan. Undated clipping, Mitford papers, Ohio State.

212 **Saffold family:** U.S. Census report, Carroll County, Mississippi, April 17, 1930.

212 **Bertha Mae Crowell:** author interviews, December 2007.

216 **"I am the wife of Willie McGee":** Rosalee McGee letters, CRC papers.

217 **"many other crimes":** Ibid.

217 **"the jailer got angery":** Ibid.

218 **"Lawyer Poole":** Ibid.

218 **"Willie is almost crazy":** Ibid., October 13, 1949.

218 **Patterson letters:** Ibid., October 11, 1949.

218 **press release:** "A Wife Pleads to Nation for Innocent Husband: 'Please Don't Let Willie McGee Die!' " October 31, 1949, Kaufman papers.

218 *Compass* **series:** *Compass,* June 14–19, 1950.

218 **Marvin Murray:** *Compass,* June 16, 1950.

219. **Murray execution:** *Jackson Advocate,* July 3, 1948.

219 **informational swap meet:** author interviews with Tracey McGee, Donna Poole Mills, Liz Abzug, Bridgette McGee Robinson, and Della McGee, July 2007.

221 **Jim Crow spokespeople:** Bessie McGee letter to Abraham Isserman, June 1948, CRC papers, and *DW*, June 18, 1950; Carter, *Scottsboro*, 244–45; *Daily Worker*, February 6, 1951; Haywood Patterson subject files, Michigan CRC papers, Wayne State University.

222 **Dixon Pyles, Rose McGee:** interview transcripts, Mitford papers, Ohio State University.

225 **Lottie Gordon:** Rosalee McGee letters, February 23, 1950, CRC papers.

226 **"how meny children":** Ibid., March 21, 1950.

226 **Christmas card:** box 10, frames 0456–57, CRC papers.

226 **"i work so hard":** Ibid., April 4, 1950.

227 **Kinderland:** Gordon letters to Rosalee McGee and S. Davidovitch, CRC papers.

227 **Rosalee speeches, travel:** *DW*, May 18, 22, 24, June 18, 1950; *NYT*, June 18, 29, 1950; *Jackson Advocate*, July 15, 1950; *Compass*, July 28, 1950.

228 **"bad company":** *LLC*, July 19, 1950.

228 **Katharine Carr Esters:** author interview, November 2007; Esters, *Jay Bird Creek and My Recollections*.

232 **Boys & Girls Club:** see "Small Town, Big Dream," http://www.bgca.org/connections/06_winter/story2.html.

TEN: COMMUNISTS COMING HERE

233 **McCarthy:** Matusow, *Joseph R. McCarthy*, 19–26; Oshinsky, *A Conspiracy So Immense*, 103–14; *NYT*, February 12, 21, 1950.

233 **China, Germany, A-Bomb:** Donovan, *Tumultuous Years*, 51, 84, 98–101; *NYT*, September 24, October 2, 8, 24, 1949.

234 **Hiss:** *NYT*, January 22, 1950.

234 **Fuchs:** Roberts, *The Brother*, 195; *NYT*, February 4, 1950.

234 **Greenglass, Rosenbergs:** Roberts, *The Brother*, 244–45, 269, 271; *NYT*, June 17, July 18, August 12, 1950.

234 **Emanuel H. Bloch:** *NYT*, July 18, 1950.

234 **North Korea:** *NYT*, June 25, 1950.

234 **CRC's McGee crusade:** *JDN*, July 17, 19, 23, 1950; *LLC*, July 18, 1950.

235 **Sullens:** Skates, *A Southern Editor Views the National Scene*; "Punch Lines by Sullens," *Collier's*, September 13, 1947; McCain, *The Story of Jackson*, volume 2, 12–15; *JDN*, December 24, 1950; November 20–21, 1957.

235 **pugnacious Sullens:** "Southern Scorcher," *Time*, January 18, 1943.

235 **"Chimneyville":** McCain, *The Story of Jackson*, volume 1, 196–202.

237 Johnson, Sullens fight: *JDN*, May 3, 1940; *CL*, May 3, 1940; Johnston, *Politics: Mississippi Style*, 18–21, 46, 55; "Pizen Slinger," *Time*, May 13, 1940; "Punch Lines by Sullens," *Collier's*, September 13, 1947; *WaPo*, May 3, 1940; author interview with Paul B. Johnson III.

237 Sullens and Bilbo: Green, *The Man Bilbo*, 52; Morgan, *Redneck Liberal*, 228–29; Skates, *A Southern Editor Views the National Scene*, 239–40; *CL*, June 26, 1931.

238 "Remember her": *JDN*, November 3, 1928.

238 "write and wire": CRC press release, October 22, 1949, Kaufman papers.

238 15,000 people: *Compass*, July 29, 1950.

238 mysterious CRC activity: *LLC*, July 18, 1950.

238 Ella Fitzgerald: "M.I.S.S.I.S.S.I.P.P.I.," *Music Business*, July 1950.

238 *Compass* series: June 14–19, 1950.

238 the *Compass* . . . had a place: *NYT*, May 2–3, 17, 1949; June 1, 1949. (The *Compass* debuted in May 1949 and ceased publication in November 1952, *NYT*, November 4, 1952.)

239 "beginning to boil": William Patterson letters to Jack Raskin, July 12, 1950, Michigan CRC files, Wayne State University.

240 R. H. Harris: *JDN*, July 19, 1950.

240 "Communists Coming Here": *JDN*, July 19, 1950.

240 "explosive case": Abzug interviews, Columbia.

240 Patterson on Abzug: William Patterson letter to Jessica Mitford, May 29, 1975, Mitford Collection, Ohio State University.

241 *error coram nobis*: *NYT*, August 20, 1927, January 5, 1954, May 20, 1955, January 26, 1979, March 16, 1986; *WaPo*, October 23, 1983; Zaim, *The Journal of Mississippi History*, Fall 2003, 238.

241 McGee's petition: *Mississippi v. Willie McGee*, Petition for Writ of Error Coram Nobis, No. 1268, July 21, 1950.

241 tea leaves: *LLC*, July 21, 1950.

242 Swartzfager's reply: *Mississippi v. Willie McGee*, State's Answer, July 22, 1950.

242 Poole in Laurel: Poole, Bloch, Abzug affidavits, July 1950, MDAH.

243 *coram nobis* dismissal: *LLC*, July 22, 1950; Collins, *Mississippi v. Willie McGee*, July 22, 1950.

243 B. Frank Carter: Affidavit, Hinds County Circuit Court, July 24, 1950.

243 Poole disbarment: *LLC*, July 22, 1950; *DW*, July 24, 1950.

243 Jackson in the 1950s: *Memphis Commercial Appeal*, January 19, 1953; Jackson City Directory, 1952–53; *Beautiful Jackson: In Pictures*; author correspondence with Jerry Dallas.

243 "a new industrial empire": *Memphis Commercial Appeal*, January 19, 1953.

243 Jackson businesses: Jackson City Directory, 1950; Dallas, "Capitol Street, Jackson, Mississippi—Then and Now," http://usads.ms11.net/dallas.html.

244 **new and old capitols:** *Oxford Eagle,* February 16, 1950; *Mississippi: The WPA Guide to the Magnolia State,* 214–15, 217–18.

244 **Jackson office buildings:** *CL, JDN,* September 7, 1986; *JDN,* May 14, 1953; *CL,* April 6, 1956, February 5, 1986; Welty, *One Writer's Beginnings,* 82–83.

244 **. . . and hotels:** Eastland papers, Ole Miss; McCain, *The Story of Jackson,* volume 2, 60; subject files, MDAH.

244 **Farish Street:** Mississippi: The WPA Guide to the Magnolia State, 221; James Rundles interview.

245 **Greene on CRC:** *Jackson Advocate,* July 22, 1950.

245 **police, American Legion:** *JDN,* July 19, 22, 1950.

245 **"lies and propaganda":** *LLC,* July 20, 1950.

245 **Klan, Spinks:** *JDN,* July 17, 1950; *NYT,* August 7, 1947, March 26, 1950.

246 **FBI reports:** FBI file, "Willie McGee."

246 **manageably sized group:** *CL,* July 20, 23, 1950.

246 **black CRC members:** FBI file, "Willie McGee."

246 **Gene Weltfish:** Gacs, *Women Anthropologists,* 372–77; *NYT,* December 22, 1942, August 5, 1980.

246 **Franz Boas:** *NYT,* December 22, 1942; Stocking, *The Shaping of American Anthropology,* 307–16.

246 ***The Races of Mankind:*** Benedict, *Race, Science and Politics,* 167–69, 182–83; Price, *Threatening Anthropology,* 113–15; *WaPo,* April 28, March 9, 1944; *NYT,* March 6, 1944.

247 **Stoll and Ordower:** author interviews with Anne Stoll (September 2004) and Steven Ordower (March 2005).

248 **germ warfare:** *NYT,* September 26, 1952; *Time,* "Brother, You Don't Resign," October 6, 1952.

248 **Weltfish and Columbia:** *NYT,* September 26, 1952, April 1, 1953.

248 **Winifred Feise:** *CL,* July 21, 1950; author interview with Winifred Feise, October 2006; *NYT,* April 6, 8, 1956.

248 **Johnson, Dombrowski:** *NYT,* October 6, 1932, January 10, 1949; Egerton, *Speak Now Against the Day,* 299–301.

248 **"two men and two women":** *LLC,* July 14, 1950; *CL,* July 21, 1950.

249 **"It was not a rape.":** author interview with Winifred Feise.

249 **train station:** subject file, MDAH Historic Preservation Division.

250 **clemency delegation:** FBI file, "Willie McGee"; *JDN,* July 25, 1950; *Compass,* July 26, 1950.

250 **McGehee ruling:** *LLC,* July 25, 1950; *JDN,* July 26, 1950.

250 **Harry Raymond:** *JDN,* July 25, 1950; *NYT,* March 8, 25, 1930; April 22, August 26, 1930.

250 **Harold J. Lightcap:** See "Tribute to a Workingclass Journalist," eulogy for Harry Raymond by Simon W. Gerson, Gerson papers, Tamiment Library, NYU.

250 **Rose Lightcap:** *NYT,* August 11, October 25, 1950.

251 **seating arrangements, legionnaires:** *Compass,* July 26, 1950.

251 **clemency hearing:** *JDN,* July 25, 1950; *Compass, DW, NYT,* July 26, 1950; FBI file, "Willie McGee."

254 **"aged Jacksonian":** *JDN,* July 26, 1950.

254 **violence stories:** *NYT,* July 27, 1950; *JDN,* July 26, 1950; *DW,* July 27–28, 1950; FBI file, "Willie McGee."

255 **train station attack:** *Compass,* July 27, 1950.

256 **Fifth Circuit:** *NYT,* July 26, 1950.

256 **airport violence:** *JDN,* July 26, 1950.

256 **Grossman's demands:** FBI file, "Willie McGee."

257 **Burton stay:** Burton papers, LOC; *Compass,* July 27, 1950; U.S. Supreme Court telegram, July 26, 1950.

257 **Rosalee learns of stay:** *JDN,* July 26, 1950; FBI file, "Willie McGee."

257 **Jackson aftermath:** *CL,* July 27, 1950; *JDN,* July 27, 1950; FBI file, "Willie McGee."

258 **"this writer":** FBI file, "Willie McGee."

259 **Klan gunfight:** Ibid.; *JDN,* July 27, 1950.

ELEVEN: A LONG, LOW SONG

261 **"They are all hot":** Willie McGee letters, CRC papers.

261 **Laurel reaction:** *LLC, JDN,* July 27, 1950.

262 **"nastiest group":** *LLC,* August 9, 1950.

262 **letters to Wright:** Willie McGee case correspondence, MDAH.

263 **letters to McGehee:** *JDN,* August 11, 1950.

264 **letters to Burton:** Burton papers, LOC.

265 **"fomenting discord":** Colmer remarks on the floor of the U.S. House, July 31, 1950, Colmer papers, University of Southern Mississippi.

265 **Martinsville stay:** *DW,* July 27, 1950.

265 ***Daily Worker* editorial:** *DW,* July 28, 1950.

266 **Thackrey editorial:** *Compass,* July 27, 1950.

266 **Supreme Court rosters:** Urofsky, *Division and Discord: The Supreme Court under Stone and Vinson, 1941–1953.*

266 **Raberthe Hanks:** Hanks letter to Aubrey Grossman, March 8, 1952, Danny Grossman papers.

267 **"I can't even visit Willie":** Rosalee McGee letters, CRC papers.

267 **Rosalee's work problems:** Ibid.

268 **death of sister:** Ibid., October 2, 1950.

268 **Percy Greene:** Ibid., October 24, 1950.

268 **Gracie Lee:** Ibid., October 7, 1950.

269 **wish list:** Rosalee McGee letters, December 29, 1950, CRC papers.

269 **"pajama suit":** Willie McGee letters, November 21, December 26, 1950, CRC papers.

269 **Poole disbarment:** *LLC*, July 22, 1950; *DW*, July 24, 1950.

269 **libel case:** Poole interview, 1952, CRC papers; *JDN*, *CL*, June 30, 1950.

271 **Poole withdraws:** *JDN*, August 16, 1950.

271 **Easterling response:** Undated clip, Kaufman papers, Smith College.

271 **contempt of Congress:** Goodman, *The Committee*, 179–81.

272 **Patterson, Lanham.** *Compass*, August 6, 1950; *NYT*, August 6, 1950, April 10, 1951; "Gentleman from Georgia," *Time*, August 14, 1950.

272 **contempt charges:** *NYT*, August 27, 1950.

272 **Rosa Lee Ingram:** Horne, *Communist Front?*, 205–6; Patterson, *We Charge Genocide*, 99.

273 **one hint:** FBI file, "Willie McGee."

274 **Rosalee's affair story:** Rosalee McGee affidavit, July 25, 1950.

275 **appeal filed:** Abzug letter to J. P. Coleman, November 24, 1950; *NYT*, November 23, 1950.

275 **"without proof so far":** *CL*, November 26, 1950.

275 **Louis Lautier:** *Atlanta World*, November 29, 1950.

276 **Schwartz:** MLS memo, 254 Misc., 1950, Reed papers, University of Kentucky.

277 **Burnett:** JGB memo, January 11, 1951, Douglas papers, LOC.

277 **Supreme Court declines:** *NYT*, January 16, 1951.

277 **"No More Interference":** *JDN*, January 17, 1951.

277 *Worker* **reaction:** *DW*, January 17, 1951.

277 **"My hart is hurt":** Bessie McGee letters, CRC papers.

278 **"I was dead broke":** Rosalee McGee letters, CRC papers.

278 **confusion and hurt feelings:** see "The Patterson-Wilkins Correspondence," NAACP press release, November 23, 1949, and William Patterson to Thurgood Marshall, June 15, 1950, NAACP papers.

278 **mistrust his intentions:** Chicago field report on William Patterson, November 4, 1947; FBI file, "William Patterson," 7–52, 128–30.

279 **Martinsville:** Rise, *The Martinsville Seven*; Patterson, *The Man Who Cried Genocide*, 156–68; "The Martinsville Seven Case," unpublished report by Robert Harris for Len Holt, August 21, 1964, Patterson papers, Howard University;

Daily Worker coverage; Tuskegee news clippings file, reel 234; SRC clippings file, "Martinsville, VA, Rape Case 1949–1951."

279 **"cannot . . . be associated"**: *Atlanta Daily World*, June 18, 1949; Rise, *The Martinsville Seven*, 63–65.

279 **"guilt or innocence"**: *The Nation*, March 3, 1951, 212.

279 **"alleged victim"**: Patterson, *The Man Who Cried Genocide*, 161.

280 **Battle grants stay:** NYT, November 11, 1950.

280 **Vinson and Burton:** NYT, February 2, 5, 6, 1951.

280 **"mass pilgrimage" . . . "vigil":** *DW*, January 29, 1951.

281 **executions:** *NYT*, February 3, 6, 1951; *DW*, February 5, 1951.

281 **"funeral pyre":** *DW*, February 7, 1951.

281 **"Communist calliope":** *Time*, February 12, 1951.

281 **"Martinsville Chant":** William Patterson papers, Howard University.

282 **"unconcern":** Moon, "The Martinsville Rape Case," *The New Leader*, February 12, 1951.

282 **McGee's affair stories:** See Dixon Pyles interview with *Daily Worker* investigator, 1952, CRC papers, and Willie McGee affidavit, February 3, 1951, Hinds County Chancery Clerk's Office, Jackson, Mississippi, CRC papers.

TWELVE: BARE-LEGGED WOMEN
285 **new execution date:** *LLC*, February 5, 1951.

285 **affair story revealed:** *DW*, February 25, 1951; *Daily People's World*, March 2, 1951; "Fact Sheet On Willie McGee," Kaufman papers, Smith College.

285 **habeas corpus plea, denial:** "Petition for Writ of Habeas Corpus," *McGee v. Jones and Brogan*, March 5, 1951; *CL*, March 6, 1951.

286 **new flourishes:** Raymond, *Save Willie McGee*, February 1951.

286 **second alibi:** Hettie Johnson affidavit, March 4, 1951, MDAH.

287 **stay appeal:** *NYT*, March 16, 1951; *CL*, March 6, 1957.

287 **"Mississippi":** Mitford, *A Fine Old Conflict*, 160–94.

288 **White Women's Delegation:** Ibid. 160–65.

288 **her memoir of her fifteen years:** Ibid. 62–64, 279.

288 **Faulkner visit:** Ibid., 181–183; *Daily People's World*, April 13, 1951.

288 **Rowan Oak:** Blotner, *Faulkner*, 258–63; author visit.

289 **Faulkner press release:** *LLC*, March 28, 1951.

289 **"an outrage":** delayed *Daily People's World* clip, datelined March 20, 1951, Mitford papers, Ohio State University.

290 **Faulkner retreats:** *JDN*, March 26, 1951; *Boston Guardian*, March 31, 1951;

Meriwether, *Essays, Speeches & Public Letters by William Faulkner*, 211–12; Blotner, *Faulkner*, 539.

290 "fictitious imaginations": *LLC*, March 28, 1951.

290 "Those people, all women": William Faulkner to Robert M. Bridgeforth, March 30, 1951, MDAH.

290 Faulkner had a knack: Williamson, *William Faulkner and Southern History*, 300–6.

291 "Gothic fascist": Blotner, *Faulkner*, 411.

291 "I'd fight for Mississippi": *NYT*, March 15, 1956; United Press, March 16, 1956; *The Reporter*, March 22, 1956.

292 Patton: "Trouble Now Over at Oxford," unlabeled clip from MDAH subject file, "Lynching to 1925"; *JDN*, September 8, 9, 1908; *NYT*, September 9, 1908.

292 Higginbotham: *NYT*, September 19, 1935; *CL*, September 19, 1935.

292 "Dry September": Faulkner, *Collected Stories of William Faulkner*.

292 W. H. James, Faulkner: *Memphis Commercial Appeal*, February 2, 15, 1931.

293 *Intruder*: Faulkner, *Intruder in the Dust*, 1948; Blotner, *Faulkner*, 490–91, 500–3, 508–10.

294 Wilson review: "William Faulkner's Reply to the Civil-Rights Program," *The New Yorker*, October 23, 1948, 120–28.

295 MGM: *NYT*, July 18, 1948.

295 Oxford, *Intruder*: Carter, "No Phony Magnolias," *WaPo*, May 1, 1949; undated *Oxford Eagle* profile of Juano Hernandez, Faulkner papers, University of Mississippi; *NYT*, April 10, 1949; *Oxford Eagle*, October 6, 1949; *Memphis Press-Scimitar*, October 12, 1949, Faulkner papers.

296 Mitford in Oakland: *A Fine Old Conflict*, 98–138, 160–63.

297 three other CRC delegates: *Daily People's World*, April 13, 1951. (In *A Fine Old Conflict*, Mitford changed the names of several characters: Wachter and Hopson were called "Rita Baxter" and "the Youth Comrade.")

297 Mitford background: Lovell, *The Sisters*; Mitford, Jessica, *A Fine Old Conflict* and *Daughters and Rebels*; Mitford, Nancy, *The Pursuit of Love* and *Love in a Cold Climate*; Pryce-Jones, *Unity Mitford: An Enquiry Into Her Life and the Frivolity of Evil*; FBI file, "Jessica Mitford'" author correspondence with Constancia Romilly, Lester Brody, and Peter Y. Sussmon.

298 Hitler meets Unity: DeCourcy, *Diana Mosley*, 143–45.

298 "perfect Nordic beauty": *NYT*, October 21, 1939.

298 Diana, Mosley wedding: DeCourcy, *Diana Mosley*, 173–75.

298 arrested and released: *WaPo*, November 18, 1943, June 30, 1948.

298 "mysteriously ill": *NYT*, January 3–4, 1940.

298 put a pistol to her head: DeCourcy, *Diana Mosley*, 205.

299 Inch Kenneth: *NYT*, February 31, 1940, May 31, 1948; DeCourcy, *Diana Mosley*, 295–96.

299 **Jessica, Esmond:** Lovell, *The Sisters*; 177–79, 217–40.

299 **Spanish Civil War:** *NYT*, December 27, 1936.

300 **"The story . . . made headlines":** Lovell, *The Sisters*, 230.

300 **"Threats of imprisonment":** *NYT*, May 19, 1937.

300 **They moved to America:** Mitford, *A Fine Old Conflict*, 18–22.

300 *Washington Post* articles: the *Post* series began on January 28, 1940, and ran periodically over the next few months.

300 **Romilly's death:** *WaPo*, December 4, 1941; *NYT*, December 5, 1941; Mitford, *A Fine Old Conflict*, 22.

301 **employee evaluation:** Mitford FBI file, April 8, 1943, memo.

301 **"boring and oppressive":** *A Fine Old Conflict*, 30.

301 **joins Communist Party:** Ibid. 62–64.

301 **Mitford in Needles:** *Daily People's World*, March 12, 1951.

302 **. . . in St. Louis:** Mitford, *A Fine Old Conflict*, 172; Tuskegee news clippings file, reel 234, frame 0650.

302 **second group:** *DW*, March 28, April 17, 1951.

302 **"story of sick horror":** *Daily People's World*, March 12, 1951.

302 **Mitford in Jackson:** *A Fine Old Conflict*, 172–81.

303 **"bare-legged Chicago women":** *JDN*, March 17, 1951.

303 **Mayor Thompson:** *JDN*, March 16, 1951.

303 **careful tally:** delayed *Daily People's World* clips, datelined March 18 and 19, 1951, Mitford papers, Ohio State University.

304 **skeptical teacher:** *Daily People's World*, March 19, 1951.

304 **MacGillivray:** YWCA subject file, MDAH; author interview with Simmie Roberts.

304 **Hudgins:** *Daily People's World*, March 19, 1951.

305 **CRC chapter activity:** much of the FBI file on Willie McGee consists of field reports about McGee-related meetings held by CRC chapters around the U.S.

305 **Washington vigil, Rosalee travels:** *Daily People's World*, February 26, 1951; Rosalee's activities in the spring of 1951 are described in the Willie McGee FBI file, press releases in the CRC papers, and in various newspaper stories in the Jessica Mitford papers.

305 **stay arguments:** "Petition for Stay of Execution," *McGee v. Mississippi*, March 15, 1951, National Archives, Washington, D.C.

305 **"very bad practice":** *JDN*, March 15, 1951; *NYT*, March 16, 1951.

305 **letters to Black:** Black papers, LOC.

306 **campus controversy:** Ibid.; *Michigan Daily*, March and April 1951.

306 **Black orders stay:** *NYT*, March 16, 1951.

307 "Justice Again Ravished": *JDN*, March 18, 1951.

307 Supreme Court hears arguments: *NYT*, March 21, 1951.

307 Burnett: William O. Douglas papers, case 417, 1950, March 23, 1951.

308 Schwartz: Ibid.

308 McGee denied: *NYT*, March 27, 1951.

THIRTEEN: SORROW NIGHT

309 W. O. Chet Dillard: correspondence and author interview, November 2007; Dillard, *Clearburning*, 35–65.

312 civil rights suit: *CL*, May 6, 1951.

312 Coe drops out: Coe to Abzug, April 25, 1951, Coe papers, Emory University.

313 Abzug on arrests: Abzug interviews, Columbia.

313 clemency hearing: *CL*, May 5, 1951; *LLC*, May 5, 1951.

313 "Rightly or wrongly": Abzug and Coe, pardon petition to Fielding Wright, May 5, 1951, Toler papers, Mississippi State University.

314 "bestial hands": Carroll Gartin statement to Fielding Wright, May 5, 1951, Toler papers, Mississippi State University.

314 no clemency: *CL*, May 8, 1951.

314 mass arrests: *NYT*, *JDN*, May 6, 1951; *DW*, May 7, 1951; Ken Toler memo to *Life*, Toler papers, Mississippi State University; Abzug interviews, Columbia; Honey, *Black Workers Remember*, 203–6.

315 Lincoln Memorial, White House: *CL*, *DW*, May 7, 1951; Randall, "Democracy's Passion Play: The Lincoln Memorial, Politics, and History as Myth," 249–50; *People's Daily World*, May 7, 1951.

316 aborted Laurel trip: *CL*, *JDN*, May 6, 1951.

317 May letters: Willie McGee letters, CRC papers.

317 McGee talks to reporters: *CL*, May 8, 1951.

317 McGee statement, lawsuit: *JDN*, May 8, 1951; "Note to Editors and Organizations," CRC press release, May 14, 1951, NAACP papers; London interview with Spivak, 1952, CRC papers.

318 Mize says no: *CL*, May 8, 1951.

318 "McGee was visibly nervous": Ibid.

318 Deavours, Tabor: author interviews, November 2007.

320 electric chair: subject files, MDAH.

320 Willie Mae Bragg: *CL*, October 13, 1940.

321 Bill Minor: author interview, May 2005.

321 crowd description: author interviews with Bill Minor, "Warren Tabor," and Wayne Valentine Jr.

324 **"he paid too much"**: Rowan, *South of Freedom*, 191.

324 **Max Lerner**: *New York Post*, May 8, 1951.

325 **"Let me sign this thing!"**: *Daily People's World*, March 13, 1951.

325 **Oppenheim**: Ibid., March 16, 1951.

325 **Harvey Bellet**: *NYT*, April 1, 1951.

325 **Abyssinian Baptist Church**: Harlem CRC pamphlet, MDAH.

325 **"Negro white unity"**: Anne Shore letter to William Patterson, March 13, 1951, Michigan CRC papers, Wayne State University.

325 **Chicago march**: *Chicago Defender*, April 28, 1951; author interview with John Polk Allen, September 2004.

326 **Barkley**: *Daily People's World*, May 1, 1951.

326 **Walter White urged chapter members**: Walter White memo to "NAACP Branches, Youth Councils and College Chapters," March 7, 1951, NAACP papers.

326 **somebody else's news**: See "McGee and the Martinsville 7," *Chicago Defender*, May 19, 1951.

327 ***Freedom* extra**: Willie McGee clippings, 1948–51, Michigan CRC papers, Wayne State University.

327 **Diego Rivera**: undated clipping, Mitford papers, Ohio State University.

327 **Shostakovich**: *JDN*, April 21, 1951.

327 **London theater demonstration**: Undated *Daily People's World* clip, Mitford papers, Ohio State University.

327 **Lumpkin**: *JDN*, April 30, 1951.

327 **Truman letters**: Truman papers, Truman Library; "Text of Open Letter to the President," May 2, 1951, NAACP papers.

328 **front-page news in France**: "French Legislators Mourned McGee," undated CRC press release, NAACP papers.

328 **Paris protests**: *DW*, May 8, 1951.

328 **China, Soviet Union**: *LLC*, April 9, 1951; "Execution of M'Gee Blasted by Moscow," Toler papers, Mississippi State University.

329 **Fifth Circuit appeal**: *New Orleans Times-Picayune*, May 8, 1951.

329 **appeal to Truman**: McGee petition, May 7, 1951, Coe papers, Emory University.

330 **Troy Hawkins arrival**: *CL*, May 8, 1951.

330 **Ernest Goodman**: "Counsel for the Common People," videotaped interview with Ernest Goodman, 1995, produced by William Bryce, Walter P. Reuther Library, Wayne State University.

330 **final appeals**: *NYT*, *New Orleans Times-Picayune*, May 8, 1951.

331 **crowd shot**: *Life*, May 21, 1951, 44–45.

331 **decoy:** author interview with Wayne Valentine Jr., November 2007.

332 **McGee execution:** *CL, JDN, LLC, New Orleans Times-Picayune, NYT,* May 8, 1951.

332 **broadcast:** "Willie McGee Execution," Jim Leeson audio recording, May 7–8, 1950, University of Southern Mississippi oral history collections.

334 **"blood-curdling cries":** Abzug interviews, Columbia University; Goodman interview, Wayne State University.

335 **Robeson, Sullens:** unidentified newspaper story in Mitford papers, datelined May 1951; *JDN,* "The Low Down on the Higher Ups," May 8, 1951.

335 **Josephine Baker:** *Pittsburgh Courier,* May 12, 1951; "Josephine Baker Homage to McGee," undated CRC press release, NAACP papers.

335 **looked thoroughly defeated:** *Life,* May 21, 1951, 44–45.

335 **McGee's last letter:** Hall papers, New York State Library.

EPILOGUE: WHISKEY IN A PAPER SACK

337 **Gus DeLoach:** author interview, November 2007.

338 **Jon Swartzfager:** author interview, November 2007.

339 **Swartzfager:** Luke Lampton interview with Paul Swartzfager.

340 **federal courts:** Zaim, *Journal of Mississippi History,* Fall 2003, 216.

341 **Patterson imprisoned:** *NYT,* June 29, November 20, 1954; January 28, 1955.

341 **"never forget":** William Patterson letter to MaryLouise Patterson, July 17, 1954, William Patterson papers, Howard University.

342 **CRC folds:** *NYT,* January 8, 1956.

342 **"Secret Speech":** *NYT,* June 5, 1956.

342 **Fast and Mitford:** *A Fine Old Conflict,* 255–80; *NYT,* February 1, 1957.

342 **Patterson on *A Fine Old Conflict*:** Mitford to Patterson, August 9, 1977, Mitford papers, Ohio State University; Patterson to Mitford, September 9, 1977, Patterson papers, Howard University.

343 **McGee case summarized:** *We Charge Genocide,* 77.

343 **CRC cried "frame-up":** Michigan CRC files on Haywood Patterson, Wayne State University.

343 **U.N. petition:** Patterson, *The Man Who Cried Genocide,* 169–208; Patterson, ed., *We Charge Genocide: The Historic Petition to the United Nations for Relief from a Crime of the United States Government Against the Negro People,* 3, 109, 116; *NYT,* November 21, 1951.

343 **Paris speech:** Patterson papers, Howard University.

344 **Channing Tobias:** Patterson, *The Man Who Cried Genocide,* 184–89; *NYT,* November 5, 1951, November 6, 1961.

344 **CRC "swindle":** *Pittsburgh Courier,* May 19, 1951.

344 **Baker, McGee:** "Mrs. Rosalie McGee" affidavit, Parish of Orleans, New Orleans, Louisiana, May 17, 1951, CRC papers.

344 **"I no it did good":** Rosalee Safford to CRC, July 14, 1951, CRC papers.

345 **Rosalee claims harassment:** *Norfolk Journal and Guide,* May 10, 1952.

345 **Prisoners Relief Department:** *Reports of the Subversive Activities Control Board, Volume 1,* 1966, 647.

345 **1955 hearing:** *DW,* April 21, 1955.

345 **Jesse James Harris:** author interview, September 2008.

346 **Hawkins libel suit:** *CL,* August 2, 1951; *Hawkins v. Freedom of the Press Company, Inc.,* National Archives, New York.

346 **Grayson L. Tucker:** Spivak interview, 1952, CRC papers.

346 **CRC activists:** the Detroit CRC branch was especially active in looking for new witnesses. See Anne Shore letter to Bella Abzug, March 20, 1951, Michigan CRC papers, Wayne State University.

346 **procedural back-and-forth:** *Hawkins v. Freedom of the Press Company, Inc.,* National Archives, New York.

347 **libel settlement:** *NYT,* May 6, 1955.

347 **She traveled to New York:** author interviews with Ann, Sandra, and Dorothy Hawkins.

347 **Abzug on Poole and London:** Luke Lampton interview with Bella Abzug.

347 **Abzug and Coe letters:** June 13, 20, 1951, Coe papers, Emory University.

348 **Poole libel case:** Dixon Pyles interview transcript, Mitford papers, Ohio State University.

348 **Poole's practice collapsed:** Chancery Court, Hinds County, Mississippi, "Petition for Disbarment of John Poole," 1954.

348 **Poole disbarred:** Ibid.; *CL,* May 5, 1954.

349 **chess champion:** Poole family papers.

349 **suicide:** *CL,* November 14, 1980.

Index